PRIVATE LAW AND POWER

The aim of this edited collection of essays is to examine the relationship between private law and power—both the public power of the state and the 'private' power of institutions and individuals. Its objectives are to describe and critically assess the way that private law doctrines, institutions, processes and rules express, moderate, facilitate and control relationships of power. The aim is to scrutinise this subject from the viewpoints of both history and modernity.

The various chapters of this work examine the dynamics of the relationship between private law and power from a number of different perspectives—historical, theoretical, doctrinal and comparative. They have been commissioned from leading experts in the field of private law, from several different Commonwealth Jurisdictions (Australia, the UK, Canada and New Zealand), each with expertise in the particular sphere of their contribution. They aim to illuminate the past and assist in resolving some contemporary, difficult legal issues relating to the shape, scope and content of private law and its difficult relationship with power.

Volume 22 in the series Hart Studies in Private Law

Private Law and Power

Edited by
Kit Barker, Simone Degeling, Karen Fairweather
and Ross Grantham

•HART•
PUBLISHING
OXFORD AND PORTLAND, OREGON
2017

Hart Publishing
An imprint of Bloomsbury Publishing Plc

Hart Publishing Ltd
Kemp House
Chawley Park
Cumnor Hill
Oxford OX2 9PH
UK

Bloomsbury Publishing Plc
50 Bedford Square
London
WC1B 3DP
UK

www.hartpub.co.uk
www.bloomsbury.com

Published in North America (US and Canada) by
Hart Publishing
c/o International Specialized Book Services
920 NE 58th Avenue, Suite 300
Portland, OR 97213-3786
USA

www.isbs.com

First published 2017

British Library Cataloguing-in-Publication Data
A catalogue record for this book is available from the British Library.

ISBN: HB: 978-1-50990-599-7
ePDF: 978-1-50990-601-7
ePub: 978-1-50990-600-0

Library of Congress Cataloging-in-Publication Data
A catalogue record for this book is available from the Library of Congress.

Names: Barker, Kit, editor.

Title: Private law and power / Edited by Kit Barker, Simone Degeling, Karen Fairweather and Ross Grantham.

Description: Portland, Oregon : Hart Publishing, 2017. | Series: Hart studies in private law ; volume 22 | Includes bibliographical references and index.

Identifiers: LCCN 2016048078 (print) | LCCN 2016048395 (ebook) | ISBN 9781509905997 (hardback : alk. paper) | ISBN 9781509906000 (Epub)

Subjects: LCSH: Civil law—Commonwealth countries. | Public law—Commonwealth countries. | Power (Social sciences) | Power (Philosophy)

Classification: LCC K623 .P748 2017 (print) | LCC K623 (ebook) | DDC 346/.11241—dc23

LC record available at https://lccn.loc.gov/2016048078

Series: Hart Studies in Private Law, volume 22

Typeset by Compuscript Ltd, Shannon
Printed and bound in Great Britain by TJ International Ltd, Padstow

PREFACE

This collection of essays examines the relationship between private law and power, examining both the public power of the state and the 'private' power of institutions and individuals. Drawing on a variety of different areas of private law, it assesses the ways that private law doctrines, institutions, processes and rules express, moderate, facilitate and control relationships of power. The subject is scrutinised from the viewpoints of both history and modernity.

In one sense, all private law is an expression of the power of the state—a system of adjudicative rules pronounced by authority, whether judicial or legislative in nature. Private law's more detailed doctrines and rules are, however, also important in providing individuals with their own powers (for example, through the institutions of contract, property, trust and incorporation); and they operate as a key mechanism for redressing abuses both of the public powers of the state and of the private powers of institutions (corporations, religious institutions) and individuals *inter se*. The rise of the limited liability corporation, the increased pervasion of the state into social welfare provision and economic markets; the abolition of Crown immunities in tort, and the rise of consumer-welfarism have all altered the power dynamics operating within and around private law doctrine. Changes in dynamic are evident not simply in changes in the substantive rules of private law themselves over the years, but also in its procedural rules, such as class action provisions, and in the emergence of a market for third party litigation funding. Despite its increased sophistication and flexibility in the modern day, private law struggles to respond to historic institutional abuses of power, such as cases of institutionalised child sexual exploitation; as well as with the inequalities created by increasingly powerful corporate actors in economic markets. Private law is the forum in which the impact of these inequalities and inequities upon personal interests is confronted and addressed.

The various chapters of this work examine the dynamics of the relationship between private law and power from a number of different perspectives: historical, theoretical, doctrinal and comparative. They draw on aspects of the law of torts, contract, equity, property, trusts, consumer law, company law and civil procedure. Our hope is that they will help both to illuminate the past and assist in resolving some contemporary, challenging legal issues relating to the shape, scope and content of private law and its difficult, ongoing relationship with power.

FOREWORD

In 1914, before the onset of United States legal realism, Roscoe Pound spoke of the temporary expedient of justice where the advantages claimed are 'directness, expedition, conformity to the popular will for the time being, freedom from the bounds of purely traditional rules, freedom from the technical rules of evidence and power to act upon the everyday instincts of ordinary [people]'. Pound was speaking of justice *without law.* Law constrains all of these matters. This collection of essays is about how private law constrains power, including State, corporate, or individual power. It is also about how private law is, and should be, itself constrained.

There are extremely difficult questions underlying the extraordinary essays in *Private Law and Power.* The first question: what is private law? It is commonly conceived as the law that is applied between private persons rather than the law between those persons and the State. However, the divide between the private and the public is very difficult. One of the themes of this book is the way that private law is enforced by the State. An understanding of the divide between private and public also immediately invites the question of what is meant by the State. It is made more difficult by public law rights that have been given private effect. One example is the use of the 14th Amendment to the United States Constitution for private rights described as 'substantive due process'. Another is the use of s 6 of the *Human Rights Act 1998* in the United Kingdom to develop private rights.

A second deep seated question: what is the function of private law? On one view, private law exists only as a tool of corrective justice, to rectify or correct. This view has deep roots. In *Nichomachean Ethics,* Aristotle described corrective justice as operating 'such that each party has the same both before the transaction and after it'. A formalist conception of corrective justice sees the process of rectification as independent of any distributive policy concerns that arise outside this formal conception of the legal system. The most brilliant exponent today of this formalist view is Professor Weinrib. In his introduction in this book, Professor Barker describes the body of disciples of Professor Weinrib as Weinribians.

A third question: how should private law operate to fulfil its function? It is here that the book turns to questions of power. These questions of power operate at many levels. At the structural level, as Professor Cane observes, we could compare the traditional English conception of courts exercising private and public law power with the French approach to separate courts exercising public law power (headed by the *Conseil d'Etat*). With the growth and expansion of administrative tribunals, the older Diceyan model of operational equality has evaporated. Then there is the question of the operation of private power. In the French debates which preceded the 1804 adoption of the Napoleonic Code, Jean-Étienne-Marie Portalis argued that the Code ought only to express matters at a high level of abstraction. He thought that it was better to leave it to the 'judge and the jurist, imbued with the general spirit of the laws, to direct their application'. The common law has always preferred rules. General principles, once a characteristic trait of equity, are now subordinated to a gap-filling function. As Sir Sydney Kentridge wrote, when acting as a Justice of the South African Constitutional Court, 'If the language used by the lawgiver is ignored in favour of general resort to "values" the result is not interpretation but divination'.

To some, particularly United States realists, the obsessively technical and formal interstices of the law are boring. This book would have little lure for them. United States private law was not always so exciting. In *The Federalist Papers*, Hamilton, echoing Montesquieu, wrote of the judiciary as having neither force nor will, but merely judgment. But realist scholarship in the United States is now often marked by an exciting focus on policy. Private law in the United States, developed and refined over the two millennia since the Roman jurists, has now been subjugated by the realists to a sub-division of an independent field of learning which is less than a century old. This is the field of economics. The same future may loom in Europe. The European courts in Luxembourg and Strasbourg have brought more realism to the formal jurisdictions such as England and Germany than the other way round. *Private Law and Power* is a response to this siren call of policy, which has so far been resisted in the private law in jurisdictions such as Australia and England which feature prominently in the essays. In Australia, as Dyson Heydon wrote in 2011 without lament at the absence of United States realism, the 'attainment of just outcomes is often accompanied by boredom'. The extraordinary essays in this book are part of the search for underlying truth in the structure, nature, and operation of private law, rather than a functional approach to private law as economics or applied policy. The beauty of that search is not yet lost on this continent.

James Edelman
Federal Court of Australia
11 May 2016

ACKNOWLEDGEMENTS

This book came about as the result of a symposium jointly hosted by the Australian Centre of Private Law in the TC Beirne School of Law, The University of Queensland and the Bar Association of Queensland in Brisbane on the 11th September 2015. Some of the papers were presented on that day and others were commissioned independently by the editors in order to complement the themes explored on that occasion.

We would like to express our gratitude to all those who participated in the very lively and productive day of discussion in Brisbane, and to the Bar Association of Queensland for making its excellent facilities available to us. For their assistance in staging the event, we would like to say a special thank you to Jane Gay, Helene Breene and Holly Bartolo. We would also like to thank Bill Asquith of Hart Publishing for his enthusiasm for the project and to acknowledge the financial support accorded to the Centre of Private Law by the University of Queensland, which made the event—and hence the book—possible.

Kit Barker, Simone Degeling, Karen Fairweather and Ross Grantham
March 2016

CONTENTS

Preface v
Foreword vii
Acknowledgements ix
List of Contributors xiii

Part 1: Issues

1. The Dynamics of Private Law and Power 3
Kit Barker

Part 2: Power, History and Society

2. Power, History and the Law of Contract in Eighteenth Century England 31
Warren Swain

3. Redressing Inequality in Personal Credit Transactions: 1700–1974 53
Karen Fairweather

4. Tort Law and Government Liability in the Administrative State 83
Peter Cane

Part 3: Doctrines, Institutions and Process

5. Property and Power: The Judicial Redistribution of Proprietary Rights...107
Craig Rotherham

6. Trustees' Powers and Social Justice 137
Matthew Harding

7. Undue Influence and the Spiritual Economy..159
Simone Degeling

8. A Public Law Tort: Understanding Misfeasance in Public Office...............177
Donal Nolan

9. Public Power, Discretion and the Duty of Care 207
Kit Barker

10. The Legitimacy of the Company as a Source of (Private) Power 239
Ross Grantham

11. Reshaping Responsibility: The Emerging Private Law of Institutional Wrongs 263
Mayo Moran

12. Class Actions: Uses and Abuses of the Process of Courts 285
Justice Philip McMurdo

Index 301

LIST OF CONTRIBUTORS

Kit Barker is Professor of Law at the TC Beirne School of Law, The University of Queensland, Australia.

Peter Cane is an Emeritus Professor of the Australian National University currently based at Christ's College, Cambridge.

Simone Degeling is Professor of Law at UNSW Australia.

Karen Fairweather is Lecturer in Law at the TC Beirne School of Law, The University of Queensland, Australia.

Ross Grantham is Professor of Commercial Law and former Dean of the Faculty of Law at the TC Beirne School of Law, The University of Queensland, Australia.

Matthew Harding is Professor of Law at Melbourne University, Australia.

Mayo Moran is Provost of Trinity College, Professor of Law and former Dean of the Faculty of Law at the University of Toronto, Canada.

The Hon Justice Philip D McMurdo is a judge of the Queensland Court of Appeal, based in Brisbane, Australia and a fellow of the Australian Academy of Law.

Donal Nolan is Professor of Private Law at the University of Oxford and Francis Reynolds and Clarendon Fellow and Tutor in Law at Worcester College, Oxford.

Craig Rotherham is Professor of Law in the Faculty of Social Sciences at Nottingham University, The United Kingdom.

Warren Swain is Professor of Law at the Faculty of Law, the University of Auckland, co-director of the New Zealand Centre for Law and Business and Professor of Law at the TC Beirne School of Law, The University of Queensland, Australia.

Part 1

Issues

1

The Dynamics of Private Law and Power

KIT BARKER*

'Where I found the living, there I found the will to power'
(Friedrich Nietzsche, *Thus Spoke Zarathustra: a Book for All and None* II:12)

I. Introduction

The relationship between law and power lies at the heart of, if indeed it does not entirely define, the corpus of legal rules we have come to know as public law. It is equally important, this book serves to suggest, in private law. In one sense, this could not be otherwise, since all modern private law is an expression of the power of the state—a system of rules pronounced by either judicial, or legislative authority. Beyond this, however, private law's doctrines and rules provide individuals with their own powers of self-advancement and purposive disposition (through contract, property and trust); and they serve to address and redress the effects of important misuses of power by the State, private institutions and individuals. Its facilitative institutions hence bestow on private parties the power to chart for themselves lives which are more autonomous in the modern, liberal sense,[1] whilst its protective rules (in the form of tort law, unjust enrichment law, equitable doctrines and remedies and so on) set perimeters around their most basic personal interests, which render those interests resistant to abuse by those seeking to exploit them, and which provide meaningful forms of redress in the latter event.

Private law's power-conferring and protective rules are close to the everyday experience of individuals in ways that constitutional, administrative and criminal law doctrines are (perhaps thankfully) generally not. This is not to deny the crucial importance of public law's structural relationship with power. But, because we all

* I dedicate this chapter to my late brother, Alan—a man as generous in human spirit as he was sceptically challenging of the structures of human authority.
[1] J Raz, *The Morality of Freedom* (Oxford, Clarendon Press, 1986).

engage with each other, person-to-person, each time we set foot outside our doors, private law has a way of seeping into our lives at a visceral, personal level. Power invisibly affects the price we pay when we fill our petrol tank in the morning, or buy our first cup of coffee; it bears upon our obligations at work; it affects the freedom of our consent to medical procedures, hire-purchase agreements, or personal, sexual intimacies; it implicates our ability to get back money that we paid to others when we were held in the grip of error, terror, trust, ignorance, addiction, and so on. It is because private law enters our personal and economic interactions, one with another, in this way, that our encounters with it are regular, familiar and microscopic. Private law is the law of daily life, and power one of life's inescapable, empirical facts. How, then, could private law and power *not* be intimately involved with one another?

Although private law has always been tied to power, there is much to suggest that the intensity of the relationship between the two has increased. One reason for this lies in the growth of the positive state, whose regulatory and welfare functions now reach further into our personal lives than at any previous time. As the state's protective powers have increased, so too has its capacity to harm private interests. Another lies in the rise of the multinational corporation, whose influence over not just the economic, but the social aspects of our being is now sobering. At the same time, within the institution of private law itself, power has shifted, since the mid-seventeenth century, from juries to judges; and, with the proliferation of legislative interventions in the private law, from judges to legislatures. Often, the last of these shifts has advanced the protections available for the most vulnerable in our societies, but equally, there are occasions when it has also operated to their detriment, curtailing private rights in favour of vested interests and markets.[2] The power of legislatures has thus served to shape private justice in ways that tend to democratise it and (generally) to increase aggregate social welfare, but also inevitably to fully politicise it (in a strong sense) and thereby to expose it, on occasion, to exploitation by powerful groups that have special access to the ears of government.

Recent years have also highlighted the power of private, unincorporated institutions, such as the Catholic Church, within whose walls some of the most terrible abuses of children and vulnerable adults have taken place.[3] The structure of these private institutions, many of them accorded the benefits of charitable status and public subsidy, has proven remarkably resistant to the normal processes of civil justice and they continue to evade full institutional responsibility in some jurisdictions. Such instances raise serious questions about the capacities of private law itself to respond to some of society's most important, historic abuses, inviting a reappraisal of its internal rules and processes.[4]

[2] For recent examples in Australia, see Chapter 9, Part IV.

[3] See most recently in Australia, Commonwealth Royal Commission into Institutional Responses to Child Sexual Abuse, *Redress and Civil Litigation Report* (Sydney, Commonwealth of Australia, 2015).

[4] Most obviously, limitation rules, evidential rules and standards of proof, vicariously liability doctrine and non-delegable duties.

At the procedural level, recent civil justice reforms have also sought to change the dynamics of power in private law—supposedly by increasing access to justice for individuals through new class action procedures and other measures designed to decrease cost.[5] The power that has been added to the private litigant's elbow by these measures has at the same time been degraded by swingeing cuts to civil legal aid.[6] The withdrawal of state support for civil litigants has in turn encouraged devolution of the real power of civil suit away from victims, in many cases, to third party litigation funders and commercial markets. The diversion of suits away from the judicial process into informal arbitration and conciliation processes may also be seen as both empowering and disempowering, depending on one's point of view. On the one hand, it facilitates resolutions that would otherwise simply not take place, or only at very significant cost. On the other hand, it re-seats the power of adjudication within the private sector, away from the scrutiny of courts and the public eye. Not only does this further diminish the judicial role, it may also, ironically, reduce the vindicatory power of the civil law system itself, by occluding the veins of legal precedent, de-formalising justice and hiding its face from external view.[7] This phenomenon is less apparent in civilian jurisdictions than it is in common law ones.[8] It reflects a recent enthusiasm in the United States, United Kingdom and Australia for privatising core state functions and devolving key public services (of which justice is surely one) to the market.

II. Aims and Overview

The purpose of this work is to investigate the dynamics of power within, and around, private law at this controversial time, looking across some of its institutions, doctrines, remedies and procedures. The survey extends both longitudinally across time (from at least as far back as the seventeenth century to the current

[5] See, eg, The Right Hon Lord Woolf, *Access to Justice, Final Report* (1996) (UK) and the consequent *Civil Procedure Rules 1999*; Australian Government Attorney General's Department Report by the Access to Justice Taskforce, *A Strategic Framework for Access to Justice in the Federal Civil Justice System* (Sept, 2009).

[6] Statistics produced by the Legal Action Group (UK) illustrate a decline in the total number of state acts of assistance to civil litigants of more than two thirds in the period 2009–014: www.lag.org.uk/policy-campaigns/graphs-showing-the-cuts-to-civil-legal-aid.aspx. For damning criticisms of these measures, one need look no further than the House of Commons Committee of Public Accounts, Thirty Sixth Report of Session 2014–2015, *Implementing Reforms to Civil Legal Aid* (HC 808, 19th Jan 2015).

[7] For references to the wide range of discussion on the issues caused by the vanishing trial, see H Genn, 'Why the Privatisation of Civil Justice is a Rule of Law Issue' (36th FA Mann Lecture, 19th November, 2012); C Giabardo, 'Private Law in the Age of the Vanishing Trial' ch 26 in K Barker, K Fairweather and R Grantham (eds), *Private Law in the Twenty First Century* (Oxford, Hart Publishing, 2016).

[8] ibid.

day), and latitudinally across several different common law jurisdictions—the United Kingdom, Australia and Canada, although some consideration is also given to the law of the United States and France. The areas of law drawn into focus are the law(s) of contract, tort, property, trust, equity, company law and civil procedure rules governing class actions and litigation funding. Views as to whether all of these contributions relate squarely to 'private law' will inevitably differ, since different classifications of 'public' and 'private' law are possible.[9] If one conceptualises private law as that part of the law that governs the protection of our private interests as individuals, as opposed the rights we enjoy because we are public citizens, most, but not all (or not all of all) contributions fall within it.[10] On this definition, statutory rules that serve to define or alter the substance of common law rules of contract or tort (such as the Unfair Contract Terms Act 1977 in the United Kingdom, or the Civil Liability Acts in Australia) form part of the very fabric of modern private law and therefore lie clearly within its domain. By contrast, human rights provisions such as section 7 of the Human Rights Act 1998 (UK), which give private citizens the right to bring actions in common law courts for the state's failure to observe or implement the fundamental rights and protections set out in the European Convention on Human Rights, protect rights which those individuals enjoy as part of the polity of public citizens, not their private interests *per se*; and so fall outside private law, even if they also operate, as they do in the United Kingdom, indirectly to add momentum to the development of the private law in civil disputes.

Part 2 ('Power, History and Society') commences with three chapters that take a broad, historical and contextual approach to the relationship between private law and power, looking at aspects of the law of contract, consumer law and tort law. Part 3 ('Doctrines, Institutions and Process'), contains contributions focusing on the relationship between power and more specific private law doctrines, institutions, remedies and processes, although there is much cross-over between the two Parts. The following discussion does not address the contributions in the order they appear, but draws them into a thematic analysis of what I perceive to be the main dimensions of the relationship between power and private law. In the final section, I draw some brief conclusions about these dimensions and about the nature of the dynamics that are in play within, and between them.

[9] For a recent discussion of the wide range of views, see K Barker, 'Private Law: Key Encounters with Public Law,' ch 1 in K Barker and D Jensen (eds), *Private Law: Key Encounters with Public Law* (Cambridge, Cambridge University Press, 2013) esp 20–21. Note that the definition of private law following in the text on this occasion corresponds with the first of the distinctions between private and public that Barker lists (the distinction between individual and collective interests). The definition later assumed by Nolan in Chapter 8 corresponds instead to the third distinction Barker names (the distinction between law governing relations between citizens inter se and between citizens and the state).

[10] The clearest examples of pure public law, on this definition, are the civil procedure rules (considered in Chapter 12) but these are so intimately connected to the practice of private law that we consider their inclusion in this work to be justified.

III. Meanings and Sources of Power

The word 'power' stems from the Latin root, *posse*, meaning 'to be able'. One meaning of power is therefore 'capacity', or 'ability'. This idea clearly informs private law doctrines in which the actual or presumed mental *incapacity* of an adult or child provides the basis for relieving him or her of a contractual obligation, an act of disposition through the law of restitution, or a legal liability (in tort). Infants are presumptively not bound by their agreements; automatons are not liable for their carelessness or trespasses in tort, and so on. Power in this sense is hence assumed by private law as a basic precondition of legal responsibility, as it is in the criminal law.

A second, more specific sense of the term is the ability of one person to change the physical or mental state of another. Power in this sense relates not simply to *internal* capacities that we possess or lack in ourselves, but to our capacity to *affect* the *external* world around us, especially other people. Private law operates upon this conception of power too—for example, through the doctrines of misrepresentation, duress and actual undue influence (equity's more subtle version of duress),[11] which operate in both contract and unjust enrichment law in instances in which one person compels, deceives or influences another in ways that bring about disadvantage to the one, and advantage to the other. The same conception is present in the tort of deceit and in many cases of trespass to land, goods and the person. Power of this type (what Professor Grantham in Chapter 10 refers to as the capacity to 'impose one's will and purposes on others') can stem from a wide variety of different sources—asymmetries of information, opportunity, wealth and physical strength being just some. The conception of power as the capacity to 'purposively impose one's will' on another, which Grantham uses to describe corporate power, is redolent of Kant, and those who are keen to endorse the Kantian/Weinribian conception of private law[12] might even be tempted to cast the whole of private law's remedial rules as mechanisms for redressing inequalities which one party has brought about by subjecting another to his or her own purposes. This is not a vision that all contributors to this volume share. As we shall see in Chapter 7, Professor Degeling doubts whether it is possible to conceive of many equitable doctrines and remedies in Kantian terms. Cases of presumed undue influence, she argues, are not cases in which one person has exercised power by subjecting the will of another to his own by changing the latter's conditions in the world, but

[11] *Williams v Bayley* (1866) LR 1 HL 200. Note that this phrase is sometimes also used to refer to cases of influence, not pressure (threat), where the onus is on the plaintiff to prove the relation of influence.

[12] E Weinrib, *The Idea of Private Law* (Cambridge, Mass, Harvard University Press, 1995). On Kant's legal philosophy generally, see A Ripstein, *Force and Freedom: Kant's Legal and Political Philosophy* (Cambridge, Mass, Harvard University Press, 2009).

rather ones in which the law operates paternalistically to protect the free choice of persons lacking rational agency, on account of the trust they place in others. Similar doubts about the Weinribian vision have been expressed by Dennis Klimchuk in the context of his analysis of the rationale for the restitution of payments made under a spontaneous (uninduced) mistake, the explanation for which he attributes to a very localised form of distributive justice, not corrective justice as conceived by Aristotle, or Weinrib.[13] Perhaps the most vociferous of Weinrib's critics in the restitutionary context is Hanoch Dagan, for whom the law of mistake needs to be understood socially and distributively as a private law project for the protection and enhancement of personal autonomy and general utility, not as a product of Kantian norms.[14]

A third conception of power in private law stems from Hohfeld's analytical scheme.[15] In that scheme, powers are abilities that one party has to change legal relationships. This conception differs from the previous one in so far as it conceptualises power *legally*; legal powers being abilities to change the legal, not just the physical order. On one view (which I hesitate to attribute to Hohfeld himself, but which may nonetheless be helpful), the measure of a person's legal power might be judged according to the number of legal relationships he or she has the ability to change, and according to the type of legal change that he or she is able to effect. One who can change only the legal relationship of himself to one other party has only a small amount of legal power on this understanding, whereas a person who is able to change the duties of the world at large has lots of power(s). Similarly, one who has the power to not just change legal rights and duties, but also to create further powers (whether in others or himself) would seem to have hit the jackpot, for there is surely no greater *form* of power than the power to create more power. States clearly have such 'apex' or 'exponential' powers to grant power to others (especially local authorities, police forces and other public agencies), as well as being able to grant rights and impose duties, through legislative acts. Judges adjudicating private law disputes have powers to create primary and secondary legal duties, to grant privileges, immunities and so on. They also have powers (often statutory) to grant powers to public agents (bailiffs) to distrain on a defendant's private property in the event of judgment default and thereby to change his rights of possession and ownership, in order to satisfy remedial duties he owes a successful plaintiff. The substantive doctrines of private law, as developed by both courts and parliaments, grant powers to individuals to create and change their own rights and duties in relation to property and contract and to vest trustees with powers to change the legal rights of beneficiaries, subject to the trustees' duties to act in the

[13] D Klimchuk, 'Unjust Enrichment and Corrective Justice' ch 6 in C Rickett and R Grantham (eds), *Structure and Justification in Private Law: Essays for Peter Birks* (Oxford, Hart Publishing, 2008).

[14] H Dagan, *The Law and Ethics of Restitution* (Cambridge, Cambridge University Press, 2003) ch 3 esp 37–52.

[15] W Hohfeld, *Fundamental Conceptions as Applied in Judicial Reasoning* (ed), W Cook, New Haven, Yale University Press, 1919).

beneficiaries' best interests. Individuals have procedural powers to initiate proceedings in courts of law that may, in turn, bring about changes in a defendant's rights and duties. And so on.

When scrutinised from the Hohfeldian point of view, private law is hence illuminated as a complex web of power relationships with various different sources, and clear points of contact. Courts' public powers operate to reinforce parties' private ones, as well as to ensure that the law responds to precisely the sorts of factual incapacity and inequality identified in the previous two paragraphs. The importance of the connections between the private powers, rights and duties of litigants and the public powers of courts must, I suggest, lie at the heart of any complete understanding of the private law system in the modern day.

These three conceptions of power as (respectively) factual personal capacity, capacity to change the external world (to influence others), and the ability to change the normative legal order are clearly not the only ways of conceiving of power,[16] or of understanding its sources or complexities in the modern world, but they are the ones that are most centrally relevant to the discussions of private law that take place in this book.

IV. Individual Power, Social Power

Some of the ways in which private law operates to redress the consequences of deficiencies in individual, personal capacity and rational choice caused by youth, ignorance, informational deficit, pressure (threats) and relationships of trust are explored by Professor Swain in Chapter 2, Dr Fairweather in Chapter 3 and Professor Degeling, in Chapter 7.

Professor Swain's study of power in the English law of contract in the eighteenth century is not concerned only with personal inequalities of this sort, although he does draw out some of the early doctrines and remedies that served to protect the weak and vulnerable in their contractual dealings with others. He is also (perhaps more?) interested in the dynamics of power created by 'economic, political and social forces' during that period, and with the balance of power between 'the people, judges, juries, parliament, and mercantile interests. In this he shares some of the instincts and interests of the realist movement in conceptualising power as the *capacity to drive change* and as something both external and internal to the law. His main thesis is that the nineteenth century was not as great a break with past tradition as is sometimes assumed, in terms of representing a sudden, politicised embrace of market values over communitarian conceptions of contract. Respect

[16] For a fascinating exploration of some of the philosophical debate, see A Berndtson, 'The Meaning of Power' (1970) 31 *Philosophy and Phenomenological Research* 73. For a counterpoint in the criminal law sphere, considering the power of law itself as a dominant framework and its Foucauldian counterpoints, see C Smart, *Feminism and the Power of Law* (London, Routledge, 1989), ch 1.

for mercantile interests was evident within the law from an earlier stage, just as the traditional equitable concerns about fairness did not simply vanish in the nineteenth century, but were restructured. Nor, interestingly, were equitable doctrines only ever concerned with the protection of the weakest in society. As often as not, they served to protect powerful, aristocratic elites, the succour offered to young heirs of vast estates via the 'unconscionable bargain' doctrine being perhaps one of the starkest examples. From this point of view, the dawn of the new industrial age in the nineteenth century was as much a power struggle between the aristocratic and industrial classes—between old money and new—as it was between a conception of contract 'as fairness' and contract 'as laissez-faire, free-market exchange'. Swain's chapter resonates vibrantly with the view expressed by Brian Tamanaha in the United States that the formalist-realist 'divide' in law is not one that can be marked out clearly in legal history.[17] Social, political and economic forces operate in the common law by way of flux, in an equilibrium of continuity and evolutionary change, not by way sudden, violent paroxysm.

Dr Fairweather and Professor Degeling are more directly concerned to interrogate the granular detail of private law's responses to imbalances in personal power between individuals, although both contributions also have broad social and philosophical implications. Fairweather provides a historical account of the very wide range of private and public law mechanisms designed to protect individuals in the consumer credit context from the early 1700s through to the Crowther Report of 1971 and the ensuing Consumer Credit Act 1974 (UK). Degeling focuses on the law of (presumed) undue influence and its potential application in aid of those who fall victim to the seductions of the modern 'spiritual economy'. The latter phrase is a euphemism for a wide array of religious cults and providers of 'self-development' experiences such as 'large groups awareness training courses' ('LGATs'), which are increasingly popular and which pose a potential trap for those seeking new forms of meaning either within, or outside themselves in the psychic crisis of the modern day. Both of these treatments are rich in insight.

Fairweather makes two, especially important observations of broader significance. The first is that regulatory measures to combat exploitation in the consumer credit context have almost always struggled to keep up with the ingenuity of markets. The clear, historical implication of this is that economic power is evolutionarily highly adaptable and prone always to respond to constraint by regenerating itself in new and ever-more-complex forms. The second, rather startling observation is that the philosophical assumption upon which the Crowther review was based—that borrowers are 'rational' adults who are 'fully capable of managing their financial affairs'—is false. Indeed, it appears to contradict the very insights that informed the review in the first place. This being so, the strategy which was ultimately adopted in the ensuing, rationalising legislation in the United

[17] B Tamanaha, *Beyond the Formalist-Realist Divide: The Role of Politics in Judging* (Princeton, Princeton University Press, 2010). See also, 'The Bogus Tales about Legal Formalists' *St Johns's Legal Studies Research Paper 08-0130* (April, 2008) available at: SSRN: http://ssrn.com/abstract=1123498.

Kingdom—one of combatting inequality by seeking to redress informational asymmetry—is only a partial solution to the power problem, because the relevant sources of inequality are far more diverse than simply lack of access to accurate information. *Scientia non est potentia*[18]—knowledge *is not* power, merely one of a number of background preconditions required for power to exist. Other sources of inequality that affect the bargaining power of those seeking credit lie in the existence of market monopolies, personal circumstances of poverty or need, and the common, psychological impairments that we all experience when assessing risk, such as cognitive bias.

What is therefore really needed to more effectively eliminate *inequality* in the field of consumer credit is a set of measures to increase the range of moderate-cost loan facilities available to borrowers; measures that are beyond the reach of private law and which lie in the hands of the market itself. Such measures would help, Fairweather suggests, to enhance consumer autonomy in the perfectionist liberal sense popularised by Joseph Raz.[19] They could be incentivised, one might speculate, by government tax concessions, by organisations' proper sense of social responsibility, or (a little more likely, but perhaps not much) by the reputational advantages that social responsibility can bring in a world in which there have recently been so many reckless and unethical lending practices. But solutions of this sort are still a long way off. As long as imperfection exists in the lending market, the problem of inequality of bargaining power seems set to persist.

Fairweather's intuition, that what consumers need is more options, connects in an important way, I suggest, with Professor Degeling's chapter on undue influence doctrine. In particular, the way in which Degeling suggests that we could understand and apply that doctrine in cases involving parties handing over assets to spiritual advisors is based on a conception of private law that also endorses the importance of the value of positive autonomy. Whether undue influence doctrine forms part of unjust enrichment law, or consists in a wrong giving rise to compensatory damages (Degeling admits of both possibilities) the doctrine is not, she argues, based on any idea of purposive exploitation, active or passive. Private law's remedial responses stem from the mere fact that a defendant has received value 'under the guise of authority'. The point here is therefore that a party receiving money or other assets from an apparently willing spiritual devotee need do nothing in terms of applying his or her purposive agency to the world so as to bring about either the relationship of devotion, or the transfer of value, in order for the law to intervene. The law does so purely on the presumption that, where background trust exists so as to shape a donor's perceptions, cognitions and preferences, the choices he makes are not truly free in the modern, Razian sense,

[18] This is a rather obvious play on the phrase *scientia potentia est*, often attributed to Thomas Hobbes in *De Homine* (1658). Hobbes worked as secretary to Sir Francis Bacon, in whose *Meditationes Sacrae* (1597) a similar phrase appears ('*scientia potestas est*'). In neither instance is knowledge, or 'science', actually *equated* with power.

[19] Raz (n 1).

and he must therefore, at the very least, be relieved of responsibility for the consequences of any economic transaction entered into whilst subject to the influence. The donor must be presumed not to be a true author of his own choices, but effectively to be writing his life for someone, or something else.

This vision also entails a rejection, I intimated above, of the Kantian/Weinribian conception of private law, at least in cases in which no purposive exploitation of weakness has taken place. It will be controversial for Weinribians (in a way that Fairweather's suggestions are not) because it involves unelected judges in the promotion of paternalistic ends, not legislatures. I wonder, however, whether this is a serious concern. The potential vulnerabilities of those committing to fundamental spiritual ideologies or quasi-clinical psychological courses are so evident in the fabric of our public experience these days that it seems unreasonable to baulk at the suggestion that judges should be able to provide relief where such vulnerabilities actually exist. If there is any controversy in Degeling's view, it is more likely, I think, to relate to the presumption that any relationship between the organiser of an LGAT and a participant is one in which such vulnerability necessarily exists (subject to disproof by the organisation running the course). An alternative approach, she seems to acknowledge, would be to leave it to the participant to prove that the relationship had this character at the time he or she made the relevant disposition before the presumption of influence is raised, on the basis that there is otherwise a risk of unduly infantilising those seeking to make spiritual commitments, or advance their own emotional welfare, and to give money away in the process. Whether all LGAT relationships should drop into the traditional 'spiritual advisor' category probably requires more extensive empirical research into the form and risks of these relationships. That research may well ultimately prove the wisdom of Degeling's suggestion.

V. Governmental Power

The relationship between private law and governmental power is critical not just to the structural operation of the private law systems as whole, but also to its individual doctrines. Since government in the expanded, positive, administrative state now has more potential to harm private interests through maladministration in executing its regulatory and welfare functions, the law of tort is especially heavily implicated.[20] Both negligence proceedings and actions for misfeasance in public

[20] See generally, M Aronson and H Whitmore, *Public Torts and Contracts* (Sydney, Lawbook Co, 1982); S Arrowsmith, *Civil Liability and Public Authorities* (Winteringham, Earlsgate Press, 1992); P Hogg & P Monaghan, *Liability of the Crown* 3rd edn (Toronto, Carswell Press, 2000); C Harlow, *State Liability* (Oxford, Oxford University Press, 2004); C Booth & D Squires, *The Negligence Liability of Public Authorities* (Oxford, Oxford University Press, 2006); C Nicholls et al, *Corruption and Misuse of Public Office* 2nd edn (Oxford, Oxford University Press, 2011); W Wade and C Forsyth, *Administrative Law* 11th edn (Oxford, Oxford University Press, 2014), ch 20; E Chamberlain, *Misfeasance in a Public Office* (Toronto, Carswell Press, 2016); P Cane, *Controlling Administrative Power: An Historical Comparison* (Cambridge, Cambridge University Press, 2016) ch 10 esp 368–98.

office are now commonplace against government in respect of harm to the person, property and (though less successfully in most jurisdictions) pure economic interests. Three chapters of this work are devoted specifically to examining the dynamic between private law and governmental power in the tort context. A fourth (Professor Moran's) considers this relationship within the context of a discussion about institutional responsibility more generally and I therefore postpone consideration of it until Part VIII. Inevitably, given the increased outsourcing of traditional state functions to markets, there can no longer be any rigid separation of the notions of governmental and private institutional power. Some interplay in the dynamics of the two spheres is unavoidable.

A. Configurations of Liability

In Chapter 3, Professor Cane focuses on the role of tort law in the modern administrative state as a system of civil liability rules, one purpose of which is to control state power in much the same way as doctrines of administrative law. In a broad-ranging survey of the law of the United Kingdom, France, the United States and Australia, he offers explanations for the very different ways in which state civil liabilities and immunities to suit are configured and understood in each jurisdiction, rooting his explanations in a penetrating analysis of each society's social and institutional history and its relationship with power. He asks, in particular, why the United Kingdom never developed a separate system for civil claims against the state, akin to that which exists in France,[21] and speculates about what such a system might have looked like, had it been allowed to develop north of the English Channel. In this regard, he outlines three different possible models of public liability: (i) a 'responsibility' model (a general, French-style principle of direct liability for state illegality, distinct from ordinary tort law, but administered by ordinary courts); (ii) a 'corrective' (justice) model (which would deal with state liabilities in tort in the same way as those of private individuals according to the Diceyan vision,[22] and which would probably strip out any additional liabilities to the public law of human rights) and (iii) the 'instrumental model (which could take a number of different forms, but which would probably involve supplementing a Diceyan tort law with additional regulatory and ex gratia administrative compensation schemes designed to deal with harm caused by maladministration).

The lynchpin of Cane's fascinating thesis appears to be that the way in which tort claims against the state are currently configured and understood in the various jurisdictions is, in part, a function of the way in which the state itself is understood (either as a substitute for the private person of a monarch, as in the United Kingdom, or as a metaphysical, 'corporatist' public entity in its own right, as in

[21] For an excellent comparative review of the English and French systems, see D Fairgrieve, *State Liability in Tort: A Comparative Study* (Oxford, Oxford University Press, 2003).

[22] AV Dicey, *Introduction to the Law of the Constitution* 7th edn (London, Macmillan & Co, 1908) esp 189–91, 198–99.

France); and in part a function of the way power is distributed in each system (such power being concentrated in France and the United Kingdom; and more widely diffused in the United States). The result is that in the United Kingdom, the state is treated very much in the same way as an individual for the purposes of tort liability at a formal level, being subjected to scrutiny in normal private law courts according, more or less, to the Diceyan vision; and tort liabilities of the Crown tend, in the main, to be vicarious liabilities for the acts of its personal agents, additional to the liabilities of the agents themselves. Any adjustments to liability that are necessary to take account of the state's special public functions take place at the lower level of substantive tort rules, not at the level of general immunities, or different processes. By contrast, in France, the state is conceived of as an entity very much distinct from the monarchs that preceded the Revolution of 1789 and traditional courts, whose benches were probably packed with anti-republican conservatives, were regarded as the last agencies to be trusted in the new regime. The result is that powers of redress against the state ended up in the hands of the executive itself, and a separate system of governmental liability ensued. In France, it was thought that the people (re-conceptualised abstractly as the government) needed protection from the obstructive practices of courts; whereas in England, conversely, it was thought that they needed protection by independent courts against government. The position in the United States is complex and more obscure. Federal immunity remains the basic starting point in tort cases, the state itself is conceptualised still in individualistic terms, as in the United Kingdom, but the Diceyan vision never really appealed in the same way. The result is a law of tort that is administered by ordinary courts, but which has a more 'public' character than either its English or Australian counterparts, operating as it does alongside actions for breach of the Constitution to provide a powerful mechanism of governmental accountability. This makes it far more instrumental in outlook that either English or Australian law.

In the current environment, it seems very unlikely that a French-style 'responsibility' model of civil liability will be adopted in the United Kingdom, and even less likely that it will appeal to governments in Australia. Suggestions made by the Law Commission of England and Wales that the state's civil liability for maladministration should be should be broadened, subject to something akin to the 'faute lourde' standard that is sometimes deployed in French law, were effectively snubbed in the light of their likely financial implications for the public purse.[23] For similar reasons, the Harlow vision of special ex gratia public compensation schemes for maladministration, supplementing the existing tort system,[24] looks like a heady pipe-dream in the current political climate prevailing in both countries. Of the three models alluded to by Cane, the second one therefore looks

[23] Law Commission (England and Wales) *Administrative Redress: Public Bodies and the Citizen* (Law Comm CP No 187, 2008) [4.99]–[4.104]. The idea was dropped in the face of stiff opposition: Law Comm Rep No 322, 2010.

[24] Harlow (n 20).

the most likely to take hold in the United Kingdom. Until Australia increases the power and reach of its human rights provisions considerably, so as to give its international obligations some purchase for its own citizens,[25] such additional recourse is also not in prospect in that jurisdiction. Indeed, it might yield tensions with the framework of statutory restrictions on public liability that has recently been brought into effect.[26] The result is likely to be that courts will continue to pursue a bumpy Diceyan path, utilising ordinary tort principles in ordinary courts to provide recourse for citizens harmed by governmental power, subject to some adjustments, and manoeuvring their way as best they can around the special protections that have now been implemented by legislatures in some domestic jurisdictions. As Cane explains, Australians have been firmly committed to the egalitarian, Diceyan vision from a very early stage and have probably been more generous in respect of public liability in respect of the exercise, or non-exercise, of statutory powers than English courts, in part as a function of the way in which the state was forced to become the main provider of welfare services, and therefore a significant source of risk to citizens, from a very early stage.

B. Abuse of Power

The idea that certain parts of tort law are really 'public' law and specifically designed to control the power of public actors is pursued further by Professor Nolan in Chapter 8. Nolan construes the action for misfeasance in public office as one that belongs neither in tort law, nor in other departments of private law, but squarely in public law—its essence lying in the prudential (instrumental) need to preserve public trust and bonds of allegiance to government and hold officials to account for abuses of the public trust. Misfeasance hence involves breaching a public duty, which has no corresponding Hohfeldian right-holder, much like a crime.[27] And the only reasons for preserving the action, as opposed to achieving these allegiance-oriented instrumental ends via the criminal and administrative law are pragmatic: the criminal law route would involve asking state officials to prosecute other state officials, which is unlikely to lead

[25] Currently, such protections as do exist in the Australian Capital Territory (Human Rights Act 2004 (ACT)) and Victoria (Charter of Human Rights and Responsibilities Act 2006 (Vic)) do not bind courts to give effect to human rights in their determinations of individual disputes, nor do they give individual citizens rights to seek damages against the state in cases in which human rights are not respected by the common law. Such structures, it is thought, would be inconsistent with the power of the High Court to determine the norms of the common law system in Australia as a whole.

[26] On which see Chapter 9, Part IV; M Aronson, 'Government Liability in Negligence' (2008) 32 *Melbourne University Law Review* 44; J Bell-James and K Barker, 'Public Authority Liability for Negligence in the post-Ipp Era: Sceptical Reflections on the "Policy Defence"' (2016) 40 *Melbourne University Law Review* 1.

[27] On the connections more generally between tort and crime, see now M Dyson (ed), *Unraveling Tort and Crime* (Cambridge, Cambridge University Press, 2013) and M Dyson, *Comparing Tort and Crime* (Cambridge, Cambridge University Press, 2015).

to efficient policing, and judicial review offers no compensation for past misconduct, and has inappropriately short time limits. This is a coherent and well-argued position that acknowledges the random way in which much of tort law came to be classified in the common law system historically, and which fits many of the elements of the tort, as currently conceived. The vision is that misfeasance is the leading edge of a public law of tort that is concerned to discipline public power and compensate the most egregious forms of abuse.

There are two residual puzzles: first, why, if the tort is part of public laws is proof of actual damage necessary for a plaintiff to sue upon it; and, second, why are damages awarded on a fully compensatory basis, rather than simply by way of penal sanction? Nolan's ingenious solution to the first conundrum is that the damage requirement needs to be reconstructed as a weaker, standing rule and that the decision of the House of Lords in *Watkins*[28] was wrong. He does not offer an expansive answer to the second question, other than to say that, although doing interpersonal justice is not the aim of the tort, compensatory damages can help to serve a 'vindicatory function' in enabling 'victims' of abuse to 'obtain redress for loss' they have suffered. To my mind, this suggests that at least part of the function of the tort is indeed to protect private interests, not just public ones. On this view, the tort might still legitimately be situated within 'private law', albeit recognising that it is a hybrid construct that serves both public and private ends. There is, however, no doubting the difficulty of this question and the taxonomic issue seems secondary in importance to the moral and social functions that the tort can achieve in the modern day. Nolan's analysis is coherent, compelling, and describes an important source of empowerment for citizens in the face of an increasingly invasive state. It will never provide full protection against the harms caused by maladministration, but sets a baseline guarantee of honesty in public practice.

C. Governmental Discretion

One of the features of public power that makes it adaptable, but dangerous, is the fact that it is so regularly cast in 'discretionary' terms. The potential arbitrariness of discretionary governmental powers provides the reason why it is so important to have a vigilant administrative law to control their exercise. In Chapter 9, I seek to unlock the relationship between 'discretions,' as they are embodied in public powers, and private law duties of care owed by public bodies in the tort of negligence. This proves a difficult task, because judicial conceptions of what is meant by 'discretion' are varied. A court may simply mean that a public authority has a 'mere power', not a statutory duty to act; or that it has a complete immunity from liability; or a privilege from any duty; or, simply, that a difficult and expert judgment is involved in its decision. Given these different understandings, it is unsurprising that judges regularly draw different conclusions in negligence law from

[28] *Watkins v Secretary of State for the Home Department* [2006] UKHL 17, [2006] 2 AC 395.

their observation that a particular exercise of power involved 'discretion'. Tracking the question across both Australian and English law, I suggest that the language of discretion itself needs to be abandoned. The real questions that are relevant to the duty of care debate (as opposed to debates about the *amount* of care that should be expected of the state in exercising its functions) relate to the relationship between judicial and executive, or legislative authority. These must be considered in their own terms.

In both Australia and the United Kingdom, courts are increasingly prepared to exercise their power at least to scrutinise private law claims against government in respect of the exercise of 'discretionary' public functions, and claims are treated very much accordance with the Diceyan vision. By contrast, governments themselves have taken a very different view in the light of the global financial crisis and (in Australia) the lobbying efforts of the insurance sector. In some Australian jurisdictions, this has resulted in the implementation of a series of measures that either cast more power back into the hands of the executive itself (by giving prominent evidential weight to a public body's own procedures and practices), or which introduce special regimes of civil liability that loosely mimic the criteria of intervention in the administrative law system.[29]

These legislative criteria (which take the form of threshold liability standards of 'Wednesbury unreasonableness') connect loosely with 'faute lourde' standards of civil liability in French law, but the difference is that they are unaccompanied in Australia by any broader general principle of state liability for unlawful action, such as exists in France. The result is a clash between the culture of governments themselves (which is overtly anti-Diceyan and self-preferential in respect of the law's substantive rules) and that of courts (which seeks to address state liabilities as often as possible in the same way that it approaches the liability of private parties). The upper hand of government on this occasion is unmoderated, as I suggested above, by domestic human rights provisions of the United Kingdom type, which is unfortunate. Were democracy a perfect market, the risks of governmental self-preference would be more marginal, since rational voters would almost certainly not accept the diminutions in their private rights of action which these measures represent, at least not now that the global financial crisis has receded and insurance markets have recovered from their recent difficulties. They would probably, I speculate, elect to repeal the special public-law-style measures and restore the basic norm of equality. Unfortunately, however, the power of vested commercial interests, in the form of liability insurers, aligned perfectly with the interests of governments themselves on this occasion and measures were rushed through in short time, with minimum consideration. The measures are now firmly in place, with little prospect of being repealed, or moderated. Citizens may rely to some extent on courts' powers to interpret them in a way that obviates some of their worst effects for their private interests, but the extent of the liberties that courts can take with the statutory language is itself strictly limited.

[29] See n 26.

It will be apparent that my own view is that there are few governmental decisions (saving perhaps legislative and quasi-legislative ones)[30] that should not in principle be amenable to suit in the law of negligence, and that courts ought generally to approach public decisions regarding the use of special statutory powers in the same way that they approach the decisions of private parties charged with specialised, expert, allocative tasks. This would still give credit to public authorities at the breach stage, as one should, for their limited resources and multiple, complex commitments. It would also acknowledge the protection of any express or implied statutory immunities that have been granted them by parliament. In acknowledging that statutory immunities must always be respected, I realise that there is a risk of seeming to contradict myself, given the apparent scorn I have heaped on the recent wave of legislative provisions protecting public authorities in Australia. In fact, my point is simply that such immunities should be kept to a necessary minimum and ought to be fully empirically justified before being implemented. They are not something that should be introduced precipitously.

VI. Judicial Power, Access to Justice and Court Process

A. Judicial Power and Legislative Power

The point about recent legislative interventions in tort law in Australia brings us neatly to the role of judicial power in private law. The debates about the relative roles of courts and parliaments in developing private law doctrines are now well rehearsed.[31] They are considered to some degree in respect of the histories of consumer and contract law provided by Swain and Fairweather, to which I have already referred. At the end of the day, how one chooses to configure power in relation to the development of the private law depends on whom one trusts more—legislatures, or courts. It also depends on the extent to which one thinks that judges should be involved in the construction of social policy, and, conversely, governments in the day-to-day moral affairs of doing corrective justice. Answers to these questions are contingent and differ radically as between European systems, which observe a more deontological approach, and courts in the United States, where private law and public policy are trenchantly connected, if indeed they are

[30] This is a category of decisions commonly singled out for special protection from private law action in Australia. See, eg, *Crimmins v Stevedoring Industry Finance Committee* (1999) 200 CLR 1 (HCA) 21 (Gaudron J), (62) (Gummow J), 100-01 (Hayne J); *Graham Barclay Oysters Pty Ltd v Ryan* (2002) 211 CLR 540 (HCA) 557 (Gleeson CJ), 606-07 (Gummow & Hayne JJ, Gaudron J agreeing). Legislation in many states and territories prefers to protect a broader range of public decisions concerned with 'general allocations of resources'. See, eg, Civil Liability Act 2002 (NSW), s 42(b).

[31] See TT Arvind and J Steele (eds), *Tort Law and the Legislature* (Oxford, Hart Publishing, 2012); J Lee, *Legislation and Reform in the Law of Obligations* (Oxford, Hart Publishing, 2013).

not viewed as one and the same thing. The increase in the use of legislative techniques to develop, replicate, or adjust common law norms since the nineteenth century has been exponential and now poses a serious challenge of its own, by adding great complexity and duplication to the determination of private entitlements. Ironically, the very democratisation of private law through state legislative intervention has so complicated it in some fields as to seriously reduce its capacity to provide coherent normative guidance to either its own administrators, or its subjects. The proliferation of the sources of normative prescription in and around private law has, in fact, resulted in normative overload, with the consequence that making sense of the system of private law as a whole is increasingly problematic. This, I hazard to suggest, could be construed as a rule of law problem and it is one that we shall have to address.

B. Judicial Power and Property Rights

In Chapter 5, Professor Rotherham considers the question of judicial power directly in the context of what he casts as the power of courts to redistribute property rights in cases of private nuisance and trespass, through the award of damages in lieu of an injunction. Construing the private law concept of property as a quasi-constitutional control upon the exercise of judicial power, he notes that the United Kingdom Supreme Court has recently shown greater willingness to shake itself free of that control by shifting towards a more liberal approach to the grant of damages in the stead of specific relief in the *Fen Tigers* case.[32] This conceives of a more activist role for courts in redistributing private property rights and an approach that is also possibly more open to the influence of utilitarian public interest arguments in determinations of a plaintiff's secondary rights. Rotherham does not give away whether or not he considers these trends to be desirable in themselves, but expresses very clear concern about the lack of guidance emanating from the Supreme Court as to the circumstances in which judges ought to exercise their redistributive powers, warning us of the dangers of arbitrary, unfettered exercises of discretion. He suggests that, at a minimum, compulsory redistribution ought to be accompanied by the grant of a notional 'release fee' of the *Wrotham Park* type[33] to persons being deprived of their rights. This approach approximates favouring 'liability rules' in the famous construction of Calabresi and Melamed,[34] but was not something that the Supreme Court in *Fen Tigers* appeared to welcome.

If the denial of injunctive relief in a case of nuisance, or trespass, does involve a true redistribution of property rights,[35] it is one that is now authorised in most

[32] *Lawrence v Fen Tigers Ltd* [2014] UKSC 13, [2014] AC 822.

[33] *Wrotham Park Estates v Parkside Homes* [1974] 1 WLR 798 (Ch).

[34] G Calabresi and A Melamed, 'Property Rules, Liability Rules and Inalienability: One View of the Cathedral' (1972) 85 *Harvard Law Review* 1089.

[35] An alternative view is that merely denying an injunction does not strip the plaintiff of his or her primary property right at all, although it may considerably reduce its value. All it does is refuse to grant

jurisdictions by state power, through statutes equivalent to Lord Cairns Act. In other words, the quasi-constitutional limit upon judicial power has been relaxed by state legislatures, not discarded by courts themselves. Viewed in this light, the fact that courts are able to vary property rights is less alarming in this context than it might be in cases in which courts grant constructive trusts over assets a plaintiff never originally owned, as has sometimes occurred in restitution/disgorgement cases such as of *Attorney General v Reid*.[36] One may also accept that there could be good reasons in the modern day for weakening some of the boundaries around real property rights in cases of lesser interference. The world is destined to get very crowded very quickly, neighbours will be closer to one another than ever, and compromise accommodations may sometimes need to be forced in ways that are in their 'mutual' best interests. A more serious question is whether courts should be entitled to have regard to interests other than those of the parties to a dispute, including the interests of the 'community as a whole'.[37] How are courts to know what is in the community interest and what is their authority for deciding? Currently, they take some account of administrative decisions regarding planning permissions and the like in nuisance cases, but they have refused to give up their power to decide the issue of whether or not to issue an injunction for themselves.[38] These tensions between judicial and executive power are ubiquitous in the planning and environmental space and they are precisely the reason why decisions related to planning are normally left to the state and the public process. This may also explain why some courts still tend toward the robust protection of property rights, no matter the apparent social costs. Not only does this respect the historical importance attached to property, it avoids the controversy of arrogating powers of redistribution that remain difficult to effect without making broader social policy judgments. Precisely how private law protections for real property and the public environmental planning process should interlock with one another is probably going to be become one of the major issues of twenty-first century property law, given current predictions regarding the rate and seriousness of climate change.[39] Public planning will increasingly implicate private rights.

a secondary, remedial right to specific relief to enforce the primary right literally, favouring instead the grant of secondary remedial rights of other types. Things are different in cases in which courts grant orders which create *new primary* rights to plaintiffs over property by way of the remedial constructive trust.

[36] *Attorney General for Hong Kong v Reid* [1994] 1 AC 324 (PC).

[37] For a discussion of the same issue in the negligence context, see A Robertson, 'Justice, Community Welfare and the Duty of Care' (2011) 127 *LQR* 370.

[38] *Gillingham Borough Council v Medway (Chatham) Dock Co Ltd* [1993] QB 343; *Watson v Croft Promo-Sport Ltd* [2009] EWCA Civ 15 [32].

[39] See, eg, the current predictions of the Intergovernmental Panel on Climate Change 5th Assessment Report, *Climate Change 2014 Synthesis Report* (2015), available at: http://www.ipcc.ch/pdf/assessment-report/ar5/syr/SYR_AR5_FINAL_full_wcover.pdf

C. Access to Justice and Court Process

The substance of private law's protections are practically meaningless if individuals are too poor to access them. The topic of access to justice is vast,[40] but constitutes another key dimension of private law's dynamics with power. Powers of access for litigants can be increased by state funding, but the trend in recent years has been in precisely the opposite direction, as legal aid systems have been starved of cash in favour of other spending priorities. Attempts have instead been made to channel more proceedings into alternative dispute resolutions procedures, to cut court costs, to enable more litigants to band together in class action proceedings and—controversially, to allow the market itself to fund and direct the conduct of private lawsuits. The reasons why permitting third party litigation funding is so controversial are obvious—it can create a conflict between the private interest of the litigant and the interests of the litigation-funder, who may, by superior bargaining power, exploit a victim's weak position in order to obtain a high percentage of his or her rightful compensation.[41] It can also threaten the confidentiality of information disclosed by a defendant during settlement discussions and create vexatious litigation. It was to avert such risks that the common law traditionally recognised the torts (also crimes) of champerty and maintenance.[42] Most jurisdictions have now abolished both the crimes and the torts, although the torts remain alive and well in New Zealand, Canada and some Australian States,[43] and champertous contracts are generally void in all jurisdictions. The traditional disapproval of the involvement of third party economic interests in private litigation is clearly in tension with current public policy in seeking to privatise justice, and with existing contingency fee arrangements. The latter are only tolerated because it is thought that lawyers can be trusted, being bound by their ethical obligations not to allow their own interests to conflict directly with those of their clients. Whether the same can be said of third party litigation-funders is quite a different matter.

These issues are at the forefront of Justice McMurdo's insightful consideration of class action proceedings in Australia in Chapter 12, such actions commonly being externally funded on a commercial basis, and currently being subject to no dedicated statutory regime. As His Honour makes clear, the precise position

[40] See, generally, Genn (n 7).

[41] Whether this be damages obtained from a court, or an amount obtained in private settlement.

[42] This is part of the story of these wrongs at least. For the full history, see P Winfield, 'The History of Maintenance and Champerty' (1919) 35 *LQR* 50.

[43] In NZ, see *Waterhouse & Waterhouse v Contractors Bonding Ltd* [2013] NZSC 89 [26] (Elias CJ, McGrath, William Young, Chambers and Glazebrook JJ). Calls for the torts' abolition were rejected by the New Zealand Law Commission in 2001: *Subsidising Litigation* (NZ Law Comm Rep 72, 2001). In Canada see, eg, *Canada: McIntyre Estates v. Ontario (Attorney General)* [2002] Carswell Ont 2880 (Ont CA) [26]–[34]; *Boldt v The Law Society of Upper Canada* 2010 ONSC 3568. In Hong Kong, the crimes still exist and continue to be prosecuted: *Winnie Lo v HKSAR* [2012] HKEC 263 (HKCFA). The torts also survive in Queensland.

as regards such arrangements remains uncertain in Australia, despite two recent High Court decisions. There seems to be some degree of tolerance for them in principle, with a residual power in courts to prevent the abuse of their own process on a case-to-case basis. There are several, complex power dynamics in play here. The first is obviously the dynamic between the litigant victim and defendant, which tends to be skewed in favour of the defendant where the victim is poor, or his claim is relatively small. The second is that between the litigant victim and the third party litigation-funder, the latter of whom, in return for a potentially high proportion of the victim's rightful compensation (commensurate, no doubt, with the perceived insecurity of the investment) assumes a degree of control over the victim's litigation. The third is the dynamic of power between the court itself and the litigation-funder. The risk is that entrepreneurial private financiers will effectively end up hijacking court powers to determine disputes as a mechanism for the pursuit not of private justice, but pure commercial profit. This is a commodification of the process of justice itself. His Honour draws attention to this risk, arguing that courts' powers are limited to resolving genuine disputes between the parties to a dispute; and that they have (and should have) no power to determine matters that are not 'genuine disputes' according to law.

One solution to the risk of third party litigation funding would simply be to ban all such arrangements, but that might well undermine litigants' power to access justice in cases in which they retain a genuine interest in the dispute. It would also potentially frustrate the use of private law proceedings to hold defendants to account for instrumental reasons, assuming this to be an aim in some cases. Another solution, which represents the more difficult path that the High Court appears to be contemplating, is to try to distinguish between cases in which the interests of litigant and funder are genuinely aligned (so that the former's 'justice' interest is not being dominated by the funder's commercial one) and cases in which the they are not (such that the only interest before the court is the raw commercial interest of the funder). Disentangling these interests within the context of ad hoc determinations about abuse of process is likely to prove difficult, I suggest, and will probably not send clear enough messages to the market. The field seems to be one that is appropriate for dedicated, legislative review.

VII. Institutional Power

This brings us, finally, to institutional power in the private sense. The trust is one obvious institution of private power. Others are the Private Corporation and unincorporated associations such as the Roman Catholic Church. Both of the last two forms of institution now command enormous influence in the world. The Vatican is a small state in its own right, of course; and multinational corporations, whilst not actually states, span them, and sometimes command similar resources.

Super-national entities of this type now assume such central economic importance as to be in position to dictate public policy—economic, environmental and social. As Professor Grantham observes in Chapter 10, multinational banks have become simply too important to markets to be allowed to fail. The consequence is that it is the very victims of these institutions' most arbitrary excesses of power—the public—who end up subsidising the effects of their misconduct through government bail-outs.

A. The Corporation

Grantham's task is to seek a basis for the legitimacy of corporations as a source of private power in the twenty first century. His account of the nature and extent of the economic dimension of the company's power is startling, but it is perhaps his analysis of the unseen, or unacknowledged social power of such institutions that is most sobering of all and which, he suggests, is most difficult to justify normatively. International corporations have left indelible stains upon the social fabric of many developing nations and the ability of many multinationals and social media entities to influence popular culture and invisibly intrude upon our personal data for commercial purposes smacks, Grantham suggests, of the dystopian world of George Orwell and Aldous Huxley. His observations chime well beyond the field of corporations law itself. The power of multinationals and their intimate relationships with privatised media outlets arguably provide very good reasons for stripping them of any remaining standing to sue for defamation—a measure recently implemented throughout Australian jurisdictions via uniform legislation[44] and which has long been accepted in the case of state agencies and political parties.[45] Such entities are otherwise able to stifle free speech about issues that are of genuine public interest. When corporations operated only in the economic domain, this was perhaps less important. Now that they have such impact in the social policy domain as well, it embodies a new type of threat.

Justifications of the corporate form are interesting, precisely because they do not mesh perfectly with any of the theories Grantham explores: property, contract, state concession, social enterprise, or wealth-maximisation. Hohfeld conceptualised the corporation as a complex contractual or quasi-contractual associative arrangement between persons,[46] but it is no longer possible to regard the corporation as anything like a natural person, or even a collection of natural persons—it has attained something like the metaphysical abstraction of the civil state in

[44] See, eg, Defamation Act 2005 (NSW), s 9.

[45] *Derbyshire County Council v Times Newspapers Ltd* [1993] AC 534 (HL); *Ballina Shire Council v Ringland* (1994) 22 NSWLR 680; *Goldsmith v Boryhul* [1988] QB 459.

[46] W Hohfeld, 'Nature of Stockholders' Individual Liability for Corporation Debts' (1909) 9 *Columbia Law Review* 285, 288 (the corporation is nothing more an 'association of individuals').

France. Similarly, there are, Grantham points out, questions about the authority of corporate managers to engage in social policy projects (so, goodbye social enterprise theory?); and, whilst wealth-maximisation theories probably carry most weight in the current consensus, the fact that social costs and benefits are often incalculable and incommensurable means that the social power of corporations is very hard to justify, even if its economic power stands on a firm, normative footing. This social power, Grantham points out, may be something that we might ultimately welcome, but it is not something that should be allowed to creep up on us unawares. This reminds us, once again, that new forms of power emerge constantly, particularly via the open channels of the market, in ways that are often unforeseen and difficult to control.

B. The Trust

The question mark Grantham raises against the social role of corporations and the authority (and ability) of company directors to pursue social policy ends connects with the philosophical inquiry pursued by Professor Harding in Chapter 6. Harding's objective is to explain and justify the limits that are currently set on the purposes to which trustees may use their powers to administer, or dispose of the assets of a trust; in particular, the rule that they may only do so in so far as this accords with their mandate. Whilst the traditional justification for this limit tends to be framed in terms of the will of the settlors of the trust (i.e. within an individualistic framework), Harding asks whether it might be possible to justify it in social justice terms, referencing the political theory of John Rawls. One, potentially useful stroke in this design that he identifies is Rawls' idea that social justice should implicate only the design of the law's 'basic structure' (in this instance, the design of the trust?), not 'post-institutional action' (individual decisions that trustees make about administration and disposition). He confesses that the question is difficult and acknowledges some of its challenges—one of the most tricky of which stems from Cohen's criticism of Rawls' account: if social justice is something we should be doing, then why should the obligation exist only at the institutional level, rather than reaching down to post-institutional actions as well? Hesitant as Harding is, in the end, his piece highlights brilliantly the difficult interface between private law and the power of 'social forces.' On this occasion, trust rules in their current form appear to operate as a constraint upon those forces—as a barrier to the use of the trust for social justice aims other than where these are explicitly intended. If Harding is correct, however, these limits may be more consistent with these aims than initially appears to be the case.

C. The Church

Ecclesiastical institutions are not powerful simply because they are wealthy, but also because they engender intimate relationships of personal trust. The abuses of such trust that have occurred historically within their watch, to the detriment of vulnerable children and adults, have become headline news everywhere in the world. Such tragedies form the focus of the recent Royal Commission investigation into institutional responses to child sexual abuse in Australia.[47] These abuses are precisely the sort that private law ought to be able to redress, but claims against individual perpetrators have proven difficult. For example, the offending priest may be dead, or impecunious, and the reliability of witness evidence may have been prejudiced by the passage of time. Cultures of secrecy, fears of reprisal, senses of shame and long-lasting psychiatric damage also regularly obscure the emergence of truths, as does reliance by the Church on the technicalities of its unincorporated status. One particularly common strategy that has proven successful in Australia, but less so in other jurisdictions (known as the 'Ellis defence')[48] is for the Church to take a recognised corporate or trust form for the purposes of advancing its economic interests in the world, but then to vanish before one's eyes, or dissolve as a legal personality into a sea of unincorporated personal associations, when victims come looking for redress. This is a spectacular example of the way in which power can change its form to suit its own devices and evade the grasp of legal or social control.

Such instances, alongside examples of state wrongdoing, form part of Professor Moran's analysis of what she refers to as an emerging private law of institutional wrongs. Tort law, she argues, is in the process of developing in such a way as to offer significant new possibilities for reshaping institutional responsibility and redressing imbalances of power. The sources of change, she suggests, lie in a more generalised conception of the duty to take care stemming originally from Lord Atkin,[49] from the gradual elimination of state and charitable immunities from suit, from a shift of legal responsibility paradigms away from 'single wrongdoer' and 'single legal cause' models to paradigms that spread responsibility more widely beyond its immediate perpetrator, and to changes in our understandings of vicarious liability doctrine. That doctrine is shifting in its focus, precisely in response to such cases, away from traditional conceptions that attach liability to employing institutions in accordance with an implied authorisation thesis, toward one that is tantamount to fixing direct responsibility on the institution itself for creating risks for the vulnerable, which risks lie within its domain of control. Although the process is not complete, this model offers a potential source of new hope and imagines private law as a powerful tool of institutional accountability.

Such developments are still sorely needed. If they are brought to fruition alongside appropriate abandonments of traditional limitation of actions restrictions,[50]

[47] See n 3.

[48] *Trustees of the Roman Catholic Church for the Archdiocese of Sydney v Ellis* (2007) 70 NSWLR 565, [2007] NSWCA 117.

[49] *Donoghue v Stevenson* [1932] AC 562 (HL). Another lynchpin was *Dorset Yacht Co Ltd v Home Office* [1970] AC 1004 (HL).

[50] See, eg, Limitation of Actions Amendment (Criminal Child Abuse) Act 2015 (Vic); Limitations Amendment (Child Abuse) Bill 2015 (NSW).

they may restore to private law some of the power to act as a tool of corrective justice, vindication and accountability that it has lacked. This may help to restore public faith its capacities. Even then, however, it is unlikely to yield a complete solution to problems of historic abuse of power. For these reasons, it has been suggested that a redesign of institutional, administrative systems of ex gratia reparation may be in order.[51] Currently, those offered by the Catholic Church in Australia appear woefully inadequate both in terms of the amount of money they offer victims, and in terms of defects in process (secrecy of outcomes, absence of the appearance of independence, arbitrary cut-offs without extension periods) that are likely to undermine public confidence in them. One solution that two of the editors of this work have elsewhere proposed is that the power of private law's corrective norms (full redress) and institutional features (transparency, consistency, openness to review) could usefully be used to inform and enhance the design of future schemes of administrative reparation offered by those institutions that have accepted responsibility for the events in question.[52] In that way, the ethical power of private law's institutions and norms might constructively be combined with the more efficient, less formal and more cost-effective mechanisms that tend to accompany public systems of monetary support. Even if, therefore, private litigation does not always provide a viable solution, private law's conceptions of justice can useful serve to inform administrative solutions. That will not simply empower private law itself, allowing its values to be taken more seriously in the public domain, but it will also empower victims of historic, institutional abuse by providing them with a more meaningful and complete form of justice.

VIII. Conclusions

The dynamics of private law and power are complex and forever changing. Those dynamics are both internal to the law's doctrines and remedies and external, in the sense that those rules are located within a public system with political ends that strives for common goods. The ends of the public system are fed into the private law system through democratic, legislative processes, to be applied by judges, who retain interpretative powers of their own, and who also have their own powers to develop the common law alongside those legislative rules in a way that is complementary, harmonious and respectful of constitutional conventions regarding the proper allocation of decision between the different organs of the modern state. As legislative incursions increase through the twenty-first century, judges'

[51] See S Degeling and K Barker, 'Private Law and Grave Historical Injustice: The Role of the Common Law' (2016) 41 *Monash University Law Review* 377; 'Designing Reparation: Lessons from Private Law' (Canberra, ANU Press, 2016) (in press).

[52] ibid.

power will be further reduced, but it will never cease to be a crucial, moderating force. As legislative norms increase, and assuming that these norms will never be able to prescribe for their own application in every situation, the importance of judges' powers of statutory interpretation will similarly increase. Here too there is scope for manoeuver, albeit within a smaller space. Power contained always finds another place in which to expand.

To the extent that 'the people' themselves, as constitutive of the common weal, retain power over the content of private law, it is now solely through the democratic process, not, as it once was, through having the final say in a jury box in accordance with a logic that they need not disclose. That is clearly an important historical development that has legitimised the norms of private law and rendered them both more transparent and predictable. At the same time, however, imperfections in the processes of democratic government always carry risks of their own for private law and private interests. Governments still show alarming tendencies toward self-preference in setting civil liability rules in some quarters and jurisdictions; and they sometimes fall prey to the influence of powerful, multinational commercial interests. This can have serious repercussions for the protection of the private rights of the less powerful in society, resulting in redistributions of resource that cut back on corrective justice for vulnerable victims of wrongdoing in the name of creating a healthier economy with trickle-down benefits that may never, in fact, trickle down. Measures of this sort may simply see the coffers of powerful wrongdoers (or of those underwriting their liabilities), filled at the expense of innocent victims whose compensation will, in corresponding measure, run out in a mere matter of years.[53] The costs of that failure are born both by them and by society as a whole through the levers of the social security system.

To safeguard against risks such as this, and against manipulations of the 'democratic market' by those with vested commercial interests in the content of private law, we must be vigilant to protect the legislative process itself against the undue influence of private institutional power. This may involve changing aspects of the public system, such as conventions surrounding lobbying and systems of political donation. The same lesson, I suggest, must be learned in respect of rights of access to justice, where a moderate course must be steered that does not permit rights of action themselves to be commodified, so as to become simply the next investment product for all to buy and sell. Once the full power of naked commercial interest is unleashed in the civil process, the dynamics of power change the nature of game itself—from one in which the market is used to fund justice, to one in which justice is instead used to fund the market.

[53] For the shocking statistics in this regard, see G Grant, K Burns et al, 'When Lump Sums Run Out: Disputes at the Borderlines of Tort Law, Injury Compensation and Social Security,' ch 15 in K Barker, K Fairweather and R Grantham (eds), *Private Law in the Twenty-First Century* (Oxford, Hart, 2016).

Looking past private law at the systemic level to its individual substantive doctrines and rules, there are further, complex dynamics. On the one hand, there are some signs of the weakening of property rights which could operate to the detriment of individual interests in favour of the public good and allow them more regularly to be steam-rollered, or compulsorily purchased by other persons or commercial interests, through judicial fiat. On the other hand, it might be suggested that this more flexible strategy is consistent with a commitment to the promotion of the general autonomy of all, conceived of in a positive, social sense. I have suggested at various points in this chapter that private law doctrine itself may be shifting gradually toward a more positive conception of autonomy, away from any Kantian ideology, promoting welfare pure and simple in some instances. I remain hesitant about that as a general proposition, because in commercial markets between equals, the commitments to norms of self-reliance are still very strong. But several contributions to this work point to the importance of the autonomy agenda in discrete contexts that lie outside the mainstream of the competitive market. This shift from the protection of individual liberties in the negative sense to their protection in the positive sense, if more widely instantiated in the law, could be understood as the judicial version of the switch the state has made through the twentieth century from negative to positive mode. If positive autonomy in the sense of access to the full authorship of one's life through access to a reasonable range of options is to be attained in the perfectionist liberal sense, however, private law can only ever be a partial solution. The market also has its part to play in the creation of those options and may need to be regulated to promote that effect. Indeed, it will only ever be through a combination of private law rules, public systems and economic markets that power in the sense that is most important to us—the ability to become true authors of our own lives—is likely to be realised. Even then, our power may never be truly complete.

Part 2

Power, History and Society

2

Power, History and the Law of Contract in Eighteenth Century England

WARREN SWAIN

> What dramatically distinguished nineteenth century law from its eighteenth century counterpart was the extent to which common law judges came to play a central role in directing the course of social change. Especially during the period before the Civil War, the common law performed at least as great a role as legislation in underwriting and channelling economic development. In fact, common law judges regularly brought about the sort of far-reaching changes that would have been regarded earlier as entirely within the powers of the legislature.[1]

Morton Horwitz was writing about the transformation of the law in America during the period between 1780 and 1860, but the impact of his ideas would extend a long way beyond his subject matter.[2] Horwitz's approach was a reaction to what he saw as 'conservative legal history'[3] with its 'emphasis on continuity and a corresponding de-emphasis of change'.[4] The best legal historians have always had a least half an eye on social context.[5] And yet if 'power' is taken broadly to mean the influence of economic, political or social forces, it is a fairly peripheral matter within the traditional legal histories of private law. The main emphasis is squarely

[1] MJ Horwitz, *The Transformation of American Law 1780–1860* (Cambridge Mass, Harvard University Press, 1977) 1.

[2] From a non-American perspective, see D Sugarman, '"Great Beyond His Knowing": Morton Horwitz's Influence on Legal Education and Scholarship in England, Canada, and Australia' in D Hamilton and A Brophy (eds), *Transformations in American Legal History Law Ideology, and Methods Essays in Honor of Morton J Horwitz Volume II* (Cambridge Mass, Harvard University Press, 2010) 504–42.

[3] MJ Horwitz, 'The Conservative Tradition in the Writing of American Legal History' (1973) 17 *American Journal of Legal History* 275.

[4] ibid, 276.

[5] This is certainly true of the greatest legal historian of them all, Frederic Maitland. Some legal history truly deserves the epithet social history. The outstanding example is James Willard Hurst's *Law and Economic Growth: The Legal History of the Lumber Industry in Wisconsin 1836–1915* (Cambridge Mass, Harvard University Press, 1964).

upon developments within the law itself, or what is sometimes called the internal point of view.[6]

Horwitz approached the material as a disciple of the Critical Legal Studies movement.[7] As such, he was acutely sensitive to the dynamics of power. The great value of his thesis was to remind legal historians that it is not enough to describe legal change. Good legal history seeks to explain it as well, whether those explanations can be found within the law, or outside it. Horwitz's central claim was that nineteenth century judges departed from their predecessors. They no longer saw their role as limited to adjudicators of the case before them, but rather as framers of general rules based on considerations of social and economic policy.[8]

Many of these themes were taken up by Patrick Atiyah[9] in his *The Rise and Fall of Freedom of Contract*[10] where he wrote that '[t]he period between 1770–1870 saw the emergence of general principles of contract law closely associated with the development of the free market and the ideals of the political economists'.[11] In his account, this approach marked a change from an earlier time when judges were more inclined to promote principles of fairness between contracting parties. The focus is on England rather than America. As such, it provides the best starting point when considering the dynamics of power in eighteenth century contract law.

I. Fairness, Community and the Law of Contract

According to Atiyah, '[t]he extreme individualism, the belief that all prices are a matter of subjective choice, the stress on will and intention, of the nineteenth century were not found in the law of the eighteenth century to any significant degree'.[12] Atiyah is anxious to draw a clear line between the old and the new. On this view, before 1770, the law of contract was infused, much more than it was subsequently, with principles of fair play and equity. If he is right, then power, in so far as it can be located within contract law, rested with the people rather than the political and economic elites. There is an obvious parallel with EP Thompson's

[6] D Ibbetson, 'What is Legal History a History of?' in A Lewis and M Lobban (eds), *Law and History* (Oxford, Oxford University Press, 2004) 33–40.

[7] For a detailed account of the influence of the CLS movement on legal history, see R Gordon, 'Critical Legal Histories' (1984) 36 *Stanford Law Review* 57. For a summary of influence of CLS more broadly, see N Duxbury, *Patterns of American Jurisprudence* (Oxford, Oxford University Press, 1995) 421–509.

[8] Horwitz (n 1) 2.

[9] Atiyah attended some of Horwitz's seminars at Harvard and has acknowledged his influence: P Atiyah, 'An Autobiographical Fragment' in G Wilson (ed), *Frontiers of Legal Scholarship* (Chichester, Wiley, 1995) 45–46.

[10] P Atiyah, *The Rise and Fall of Freedom of Contract* (Oxford, Oxford University Press, 1979).

[11] ibid, 398.

[12] Atiyah (n 10) 167.

description of the 'moral economy' which 'supposed definite, and passionately held, notions of the common weal—notions which, indeed, found some support in the paternalist tradition of the authorities; notions which the people re-echoed so loudly in their turn that the authorities were, in some measure, the prisoners of the people'.[13] In sixteenth century England the idea of the 'commonwealth' or 'common weal' encapsulated the way in which many people thought about society.[14] It stood for a communitarian, rather than egalitarian system of social order based around 'estates', whose members owed mutual obligations to each other and to members of the other 'estates'.[15] In this value system, unchecked economic freedom was disparaged.[16] The theory of 'common weal' was grounded in both legal[17] and social reality. Outside of London, the population lived in small, rural communities[18] bound together by ties of kinship, friendship and neighbourliness.[19] These values had not entirely disappeared by the end of the eighteenth century. The growth of domestic trade, international trade, agricultural innovation and the beginnings of industrialisation changed things. Not least of all, it brought urbanisation in its wake.[20] Yet even though economic relations were becoming more impersonal, a strong element of the personal and local remained. A flavour of this can be found in the diary of Thomas Turner, a Sussex shopkeeper, who described the anxiety that he felt about recovering a debt from one of his customers in 1758:

> Oh, what a confusion and tumult there is in my breast about this affair! To think what a terrible thing it is to arrest a person, for by these means he may be entirely torn to pieces; but, on the other hand, this debt hath been standing above four years ... and I am so oppressed for want of money that I know not which way to turn.[21]

The extent to which the law of contract concerned itself with fairness, reflected community values or a particular vision of economic morality, is not easy to ascertain. There are some situations in which fairness was a factor. From the sixteenth century the Court of Chancery would routinely offer relief against

[13] E Thompson, *Customs in Common* (London, Penguin, 1993) 188–89. The context was very different. Thompson was discussing the price of bread and the relationship between the crowd (the ruled) and the rulers.

[14] K Wrightson, *Earthly Necessities* (London, Penguin, 2002) 27–29.

[15] For an account of the Tudor Commonwealth, see W Jones, *The Tudor Commonwealth 1529–1559* (London, Athlone Press, 1970) 192–201.

[16] Wrightson (n 14) 29; Jones ibid.

[17] See Christopher Brooks, *Law, Politics and Society in Early Modern England* (Cambridge, Cambridge University Press, 2008) 241–77.

[18] E Wrigley, 'Urban Growth and Agricultural Change: England and the Continent in the Early Modern Period' (1985) 15 *Journal of Interdisciplinary History* 683.

[19] These types of relations were crucial in the credit market: C Muldrew, *The Economy of Obligation* (London, Palgrave, 1998).

[20] For a discussion of all of these events, see J Mokyr, *The Enlightenment Economy* (New Haven, Yale University Press, 2009).

[21] R Blencowe and M Lower (eds), T Turner, *The Diary of a Georgian Shopkeeper* (Oxford, Oxford University Press, 1979) 26. Informal pressure, without resorting to the law, could sometimes succeed: J Price (ed), *Joshua Johnson's Letterbook, 1771–1774* (London, London Record Society, 1979) [90], [93].

penalty clauses.[22] The superior methods for gathering evidence in Chancery meant that it was not too difficult to ascertain whether the sum claimed was in excess of the actual loss suffered and therefore ought to be treated as an unenforceable penalty.[23] The common law courts might also intervene in cases of extreme contractual unfairness. The defence of duress, for example, can be traced to the Middle Ages.[24] But it was usually difficult to assess whether a transaction was unfair. Until the nineteenth century, the common law courts did not enjoy the luxury of hearing evidence from the parties themselves.[25] Many low value claims were litigated in the Courts of Conscience before a single Commissioner.[26] The high turnover of business in these courts suggests that there was little time for consideration of the rights and wrongs of individual cases.[27]

There is little proof that the courts routinely intervened where a bad, disadvantageous or hard bargain was entered into.[28] Those cases where contracts were struck down are exceptional and involve factors in addition to an unfair price.[29] In the two main contract actions, debt on a bond and assumpsit, the value received in return for the promise was irrelevant. In the former, the bond was dispositive in character. In the latter, the consideration did not need to be adequate or fair.[30] There was no English version of *laesio enormis*.[31] An inadequate price was evidence of fraud or some other ground to set aside a contract in Chancery, but it was usually said to be insufficient on its own.[32] Towards the end of the eighteenth century Equity judges actually seem to have been more inclined to treat inadequacy, if very gross, as sufficient grounds for intervention.[33] This was still not a power to be exercised lightly. Lord Thurlow was at pains to stress: 'if the court should take

[22] E Henderson, 'Relief from Bonds in the English Chancery: Mid-Sixteenth Century' (1974) 18 *American Journal of Legal History* 298.

[23] In Chancery the defendant could generally be compelled to answer questions under oath: M Macnair, *The Law of Proof in Early Modern Equity* (Berlin, Dunker & Humblot, 1999) 54–60.

[24] A Simpson, *A History of the Common Law of Contract* (Oxford, Oxford University Press, 1996) 99.

[25] (1843) 6 & 7 Vict c 85; (1851) 14 & 15 Vict c 99. C Allen, *The Law of Evidence in Victorian England* (Cambridge, Cambridge University Press, 1997) 96–8, 100–10.

[26] On the Courts of Conscience, see W Holdsworth, *A History of English Law*, vol 1 (London, Methuen, 1922) 190–91; M Finn, *The Character of Credit* (Cambridge, Cambridge University Press, 2003) 197–235. The Court of Conscience was still sometimes called the Court of Requests in recognition of its origins, see WHD Winder, 'The Courts of Requests' (1936) 52 *LQR* 369.

[27] W Hutton, *Courts of Requests. Their Nature, Utility and Powers Described* (Birmingham, Pearson and Rollason, 1787).

[28] J Barton, 'The Enforcement of Hard Bargains' (1987) 103 *LQR* 118.

[29] See D Ibbetson, *A Historical Introduction to the Law of Obligations* (Oxford, Oxford University Press, 1999) 210–11.

[30] D Ibbetson, 'Consideration and the Theory of Contract in the Sixteenth Century Common Law', in J Barton (ed), *Towards a General Law of Contract* (Berlin, Duncker & Humblot, 1990) 67, 72–77. The classic statement on this question is found in *Sturlyn v Albany* (1587) Cro Eliz 67, 150, 78 ER 327.

[31] *Nott v Hill* (1682) 2 Chan Cas 120, 22 ER 875.

[32] *Heathcote v Paignon* (1787) 2 Bro CC 167, 175, 29 ER 96.

[33] *Gwynne v Heaton* (1778) 1 Bro CC 1, 28 ER 949.

such a ground as to rest the case upon the market price, every transaction of this kind would come into the court of equity'.[34]

The 'sound price' doctrine is central to the debate about contractual fairness. The evidence that the courts sweetened the strictness of *caveat emptor* by imposing an implied warranty of quality when a sound price was paid is difficult to disentangle.[35] Sir William Blackstone made no mention of such a rule.[36] The few legal writers who discussed the doctrine disagreed on its scope. John Joseph Powell wrote that, 'if a man sell a horse for a price, which it would not be worth unless it were sound, the contract will be void'.[37] Richard Wooddeson did not go as far but stated that 'a fair price implies a warranty'.[38] A third version was to be found in some obiter remarks made by Lord Mansfield in *Stuart v Wilkins*, where he suggests that a warranty would be implied where a sound price was paid and the seller knew of the defect.[39] A decade before, the same judge is reported to have said that, 'if [horse sellers] at any time … took a sound price for a horse they knew not to be sound, or concealed any defect, the not warranting him should not avail them at all'.[40] Horses sold with an express warranty were usually more expensive. The cheaper sales at a horse repository usually excluded a warranty as part of the conditions of the sale, or made any warranty—even when express—practically difficult to enforce.[41] The impact of any sound price doctrine may therefore have been quite small, at least in horse sales. It remains an unsolved puzzle how long the sound price doctrine lasted and what form it took. All that can be said with any confidence is that by the start of the nineteenth century the doctrine had fallen out of favour.[42]

One of the main hurdles in trying to reconstruct the motives of eighteenth century judges is that multiple factors were often influential in reaching a decision. On occasion, the courts were quite explicit in affording protection from

[34] *Heathcote* (n 32) 175. For similar statements, see *Nichols v Gould* (1752) 2 Ves Sen 422, 423, 28 ER 270; *Griffith v Spratley* (1787) 1 Cox 383, 388, 29 ER 1213.

[35] For two, opposite interpretations see Horwitz (n 1) 167 and A Simpson, 'The Horwitz Thesis and the History of Contracts' (1979) 46 *University of Chicago Law Review* 533, 581–83.

[36] Given how little attention was paid to contract law generally by Blackstone in W Blackstone, *Commentaries on the Laws of England*, 4 vols (Oxford, Clarendon Press, 1765–69), too much weight should not be put on the omission.

[37] JJ Powell, *Essay Upon the Law of Contracts and Agreements*, vol 1 (London, J Johnson, 1790) 150.

[38] R Wooddeson, *A Systematical View of the Laws of England*, vol 2 (London, Thomas Payne, 1792) 415.

[39] (1778) 1 Doug 18, 20, 99 ER 15. This version is most fully articulated in a manuscript report: LI MS Hill 13 f 258.

[40] *London Chronicle* (London, 14 August 1764). The decision survives in Lord Mansfield's note book, *Worth v Pank* (1764) in J Oldham, *The Mansfield Manuscripts and the Growth of English Law in the Eighteenth Century*, vol 1 (Chapel Hill, The University of North Carolina Press, 1992) 266.

[41] W Swain, 'Horse Sales: the Problem of Consumer Contracts from a Historical Perspective' in J Devenney and M Kenny (eds), *European Consumer Protection Theory and Practice* (Cambridge, Cambridge University Press, 2012) 282, 293–94.

[42] *Parkinson v Lee* (1802) 2 East 314, 102 ER 389.

exploitation. Sailors dealing with their prize money could expect a sympathetic hearing.[43] Things were usually more complicated. Unfairness took many forms. A series of decisions from Lord Nottingham's time onwards were concerned with credit transactions, many of which involved heirs raising money on the back of their expected inheritance.[44] There was no single ground for intervention. Chancery judges were partly motivated by a desire to avoid circumvention of the usury laws, which by this time operated as a cap on permissible interest, rather than an outright prohibition.[45] There was also a concern about the exploitation of young heirs.[46] But perhaps the dominant factor in the mind of judges was the fact that such transactions were seen as a threat to the landed interest.[47] As the eighteenth century progressed Equity began to adopt a harsher line against this sort of contract. In *Twistleton v Griffith*, Lord Cowper made no secret of his motives:

> he saw no inconvenience in the objection, that at this rate, an heir, without difficulty, could not sell a reversion; this might force an heir to go home, and submit to his father, or to bite on the bridle, and endure some hardships, and in the meantime he might grow wiser, and be reclaimed.[48]

For a time, any agreement with an heir regarding his expectancy was unenforceable. This apparently 'established principle' was a departure from the more flexible rule a century before.[49] In turn, the new approach would be overturned. By the mid-nineteenth century the usury laws had been abolished.[50] New forms of money lending, some of which were regulated by statute,[51] began to evolve. Heirs could deal with their reversions without getting special protection.[52] In *Earl of Aylesford v Morris*, Lord Selbourne explained that the unreformed rules were

[43] *Baldwin v Rochford* (1748) 1 Wils 229, 95 ER 589; *Taylour v Rochford* (1751) 2 Ves Sen 281, 28 ER 546; *How v Weldon* (1754) 2 Ves Sen 516, 28 ER 330. Prize money consisted of the proceeds from cargo captured from enemy ships: E Roscoe, *A History of the English Prize Court* (London, Lloyds, 1924) 52.

[44] W Swain and K Fairweather, 'Usury and the Judicial Regulation of Financial Transactions in Seventeenth and Eighteenth Century England' in M Kenny, J Devenney and L Fox-O'Mahony (eds), *Unconscionability in European Private Financial Transactions* (Cambridge, Cambridge University Press, 2010) 147, 154–59.

[45] *Draper v Draper* (1677); *Berry* (1680) in DEC Yale (ed), *Lord Nottingham's Chancery Cases* (London, Selden Society, 1961) 602, 868.

[46] *Fairfax v Trigg* (1675), ibid 448.

[47] On the political significance of the landed classes at this time, see P Langford, *Public Life and the Propertied Englishman 1689–1798* (Oxford, Oxford University Press, 1994).

[48] (1716) 1 P Wms 312, 313, 24 ER 403. For similar statements, see *Cole v Gibson* (1734) 3 P Wms 290, 293, 24 ER 1070; *Walmesley v Booth* (1741) 2 Atk 27, 28, 26 ER 412; *Baugh v Price* (1752) 1 Wils KB 320, 322, 95 ER 640.

[49] *Gwynne v Heaton* (1778) 1 Bro CC 1, 9–10, 28 ER 949.

[50] (1854) 17 & 18 Vict c 90.

[51] Pawnbroking transactions, which largely involved the poor, had long been regulated by statute: W Swain and K Fairweather, 'The Legal Regulation of Pawnbroking in England' in J Devenney and M Kenny (eds), *Consumer Credit, Debt and Investment in Europe* (Cambridge, Cambridge University Press, 2012) 142–59. More general regulation came in the form of the Money Lending Act (1900) 63 & 64 Vict c 51.

[52] (1867) 31 Vict c 4.

seen as an 'impediment to fair and reasonable, as well as to unconscionable, bargains'.[53]

It would be easy to conclude that the nineteenth century saw values of fairness and paternalism sidelined in the context of contract claims. The truth is much more complex. Attitudes towards credit transactions had been shifting for centuries. The religious objections to usury had long ago been recast into ones of public policy. Interest rate caps disappeared with barely a whimper of protest in 1854.[54] Economic morality evolved over time. So did the identity of the dominant economic actors. New industrial wealth gradually began to eclipse the traditional landed aristocracy.[55] Yet the law's reactions should not be exaggerated either. Chancery judges who were never entirely adverse to the free market did not suddenly become converts to its unrestricted excesses. Close examination of the authorities shows that, whilst there were some changes in Equity's application, the most fundamental shift involved the way in which the law was structured.[56] Undue influence took over as the main organising concept. The open textured structure of the eighteenth century was replaced with something more rigid. Except at the margins, the willingness or otherwise of Equity to grant relief may have evolved rather less. The argument that there was a shift away from some idealised system where fairness was dominant is ultimately unconvincing. It is based on an idealised notion of the pre-nineteenth law of contract. An element of fairness and honesty may have been recognised as part of the English character,[57] but this only went so far in the law of contract. Greater continuity existed in other ways as well. Not least of these was in the relationship between merchants and judges.

II. Lawyers and the Mercantile Interest[58]

Reading some accounts of the history of contract law it would be easy to conclude that lawyers paid little heed to the needs of merchants before the nineteenth century.[59] There is a great deal of evidence to the contrary. As far back as the mid-fifteenth century, whilst the majority were prepared to accept that a threat to a

53 *Earl of Aylesford v Morris* (1873) LR 8 Ch App 484, 490.

54 Editorial, 'Repeal of the Usury Laws', *The Law Times* (London, 19 August 1854). I am grateful to Ms Karen Fairweather for this reference.

55 It might be said to be the beginning of the end: D Cannadine, *The Decline and Fall of the British Aristocracy* (New Haven, Conn, Harvard University Press, 1990).

56 For a detailed account see W Swain, 'Reshaping Contractual Unfairness in Eighteenth and Nineteenth Century England' (2014) *Journal of Legal History* 131.

57 P Langford, *Englishness Identified. Manners and Character 1650–1850* (Oxford, Oxford University Press, 2000) 122–28, 148–57.

58 Some of the material in this section is discussed in more detail in W Swain, *The Law of Contract 1670–1870* (Cambridge, Cambridge University Press, 2015) 42–106.

59 This view is at least as old as Lord Campbell, *The Lives of the Chief Justices of England*, vol 2 (London, John Murray, 1849) 402–403. More recently see, Horwitz (n 1) 167.

man's goods amounted to duress, Choke J said that, were such an argument to succeed, it 'would invalidate most of the obligations in England'.[60] His more cautious views would eventually prevail.[61] The need to protect the institution of contract and the economic implications that flowed from it was seen as more crucial than ensuring fairness. With the passing centuries, the common lawyers began to take a much more prominent role in mercantile affairs. In Medieval times, mercantile disputes were heard in the City and Borough Courts.[62] These courts began to decline under the Tudors but it was the seventeenth century before the Common Law took a decisive stranglehold in the affairs of merchants. It did so in the context of negotiable instruments, which were gradually integrated into the Common Law. The process can hardly be described as smooth. Promissory notes were particularly problematic. But to say that the mercantile or commercial interest only exerted a major influence in the nineteenth century is plainly false.

None of this means that the relationship between merchants and lawyers was always harmonious. The mercantile writer Marius counselled that 'the right dealing merchant doth not care how little he hath to do in the Common law'.[63] Seventy years later, in *The Complete English Tradesman*, Daniel Defoe described lawsuits as the 'plagues of a tradesman's life'.[64] The expense of litigation is one source of dissatisfaction.[65] Josiah Child's complaint was more specific:

> After great expences of time and money, it is as well if we can make our own counsel (being common lawyers) understand one half our case, we being amongst them as in a foreign country, our language strange to them, and theirs strange to us.[66]

Sixty years later, the supposedly poor state of the common lawyers' knowledge of mercantile practice still had the ability to irritate merchants. Malachy Postlethwayt, a merchant and writer on economic and business matters, argued that a 'student of the law cannot have too minute and comprehensive a knowledge of the practical arts of merchants'.[67]

The perception that lawyers were remote from the concerns of merchants may have been genuinely held, but seems unlikely to have entirely reflected reality.

[60] (1467) YB 7 Ed 4 fl 21a–22a pl 24. The decision is discussed by Ibbetson (n 29) 72; Simpson (n 24) 99.

[61] Simpson (n 24) 99. By the eighteenth century, duress to goods could be used to reclaim money paid: *Astley v Reynolds* (1731) 2 Stra 915, 93 ER 939. As late as the 1840s, it was still not a vitiating factor: *Skeate v Beale* (1841) 11 A & E 983, 113 ER 688.

[62] The London Mayor's and Sherriff's Courts were particularly significant: P Tucker, *Law Courts and Lawyers in the City of London 1300–1550* (Cambridge, Cambridge University Press, 2007).

[63] J Marius, *Advice Concerning Bills of Exchange*, 2nd edn (London, William Hunt, 1655) preface. These remarks did not appear in the first edition of 1651.

[64] *The Complete English Tradesman*, 2nd edn (London, Charles Rivington, 1727) 284.

[65] W Prest, 'The Experience of Litigation in Eighteenth-Century England' in D Lemmings (ed), *The British and Their Laws in the Eighteenth Century* (Woodbridge, Boydell Press, 2005) 133–54. R Boote, *An Historical Treatise of an Action or Suit at Law* (London, A Sowle, 1766) iii noted the 'obscurity and expense' attendant upon a law suit.

[66] J Child, *A Discourse about Trade* (London, W Johnston, 1690) 113–14.

[67] M Postlethwayt, *The Merchant's Public Counting House* (London, John and Paul Knapton, 1750) 55.

Lawyers were especially sensitive to market forces,[68] and had the opportunity to gain 'extensive knowledge of the world'[69] through their involvement in business activity beyond litigation. Attorneys had traditionally filled a variety of roles,[70] and some barristers worked as advisers and standing counsel to commercial bodies.[71] For those not directly involved in business activities there were likely to be some social connections with merchants as fellow members of the 'middling sort'[72] through coffee house culture and elsewhere.[73] A growing body of mercantile literature began to be published.[74] The practice of citing mercantile literature in argument was comparatively rare but not unknown before 1750.[75] As the century progressed, it became more common.

There were also plenty of more formal channels for canvassing mercantile opinion. In the 1670s Sir Mathew Hale explained that:

> The court use to ascertain themselves by Speech with Merchants or Civilians, or else it comes in question upon the general Issue; and then if it be a question touching the Customes of Merchants, Merchants are usually Jurors at the request of either party, and Merchants produced on either side are produced to ascertaine the Court and Jury touching the Custome of Merchants; and if it be a question touching the Marine Law, Merchants, Mariners and Civilians are heard.[76]

Merchants gave advice outside the courtroom[77] as well as giving evidence at trial.[78] On one occasion, Holt CJ is reported to have 'had all the eminent merchants in

[68] D Lemmings, *Gentlemen and Barristers* (Oxford, Oxford University Press, 1990) 176.

[69] P Corfield, *Power and the Professions in Britain 1700–1850* (London, Routledge, 1995) 73.

[70] P Mathias, 'The Lawyer as Businessman in Eighteenth-Century England' in D Coleman and P Mathias (eds), *Enterprise and History* (Cambridge, Cambridge University Press, 1984) 151–70; C Brooks, *Pettyfoggers and Vipers of the Commonwealth* (Cambridge, Cambridge University Press, 2004) 196–203; M Miles, '"Eminent Practitioners": The New Visage of Country Attorneys c.1750–1800' in G Rubin and D Sugarman (eds), *Law, Economy and Society, 1750–1914: Essays in the History of English Law* (Abingdon, Professional Books, 1984) 470–503.

[71] Lemmings (n 68) 173–75.

[72] N Rogers, 'The Middling Orders' in H Dickinson (ed), *A Companion to Eighteenth-Century Britain* (Oxford, Blackwell, 2002), ch 13.

[73] B Cowan, *The Social Life of Coffee: The Emergence of the British Coffee House* (New Haven, Yale University Press, 2005) 104–5; P Earle, *The Making of the English Middle Class* (London, Methuen, 1991) 54.

[74] The first wave of mercantile literature can be traced to the seventeenth century; J Appleby, *Economic Thought and Ideology in Seventeenth-Century England* (New Jersey, Princeton University Press, 1978) 24–51.

[75] Examples include: *Ward v Evans* (1702) 2 Ld Raym 928, 92 ER 120; *Thorold v Smith* (1706) Holt 462, 463, 90 ER 1155; *Wegersloffe v Keene* (1719) 1 Str 214, 217, 193 ER 480; *Lumley v Palmer* (1734) Cas t Hard 74, 75, 95 ER 46; *Colehan v Cooke* (1743) Willes 393, 125 ER 1231; *Simmonds v Parminter* (1747) 1 Wils KB 185, 95 ER 564.

[76] M Prichard and D Yale, *Hale and Fleetwood on Admiralty Jurisdiction* (London, Selden Society, 1992) 57.

[77] This practice was an old one: *Vanheath v Turner* (1621) Win 24, 124 ER 20; *Pickering v Barkley* (1649) 2 Rolle Abr 248, pl 10. For a very early example see *Dederit v Abbot of Ramsey* (1315), H Hall (ed), *Select Cases Concerning the Law Merchant* (London, Selden Society, 1929) 86.

[78] *Dehers v Harriot* (1691) 1 Show 163, 164, 89 ER 513; *Tassell v Lewis* (1695) 1 Ld Raym 743, 91 ER 1397.

London with him at his chambers'.[79] The mercantile jury was at the hub of commercial contract litigation and, as James Oldham shows, mercantile jurors were highly influential in the development of legal doctrine.[80] Contact with mercantile jurors was a particularly effective way for a judge to build up a body of knowledge on mercantile practice over a long period of time.[81]

Although it was relatively easy to ascertain, mercantile practice was not invariably adopted as a legal rule. Holt CJ, having by his own admission spoken with 'two of the most famous merchants in London',[82] still reached a different conclusion. On another occasion, having referred to the well-known mercantile writer, Malynes, it was not the existence of the practice that Holt CJ doubted, but whether it should be applied: 'I am of the opinion, and always was (notwithstanding the noise and cry, that it is the use of Lombard Street, as if the contrary opinion would blow up Lombard Street) that acceptance of such a note is not actual payment'.[83] Yet the same judge was still prepared to justify a particular outcome because the contrary 'would destroy commerce and public transactions of this nature'.[84]

Holt CJ was particularly worried about the attempt to allow promissory notes to be enforced using the action of assumpsit and in *Clerke v Martin*[85] he warned:

> The maintaining of these actions upon such notes, were innovations on the rules of the common law; and that it amounted to setting up a new sort of specialty, unknown to the common law, and invented in Lombard Street, which attempted in these matters of bills of exchange to give laws to Westminster Hall.[86]

Gould J was less hostile.[87] It is important to be clear about the nature of Holt CJ's objection, which had more to do with preserving the integrity of the doctrine of consideration, than creating obstacles for merchants. When, in *Potter v Pearson*,[88] it was claimed that a promissory note was justified by the customs of London, the obvious retort was: 'it is a void custom, since it binds a man to pay money

[79] *Mutford v Walcot* (1700) 1 Ld Raym 574, 575, 91 ER 1283.

[80] J Oldham, *The Varied Life of the Self-Informing Jury* (London, Selden Society, 2005); J Oldham, 'The Origins of the Special Jury' (1983) 50 *University of Chicago Law Review* 137.

[81] In *Thwaits v Angerstein, The Times*, (London, 14 November 1798), Kenyon CJ 'professed himself totally ignorant of navigation, except in so far as he had learned it from his apprenticeship in his judicial office. He had received a great deal of information from the different classes of merchants by whom he had the honour of being assisted in the administration of justice', cited by E Kadens, 'The Puzzle of Judicial Education: The Case of Chief Justice William De Grey' (2009) 79 *Brooklyn Law Review* 143, 159.

[82] *Buller v Crips* (1703) 6 Mod 29, 30, 87 ER 793.

[83] *Ward v Evans* (1702) 2 Ld Raym 928, 930, 92 ER 120.

[84] *Anon* (1698) Holt 296, 297, 9 ER 1063.

[85] (1702) 2 Ld Raym 757, 1 Salk 129, 364, 92 ER 6.

[86] (1702) 2 Ld Raym 757, 758. Holt CJ would claim the following year that other judges agreed with him, *Cutting v Williams* (1703) 7 Mod 154, 87 ER 1160.

[87] (1702) 2 Ld Raym 757, 758.

[88] (1703) 2 Ld Raym 759, 92 ER 7.

without any consideration. For the rule is, *ex nudo pacto non oritur actio*'.[89] In *Buller v Crips*[90] Holt CJ explained:

> And the notes in question are only an invention of the goldsmiths in Lombard Street, who had in mind to make a law to bind all those who did deal with them: and sure to allow such a note to carry any lien with it were to turn a piece of paper, which is in law but evidence of a parol contract into a specialty: and besides, it would impower one to assign that to another which he could not have himself.[91]

The doctrine of consideration was just too woven into the fabric of the Common Law to be ignored.[92] Yet formal appearances were all-important as well. In this spirit, Holt CJ was quite willing to suggest an alternative: bills of exchange between two rather than three persons could be used. He argued, 'if there be such a necessity of dealing that way, why do not dealers use that way which is legal?'.[93] Provided the right steps were taken, common law and mercantile practice could be reconciled. As a special and much narrower type of contract than a promissory note, a bill of exchange did not threaten the Common Law to anything like the same extent. It needed legislation before promissory notes could be properly absorbed.[94] Even then, the exact role of consideration in such cases was difficult to resolve.[95]

Holt CJ is sometimes, quite wrongly, seen as hostile to merchants. Lord Mansfield, on the other hand, was described by his friend and contemporary Buller J as 'the founder of commercial law of this country'.[96] The dedication to the Chief Justice in James Park's work on marine insurance read, 'your extensive knowledge, joined to an unwearied application to every part of commercial jurisprudence … has endeared your Lordship's name to the Merchants of London'.[97] During Lord Mansfield's tenure, the decisions on negotiable instruments were largely an exercise in tidying up the existing law.[98] Marine insurance was already established in the Common Law, but there were relatively few authorities.[99] Sir William Blackstone, writing in the 1760s, would describe recent developments in the area as amounting to a 'very complete title in a code of commercial jurisprudence'.[100]

[89] ibid.
[90] n 82.
[91] ibid.
[92] J Baker, 'The Law Merchant as a Source of English Law' in W Swadling and G Jones (eds), *The Search for Principle: Essays for Lord Goff of Chieveley* (Oxford, Oxford University Press, 2000) 79, 93; J Rogers, *The Early History of the Law of Bills and Notes* (Cambridge, Cambridge University Press, 1995) 184 described Holt CJ's attitude as 'entirely understandable'.
[93] *Buller* (n 82) 30.
[94] Promissory Notes Act (1704) 3 & 4 Anne c 9. It was made perpetual in (1708) 7 Anne c 25 s 3.
[95] *Brown v Marsh* (1721) Gilb Rept 154, 25 ER 108.
[96] *Lickbarrow v Mason* (1787) 2 TR 63, 73, 100 ER 35.
[97] *System of the Law of Marine Insurances*, 2nd edn (London, T Whieldon, 1790) iii.
[98] Swain (n 58) 82–90.
[99] D Ibbetson, 'Law and Custom: Insurance in Sixteenth Century England' (2008) 29 *Journal of Legal History* 291.
[100] W Blackstone, *Commentaries on the Laws of England*, vol 2 (Clarendon Press, Oxford, 1766) 461.

Thomas Parker maintained that Lord Mansfield had rendered the law so 'plain and clear'.[101] John Weskett was less sanguine:

> What, in any country, could be more preposterous and intolerably grievous; or more reproachful to a great commercial Nation, in particular; than the Administration of private Justice, in the Affairs of MERCHANTS should be solely in the Hands of Inconclusiveness![102]

This is a more realistic assessment. Lord Mansfield himself, speaking in 1761, complained that:

> The daily negotiations and property of merchants ought not to depend upon subtleties and niceties, but on rules, easily learned and easily retained, because they are the dictates of common sense drawn from the truth of the case.[103]

Two decades on, there was still much to do: 'All questions on mercantile transactions, but more particularly upon policies of insurance, are extremely important and ought to be settled'.[104] Mercantile juries were vital.[105] Those involved in the insurance and shipping industries were also called as expert witnesses.[106] Underwriters[107] and others with knowledge of particular types of insurance[108] were consulted informally. John Wesket may even have had Lord Mansfield in mind when he complained that a judge may be 'as often misled as assisted, by these extrajudicial and *ex parte* conversations'.[109]

Developments in insurance and negotiable instruments clearly demonstrate that merchants helped to shape the law long before the nineteenth century. Speaking in the 1740s, Willes CJ refers to a well established tradition: 'Courts of law have always in mercantile affairs endeavoured to adapt rules of law to the course and method of trade in order to promote trade and commerce instead of doing it hurt'.[110] Marine insurance also highlights another important point. The commercial interest is rarely easy to categorise. It does not express a single idea. Merchants

[101] T Parker, *The Laws of Shipping and Insurance, with a Digest of Adjudged Cases; Containing the Acts of Parliament Relative to Shipping, Insurance and Navigation* (London, W Strahan and M Woodfall, 1775) v.

[102] J Weskett, *A Complete Digest of the Theory, Laws, and Practice of Insurance* (London, Frys, Couchman and Collier, 1781) xvi.

[103] *Hamilton v Mendes* (1761) 2 Burr 1198, 1214, 97 ER 787.

[104] *Nutt v Hague* (1786) 1 TR 323, 330, 99 ER 1119. See also *Milles v Fletcher* (1779) 1 Doug 231, 232, 99 ER 151; *Simond v Boydell* (1779) 1 Doug 268, 270–71, 99 ER 175.

[105] *Lewis v Rucker* (1761) 2 Burr 1167, 1168, 97 ER 767.

[106] D Dwyer, 'Expert Evidence in the English Civil Courts 1550–1800' (2007) 28 *Journal of Legal History* 93, 100 provides examples of expert witnesses mentioned in the printed reports at this time across a range of litigation. The evidence of expert witnesses could have a vital bearing on the outcome. For example, in *Harrington v Halked* (1778), Oldham (n 40) 549–50 and Parker (n 101) 302–3 indicate that sea captains were called to comment on a ship's course on a question of deviation.

[107] *Glover v Black* (1763) 3 Burr 1394, 97 ER 891; *Camden v Cowley* (1763) 1 W Bla 417, 96 ER 237, Oldham (n 40) 500–1; *Wilson v Smith* (1764) 3 Burr 1550, 1556, 97 ER 975.

[108] *Salvador v Hopkins* (1765) 3 Burr 1707, 1714, 97 ER 1057.

[109] Weskett (n 102) xviii.

[110] *Stone v Rawlinson* (1745) Willes 559, 561, 125 ER 1320.

are not an homogenous group. Within the mercantile community there are competing pressures. This can be seen in the way in which Lord Mansfield attempted to strike a balance between the insurer and the insured through the disclosure rules laid down in *Carter v Boehm*.[111] Judges of the time were just as sensitive to the economic consequences of their rulings as modern judges. Sometimes they even admitted that such factors were relevant. Burnet J in *Ryall v Rowles*[112] said:

> This case is of so extensive a consequence to trade in general, it may be attended with such inconvenience either way, and in most respects is so wholly new, and no judicial determination, that I shall endeavour to lay my thoughts in as clear light as possible.[113]

III. Judges, Public Policy and Morality

Public policy has played a role in contract law for centuries.[114] Some contracts are rendered unenforceable because of it. Several examples have already been mentioned, including contracts with sailors over their prize money and heirs dealing with their inheritance. Contracts for the sale of offices,[115] champerty[116] and contracts in restraint of trade[117] also fell foul of public policy. Beyond established categories such as these, most modern judges enter into an explicit discussion of public policy in contract law with great reluctance. To do so would be to ride the unruly horse of public policy.[118] In the 1870s Sir George Jessel, MR, noted that:

> It must not be forgotten that you are not to extend arbitrarily those rules which say that a given contract is void as being against public policy, because if there is one thing which more than another public policy requires it is that men of full age and competent understanding shall have the utmost liberty of contracting, and that their contracts when entered into freely and voluntarily shall be held sacred and shall be enforced by Courts of justice.[119]

These concerns are not new. Tensions have always arisen once the courts go beyond the uncontroversial proposition that illegal contracts will not be enforced.[120]

[111] (1766) 3 Burr 1905, 97 ER 1162. For a discussion of this seminal decision see S Watterson, 'Carter v Boehm (1766)' in C Mitchell and P Mitchell (eds), *Landmark Cases in the Law of Contract* (Oxford, Hart Publishing, 2008) 59–118.

[112] (1749) 1 Ves Sen 348, 27 ER 1074.

[113] ibid, 357.

[114] W Knight, 'Public Policy in English Law' (1922) 38 *LQR* 207; P Winfield, 'Public Policy in the English Common Law' (1928–1929) 42 *Harvard Law Review* 76.

[115] *Card v Hope* (1824) 2 B & C 661, 107 ER 527.

[116] *Stanley v Jones* (1831) 7 Bing 369, 131 ER 143.

[117] J Heydon, *The Restraint of Trade Doctrine*, 3rd edn (Sydney, Butterworths, 2008) 1–32; *Mitchell v Reynolds* (1711) 1 P Wms 181, Fort 295, 10 Mod 130, 24 ER 347, 92 ER 859, 88 ER 660.

[118] *Richardson v Mellish* (1824) 2 Bing 229, 252 (Burrough J), 130 ER 294. For a contrary view see Lord Denning in *Enderby Town Football Club v Football Association* [1971] Ch 591, 607.

[119] *Printing and Numerical Registering Company v Sampson* (1874–75) LR 19 Eq 462, 465.

[120] *Fletcher v Harcot* (1622) Hutton 65, 123 ER 1097; *Allen v Rescous* (1676) 2 Lev 174, 83 ER 505; *Collins v Blantern* (1767) 2 Wils 347, 95 ER 850.

Public policy in this wider sense is the ultimate representation of power within contract law. It amounts to a judicial expression of the power of the State and, in earlier times, of the dominant State religion and morality. The precise scope of public policy in contract law is much more difficult to pin down. In *Jones v Randall* Lord Mansfield argued that:

> It is admitted by the counsel for the defendant that the contract is against no positive law. It is admitted too, that there is no case to be found which says it is illegal: But it is argued, and rightly, that notwithstanding it is not prohibited by any positive law, nor adjudged illegal by any precedents, yet it may be decided to be so upon principles: and the law of England would be a strange science indeed if it were decided upon precedents only.[121]

Lord Mansfield was plainly prepared to go beyond illegality. It is less clear how much further he believed his jurisdiction ought to stretch. The actual wager at issue in *Jones v Randall* was found to be 'not prohibited by any positive law nor contrary to any principle of sound policy or morality'.[122] There appears to be an attempt here to anchor public policy in principle. Lord Mansfield was not alone in thinking like this.[123] It suggests that there was an element of restraint in the use of public policy in contract actions. This idea probably better reflects the eighteenth century than the claim of the legal writer Joseph Chitty in 1826 that 'the common law prohibits everything which is unjust, or *contra bonos mores*'.[124]

Some subjects that agitated moralists were also capable of troubling judges. There is no better example than the decisions on wagers.[125] Certain kinds of wagers were illegal contracts under statute.[126] Many others were not.[127] The extraordinary wagers, and consequential litigation, concerning the gender of the Chevalier D'Eon, the French Ambassador, came to a head in *Da Costa v Jones*.[128] The wager was unenforceable because it brought discredit on the character of D'Eon: it was 'manifestly a gross injury to a third person'.[129] Lord Mansfield chose his words carefully. He seemed anxious to avoid laying down broader restrictions.

[121] (1774) 1 Cowp 37, 38–39, 98 ER 954.

[122] ibid.

[123] S Waddams, *Principle and Policy in Contract Law* (Cambridge, Cambridge University Press, 2011) 151–52.

[124] J Chitty, *A Practical Treatise on the Law of Contracts Not Under Seal* (London, S Sweet, 1826) 214.

[125] For an example of the moralist case, see R Hey, *A Dissertation on the Pernicious Effects of Gaming* (Cambridge, J Archdeacon, 1783).

[126] (1708) 7 Ann c 16; (1710) 9 Anne c 14; (1740) 13 Geo 2 c 19; (1745) 18 Geo 2 c 34; (1746) 19 Geo 2 c 37; (1774) 14 Geo 3 c 48.

[127] For older authority on the enforcement of a wager see: *Andrews v Herne* (1661) 1 Lev 33, 83 ER 283; *Walcot v Tappin* (1661) 1 Keb 56, 83 ER 808. For discussion see: Simpson (n 24) 534–5; J Baker, *The Oxford History of the Law of England Volume VI 1483–1558* (Oxford, Oxford University Press, 2003) 820, 859.

[128] (1778) 2 Cowp 729, 98 ER 1331.

[129] ibid, 736. For a detailed discussion of the decision see: W Swain, 'Da Costa v. Jones (1778)' in Mitchell and Mitchell (n 111) 119–34.

He rejected the argument that the wager could not be enforced because it tended to introduce indecent evidence.[130] Tellingly, he took the opportunity to reiterate that generally, unless a wager fell under a statute, it was valid.[131]

There are a number of instances where wagers falling outside the statutes were invalidated on grounds of public policy.[132] Some judges of the time went further. Ashhurst J pleaded that 'In my opinion the Courts have gone far enough in encouraging impertinent wagers'.[133] It would be better, he said, if the courts had originally declined to enforce all wagers. Buller J also took a very robust line against wagers.[134] Nineteenth century observers had widely different views on the extent to which other judges would strike out a wager.[135] By 1845 statute had intervened and such speculation was now redundant.[136] But these decisions also illustrate the fact that some judges were prepared to encroach much further into the territory of the legislature than others.

Even when a particular public policy was expressed through a statute, there was a tension between a desire not to allow the spirit of the law to be broken, and a desire to recognise that people should be able to contract freely. In the context of usury, Lord Mansfield stressed the need to go behind the words of the transaction to look at the intentions of the parties.[137] One contemporary, who wrote that 'the laws in force against usury have been notoriously eluded',[138] was clearly not convinced that this went far enough. Chancery may have done better. But even Equity was not always transparent. Agreements designed for the purpose of procuring marriage,[139] or an agreement in which a bankrupt entered into a deed of composition with his creditors for a given sum and at the same time entered into a separate agreement with one creditor for a larger sum, in order to induce him to sign the deed,[140] could be set aside. The justification used was that contracts of these sorts were fraudulent.[141] Fraud was one of the traditional heads under which Equity

[130] *Da Costa* (n 128) 734.

[131] ibid.

[132] *Allen v Hearn* (1785) 1 TR 56, 59, 99 ER 969 (election); *Lacaussade v White* (1798) 2 Esp 626, 7 TR 535, 170 ER 478, 101 ER 1118 (contingency of peace); *Brown v Leeson* (1792) 2 H Bla 43, 126 ER 419 (dice); *Henkin v Guerss* (1810) 12 East 247, 104 ER 97 (point of law in which parties had no interest); *Sigel v Jebb* (1820) 3 Stark 1, 171 ER 747 (chess).

[133] *Atherford v Beard* (1788) 2 TR 610, 615, 100 ER 328.

[134] *Good v Elliot* (1790) 3 TR 693, 697, 100 ER 808.

[135] Chitty (n 124) 155–56 but *cf* G Oliphant, *The Law Concerning Horses, Racing, Wager and Gambling* (London, S Sweet, 1847) 188.

[136] (1845) 8 & 9 Vict c 109.

[137] *Richards v Brown* (1779) 2 Cowp 770, 776, 98 ER 1352; *Lowe v Waller* (1781) 2 Doug 736, 740, 99 ER 470.

[138] Anon, *Reflections on Usury* (London, R Faulder, 1783) 13.

[139] R Powell 'Marriage Brocage Agreements' (1953) 6 *Current Legal Problems* 254; *Drury v Hooke* (1686) 1 Vern 412, 23 ER 553; *Hall v Potter* (1695) 1 Show PC 76, 1 ER 52; *Stribblehill v Brett* (1703) 2 Vern 445, 23 ER 885; *Cole v Gibson* (1750) 1 Ves Sen 503, 27 ER 1169.

[140] *Spurret v Spiller* (1740) 1 Atk 105, 26 ER 69.

[141] *Earl of Chesterfield v Janssen* (1750) 2 Ves Sen 125, 256, 28 ER 82.

intervened.[142] The fact that Lord Hardwicke chose to categorise these contracts as fraudulent may have a number of explanations. Not least of these was that Lord Hardwicke was anxious to impose some sort of order on the material.[143] It may also reflect an uneasy relationship with public policy that extended into Chancery.

Eighteenth century judges accepted that public policy played a part in contractual enforceability. Moral considerations were certainly raised, albeit less often. In *Walker v Perkins*[144] a contract between a man and a woman that she would cohabit with him in return for payment of an annuity was held to be void. Lord Mansfield commented that the contract was 'the price of prostitution, premium prostitutionis: for if she becomes virtuous, she is to lose the annuity'.[145] It is a fair bet that any other judge of the time would have reached the same conclusion. But as the cases on gambling show, a consensus may often be quite difficult to achieve. A certain anxiety surrounded resorting to public policy. Power here plays a negative role too. It acted as a restraint on judges.[146] It made them wary about how they express public policy concerns in a contractual setting. It had to be done with care and sometimes this meant surreptitiously. These attitudes became more pronounced in the nineteenth century. But this was not a fundamental shift. In other respects eighteenth century judges began to accumulate influence rather than decline to exercise it. A century later this process would have major implications. Once again, it is part of an older tradition.

IV. Legal Procedure and Fairness

It is not difficult to see how fairness, commercial expectations and public policy fit into a discussion of power and private law. At first sight, legal procedure may appear to be rather more remote from these concerns. Power here has a slightly different connotation and one that is even more difficult to assess. It was less about influence on legal development from outside and more a power struggle in its own

142 H Rolle, *Un Abridgment des Plusieurs Cases et Resolutions del Common Ley* (London, A Crooke, 1668) 374; E Coke, *Institutes of the Laws of England*, vol 4 (London, M Flesher, 1644) 84; D Yale (ed), *Lord Nottingham's Manual of Chancery Practice and Prolegomena of Chancery and Equity* (Cambridge, Cambridge University Press, 1965) 191.

143 Hence the growing importance of precedent in Equity at this time: C Croft, 'Lord Hardwicke's Use of Precedent in Equity' in Thomas Watkin (ed), *Legal Record and Historical Reality* (London, Hambledon, 1989) 121–55.

144 (1764) 3 Burr 1568, 97 ER 985.

145 ibid, 1569.

146 The difficult relations between the State and the judges a century earlier were still recent enough to form part of the institutional memory of lawyers: R Kay, *The Glorious Revolution and the Continuity of Law* (Washington DC, The Catholic University Press, 2014) 181–215.

right, within the legal system, between the judges and juries. The jury had been at the heart of English law for centuries.[147] As one writer explained:

> They are incorporated with our Constitution and are the most valuable part of it; nay, may be termed the very vitals of it; without them no man's life can be impeached, no man's liberty or property ought to be taken from him.[148]

Public perceptions of the jury were not always favourable[149] and, over the course of a century or more, the civil jury would be toppled from its position of dominance. The jury's role was to answer the question or issue put to it after pleading was finished and issue joined.[150] In contract actions, joinder of issue was usually reached when the defence submitted a general blank denial of liability. By 1700 the jury was an impartial tribunal of fact along modern lines[151] but very little is known about how a decision was reached.[152] The process was not recorded and reasons were not given.[153] A ballad of the time advised jurors to 'be judges of fact, though not judges of laws'.[154] Applying the division between fact and law in practice was not easy: as the barrister in Sir John Hawles's *The English-mans right a dialogue between a barrister at law and a jury-man* explained, 'yet must your jury apply matter of fact and law together and from their consideration of, and a right of judgment upon both, bring forth their verdict'.[155]

Hawles illustrated his point with reference to the general issue.[156] In his day and for a long time afterwards, many issues that came to be expressed as clear legal rules remained bundled up with the facts and hidden behind a blank jury verdict. In a straightforward contract dispute, the most obvious strategy for a defendant is to give reasons for the non-existence of the contract, for example, through mistake, fraud, lack of intention, or failure to reach an agreement. These were largely issues that could be raised in evidence, the general issue of 'non-assumpsit' having been pleaded, but for much of the time clear definitions of mistake etc. were absent.[157]

[147] The Declaration of Rights of 1689 contained a clause on juries: see J Hoppit, *A Land of Liberty? England 1689–1727* (Oxford, Oxford University Press, 2000) 24.

[148] Anon, *A Compendious Library of the Law* (London, E and R Nutt, 1740) 122.

[149] Oldham (n 80) 141–44; Anon, *The Advantages of Settling Disputes by Arbitration* (Carlisle, F Jollie, 1795) 9: 'the want of local knowledge in jurors, is an evil of no small magnitude'.

[150] For an overview of the pleading process and the jury see, J Baker, *An Introduction to English Legal History*, 4th edn (London, Butterworths, 2002) 71–96.

[151] Earlier jurors had been more like witnesses: J Mitnick, 'From Neighbor-Witness to Judge of Proofs: The Transformation of the English Civil Juror' (1988) 32 *American Journal of Legal History* 201.

[152] The way in which modern juries reach verdicts continues to be debated at great length. For an overview, see D Devine et al, 'Jury Decision Making: 45 years of Empirical Research on Deliberating Groups' (2001) 7 *Psychology Pubic Policy and Law* 622.

[153] Sometimes a sense of the process can be gained from reading judicial notebooks.

[154] W Pulteney, *The Honest Jury or Caleb Triumphant. A New Ballad* (London, W Pultney, 1729) 3.

[155] (London, Richard Janeway, 1680) 11.

[156] ibid.

[157] For a rare example of fraud bubbling to the surface, see *Bright v Eynon* (1757) 1 Burr 390, 97 ER 365.

In determining the existence and content of a contract, jurors were allowed and even encouraged to bring their own expertise to bear. The mercantile juries are the most obvious example.[158] This is not to say that the relationship between judge and jurors was never strained. *Hollingsworth v Tattersall*[159] may not be atypical. A jury in a horse sale case found for the buyer, contrary to Lord Mansfield's direction. The result is said to have left him, 'much dissatisfied with the verdict' and shaking his head at the 'extraordinary conduct of the jury'.[160]

Juries enjoyed considerable power, but were not entirely left to themselves.[161] Judges were increasingly watchful. Holt CJ explained in *Ash v Ash* that:

> The jury were very shy of giving a reason of their verdict, thinking that they had an absolute despotick power, but I did rectify that mistake; for the jury are to try causes with the assistance of the judges; and ought to give reasons when required; that if they go on any mistake, they may be set right.[162]

From the mid-seventeenth century,[163] judges began gradually to take control of the jury on the back of procedural reforms. The motion for new trial began to be used for matters that appeared off, as well as on, the record.[164] As a result of apparently technical change, it became easier to mount a challenge to the jury's verdict than had been possible using the old action of attaint.[165] The motion was heard before judges in banc at Westminster in reliance on an account in the trial judge's notebook.[166] A jury verdict could be challenged if the jury had failed to follow a judge's direction. By the early eighteenth century, the scope of the motion for new trial was further expanded to include situations where the judge had erred in his direction.[167] In these cases the judges sitting in banc were essentially being asked to consider whether the trial judge, in his direction to the jury, had got the law right. Questions of law could also be raised in banc more directly and effectively than the

[158] Oldham (n 80) 24–31.

[159] (1778). The case is reported in the newspapers: *London Chronicle* (London, 30 May 1778); *Morning Post* (London, 1 June 1778). The trial notes survive: Oldham (n 40) 332–33.

[160] *Morning Post*, ibid.

[161] J Baker, *The Law's Two Bodies* (Oxford, Oxford University Press, 2001) 63.

[162] (1696) Holt 701, 702, 90 ER 1287.

[163] Baker (n 150) 81–5.

[164] *Wood v Gunston* (1655) Style 462, 466, 82 ER 864. For a flavour of the content of court records, see J Baker, 'Records, Reports and the Origins of Case-Law in England' in J Baker (ed), *Judicial Records, Law Reports, and the Growth of Case Law* (Berlin, Duncker and Humblot, 1989) 15, 34–36.

[165] B Sellon, *The Practice of the Courts of King's Bench and Common Pleas*, vol 1 (London, A Strahan and W Woodfall, 1792) 502: 'the writ of attaint is now a sound in every case it does not pretend to be a remedy'. Though not used it was not formally abolished until 1825: (1825) 6 Geo IV c 50 s 60.

[166] Sellon ibid 504; J Archbold, *The Practice of the Court of King's Bench*, vol 2 (London, J Butterworth, 1819) 227. In *Atkins v Drake* (1824) M'Cle & Young 213, 229, 148 ER 388, Alexander CB described the process.

[167] For a complete list of situations where the motion could be used, see J Morgan, *Essays Upon the Law of Evidence, New Trials, Special Verdicts, Trials at Bar and Repleaders*, vol 2 (London, J Johnson, 1789) 1.

old special verdict had allowed[168] by reserving points of law[169] and case stated.[170] Taken together, greater control of juries and the relative ease of extracting issues of law for deliberation, helped to firm up the roles of judge and jury and the line between law and fact.[171] In the 1760s Wilmot J had stated that:

> For, though when facts and law happened to be so complicated and intermixed that a jury can not help taking both into their consideration, it may be difficult or even impossible for them to avoid founding their verdict upon both; yet they are not at liberty to determine contrary to the law: they ought to take their notion of law, from the direction of the Judge who tries the cause.[172]

A mere twenty years later, Buller J was adopting a more robust approach: 'In a question of law however unpleasant it may be to us, we must not yield to the decision of a jury'.[173]

All of these developments laid the foundations for the nineteenth century emasculation of the jury.[174] These in turn completely changed the way that contract litigation was structured.[175] The trial process was no longer quite so hidden from view. Judges began to give definitions in law for those matters that were identified by the plea. By the mid-nineteenth century, matters that in the past had been addressed under the general issue came to be expressed as clear, distinct and carefully defined legal doctrines. The role of the jury was confined to applying the facts to the legal definition provided by the judge. As part of this process, judges, along with legal writers, began to articulate general principles of contractual liability. These would form the basis of the classical model of contract. This most emphatically does not necessarily mean that the principles were novel, even if they had not been (fully) articulated as legal rules.

[168] For a summary of the operation of the special verdict, see W Tidd, *The Practice of the Court of King's Bench in Personal Actions*, vol 1 (London, A Strahan and W Woodfall, 1790) 595–96.

[169] M Prichard, 'Non-suit: A Premature Obituary' (1960) 18 *CLJ* 88; *Baskerville v Brown* (1761) 2 Burr 1229, 97 ER 804; *Dally v Smith* (1771) 4 Burr 2148, 98 ER 120; *Clay v Willan* (1789) 1 H Bla 298, 126 ER 174.

[170] This method was particularly favoured by Lord Mansfield. See J Oldham, 'The Seventh Amendment Right to Jury Trial: Late Eighteenth Century Practice Reconsidered' in K O'Donovan and G Rubin (eds), *Human Rights and Legal History Essays in Honour of Brian Simpson* (Oxford, Oxford University Press, 2000) 225, 235. It worked by giving a general verdict, usually for the plaintiff, subject to an opinion of the court in banc on a question draw up by counsel on both sides on a point of law.

[171] Judges were still reluctant to intervene in relation to findings of fact: see *Smith v Frampton* (1695) 1 Ld Raym 62, 91 ER 938.

[172] *Grant v Vaughan* (1764) 3 Burr 1516, 1526, 97 ER 957.

[173] *Appleton v Sweetapple* (1782) 3 Doug 137, 140, 99 ER 579. For similar remarks elsewhere, see *Tindal v Brown* (1786) 1 TR 167, 169, 99 ER 1033; *Sproat v Matthews* (1786) 1 TR 182, 187, 99 ER 1041.

[174] M Lobban, 'The Strange Life of the English Civil Jury, 1837–1914' in J Cairns and G McLeod (eds), *The Dearest Birth Right of the People of England* (Oxford, Hart Publishing, 2002) 173–209; C Hanly, 'The Decline of Civil Jury Trial in Nineteenth-Century England' (2005) 26 *Journal of Legal History* 253.

[175] For a detailed discussion see Swain (n 58) chs 8–9.

V. Power and Contract Law: The On-going Narrative

Modern contract scholars are divided between those who prefer a formalistic model of the law of contract and those who think that judges should draw more widely on context, including matters of business practice.[176] These are not the sorts of debates that would have made much sense to eighteenth century lawyers. Contract law, at the time, was neither as formalistic as it became in the decades after 1850,[177] nor was it entirely contextual in the way that modern scholars use the term. The role of the jury made any more formalistic model of contract law impossible. Although the jury was beginning to be reined in, it retained an element of unpredictability for the time being. It would be particularly surprising if mercantile juries, in reaching their verdicts in particular, were not just swayed by commercial practice but also commercial morality.[178]

At the same time, there was a degree of flexibility in the application of eighteenth century contract law, which no longer exists.[179] The doctrine of precedent did not exert such a strong pull as it does nowadays. This did not mean that judges were puppets of interest groups. Mercantile practice made a variable impact. It was particularly important in shaping legal change when the law was unsettled, or where there was no law at all. Negotiable instruments and insurance are good examples of these phenomena. Once the law was fixed, judges were reluctant to undo it.[180] Mercantile practice might also run into resistance. This happened when the doctrine of consideration acted as a block on the Common Law absorbing the mercantile rules on promissory notes.

The idea that there is anything novel about economic and social factors having a major influence on the development of contract law is plainly fallacious. The suggestion that there was some golden age when fairness reigned does not stand up to close examination either. There were situations in which the courts, particularly the Court of Chancery, stepped in. This occurred from at least the middle of the eighteenth century and probably before Equitable intervention was structured. Certainly, there were strong themes that can be identified in the case law. There was no freewheeling doctrine of fairness. On the contrary, the courts were anxious not to undermine bargained-for agreements. The same motives explain

[176] Some of the literature includes: C Mitchell, *Contract Law and Contract Practice* (Oxford, Hart Publishing, 2013); J Morgan, *Contract Law Minimalism A Formalist Restatement of Commercial Contract Law* (Cambridge, Cambridge University Press, 2013); J Gava, 'How Should Judges Decide Commercial Contract Cases?' (2013) 30 *Journal of Contract Law* 133.

[177] The extent to which contract law became formalistic should not be exaggerated: R Ferguson, 'The Horwitz Thesis and Common Law Discourse in England' (1983) 3 *OJLS* 34.

[178] In transactions involving the sale of horses, juries seem to have been hostile towards horse sellers for example: Swain (n 41) 290–91.

[179] This is a matter of degree. Under the guise of equity, Australian contract law allows more latitude than its more formalistic English counterpart.

[180] *Medcalf v Hall* (1782) 3 Doug 113, 115, 99 ER 566.

judicial anxiety about public policy. Around the edges, there were some differences in approach between judges.

In some ways there was more scope for outside factors influencing contract law in the eighteenth century than later on. The more rigid, formalistic model of contract, which is usually known as Classical Contract Law, certainly developed a dynamic of its own. It is not necessary to be a fully fledged Legal Realist to accept that, on occasions, more was going on than the neutral language of the judgment might suggest.[181] But the pull of tradition should not be underestimated either. It provides an important restraint. Care needs to be taken not to exaggerate shifts in the law that may reflect differences in approach, as much as changes of substance.[182]

Dr Johnson is reported to have said, 'The more contracted that power is, the more easily it is destroyed. A country governed by a despot is an inverted cone.'[183] He was, of course, using contract in a different sense. Yet eighteenth century contract law was not an 'inverted cone'. It has always been particularly unsuited to a single, simple narrative. It would be surprising if the exercise of power and influence over the law of contract did not change over the centuries and it did so. Within that structure competing forces were sometimes evident. At the same time, there is a high degree of continuity between the eighteenth century and what came later. The evidence for a clear break in the 1770s is just not there. An account that looked at this thesis the other way around from the perspective of the nineteenth century would reach the same conclusion.[184] A failure to recognise these facts makes any historical account of the subject viewed from the perspective of power seriously flawed.

[181] In developing the remoteness rules, for example: R Danzig, 'Hadley v Baxendale: A Study in the Industrialization of the Law' (1975) 4 *Journal of Legal Studies* 249; J Barton, 'Contractual Damages and the Rise of Industry' (1987) 7 *OJLS* 40; F Faust, 'Hadley v Baxendale: An Understandable Miscarriage of Justice' (1994) 15 *Journal of Legal History* 41.

[182] S Hedley, 'From Individualism to Communitarianism? The Case of Standard Forms' in T Watkin (ed), *Legal Record and Historical Reality* (London, Hambledon Press, 1989) 229–42.

[183] G Hill, *Boswell's Life of Johnson*, vol 3 (Oxford, Oxford University Press, 1934) 283.

[184] For a partial attempt to do just that, see Swain (n 58) 172–200.

3

Redressing Inequality in Personal Credit Transactions: 1700–1974

KAREN FAIRWEATHER

While the phenomenon of consumerism can be traced back at least as far as the eighteenth century,[1] the idea of protecting individuals *qua* consumers is far more recent.[2] The development of a body of law with a sufficiently homogenous core that it could be regarded as a distinct branch of the law—a 'consumer law'—was one of the achievements of the last third of the twentieth century.[3] Nonetheless, the roots of consumer law lie much deeper. Perhaps the most important of these roots is inequality of bargaining power.[4] When Lord Denning MR attempted to elevate inequality of bargaining power into an independent ground of relief in 1974[5] the courts had already been grappling with it, albeit indirectly, for centuries. Although it came to be recognised that inequality of bargaining power beset consumer transactions generally, nowhere was this inequality more acute than in consumer credit transactions. As the Crowther Committee acknowledged in 1971, 'Freedom of contract has little meaning in consumer transactions. Bargaining power lies with the supplier and this is particularly the case where the transaction

[1] It has been argued that a consumer 'revolution' occurred in eighteenth century England: see N McKendrick, J Brewer and JH Plumb, *The Birth of a Consumer Society: The Commercialization of Eighteenth Century England* (Bloomington, Indiana University Press, 1982); J Mokyr, *The Enlightened Economy: An Economic History of Britain 1700–1850* (Newhaven, Yale University Press, 2010). But this is just one of five consumer revolutions that historians have claimed occurred in different periods—the Renaissanace, the Baroque, the eighteenth century, the late nineteenth century and the twentieth century: see J de Vries, *The Industrious Revolution and the Household Economy, 1650 to the Present* (Cambridge, Cambridge University Press, 2008) 37–39.

[2] The birth of consumer law is conventionally dated to 15th March 1962, when President JF Kennedy delivered his Special Message to the US Congress on Protecting the Consumer Interest.

[3] In the UK, the question of 'consumer protection' first attracted parliamentary attention in the late 1950s. The Molony Committee was appointed to 'review the working of the existing legislation relating to merchandise marks and certification trademarks, and to consider and report what changes if any in the law and what other measures, if any, are required for the further protection of the consuming public.' The Committee reported in July 1962: see Board of Trade, *Final Report of the Committee on Consumer Protection* (Cmnd 1781, 1962) ('Molony Report').

[4] See I Ramsay, 'Consumer Law, Regulatory Capitalism and the "New Learning" in Regulation' (2006) 28 *Sydney Law Review* 9.

[5] *Lloyds Bank Ltd v Bundy* [1975] QB 326.

involves the extension of credit.'[6] But, while both the construct of the 'consumer'[7] and the development of a generic concept of 'consumer credit'[8] were recent innovations, the recognition that parties to credit transactions required protection was as old as the institution of credit itself. This chapter will explore and evaluate some of the different mechanisms deployed by the courts and legislature to redress these inequalities over time.

I. Two Types of Inequality

Consumer transactions are beset by two distinct facets of inequality.[9] Inequality of *bargaining* power is used here to denote one party's greater capacity—by virtue of market conditions, the other party's personal circumstances, or a combination of both—to impose on the other the terms on which the two contract. As Lord Denning MR observed in connection with the old 'ticket cases' such as *Thompson v London Midland and Scottish Railway Co Ltd*[10] which had done so little to protect the consumer from the imposition of sweeping exclusion clauses in standard term contracts:

> [A]ll this was done in the name of "freedom of contract." But the freedom was all on the side of the big concern which had the use of the printing press. No freedom for the little man who took the ticket or order form or invoice. The big concern said "Take it or leave it." The little man had no option but to take it.[11]

Where the consumer transaction involves the extension of credit, this 'usual' inability to shape the terms of the (typically standard-term) contract is often compounded by financial distress or necessity on the consumer's part. Those entering into credit transactions are, almost by definition and to varying degrees, 'financially necessitous'. As the Crowther Committee recognised, a stronger protective code might well be justified and necessary in the case of 'adversity credit' than in cases of 'improvement credit'.[12]

Secondly, and closely related to inequality of bargaining power, is inequality of *informational* power. This type of inequality, which relates to the parties' relative

[6] *Consumer Credit: Report of the Committee* (Cmnd 4596, 1971) ('Crowther Report') para 6.1.12.

[7] The definition of a 'consumer sale' put forward by the Molony Committee in 1962 was 'a sale by way of trade of goods bought for private use or consumption to a person who does not buy for the purpose of resale or for use or consumption any trade or business': *Molony Report* (n 3) para 466.

[8] In the Consumer Credit Act 1974.

[9] There is also a third facet of inequality—the inequality of the parties' relative capacities to enforce their rights through the litigation process—that will not be considered here. For wide-ranging discussion of this problem, see CEF Rickett and TGW Telfer, *International Perspectives on Consumers' Access to Justice* (Cambridge, Cambridge University Press, 2003).

[10] [1930] 1 KB 41.

[11] *George Mitchell (Chesterhall) Ltd v Finney Lock Seeds Ltd* [1983] QB 284, 297.

[12] *Crowther Report* (n 6) para 1.2.11.

capacities to access, process and act rationally upon information material to the decision whether to enter into a contract and on what terms, was described by the Crowther Committee as a facet of inequality of bargaining power.[13] However, this characterisation can be criticised on the ground that it might be taken to assume that the redressing of informational inequalities *necessarily* enhances the consumer's capacity to decide whether, and on what terms, to enter into the contract. One of the intractable problems in consumer law generally and consumer credit law in particular is that even in situations of perfect informational symmetry[14] the supplier may be able to tell the consumer to 'take it or leave it'. This is particularly the case with low-income or 'non-status' or 'non-conforming' borrowers (that is, those with poor or no credit histories) who are excluded from access to the main stream credit market.[15] The absence of alternative sources of supply for such consumers and lack of effective competition leaves them with no genuine choice but to pay for high or extortionately priced credit.[16] For this reason, informational inequality is better conceived of as distinct from inequality of bargaining power.

Inequality of informational power is also particularly acute in the credit context. By their nature, credit products tend to complexity. While it is true that this complexity has increased dramatically since the enactment of the Consumer Credit Act in 1974, the problem is far from new. One of the difficulties is that credit products often have what Engel describes as 'multiple moving parts'—variable fees, shifting interest rates, and multiple timing requirements and trigger events.[17] The credit-grantor will be aware of, and may indeed have developed the product with a view to exploiting, the possible interactions of these 'moving parts'. Even if consumers are able to accurately predict their future behaviour and the course of future events, most of them will struggle to see through this complexity and grasp what the consequences of the contract will be for them in any given situation. Even where the credit product is not inherently complex, the way in which its terms are expressed and presented can have obfuscating effects. Complexity will present particular challenges for consumers with low levels of financial literacy or capability.[18] Furthermore, recent advances in behavioural economics have shown that the array of cognitive biases which afflict consumers, including optimism

[13] *Crowther Report* (n 6) para 6.1.12.

[14] Both in terms of access to, and capacity to process and rationally act upon, information.

[15] Although it must be acknowledged that these consumers' lack of financial capability (ie their disinterest in shopping around and inability to process information) contributes to the ineffective competition in the high-cost credit market.

[16] See, eg, UK Competition Commission, *Home Credit Inquiry: Final Report* (London, The Stationery Office, 2006); Office of Fair Trading, *Review of High-Cost Credit: Final Report* (OFT 1232) (London, OFT, 2010).

[17] K Engel, 'Can Consumer Law Solve the Problem of Complexity in US Consumer Credit Products?' in K Fairweather, P O'Shea and R Grantham (eds), *Credit, Consumers and the Law* (Abingdon, Routledge, 2016) ch 5.

[18] Financial capability is a broader concept than financial literacy in that it encompasses motivational factors and mindset as well as skills and knowledge: see New Philanthropy Capital, *Financial Capacity Outcome Frameworks* (2014) 8 available at www.thinknpc.org/publications/financial-capability-outcome-frameworks.

bias and hyperbolic discounting, affect their capacity to make rational decisions when entering into credit contracts.[19] Credit-grantors are not slow to exploit these cognitive biases; indeed it has been suggested that exploitation of this imperfect rationality may be necessary for survival in some highly competitive markets.[20]

II. A Potted History of Consumer Credit

A. Changing Modes and Patterns of Credit

Over time, modes and patterns of credit-granting changed. Until the nineteenth century, pawnbroking was the predominant mode of credit-granting to the 'industrious poor'. Items of clothing were the most common pledges, although linen, household goods and tools were also regularly pawned. For many working class families the weekly cycle of pledging was a way of life; pledging tools on a Saturday to redeem their Sunday best, which would then be put in pledge again on the Monday to secure the basic necessities of life.[21] Pawnbroking was therefore the archetype of what the Crowther Committee termed 'adversity credit'.[22] Nor were the upper classes above having to pawn their possessions on occasion. In a diary entry of 1667, Samuel Pepys mentioned how Lady Peterborough had confided in him that 'her plate and jewels are at pawn for money, and how they are forced to live beyond their estate'.[23] Writing in the 1830s, Charles Dickens observed that:

> There are grades in pawning as in everything else, and distinctions must be observed even in poverty … so, the better sort of pawnbroker calls himself a silver-smith, and decorates his shop with handsome trinkets and expensive jewellery, while the more humble money-lender boldly advertises his calling, and invites observation.[24]

The volume of money-lending transactions, whether by way of bill of sale (secured money-lending) or on promissory notes (unsecured money-lending), increased

[19] The following is a small sample of the voluminous literature on the subject: S Block-Lieb and E Janger, 'The Myth of the Rational Borrower: Rationality, Behavioralism and the Misguided "Reform" of Bankruptcy Law' (2006) 84 *Texas Law Review* 1481; C Sunstein, 'Homo Economicus, Homo Myopicus, and the Law and Economics of Consumer Choice: Boundedly Rational Borrowing' (2006) 73 *University of Chicago Law Review* 249; I Ramsay, 'From Truth in Lending to Responsible Lending' in G Howells, A Janssen and R Schulze (eds), *Information Rights and Obligations* (Aldershot, Ashgate, 2005). The problem of cognitive bias is not, of course, restricted to the credit context.

[20] O Bar-Gill, 'Seduction by Plastic' (2004) 98 *Northwestern University Law Review* 1373, 1376.

[21] See P Colquhoun, *An Account of a Meat and Soup Charity Established in the Metropolis in the Year 1797 with Observations Relative to the Situation of the Poor* (London, 1797) 10.

[22] That is, credit to help out a person who, through misfortune or improvidence, has fallen on difficult times: see *Consumer Report* para 1.2.11.

[23] HB Wheatley (ed), *The Diary of Samuel Pepys*, vols VII-VIII, 1667 (London, G Bell and Sons, 1952) 124.

[24] Charles Dickens, *Sketches by Boz and Other Early Papers, 1833–39* (London, JM Dent, 1994) 187.

dramatically throughout the course of the nineteenth century.[25] Changes brought about by the Bills of Sale Act 1878 took chattels comprised in a bill of sale duly registered under the Act outside of the reputed ownership clause of the Bankruptcy Act 1869,[26] resulting in an explosion in the use of bills of sale by money-lenders.[27] This explosion was particularly marked in the area of small-amount-lending and was accompanied by growing concern about the effects of this type of money-lending on the small borrower. With borrowing by way of bill of sale generally resorted to only by those already in financial distress, money lenders were able to take advantage of this acute inequality of bargaining power to impose harsh and oppressive terms. This inequality was amplified in cases of small-amount-lending by way of bill of sale; needing to raise sums as small as £30 by this method was often indicative of insolvency and ignorance was said to be a marked problem in those borrowing the smallest sums in this way.[28] The problem was compounded by the ingenuity and complexity of the drafting of bills of sale by money lenders. With the legislative response to these concerns, the Bills of Sale Act (1878, Amendment Act 1882) entailing the sanction of voidness for any slight deviation from the new statutory formal requirements, cumbersome registration requirements and renewed application of the doctrine of reputed ownership, lending money by way of bill of sale suddenly lost its appeal. By 1898 a dramatic decline in the incidence of this particular mode of money-lending was evident,[29] although unsecured money-lending continued unabated.

At the same time, pawnbroking was falling into decline. The sharp deterioration in the quality of goods available for pledging from around the 1880s was a significant factor.[30] The introduction in the UK in 1911 of the first contributory system of insurance against sickness was also instrumental in diminishing the pawnbroker's role as the bulwark against destitution in working class society.[31] Throughout the 1920s, conscious of having done their duty during the war, the working classes became increasingly vocal about the State's duty to maintain them, a trend which was amplified by the onset of the depression and associated mass unemployment of the 1930s. The onward march of the welfare state in the 1940s and 1950s saw the closure of pawnbrokers' shops in their hundreds.[32] By the 1970s, the importance

[25] See *Report from the Select Committee on Money Lending* (1898) ('1898 Report') qs 148–49.

[26] With the effect that the money-lender was protected (other than against the holder of a previously registered bill of sale granted over the same chattels) from claims by third party creditors regardless of the borrower's solvency.

[27] See House of Commons, *Bills of Sale. Return of the number of bills of sale given in each county of England and Wales in the year 1880, classified according to sums of money for which the same were granted; similar years for each of the years 1875 to 1879, inclusive;* and, *Summary of the returns for the whole of England and Wales in each of the years from 1875 to 1880, inclusive* (1881).

[28] *Report from the Select Committee on Bills of Sale Act (1878) Amendment Bill* (1881) qs 1623–25.

[29] 1898 Report (n 25) vii.

[30] See M Tebbutt, *Making Ends Meet: Pawnbroking and Working-Class Credit* (New York, St Martin's Press, 1983) 131.

[31] ibid, 144–45.

[32] See 'Vanishing Pawnbrokers: Only the Fittest Survive in the Welfare State' *The Times* (London, 22 June 1957).

of pawnbroking was so diminished that the Crowther Committee described it as a 'minor form of consumer credit'.[33]

By the 1890s, hire-purchase was coming into its own. Initially, the term 'hire-purchase' was used more loosely to encompass hire-purchase in its modern sense as well as transactions more accurately described as conditional sales. The distinction between the two types of transaction became significant with the enactment of the Factors Act 1889. Six years later, the test case of *Helby v Matthews*[34] was taken up to the House of Lords, establishing that a 'hire-purchase' agreement which gave the hirer an option to terminate the contract as opposed to obligating him to carry the contract through to completion was not caught by s 9 of the Factors Act. The consequence was that the hirer under such an agreement was incapable of passing title to the goods to a third party in fraud of the owner. Armed with this reassuring legal precedent, the credit industry lost no time in adopting the modern form of hire-purchase as its mechanism of choice for the financing of sales of consumer durables. It was, however, the advent of the cheap motor car in the 1920s that really cemented the hire-purchase system's place in the British economy and, by 1935, it was estimated that 80 per cent of cars, 90 per cent of sewing machines, 75 per cent of furniture, and 95 per cent of the pianos, wireless sets and gramophones sold in Britain were acquired on hire-purchase.[35]

Although hire-purchase maintained its pre-eminent position, other forms of credit also achieved prominence in the twentieth century. For the more affluent classes, the opening up of banking facilities towards the end of the nineteenth century had brought with it the overdraft system, which proved a convenient credit mechanism. Some banks also provided credit by way of loan accounts, but it was not until the late 1950s that personal loans were offered. Finally after the introduction of charge cards,[36] Barclaycard launched the first revolving credit card system in the UK in 1969, permitting the consumer to roll over the credit balance indefinitely from month to month, with interest charged on the balance. Other types of credit—credit-trading,[37] check-trading,[38] mail-order sales and

[33] *Crowther Report* (n 6) para 2.1.18. Although pawnbroking has undergone something of a resurgence in the wake of the financial crisis: see, for example, Malcolm Locke, 'Recession and high gold prices set to drive pawnbroking industry consolidation, expansion' *The Financial Times* (London, 12 October 2009) www.ft.com/cms/s/2/8efc306c-b74f-11de-9812-00144feab49a.html#axzz45Pduy4yN.

[34] [1895] AC 471.

[35] See P Johnson, *Saving and Spending: The Working-Class Economy in Britain, 1870–1939* (Oxford, Oxford University Press, 1985) 157.

[36] Under this type of credit mechanism, the balance was to be paid off in full monthly.

[37] The essence of credit-trading, which was used primarily for the acquisition of clothing and 'smaller-ticket' household items, was a sale of goods, with the property in the goods passing immediately to the purchaser but with deferred payment of the purchase price by weekly instalments, in other words a credit-sale agreement.

[38] Check-trading involved the check-trader selling (on credit) a check to the customer, who could then exchange it for goods up to its value at participating retailers and repay the check-trader the value of the check by weekly instalments. Factored into these instalments, collected during visits to the customer's home, was a 'poundage' fee.

doorstep-moneylending[39]—were primarily targeted at working class communities.[40] Common to all of these was the fact that the dealings between lender and borrower (or buyer and seller) took place in, or on the doorstep, the (typically female) consumer's home with repayments made by instalments collected during weekly home visits. A drawback of the credit-trading system was the concern about male agents pressuring women in their own homes, a problem also in evidence in the hire-purchase sector, which increasingly made use of the door-to-door sales process in sales of labour-saving devices such as vacuum cleaners.

B. Overcoming Fragmentation

By the middle of the twentieth century, a complex and fragmented patchwork of legislative rules relating to credit had grown up—the consequence of successive piecemeal, 'catch-up' responses to developing credit practices. Despite its declining importance pawnbroking retained its own legislative regime.[41] There were also the two, very different legislative regimes governing transactions with money-lenders, on the one hand,[42] and hire-purchase, credit-sale and conditional sale agreements,[43] on the other. Running alongside were the complex and highly technical provisions of the Bills of Sale Acts.[44] Cutting across all this were the rules of the common law. Credit-grantors needed to have their wits about them when navigating this complex maze of rules; the anomalous treatment of different types of credit transactions and credit-grantors inevitably gave rise to regulatory arbitrage and distortions of competition.[45] At the same time, there was uncertainty as to the legal status of some of the newer credit mechanisms. For example, the question

[39] With the decline of pawnbroking, doorstep money-lending (also known as 'home-collected credit') became the predominant form of 'adversity credit' for the working class.

[40] For a wealth of detail on working-class credit in the twentieth century, see S O'Connell, *Credit and Community: Working Class Debt in the UK since 1880* (Oxford, Oxford University Press, 2009).

[41] The Pawnbrokers Act 1872 35 & 36 Vict c 93 remained in force until 1974, albeit with some minor amendments relating to monetary limits and charges made by the Pawnbrokers Act 1922 12 &13 Geo V c 5 and the Pawnbrokers Act 1960 Eliz II c 24.

[42] Money-Lenders Act 1900 63 & 64 Vict c 51 (as amended by the Money-Lenders Act 1911 1 & 2 Geo V c 38) and the Money-Lenders Act 1927 17 & 18 Geo V c 21.

[43] Hire-Purchase Act 1938 1 & 2 Geo VI c 53 (as amended by the Hire-Purchase Act 1954 2 & 3 Eliz II c 51) and the Advertisements (Hire-Purchase) Act 1957 5 & 6 Eliz c 4.

[44] Bills of Sale Act 1878 41 & 42 Vict c 31 and Bills of Sale Act (1878) Amendment Act 1882 45 & 46 Vict c 43.

[45] These anomalies are too numerous to list in this context, but among the most significant were that: while money-lenders required a licence to carry on business, those advancing credit by way of hire-purchase or other methods of instalment selling did not; while 'money-lenders' were subject to stringent regulation under the Money-Lenders Acts, the lending of money by banks was unregulated; whereas the Money-Lenders Acts applied regardless of the size of the loan or the corporate nature of the borrower, the Hire-Purchase Act 1964 did not apply to transactions above a certain amount or where the hirer or buyer was a company.

whether check-trading and the granting of a revolving credit facility by way of credit-card constituted 'money-lending' was never authoritatively resolved.

In its wholesale review of the credit field in 1971, the Crowther Committee considered that the time had come to call a spade a spade and recognise that, commercially speaking, these different credit mechanisms all amounted to the same thing: the provision of financial accommodation. What was required was a unitary legislative regime built upon a generic concept of consumer credit.

C. A Shifting Regulatory Philosophy

The first principle of social policy on which this regime was to be founded was said to be 'to treat the users of consumer credit as adults who are fully capable of managing their own financial affairs.'[46] This guiding principle, however, sat uneasily with the Committee's earlier recognition that freedom of contract was all but illusory in the consumer credit context. Although the Committee acknowledged that there was a group of low-income and less-educated consumers who were 'woefully ignorant both of the nature of the different types of consumer credit and/or their legal rights'[47] and hence 'generally less able to make rational choices',[48] it was on the paradigm of the 'rational consumer' that the Committee's recommendations were founded. The underlying assumptions were that 'consumers will be using credit in a rational and economically efficient manner'[49] and that 'the state should interfere as little as possible with the consumer's freedom to use his knowledge of the consumer credit market to the best of his ability and according to his judgment of what constitutes his best interests'.[50] The goal was no longer the protection of the 'poor and ignorant' or vulnerable from 'rapacious' lenders (as had appeared to be the primary motivation of Parliament in enacting the bills of sale and money-lending legislation of the late nineteenth and early twentieth century), but rather an efficiently-functioning and competitive consumer credit market driven by rational consumers making welfare-maximising decisions. The ensuing Act was described by one former Director General of Fair Trading as not seeking to:

> meet its objectives through interventionist action such as interest rate-capping or direct control of the substance of contracts. Rather, it explicitly endorses freedom of contract within a framework of rules designed to ensure openness: consumer protection is attained in large part through measures to ensure that full and truthful information about credit contracts is available to consumers.[51]

[46] *Crowther Report* (n 6) para 3.9.9.
[47] ibid, para 3.8.12.
[48] ibid, para 3.6.4.
[49] ibid, para 3.8.2.
[50] ibid, para 3.9.1.
[51] *Consumer Credit Deregulation: A Review by the Director General of Fair Trading of the Scope and Operation of the Consumer Credit Act 1974* (London, Office of Fair Trading, 1994) 6 (Sir Bryan Carsberg).

III. Redressing Inequality of Bargaining Power

A. The Usury Laws

The earliest statutory interventions in the credit area can be viewed as a response to the problem of inequality of bargaining power, albeit mediated through the Christian notion of lack of charity. Both the common law and equity shied away from the idea that substantive unfairness or the harshness of the bargain could itself be a ground for denying enforcement of or setting aside a contract. Inadequacy of consideration was, however, one factor that might support a finding of equitable fraud. Where inadequacy of consideration was so 'gross' as to shock the conscience it might alone suffice to permit an inference of fraud:

> If there is such inadequacy as to shew that the person did not understand the bargain he made, or was so oppressed that he was glad to make it, knowing its inadequacy, it will shew a command over him which may amount to fraud.[52]

Examples of equitable fraud inferred from such inadequacy alone are, however, almost non-existent. It was from this equitable jurisdiction in fraud that what later came to be known as the unconscionable bargain doctrine emerged.

Lord Hardwicke's formulation of his third head of equitable fraud in *Earl of Chesterfield v Janssen* — 'taking surreptitious advantage of the weakness or necessity of another'[53] — raised the question of whether inequality of bargaining position caused by external market conditions or 'mere' financial necessity or distress (or a combination of the two) might constitute a relevant weakness for these purposes. Most of the cases in which relief could be viewed as having been granted on this ground involved extreme examples of necessity tantamount to duress. In *Lawley v Hooper*[54] and *Duke of Cadaval v Collins*,[55] for example, the transactions had been entered into to secure the plaintiff's release from debtor's gaol and to avoid the plaintiff's arrest, respectively. Historically, then, the equitable doctrine was of limited utility to parties who, by reason of their inferior bargaining position or financial necessity, were forced to enter into credit bargains on extortionate terms. Where additional ingredients, such as the application of actual pressure to a party who was 'weak'[56] or in distressed circumstances,[57] could be identified, the result might, however, be different. One notable, additional ingredient that resulted in quite different treatment was the fact that the transaction involved dealings with

[52] *Heathcote v Paignon* (1787) 2 Bro CC 167, 175; 29 ER 96, 100 (Thurlow LC). See also similar statements by Lord Thurlow in the earlier case of *Gwynne v Heaton* (1778) 1 Bro CC 1, 28 ER 949.

[53] *Earl of Chesterfield v Janssen* (1750–51) 2 Ves Sen 125, 156; 28 ER 82, 100.

[54] (1745) 3 Atk 278, 26 ER 962.

[55] (1836) 4 A & E 858, 111 ER 1006.

[56] *Gartside v Isherwood* (1783) 1 Bro CC 558, 28 ER 1297.

[57] *Proof v Hines* (1735) Cas T Talb 111, 25 ER 690, where pressure had been applied to a poor illiterate man who was reduced so low as to have to live upon 'what broken scraps of meat he could get from taverns' and was in desperate need of money.

reversionary interests, or expectancies. Such transactions were typically entered into by those with a pressing need for money but good prospects in the future. Although the earliest cases had involved young heirs just come of age,[58] by the nineteenth century the doctrine covered anyone who had a hope or expectation of succeeding to the property of an ancestor and who entered into financial dealings on the basis of that expectation.[59] In such cases, 'mere' (as opposed to gross) inadequacy of consideration was sufficient. By Lord Eldon's time, the onus was said to rest on the party dealing with the expectant heir or reversioner to establish the fairness of the transaction.[60] These cases involved a particular application of the unconscionable bargain doctrine in which the notion of advantage-taking of weakness was heavily supplemented by the policy of protecting the upper classes so shamelessly articulated by Sir Lancelot Shadwell VC in 1831:

> The mere fact that Lord Portmore was not only the heir apparent of his father, but also the expectant heir to a peerage, also brings the case distinctly within the rule laid down by this Court, and which is founded on general policy, namely that this Court will not allow the heir of a family of rank to be reduced to poverty and distress by dealing with his expectancies.[61]

Outside of this particular context though Courts of Equity had been reluctant to be seen to do more than facilitate the parties' private ordering of their own affairs and safeguard it from abusive practices.

In contrast, a democratically elected and sovereign parliament need not feel so constrained. It can, according to the political climate of the day, legitimately legislate to intervene in the substance of contracts. In modern societies, intervention in the core price terms of credit contracts is generally justified on the grounds of preventing the socially harmful consequences of extortionate credit. Even the Crowther Committee was prepared to admit that 'there is a level of cost above which it becomes socially harmful to make loans available at all'.[62] However, the usury laws as first enacted in 1487[63] were based on a concern not with the social *consequences* of such lending but rather with the moral turpitude—the sin of lack of charity, the taking advantage of one's brother's need—on which the transaction was founded. Expressing it another way, one might say that the sin of usury was the

[58] See, eg, *Nott v Hill* (1682) 2 Chan Cas 120, 22 ER 875; *Berry* (1680) [1089] (1961) 79 Selden Society 868; *Dominus Frances Pawlett v Playdell* (1679) [935] (1961) 79 Selden Society 739; *Berney v Pitt* (1686) 2 Chan Rep 395; 21 ER 697.

[59] See Sir George Jessel MR's comments in *Benyon v Cook* (1875) LR 10 Ch App 389, 391. For a comprehensive account of the development of the law relating to 'catching' bargains with expectants, see L Sheridan, *Fraud in Equity: A Study in English and Irish Law* (London, Pitman, 1957) ch 8.

[60] *Coles v Trecothick* (1804) 9 Ves Jun 234, 246; 32 ER 592, 597; *Peacock v Evans* (1809) 16 Ves Jun 512, 514; 22 ER 1079, 1080; *Gowland v De Faria* (1810) 17 Ves 20, 34 ER 8.

[61] *Earl of Portmore v Taylor* (1831) 4 Sim 182, 213; 58 ER 69, 80.

[62] Although it did not consider that a return to an interest rate ceiling was the solution: *Crowther Report* (n 6) para 6.6.6–6.6.9.

[63] 3 Hen VII c 6.

taking advantage of the borrower's inferior bargaining position. If there were any consequentialist considerations at play at all here, it was simply that, by entering into the usurious transaction, the lender imperilled his soul. All of this was a function of the fact that the secular usury laws had originally been enacted to uphold God's law.[64]

The canon law as set out in Gratian's *Decretum*, compiled and written in the twelfth century, defined usury strictly as the taking of *any* interest.[65] That position was mirrored in the early usury statutes[66] but, by the end of the sixteenth century, an Act of 1571,[67] which drew a distinction between lending at 10 per cent and below and lending at more than 10 per cent, came to be widely interpreted as sanctioning lending at 10 per cent and less.[68] Thus, the 'sin' of usury (for secular purposes at least) was now the taking of *excessive* interest, as defined by the usury statutes. Throughout the course of the seventeenth century, the legal rate of interest was reduced, first to eight per cent,[69] then to six per cent.[70] Finally in 1713 it was reduced to five per cent.[71] Despite continued hostility in some quarters to this divergence between commercial practice and the secular law, on the one hand, and God's law, on the other, the question of usury and interest rates had come to be viewed as an economic, rather than a purely moral or theological question.[72] This was an inevitable consequence of England's commercial development, its development into a global state with a global economy, and changing ideas about the relationship between divine law and the needs of the state.

The prohibition on usury applied to all loans, secured and unsecured and whether for commercial or private purposes. The usury statutes were built upon a two-pronged approach. The first prong—the stipulation that a usurious contract was void—belonged to the private law. The second prong—the offence of usury subjecting the usurer to penalties—was part of the criminal law. As became apparent, these two prongs were not merely two different consequences of the same conduct; rather, they were two distinct *species* of usury ('the offence of usury' and 'usury for the purposes of rendering the contract void'). In the majority of cases, the two species would co-exist on the facts but this was not necessarily the case. The distinction was that a person could commit the offence of usury in the

[64] The ecclesiastical courts of course retained their jurisdiction over usury. On the early history of the usury laws, see N Jones, *God and the Moneylenders* (Oxford, Basil Blackwell, 1989).

[65] On the *Decretum Gratiani*, see Landau, 'Gratian and the *Decretum Gratiani*' in W Hartmann and K Pennington (eds), *The History of Medieval Canon Law in the Classical Period, 1140–1234* (Washington DC, The Catholic University of America Press, 2008).

[66] 3 Hen VII c 6 and 11 Hen VII c 8.

[67] 13 Eliz I c 8.

[68] Although this was clearly not the intent of the Act. See Jones (n 64) ch 2.

[69] (1624) 21 Jac I c 17.

[70] (1660) 12 Car II c 13.

[71] 13 Ann c 15.

[72] See Jones (n 64) ch 2.

absence of a *contract* to take usurious interest.[73] It was sufficient for the offence of usury that the lender had *received* usurious interest. The corollary was that despite the existence of a usurious contract, the *offence* of usury was complete only if and when usurious interest was actually received.[74] In contrast, mere receipt of usurious interest was insufficient to render a contract and any securities given pursuant to it void.[75]

The penalty for the offence of usury was forfeiture of treble the value of the sum lent. One half of that penalty was to go to the Crown, the other to 'him or them that will sue for the same'.[76] This statutory wording alluded to the existence of a *qui tam* action, in other words an action brought under a penal provision of a statute giving part of the penalty to whomever would sue for it. The rationale of the *qui tam* action has been described as the protection of the community through the creation of a force of 'voluntary policemen'—common informers 'who were to be paid on the results achieved by their own zeal and enterprise'.[77]

On the private law side, the effect of voidness was to prevent the lender recovering either the interest (whether lawful or usurious) or the principal sum advanced on a usurious contract. Any securities given pursuant to such a contract were also void. In equity it was well established that the borrower would not be granted relief from a usurious contract without repayment of the principal and legal interest.[78] The position at common law was less clear-cut. A case in the Common Pleas in 1809 had followed the Chancery's approach, describing the action as 'an application to the equitable jurisdiction of the Court'.[79] However in *Roberts v Goff*, the Kings Bench refused to impose such terms on the grant of relief, asserting that 'the construction and practice of this Court have always been different'.[80] There was also the question of restitutionary claims by the borrower. Earlier case law had taken the position that the borrower was unable to recover usurious interest paid pursuant to such a contract in an action for money had and received. According to Treby CJ:

> [W]here a man knowingly pays money upon illegal consideration, the party that receives it ought to be punished for his offence; and the party that pays it is *particeps criminis*, and

[73] *Sir Wollaston Dixie's Case* (1586) 1 Leo 96, 74 ER 89; *R v Allen* (1671) 1 Mod 69, 86 ER 738; *Ferrall v Shaen* (1671) 1 Wms Saund 294, 85 ER 400; *Radley v Manning* (1674) 3 Keb 142, 84 ER 642; *Ballard v Oddey* (1678) 2 Mod 307, 86 ER 1089; *Abrahams v Bunn* (1768) 4 Burr 2251, 97 ER 173; *Floyer v Edwards* (1774) 1 Cowp 112, 98 ER 995; *Fisher v Beasley* (1779) 1 Dougl 236, 99 ER 154.

[74] *Fisher v Beasley*, ibid.

[75] *Pollard v Scholy* (1583) Cro Eliz 20, 78 ER 286; *Dalton's Case* (1600) Noy 171, 74 ER 1129; *R v Allen* (1671) 1 Mod 69, 86 ER 738.

[76] This statutory wording in s 37 Hen VII c 9 was continued in force by 13 Eliz I c 8 and the later statutes on usury.

[77] L Radzinowicz, *A History of English Criminal Law and Its Administration from 1750*, vol 2 (London, Stevens & Sons, 1956) 145–46.

[78] See *Ex parte Skip* (1752) 2 Ves Sen 489, 28 ER 313; *Mason v Gardiner* (1793) 4 Bro CC 437, 29 ER 976.

[79] *Hindle v O'Brien* (1809) 1 Taunt 413, 127 ER 894.

[80] (1820) 4 B & Ald 92, 92–93; 106 ER 872.

there is no reason that he should have his money again; for he parted with it freely, and *volenti non fit injuria.*[81]

However, the logic of characterising someone who was oppressed and obliged to submit to usurious terms as *particeps criminis* came to be questioned in the course of the eighteenth century, first in the Chancery.[82] The common law later followed suit, Lord Mansfield distinguishing between statutory provisions designed to 'protect weak and necessitous men from being over-reached, defrauded, or oppressed' (where the *in pari delicto, potior est conditio defendentis* rule did not hold) and those 'founded upon general reasons of policy and public expedience' (where it did).[83] One might have expected these private law consequences to operate as a powerful incentive for the borrower to escape from his obligations and turn informer. But another aspect of inequality of bargaining power may have been at play here. For much of the eighteenth and early nineteenth centuries money was scarce. Whether, in these circumstances, borrowers were really likely to take action that might remove from their grasp a source of future credit, must be open to doubt.[84]

Just like the ecclesiastical courts before them, the secular courts were confronted with numerous instances of 'cloaked' usury from the earliest days of the usury laws. In 1595, Miles Mosse, had described the devices employed to conceal usury as 'innumerable, as the stars in the skies, adding that 'they arise dailie spicke and span new, one in anothers necke'.[85] Lenders' ingenuity continued to flourish and, by the latter part of the eighteenth century, the perfect avoidance device—the annuity for the life of the seller—had been developed. As Mark Ord later proclaimed, 'after a long contest between the usurer and the legislature, the ingenuity of the former hath prevailed over the authority of the latter'.[86]

This chapter is not the place for detailed discussion of these numerous avoidance devices,[87] but no account of the usury laws would be complete without touching on the legal principles which permitted such circumvention. Two basic principles were at play here. The first was the principle that, if the loan principal was put at risk or 'hazard', so that it could be said that the lender would not *in any*

[81] *Tomkins v Bernet* (1693) 1 Salk 22, 91 ER 21. Also reported in Skinner as having been decided by Holt CJ on the same grounds: *Tomkyns v Barnet* (1693) Skin 410, 90 ER 182.

[82] By Lord Talbot LC in *Bosanquett v Dashwood* (1734) Cases t Talb 38, 41; 25 ER 648, 649.

[83] *Clarke v Shee* (1774) 1 Cowp 197, 210; 98 ER 1041. See also *Astley v Reynolds* (1732) 2 Str 916, 93 ER 939 and *Smith v Bromley* (1760) 2 Dougl 696, 99 ER 441.

[84] For discussion of the effects of the scarcity of money and the difficulty of raising money by way of mortgage during the Napoleonic Wars, see the evidence given to the Select Committee on the Usury Laws: Report from the Select Committee on the Usury Laws (1818).

[85] M Mosse, *The Arraignment and Conviction of Usurie* (London, 1595) 122–39.

[86] M Ord, *An Essay on the Law of Usury* (London, W Clarke and Sons & Todd, 1809) 67.

[87] On the annuity for the life of the seller, see S Campbell, 'Usury and Annuities of the Eighteenth Century' (1928) 44 *LQR* 473; W Swain and K Fairweather, 'Usury and the Judicial Regulation of Financial Transactions in Seventeenth and Eighteenth-Century England' in M Kenny, J Devenney and L Fox O'Mahony (eds), *Unconscionability in European Private Financial Transactions* (Cambridge, Cambridge University Press, 2010) ch 8. On avoidance devices more generally, see Mosse (n 85) 122–39; Jones (n 64) 118–44; R Comyn, *A Treatise on the Law of Usury* (London, R Pheny, 1817).

event recover the principal, the transaction was outside the scope of the statute.[88] The second was that it was the *intent* of the parties rather than the form of the transaction that was decisive. That had been established as early as 1598,[89] but was reiterated by Lord Mansfield in 1781 in a case involving a 'false' sale of goods:

> [T]he only question, in all cases like the present, is, what is the real substance of the transaction, not what is the colour and form. This is one of the strongest cases of the sort I ever knew litigated. It is impossible to wink so hard, as not to see, that there was no idea between the parties of anything but a loan of money.[90]

Of course, these two principles interacted. In some cases, the focus appeared to be on the degree of risk rather than the parties' true intent, but the degree of risk may, in reality, have served a purely evidential function. A risk that was so slight as to be unreal would suggest that the transaction was 'colourable'.[91] Conversely, the presence of substantial risk would generally indicate the 'lender's' acceptance of a genuine risk that he might not recover and that what was truly intended was not a loan. But by the latter part of the eighteenth century it was clear that the courts were failing to live up to their rhetoric of looking through the form of the transaction to the true intent. In *Murray v Harding*, it was accepted that, despite initial discussions about a 'loan', a refusal to lend coupled with an accepted counter-offer to enter into another type of transaction (which if entered into *bona fide* was outside the usury laws) had the effect of transforming the parties' intent.[92] Furthermore, in sales of annuities for the life of the seller, it had become the invariable practice for the buyer (the party advancing the capital sum) to insure the seller's life (the seller being the party receiving that sum in return for an agreement to make yearly payments for the rest of his life), the cost of that insurance being borne by the seller. This had the effect of rendering the risk to the principal, which might have justified treating the transaction as outside the usury laws, illusory. Yet Lord Hardwicke was a lone voice in holding that in these circumstances the transaction was not a *bona fide* sale of an annuity, but a loan of money.[93] By the late eighteenth century, it was firmly established that the practice of insuring the seller's life had no bearing on the question of the parties' true intent.[94] Furthermore, whereas in Lord Hardwicke's day the redeemability of an annuity was considered to indicate that the true intent was the lending and borrowing of money,[95] by the 1780s it was asserted that 'to sell an annuity, and make it redeemable, is not usury, because it is not a loan'.[96]

[88] *Roberts v Tremayne* (1617) Cro Jac 508, 79 ER 433.
[89] *Button v Downham* (1598) Cro Eliz 643, 78 ER 882.
[90] *Lowe v Waller* (1781) 2 Dougl 736, 740; 99 ER 470, 472.
[91] See Burnett J's comments in *Earl of Chesterfield v Janssen* (1750–51) 2 Ves Sen 125, 143; 28 ER 82, 92.
[92] *Murray v Harding* (1773) 2 Wm Bla 859, 864; 96 ER 507, 509.
[93] *Lawley v Hooper* (1745) 2 Atk 278, 26 ER 962.
[94] See F Plowden, *A Treatise Upon the Law of Usury and Annuities* (London, 1797) 155.
[95] See R Withy, *A Practical Treatise Upon the Law of Annuities* (London, J Butterworth, 1800) 13.
[96] *Irnham v Child* (1781) 1 Bro CC 92, 93; 28 ER 1006, 1007 (Thurlow LC).

Despite being widely circumvented, the usury laws were not a complete dead letter; the very fact that lenders went to such lengths to avoid their application proves as much. But their effect, it was argued, was to drive the cost of credit by forcing borrowers into the hands of those operating outside, or at the margins of the law, who levied a premium for the risk of the transaction being challenged.[97] This alleged inefficacy was a significant factor in the calls for repeal. However, a more significant pressure on the usury laws was the increased need for credit in an age of industrialisation and by the nineteenth century, the usury debate had turned into a power struggle between the commercial and the landed classes. As one commentator observed, the objections of the landed class were not confined to the purely economic concern that it would increase the cost of raising money on mortgages. Rather, the fear was that the repeal 'would place the country gentleman at the mercy of the capitalist, and give the monied men the preponderance in parliament'.[98] It was, in fact, the preponderance of the landed class in Parliament at that time that ensured that it was not until 1854 that a total repeal was achieved.[99]

B. Statutory Relief from Unconscionable Bargains

By the 1860s, equity's privileging of expectants and reversioners was considered anachronistic and Parliament sought to put dealings with reversionary interests on the same footing as dealings with interests in possession.[100] However, the fact that the relevant provision[101] was restricted to purchases made *bona fide* and without fraud or unfair dealing meant that its effect was negligible. Provided a purchase of a reversion at a 'mere' undervalue could be reframed as a transaction involving weakness on one side, the burden would still rest on the other party to prove that the transaction was fair, just and reasonable.[102] When, in the 1890s, Parliament turned its attention to the plight of the 'ordinary' borrower forced to submit to extortionate terms in money-lending transactions, there was a widely held belief amongst the legally qualified witnesses who gave evidence that the equitable doctrine was restricted to dealings with expectant heirs and reversioners. Although framing the problem as one of inequality of *informational* rather than of *bargaining* power, one High Court judge and future Lord Justice of Appeal who gave evidence to the Select Committee on Money Lending observed that 'judicial

[97] J Bentham, *Defence of Usury* (London, 1787) 23–24.

[98] JB Kelly, *A Summary of the History and Law of Usury* (London, Richard James Kennett, 1835) 177.

[99] On the repeal of the usury laws, see K Fairweather, 'The Historical Development of the Protection of Borrowers in Personal Credit Transactions: 1700–1974' (PhD thesis, University of Exeter, 2016) 85–96.

[100] Sale of Reversions Act 1867.

[101] ibid, s 1.

[102] See *Earl of Aylesford v Morris* (1873) LR 8 Ch App 484; *O'Rorke v Bollingbroke* (1877) 2 App Cas 814.

notice is taken of dementia which arises from wealth, but dementia which arises from poverty is left to take care of itself'.[103]

The repeal of the usury laws in 1854, a time when the philosophical principles of *laissez-faire* were dominant, had proceeded on the assumption that an unfettered market in credit would result in better outcomes and lower interest rates for borrowers. That assumption proved unrealistic. Part of the problem was that the repeal had been driven by considerations of 'high commercial policy', with no consideration given to the needs of the small private borrower.[104]

The acute inequality of bargaining power between money-lender and borrower was a recurrent theme in the evidence of the witnesses to the Select Committee on Moneylending. In many cases, default would be inevitable, and having once entered the transaction, the borrower found himself completely at the money-lender's mercy, forced to obtain 'renewal after renewal at increasingly extortionate rates until he is utterly ruined'.[105] As Sir James Matthew expressed it:

> [T]he money-lender may do with him as he pleases. Now, I think that is not a position in which one man ought to be placed by the law with reference to another; he ought not to have that power of coercion; he ought not to have his fellow creature in that state of subjection. It is not blackmailing, but he may so act as to approach very nearly to the confines of that offence; and, as experience shows, the exactions are, under such circumstances, sometimes excessive and extraordinary.[106]

In its Report, the 1898 Committee concluded that the minimum rate of interest charged in money-lending transactions was generally about 60 per cent. Some money-lenders charged a uniform rate of interest. Others charged as much as they could get.[107] Most lenders were charging between 60 to 170 per cent on bills of sale but interest on unsecured loans on promissory notes was much higher.[108] One notorious money-lender, Isaac Gordon, admitted in his evidence to the Committee to having charged as much as 3,000 per cent interest.[109] The problem of interest rates or 'bonuses' on renewals was particularly acute, with Gordon admitting that he generally charged a 'bonus' of up to 1,000 per cent for a renewal of a bill of exchange or promissory note.[110] On renewing the loan, the costs and interest would be added to the original principal and, as one county court judge put it, 'the whole thing starts again with compound interest, so that, although one cannot say there is any fraud about the thing, people know what it is nevertheless. It is a thing as to which, when they are once in they never get out, as far as my experience goes'.[111]

[103] Evidence of Sir James Matthew, 1898 Report (n 25) q 1459.

[104] 1898 Report (n 25) evidence of Sir George Lewis, qs 148–49; *Report from the Select Committee on Money Lending* (1897) ('1897 Report'), evidence of Judge William Owen, qs 4522–24 and evidence of Judge Lumley Smith, qs 4679–81.

[105] 1898 Report (n 25) iv.

[106] ibid, q 1441.

[107] ibid, iv.

[108] 1897 Report (n 105) evidence of Thomas Farrow, q 110.

[109] ibid, evidence of Isaac Gordon qs 3049–52.

[110] ibid, q 3067.

[111] ibid, evidence of Judge Lumley Smith, q 4648.

Harsh default clauses were a particular source of concern. One common type of default clause provided that in the event of default on any instalment, the arrears would immediately become due with interest at 216 per cent per annum. An even harsher type of default clause frequently found in money-lenders' agreements provided that, on default of any one instalment, the entire sum payable over the contemplated period of the loan, including capital and interest, would immediately become payable.[112]

During the Committee proceedings, a re-introduction of a statutory ceiling on interest rates was mooted but ultimately rejected.[113] Instead, the Committee recommended the introduction of a statutory re-opening provision giving all courts unfettered discretion to make such order that, in all the circumstances of the case, appeared reasonable. This statutory extension of the equitable jurisdiction to grant relief from unconscionable bargains was thought necessary for two reasons. Firstly, although the scope of the equitable jurisdiction was not entirely free from doubt, most equity lawyers of the day considered that there was no power to intervene simply because advantage had been taken of a borrower's financial distress in a 'pure money-lending' case.[114] Secondly, the county courts, which dealt with the vast majority of money-lending cases, had a very limited equitable jurisdiction,[115] although some county court judges had been able to alleviate the plight of some of the poorest borrowers by making creative use of their powers under s 105 of the County Courts Act 1888 to order repayment by instalments.[116]

The judiciary may have been among the most ardent advocates of a statutory re-opening provision during the Select Committee proceedings, but many of its members were not slow in voicing their dismay and frustration when actually confronted with the broad discretion bestowed on them by the ensuing s 1(1) of the Money-Lenders Act 1900. The first part of this long-winded subsection provided that:

> Where proceedings are taken in any court by a money-lender for the recovery of any money lent after the commencement of this Act, or the enforcement of any agreement or security made or taken after the commencement of this Act, in respect of money lent either before or after the commencement of this Act, and there is evidence which satisfies the court that the

[112] ibid, evidence of Judge Owen, qs 4569–71.

[113] Although the Money-Lenders Act 1927, s 7 subsequently reintroduced some direct intervention in interest rates by prohibiting both the charging of compound interest generally and the charging of default interest at more than the 'normal' contractual rate of interest.

[114] That is outside the situation of dealings with expectant heirs or reversioners. See, for example, the evidence of Judge Lumley Smith, 1897 Report (n 104) q 4661.

[115] Although the superior courts had been vested with equitable jurisdiction in the widest possible terms by s 24 of the Judicature Act 1873, the equitable jurisdiction of the county courts was limited to the express powers granted to them under s 67 of the county courts Act 1888.

[116] Rubin refers to cases where there was no choice, because of the way the law then stood, but to give judgment for the money-lender, but where the court ordered repayment in such tiny instalments that it would take sixty-six years, three hundred and eighty-five years or, in one case, nearly a thousand years, for the debt to be repaid in full: see G Rubin, 'The County Courts and the Tally Trade, 1846–1914' in G Rubin and D Sugarman (eds) *Law Economy and Society, 1750–1914: Essays in the History of English Law* (Abingdon, Professional Books, 1984) 336–37.

interest charged in respect of the sum actually lent is excessive, or that the amounts charged for expenses, inquiries, fines, bonus, premium, renewals, or any other charges, are excessive, and that, in either case, the transaction is harsh and unconscionable, or is otherwise such that a court of equity would give relief, the court may re-open the transaction.

In 1908, Farwell LJ observed that 'the Act of Parliament has cast upon the Court the necessity, very much against the will of most of the Judges who have to deal with the matter, of remodelling the terms which were entered into by persons who are *sui juris*'.[117] The construction of the subsection in fact gave rise to considerable difficulties, with one early decision threatening to frustrate the very purpose of s 1(1) just months after the Act's entry into force. In *Wilton & Co v Osborne*,[118] Ridley J concluded that the interest rate of 160 per cent charged on the loan in question 'must be regarded as excessive, and that the whole transaction was, in the sense that the charges made were excessive and extortionate, harsh and unconscionable'.[119] Nevertheless, relief was refused. In Ridley J's view, the words 'or is otherwise such that a Court of Equity would give relief' in s 1(1) qualified the preceding words, 'is harsh and unconscionable', rather than being an alternative to them. On this reading, transactions could be re-opened only if the circumstances were such that a court of equity would have granted relief prior to the Act. Since, in Ridley J's opinion, the necessary element of 'unfair dealing' was absent, this was not such a case. This erroneous construction of the subsection was soon corrected by the House of Lords in *Samuel v Newbold*, which confirmed that excessive interest and/or charges alone could render a transaction harsh or unconscionable:

Excess of interest or charges may of itself be [evidence that the transaction was harsh and unconscionable], and particularly if it be unexplained. If no justification be established, the presumption hardens into a certainty.[120]

But although the decision had clarified that relief was available on the grounds of an excessive rate of interest alone, substantive unfairness still seemed to play an evidential role. But the question was what was it that this substantive unfairness evidenced on a conceptual level? The Chancery had historically explained the equitable doctrine as defendant-sided: the grant of relief was premised on the wrongfulness of the *defendant's advantage-taking*. However, attempts to reconfigure the law of contract around the will theory in the latter part of the nineteenth century had resulted in attempts to reconceptualise the doctrine as one concerned rather with the *plaintiff's defective consent*[121] and the case law on s 1 of the

[117] *Fieldings v Pawson* unreported (11 March 1908). Transcript in appendix G of J Matthews, *The Money-Lenders Act 1900* (London, Sweet & Maxwell, 1908) 148, 155.

[118] [1901] 2 KB 110.

[119] ibid, 112.

[120] [1906] AC 461, 467 (Lord Loreburn LC). See also the earlier decision of the Court of Appeal in *In Re A Debtor* [1903] 1 KB 705.

[121] See F Pollock, *Principles of Contract at Law and in Equity: Being a Treatise on the General Principles Concerning the Validity of Agreements, with a Special View to the Comparison of Law and Equity, and*

Money-Lenders Act was shot through with this tension between plaintiff-sided and defendant-sided concerns. On the one hand, Lord MacNaghten's references in *Samuel v Newbold* to 'fair dealing' suggested a defendant-sided approach.[122] Channell J, on the other hand, who had repeatedly expressed his frustration with s 1 in a number of the reported cases,[123] took an avowedly plaintiff-sided approach, suggesting that where the judge was satisfied that:

> [T]he borrower thoroughly understood the transaction, and without any misrepresentation or any pressure other than the mere request to pay so much interest, voluntarily agreed to pay it ... he ought to find that the interest which the man so agrees to pay is reasonable, and therefore, not excessive within the meaning of the Act.[124]

On this view, the circumstance of the borrower being a competent and intelligent individual who fully understood and freely consented to the terms of the transaction would, in the absence of any other factors, render even the most extortionate rate of interest reasonable, precluding a finding that the contract was 'harsh and unconscionable'. Furthermore, on this reading, the focus of concern was inequality of *informational* power rather than inequality of *bargaining* power. Although this aspect of Channell J's judgment in *Carringtons Ltd v Smith* was not overruled by the House of Lords in *Samuel v Newbold*, it must be read in the light of the subsequent decision in *Blair v Buckworth.*[125] In allowing an appeal against Channell J's refusal to grant relief, the Court of Appeal took the view that he had placed too much weight on the borrower's competence and understanding of the terms of the transaction; this was but one factor to be taken into account and was in no way decisive.[126] In reaching this conclusion, Lord Alverstone CJ stressed that the Act was 'intended to protect borrowers against themselves'[127] emphasising that Parliament's concern had not been confined to informational inequalities.

Despite this more expansive approach, money-lenders continued to extract extortionate rates of interest from some borrowers.[128] A return to an interest rate ceiling having once again been rejected, the Money-Lenders Act 1927 introduced a rebuttable presumption that the transaction was harsh and unconscionable where the interest and/or other charges amounted to 48 per cent or above,[129] although it

with References to the Indian Contract Act and Occasionally to Roman, American and Continental Law 1st edn (London, Stevens & Sons, 1876) 518–24. Such cases were dealt with under the heading 'duress and undue influence'.

[122] *Samuel v Newbold* (n 120) 470.

[123] See, for example, his comments in *Barnett v Coronna*, The Times, 16 June 1902; *Levene v Greenwood* (1904) 20 TLR 389; *Carringtons Ltd v Smith* [1906] 1 KB 79, 86.

[124] *Carringtons Ltd v Smith* ibid, 92.

[125] (1908) 24 TLR 474.

[126] ibid, 476.

[127] ibid.

[128] See, for example, Dorothy Keeling's evidence to the Joint Select Committee of 1925 that the usual rate of interest charged by the 1,100 registered women money-lenders in Liverpool was 433 ½ per cent: *Report by the Joint Select Committee of the House of Lords and the House of Commons on the Moneylenders Bill (HL) and the Moneylenders (Amendment) Bill* (1925) qs 901 and 905.

[129] Money-Lenders Act 1927, s 10.

had been stressed that it was intended as no more than a 'useful guide' which in no way bound the court.[130] However the practical effect of the presumption proved to be the 'fixing' 48 per cent as the usual rate of interest[131] and it was ultimately abandoned when the reopening power was reformulated by the Consumer Credit Act 1974. Under the new 'extortionate credit bargain' provisions, a court would be justified in reopening a transaction if the payments to be made under it were grossly exorbitant or the agreement otherwise contravened ordinary principles of fair dealing.[132] The debtor's financial necessity or distress at the time of entering into the transaction was explicitly listed as a factor to be taken into account when deciding whether to exercise this power.[133] However, the new provision—at least as it was applied in the few cases that came before the courts—proved debtor-unfriendly in practice.[134] The main obstacles to relief were two other factors listed as relevant to the exercise of the power: rates of interest prevailing at the time the agreement was made and the degree of risk accepted by the creditor, having regard to the value of any security provided.[135] The courts apparent willingness to take creditors' assessments of risk at face value, particularly where the rate of interest was in line with rates in the particular sector of the credit market, meant that the debtors' financial necessity or distress was a factor that was easily trumped.[136]

IV. Redressing Inequality of Informational Power

A. Equitable and Statutory Relief from Unconscionable Bargains

Whereas the Chancery had been reluctant to grant relief purely on account of inequality of bargaining power, it was more willing to do so in situations of inequality of informational power. Situations of informational inequality might arise from 'constitutional' disadvantages, such as the one party's lack of education or knowledge, old age, infirmity, youth or inexperience, or the other party's greater understanding, experience, or familiarity with the terms and effect of the contracts they were in a position to impose. But in the consumer credit context such informational inequalities also commonly arise from the contract itself, for example from its

[130] See the comments of Lord Darling who had chaired the 1925 Select Committee: HL Deb 23 February, vol 63, cols 425–26.

[131] See *Crowther Report* (n 6).

[132] Consumer Credit Act 1974, ss 138(1).

[133] ibid, s 138(3)(b).

[134] See Department of Trade and Industry, *Fair Clear and Competitive: The Consumer Credit Market in the 21st Century* (White Paper, Cm 6040, 2003) paras 3.28–3.37.

[135] Consumer Credit Act 1974, s 138(4)(a).

[136] For analysis of the case law, see L Bentley and G Howells, 'Judicial Treatment of Extortionate Credit Bargains: Part 1' [1989] *Conveyancer and Property Lawyer* 164.

complexity, length, and use of obscure, technical language. While equity was more prepared to intervene in the first type of situation,[137] it rarely did so in the second. In the absence of some *special* disadvantage affecting the debtor's cognitive capacity for decision-making and setting him apart from the average debtor, equity was reluctant to intervene. The equitable doctrine's capacity to redress the informational inequalities *typically* present in consumer credit transactions was thus extremely limited.

Under s 1 of the Money-Lenders Act 1900, a more expansive view was taken of the situations of informational inequality that might justify intervention. Harsh default clauses, which had been neither explained to nor understood by the borrower made regular appearances in the case law. One common type of default clause—a perfect example of the type of complexity described by Engel as arising from 'multiple moving parts'—was a source of particular concern.[138] This type of clause provided that on default of payment of any one instalment, the entire sum payable over the contemplated period of the loan, including capital and interest, would immediately become payable. The earlier the point in time the default occurred, the greater the effect of the clause in inflating the annual rate of interest. The transaction in *Samuel v Newbold* itself had involved such a clause, which was undoubtedly a weighty factor in the decision to re-open the transaction. However, in the earlier case of *Levene v Greenwood*, Channell J, always keen to emphasise factors relevant to the quality of the borrower's *consent*, had put a rather different slant on this type of clause.[139] His concern was not simply with the substance of such clauses but rather that, while they were perfectly understood by the money-lenders who imposed them, their effect would not be readily grasped by anyone else. Channell J's approach, which was endorsed in the subsequent case law, was that the inclusion of such clauses in money-lending agreements had the effect of placing the money-lender under a positive obligation to explain their effects to the borrower; failure to do so justified re-opening the transaction as harsh and unconscionable.[140]

B. Information Disclosure and Formality Requirements

As has been seen, the Consumer Credit Act 1974 was based on the 'truth in lending' or 'information' paradigm, with interference in the substance of credit contracts

[137] See, for example, the line of cases concerning 'poor and illiterate persons': *Proof v Hines* (1735) Cas T Talb 111, 25 ER 690; *Evans v Llewellin* (1787) 1 Cox CC 333, 29 ER 1191; *Clark v Malpas* (1862) 31 Beav 80, 54 ER 1076 affirmed on appeal (1862) 4 De GF & J 401, 45 ER 1238; *Baker v Monk* (1864) 33 Beav 419, 55 ER 430.

[138] See, for example, the evidence of Judge Owen, 1897 Report (n 104) qs 4569–71.

[139] (1904) 20 TLR 389.

[140] ibid, 390. See also *Levene v Tichener* (1907) 23 TLR, where an annual interest rate of 150 per cent would have ballooned to over 1000 per cent if default had been made in the first instalment; *Harris v Clarson* (1911) 27 TLR 30, where the respective rates were 140 and 600 per cent; *Stirling v Rose* (1913) 30 TLR 67, where the rates were 60 and 240 per cent respectively.

kept to an absolute minimum.[141] This traditional paradigm, rooted in neo-classical economic thought, posits that consumers will make rational welfare-maximising credit decisions if provided with adequate information at appropriate times. Although not costless economically-speaking, information disclosure is palatable across the politic spectrum. This explains its continued appeal and favoured position in the arsenal of consumer protection mechanisms.[142] However, since 1974 the limitations of information disclosure as a tool of consumer protection have been laid bare by the insights of behavioural economics[143] and, in the wake of the global financial crisis, the information paradigm is being displaced by more paternalistic and interventionist approaches.[144]

Information disclosure in fact has a long pedigree in the credit field. The earliest example is s 10 of the Pawnbrokers Act 1784, which required pawnbrokers to display the rates of charge authorised by the Act 'in large legible Characters ... and hang up the same in some conspicuous Part of the Shop'.[145] The Pawnbrokers Act 1872 required detailed information disclosure via the printing of a statutory form of wording on pawn-tickets given to pledgors at the time of the pawning.[146] But it was not until 1881, with the Report of the Select Committee on Bills of Sale, that there was any explicit discussion of borrowers' inability to comprehend the terms of the often extremely complex agreements presented to them for signature and the need for information to be disclosed in clear and simple terms. This need was met by the introduction of a statutory form for security bills of sale.[147] Any departure from the statutory form would render the bill void. As a device intended to severely curtail lenders' ability to insert both onerous and confusing terms into bills of sale, this statutory form was rather more than a straightforward information disclosure

[141] The Consumer Credit Act 1974 Act, s 93 did retain the prohibition contained in the Money-Lenders Act 1927, s 7 on the charging of default interest at more than the contractual rate.

[142] See G Howells, 'The Potential and Limits of Consumer Empowerment by Information' (2005) 32 *Journal of Law and Society* 349, 354.

[143] See Howells ibid, arguing that one implication of the insights of behavioural economics is that the way information rules are *framed* need to be revisited but that a wider range of policy approaches also need to be considered.

[144] See, for example, the new approach towards consumer protection signalled by the Financial Services Authority in its *Mortgage Market Review* (Discussion Paper, DP 09/3, October 2009) para 1.41: 'Our policy approach to date has been underpinned by a view that mortgage consumers will act rationally to protect their own interests. We believe that we need to change that approach, recognize the behavioural biases of consumers and be more interventionist to help protect consumers from themselves.'

[145] Pawnbrokers Act 1872, s 10

[146] The ticket was to set out details of the amount advanced, the item pawned, the date of the pledge, the name and address of both parties, the charge for the ticket, the charges ('profit'), a statement of the period within which the pledge could be redeemed. A statement of the statutory rights granted to the pledger by the Act was also required.

[147] That is, a bill of sale given by way of security for the payment of money.

requirement. It mandated disclosure of certain information[148] but also prohibited the inclusion of anything else in the interests of transparency and simplicity.

The Money-Lenders Act 1900 contained only one (post-contractual) information disclosure requirement, namely, that the money-lender furnish the borrower with a copy of any document relating to the loan or any security therefor on request.[149] It was subsequently recognised that borrowers' lack of understanding of the terms of their transactions with money-lenders was a serious problem.[150] The Money-Lenders Act 1927 sought to rectify this by requiring detailed information disclosure in a memorandum of the contract signed personally by the borrower before the money was lent or the security given[151] as well as post-contractual disclosure.[152] The Hire-Purchase Act 1938 also imposed extensive information disclosure obligations requirements pre-contractually,[153] in a signed memorandum of the agreement[154] and post-contractually.[155] In its Report of 1962, the Molony Committee acknowledged that consumer ignorance remained a grave concern in the hire-purchase context. The problem was multi-faceted, encompassing failure to understand the nature of the document signed and the consequences of entering into the agreement, failure to grasp (in the typical triangular hire-purchase relationship between hirer, finance company and dealer) that the agreement was in fact entered into with the finance company rather than the dealer, ignorance as to the additional charge for credit as compared with a cash deal (effectively the rate of interest), the continuing problem of consumer ignorance of the hire-purchase price caused by the signing of blank forms and general lack of understanding of the terms of the agreement.[156] The Committee acknowledged that some aspects of

[148] Bills of Sale Act (1878) Amendment Act 1882, s 9. The statutory form was set out in the schedule to the Act. It required a statement of the consideration in respect of which the borrower granted the bill, the amount to be paid by the borrower (excluding interest), the rate of interest payable on the loan, the amounts of any instalments and dates on which such instalments would be payable or other terms as to the time of payments. The only other terms the lender was permitted to insert in the bill were those relating to insurance, payment of rent or anything else which the parties might agree for the maintenance or defeasance of the security.

[149] Money-Lenders Act 1900, s 2(1)(d).

[150] See *Report by the Joint Select Committee of the House of Lords and the House of Commons on the Moneylenders Bill (HL) and the Moneylenders (Amendment) Bill* (1925).

[151] Money-Lenders Act 1927, s 6(1) and (2). This was to contain all the terms of the contract, in particular the date on which the loan was made, the amount of the principal of the loan, and a statement of the interest on the loan expressed in a specified manner.

[152] ibid, s 8(1) and (2). On request, copies of documents relating to the loan or any security and a statement of the terms of the loan, payments already made, sums due but unpaid, the amount of sums not yet due but outstanding, were to be provided.

[153] Hire-Purchase Act 1938, s 2(1). A statement of the cash price of the goods was required to enable potential hirers to calculate the hire-purchase charges by way of comparison.

[154] ibid, s 2(2)(b). A statement of the hire-purchase price and the cash price of the goods; the amount of the instalments and the date on which they would become payable; a list of the goods to which the agreement related. A notice was also to be included setting out the Act's key protections.

[155] ibid, s 6(1). Copies of the memorandum and statements of amounts already paid, due and payable in the future were to be provided on request.

[156] *Molony Report* (n 3) paras 511–17.

the problem appeared intractable and the response of the ensuing Hire-Purchase Act 1964 was limited to the inclusion of a red box for the hirer's signature accompanied by a warning that the consumer was entering into a hire-purchase agreement.[157] The Consumer Credit Act 1974[158] and the regulations made pursuant to it[159] imposed extensive requirements relating to the form and content of consumer credit agreements with a view to ensuring that the consumer was fully informed of his rights and duties under the agreement, the rate of the total charge for credit[160] as well as the protections and remedies made available to him under the Act. An agreement would be considered properly executed only if it complied with the requirements as laid down in those regulations, embodied all the terms of the agreement (other than implied terms), all of the terms were readily legible when it was sent or presented to the consumer for signature, and was signed by the consumer and by or on behalf of the creditor or owner.[161] The effect of the agreement being considered improperly executed was that it would be enforceable against the consumer only by order of the court.[162]

C. Controls on Advertising

Misleading advertising and circularising were first identified as a source of concern by the Select Committee on Moneylending in 1898. Unscrupulous money-lenders sought to ensnare borrowers by misleading statements—typically relating to interest rates—in advertisements, circulars and prospectuses. The most common was the statement that the money-lender lent at rates of 'five per cent'. The potential borrower would assume that this meant five per cent per annum, when in fact the lender only ever lent at a rate of five per cent *per month*.[163] The concern was that the borrower might continue to labour under this induced misapprehension at the point of entering into the contract or that, even if disabused of the misapprehension prior to entry into the agreements, may already have become psychologically committed to the contract.

While not imposing direct restrictions on money-lending advertisements, the Money-Lenders Act 1900 made it an offence to fraudulently induce or attempt to induce a person to enter into a loan agreement or agree to particular terms on which money was to be borrowed through the making of false, misleading, or deceptive statements, representations, or promises, or by concealment of material

157 Hire-Purchase Act, s 3(4) and Hire-Purchase (Documents) (Legibility and Statutory Statements) Regulations 1964.

158 Consumer Credit Act 1974, s 60 empowered the Secretary of State to make regulations governing the form and content of consumer credit agreements.

159 Consumer Credit (Agreement) Regulations 1983, SI 1983/1553.

160 The Secretary of State was empowered by the Consumer Credit Act 1974, s 20 to make regulations for determining the true cost of the credit to the debtor.

161 Consumer Credit Act 1974, s 61(1).

162 ibid, s 65(1).

163 See 1898 Report (n 25) iv.

facts.[164] Two direct restrictions on money-lending advertisements were later introduced by the Money-Lenders Act 1927 Act. The first prohibited the unsolicited sending of circulars or other documents.[165] The second banned the publishing of advertisements which went beyond statements of certain specified information, which in practical terms meant that statements about interest rates were prohibited.[166] In the instalment-selling field, the Advertisements (Hire-Purchase) Act 1957 prohibited advertisements to which the Act applied unless they contained all the information required by the Act[167] and each part of that information was displayed prominently in the advertisements, in such way as not to give undue prominence to any other part.[168] Contravening the requirements of the Act was an offence.[169] The Consumer Credit Act 1974 subsequently prohibited false or misleading statements in advertisements[170] and Regulations governing the form and content of advertisements were also enacted under the power conferred by s 44.[171]

D. Doorstep Credit and Cooling-Off Periods

The various allegations levelled against the itinerant tradesman known as credit-traders included high pressure selling, overloading the (typically female) customer with credit that she (or her husband) had no reasonable prospect of repaying, sharp practices such as disguising the balance to be repaid by not marking it clearly in repayment books, and even the making of improper suggestions to married women who were in debt for the goods supplied.[172] Some of these concerns were also voiced in the context of door-to-door hire-purchase sales of labour-saving devices to housewives.[173] Salesmen had been specifically trained to overcome wives' objections to signing documents in their husbands' absence and, as they worked on a commission basis, resorted to all manner of high-pressure sales techniques and sharp practices.[174] The Molony Committee recommended the introduction of

[164] Money-Lenders Act 1900, s 4.

[165] Money-Lenders Act 1927, s 5(2).

[166] ibid, s 5(1). Contraventions of s 5 were a criminal offence.

[167] The information required, which varied according to whether the advertisement contained details of payments in respect of any goods, included: the deposit; the amount of each instalment expressed as a monetary amount; the total number of instalments payable; the length of the period in respect of which each instalment was payable; if any instalments were payable before delivery of the goods, the number of instalments so payable; the cash price of the goods: Advertisements (Hire-Purchase) Act 1957, ss 2(2) and 2(3).

[168] ibid, s 2(1).

[169] ibid, s 3(1).

[170] Consumer Credit Act 1974, s 46(2).

[171] See Consumer Credit (Advertisements) Regulations 1980, SI 1980/54. Contravention of the Regulations was a criminal offence.

[172] See O'Connell (n 40) ch 1.

[173] See, for example, HC Deb 10 Dec 1937, vol 330, col 733.

[174] See P Scott, 'Managing Door-to-Door Sales of Vacuum Cleaners in Interwar Britain' (2008) 82 *Business History Review* 761. The unhappy lot of the door-to-door salesman in the 1930s was immortalised by J MacLaren-Ross in his comic novel *Of Love and Hunger* (London, Allan Wingate, 1947).

a 'cooling-off' period in hire-purchase agreements[175] signed off trade premises with a view to protecting those who were 'over-ready' to commit themselves and unable to withstand sales pressure.[176] The Hire-Purchase Act 1964 gave hirers and buyers a non-excludable four-day cooling-off period for hirers and buyers[177] and the Consumer Credit Act 1974 later introduced a cooling-off period for all credit agreements signed by the consumer off trade premises.[178] Although the primary purpose of the cooling-off period was the neutralising of sales pressure, it can also be conceived of as a mechanism for redressing informational inequalities by affording consumers the opportunity to access more information about a product or service and/or make comparisons with competitors' products or services.[179]

E. Improving Financial Literacy and Capability

The combination of information disclosure requirements and advertising controls is designed to ensure that the consumer has both sufficient and accurate information but these efforts will be ineffective in redressing inequalities of informational power if the consumer lacks the ability to understand, process and act rationally upon that information. Although behavioural economics research has shown that consumers generally are afflicted by cognitive biases affecting their ability to process and act rationally on the information provided to them, this problem is exacerbated in the case of those consumers who suffer from low levels of financial literacy or capability. To make matters worse, low financial literacy or capability is commonly associated with low-income or non-status consumers whose bargaining power is also severely impaired by the lack of genuine options available to them. Although the terms 'financial literacy' or 'financial capability'[180] are modern ones, the concepts are not. These problems were recognised as early as 1881, when those forced to resort to borrowing small amounts by way of bill of sale were described as typically 'very ignorant'.[181] The problems caused by the ignorance of the poor in their dealings with money-lenders were a recurrent theme in the parliamentary debates on the Money-Lenders Act 1927. As one MP put it:

> The trouble is largely due to the ignorance of people … Probably a very large number of persons who have recourse to moneylenders never take the trouble to read the actual

175 And credit sale agreements.

176 *Molony Report* (n 3) para 521.

177 Hire-Purchase Act 1964, s 4.

178 Consumer Credit Act 1974, s 67. The cooling-off period applied where the antecedent negotiations included oral representations made in the presence of the consumer by someone acting as or on behalf of the negotiator.

179 See I Ramsay, *Consumer Law and Policy* 3rd edn (Oxford, Hart Publishing, 2012) 102.

180 The Financial Services Authority established a national strategy for financial capability in 2003 with the aim of providing consumers with the 'education, information and generic advice they need to make financial decisions with confidence': Financial Services Authority, *Annual Report 2003/4*. For detailed information on the strategy see www.fincap.org.uk/uk_strategy.

181 *Report from the Select Committee on Bills of Sale (1878) Amendment Bill* (1881) qs 1623–25.

terms of a contract. If they did read it through it is very doubtful if they would understand it.[182]

The peculiar complexities thrown up by hire-purchase agreements were adverted to above and, by 1962, the Molony Committee acknowledged that a multi-faceted approach, including a programme of consumer education, was required to deal with the seemingly intractable problem of consumer ignorance.[183] As the Committee observed in the consumer context more generally 'there is a vast field of consumer need which it would be impracticable to cover by legal or administrative safeguards. Consumer education should fill this gap.'[184] With the enactment of the Consumer Credit Act 1974 the new regulator of consumer credit, the Office of Fair Trading, assumed responsibility for educating the public in matters relating to the use (and overuse) of consumer credit.[185] Levels of financial literacy and capability have, nonetheless, failed to keep pace with the exponential growth in both the number and complexity of credit products available in the market since 1974.[186]

V. Conclusions

The acute inequalities of bargaining and informational power which beset consumers' dealings with credit-grantors are as old as the institution of credit itself. Legislative interventions across the period sought to redress these imbalances through a combination of mechanisms. The bargaining equalities that flow from market conditions, the consumer's financial circumstances, or the interaction of the two, are complex and deep-rooted; legal mechanisms alone may be inadequate to truly *redress* these inequalities. With their foundations in the Christian notion of lack of charity—the idea that one should not be allowed to take advantage of one's neighbour's need—the interest rate ceilings which remained in existence until 1854 can be seen as a response to inequality of bargaining power. Despite the incentives for citizens to participate in the enforcement of the usury laws through the *qui tam* action and for borrowers themselves to escape from their obligations by turning informer, it is doubtful whether the usury laws were adequately enforced in practice. Given the scarcity of money for much of the eighteenth and nineteenth centuries, it is questionable whether borrowers were really willing to jeopardise future sources of credit through such action.

[182] Major Glyn (MP for Abingdon), HC Deb 23 April 1926, vol 194, cols 1551.

[183] *Molony Report* (n 3) paras 513 and 898. The Consumer Council was set up in 1962 on the advice of the Molony Committee. One of its functions was the provision of general advice and information to the public about consumer matters.

[184] ibid, para 898.

[185] See the recommendations in the *Crowther Report* (n 6) para 7.1.4. S 4, Consumer Credit Act 1974.

[186] See The National Strategy for Financial Capability www.fincap.org.uk/uk_strategy.

Furthermore, the usury laws were blunt instruments easily circumvented. By the end of the eighteenth century, it was apparent that most judges had abandoned all attempts to live up to the earlier rhetoric of looking through the form of the transaction to its substance and intent. The usury laws were also said to be inefficacious in that they forced borrowers into the hands of those who operated at the margins of the law and extracted a premium for the risk that the transaction might be challenged.

But regardless of their practical effect, there is also a conceptual objection to describing such direct statutory interventions in the core price terms of the contract as *redressing* inequalities of bargaining power. There is, after all, a conceptual difference between enabling both parties to exercise *genuine* choice by placing them on a (more) level playing field and an *ex ante* prohibition on entry into credit contracts on certain terms. Similarly, even though the statutory power to re-open harsh and unconscionable[187] or extortionate[188] credit transactions was designed to prevent the strong from using their superior bargaining power to 'push the weak to the wall', *ex post* interference in a transaction which is the product of an impaired bargaining process is hardly the same as facilitating a fair bargaining contest in the first place. Where one party's inferior bargaining position stems from a lack of genuine choice and alternatives, the only true means of *redressing* the inequality is the creation of more genuine choices and options. This implies a much thicker version of autonomy than classical contract law was prepared to admit and may elude redress by legal mechanisms alone.[189] As Raz has observed, true autonomy—in the sense of self-authorship—depends on more than possession of the requisite mental capacities and freedom from coercion and manipulation: there must also be adequate options from which to choose.[190] A Government that is committed to autonomy must, therefore, do more than simply prevent *loss* of autonomy; rather 'Governments are subject to autonomy-based duties to provide the conditions of autonomy for people who lack them.'[191]

In the continental European context, the *monte di pietà*, first established by the Catholic Church in the second half of the fifteenth century, is an early example of an initiative designed to provide low-income borrowers with viable moderate-cost alternatives to commercial credit.[192] Something similar was attempted in England in 1707 in the establishment of a 'Charitable Corporation, for the Relief of the

[187] Money-Lenders Act 1900, s 1.

[188] Consumer Credit Act 1974, s 138.

[189] While usury laws and statutory reopening provisions might induce some lenders to offer better terms to high-risk, non-status borrowers, thus increasing their range of options, these provisions also have the propensity to exclude such borrowers from the market altogether. This was the reason for taking pawnbroking transactions not exceeding the value of £10 out of the scope of the usury laws in the late eighteenth century: see Pawnbrokers Act 1784, 24 Geo III c 42.

[190] J Raz, *The Morality of Freedom* (Oxford, Oxford University Press, 1988) 372–73.

[191] ibid, 415.

[192] On the early history of the *monte di pietà*, see C Menning, *Charity and State in Late Renaissance Italy* (Ithaca, Cornell University Press, 1994).

Industrious Poor', albeit to disastrous effect. The events that followed, described as the 'greatest scandal of the time' and involving the financial mismanagement and embezzlement of the company's funds, the flight abroad of its cashier and warehouseman, and the expulsion from Parliament of a number of its directors, ensured that such an initiative was short-lived.[193] Much more recently, the recognition that low-income or non-status borrowers need to be provided with adequate options has started to bear some fruit, with around 350 credit unions in England, Scotland and Wales now lending some £730 million as an alternative to commercial high-cost credit.[194] Another solution that has been piloted in Australia is government funding of Community Development Financial Institutions.[195]

Although mechanisms aimed at redressing inequalities in *informational* power have been in evidence since the late eighteenth century, they came to occupy an increasingly important place in credit legislation from the 1880s onwards, with the growing recognition that the complexity of credit agreements posed problems for the *average* consumer. Although equity had been able to grant relief where advantage was taken of a disparity in informational power arising from a *special disability of the weaker party*, its capacity to do so in respect of the *typical* informational inequality that arises in consumer transactions was limited. Credit-grantors increasingly came under statutory obligations to disclose key contractual information in a clear and visible manner. By the middle of the twentieth century, information disclosure requirements had been supplemented with controls on advertising with a view to preventing consumers being led into misconceptions in the pre-contractual phase. This combination lay at the heart of the Consumer Credit Act 1974, whose whole emphasis was on empowering the consumer to make rational welfare-maximising decisions through the provision of information rather than through more intrusive and paternalistic measures such as interventions in the core substance of the contract. Cooling-off periods, first introduced by the Hire-Purchase Act 1964 and retained by the Consumer Credit Act 1974, can also be viewed as furthering this policy. Although their primary purpose is the neutralising of external sales-pressure, in affording the consumer more time to access and process information about the product and make comparisons with those of competitors they may also enhance the consumer's informational power. All these mechanisms for redressing informational power can also redress inequalities of *bargaining* power at the aggregate level. By redressing the informational inequalities between consumers and suppliers, they enable consumers to send signals to suppliers reflecting 'real' preferences thus driving

[193] A Hardaker, *A Brief History of Pawnbroking* (London, Jackson Ruston and Keeson, 1892) 70–72.

[194] See Association of British Credit Unions Limited, 'Credit Unions vs Pay Day and High Cost Credit' available at www.abcul.coop/media-and-research/briefings/high-cost-credit-briefing.

[195] Australian Government, Department of Social Services, 'Community Development Financial Institutions (CDFI) Pilot Project' available at www.dss.gov.au/our-responsibilities/communities-and-vulnerable-people/programs-services/financial-management-program/community-development-financial-institutions-cdfi-pilot-project.

competition. Greater competition means greater consumer choice which, in turn, results in enhanced bargaining power.

While palatable across the spectrum of political opinion, the policy response of the Consumer Credit Act 1974 based predominantly on the 'information' or 'truth in lending' paradigm has proven to be askew for a number of reasons. Firstly, in markets in which there is no effective competition or adequate consumer choice, redressing informational inequality, even if achievable, will fall wide of the mark. Secondly, such a response assumes that consumers have the requisite financial literacy or capability to make use of the information with which they are provided. Although this obstacle may, to some extent, be overcome by educational programmes designed to improve these capacities, there is the further problem that even those with relatively high levels of financial literacy and capability may struggle to act rationally upon this information because of cognitive biases affecting their ability to accurately predict future events, their own future behaviour, and hence the way in which they will actually use the credit granted to them. Indeed, credit-grantors may design their products with a view to exploiting these cognitive biases. The burning question has therefore become whether information disclosure regimes can be more effectively designed so as to overcome these obstacles or whether the time has come to acknowledge that information disclosure is beyond redemption and that more interventionist and paternalistic[196] measures are necessary. Certainly, when set against the background of the UK's singular and sustained aversion to interest rate caps since 1854, the 2010 decision to grant interest-rate-capping powers to the new regulator of consumer credit — the Financial Conduct Authority — must be viewed as one of momentous import that calls into question many of the assumptions on which the 1974 Act was founded.[197]

[196] For the view that mandatory disclosure cannot be saved, see O Ben-Shahar and C Schneider, *More Than you Wanted to Know: The Failure of Mandated Disclosure* (Princeton, Princeton University Press, 2014).

[197] See Financial Services and Markets Act 2000 (as amended by the Financial Services Act 2012), s 137C. In December 2013, it was decided that the social harms caused by extortionate credit in the UK's 'pay-day loan' market justified price regulation. The price cap on 'high-cost short-term credit' came into effect in January 2015 and is found in Ch 5A of the Financial Conduct Authority's *Consumer Credit Sourcebook* (CONC).

4

Tort Law and Government Liability in the Administrative State

PETER CANE

I. Introduction

For the purposes of exposition and analysis, we may distinguish between two legal techniques for controlling the exercise of power, which I shall refer to as 'liability' and 'regulation' respectively. Characteristic of liability is reparation for harm in the form of monetary compensation or restitution, for instance. There are two modes of regulation, which I shall refer to as criminal and civil. Characteristic of criminal regulation are deprivation of liberty and imposition of monetary fines. Characteristic of civil regulation are mandatory, prohibitory and quashing (or 'invalidating') orders.

The modern development of civil regulation as a technique for legal control of the exercise of public power is associated with the emergence of the 'administrative state' and 'public law' from the middle of the nineteenth century. This chapter is concerned with the use, in this period, not of regulation, but of liability, as a technique for controlling the exercise of public power. It attempts to answer two main questions. First, how might we explain the fact that, even though the English legal system uses civil regulation extensively as a technique for controlling the exercise of public power, it (unlike the French system, for instance) did not develop a public law of governmental liability in general and tort law in particular? Secondly, if such a public law of governmental liability had developed, what might it have looked like? I focus on the English legal system because it was the paradigm and fountainhead of common law systems more generally, at least until the middle of the twentieth century. But I will also have things to say about Australian and US law.

The analysis will rest upon two distinctions. The first is between what I shall call, respectively, 'corporatist' and 'individualist' understandings of the 'state' as a social and political entity. Crudely, according to the individualist understanding, the state is a collection of officials and agencies that exercise public power. By contrast, according to the corporatist understanding, the state is a metaphysical entity separate from, and 'greater' than the aggregate of, the officials and agencies that exercise public power. To mark this difference, it is often said that the individualist understanding is not really a theory of 'the state' at all but rather a theory of 'government'.

The second distinction[1] is between two models of distribution or allocation of public power, which I shall call 'concentration' and 'diffusion', respectively. Diffusion of power involves dividing and sharing it between various organs of government that, as a result, must necessarily cooperate with each other to achieve their policy objectives. The US system of government is highly diffused in this sense. For instance, it divides and shares legislative power between the President (who is neither a member of, nor responsible to, the legislature) and two houses of Congress in such a way that they must work together to achieve their respective objectives. Associated with diffusion as a model of the allocation of power is a particular mode of controlling the exercise of power, which I refer to as 'checks-and-balances'. On the other hand, concentration of power allows governmental agencies to act more-or-less unilaterally and independently of other agencies. It is associated with a mode of controlling the exercise of power that I refer to as 'accountability'. Instead of forcing agencies to cooperate with each other in exercising power, and in that way to 'check and balance' each other's exercises of power, accountability sets one relatively independent agency (such as a court) to review exercises of power by another relatively independent agency (such as the executive). The English system of government is highly concentrated in this sense. Concentration allows 'strong' government and betokens trust in, and respect for, public power. By contrast, diffusion weakens government and betokens distrust of, and lack of respect for, public power.

Section II of this chapter briefly outlines the development of the English law of governmental liability and contrasts it with US law. Section III provides a short account of the development of the French system of public liability law and attempts to explain why no such system developed in England. Section IV describes three possible models of a law of public (tort) liability and analyses the relationship between each of these models and the existing law, primarily in England but also, to a lesser extent, in the US and Australia.

II. The Structure of the Law

In order to understand the foundations of the English law of government tort liability we must go back to the birth of the English common law. The social and governmental system in England after the Norman Conquest was feudal. One of

[1] Which is elaborated in much more detail in P Cane, *Controlling Administrative Power: An Historical Comparison* (Cambridge, Cambridge University Press, 2016) esp ch 1.

the social functions of feudal lords was to provide dispute-resolution services in their own courts to those inferior to them in feudal relations. Feudal inferiors could sue each other in the lord's court, but could not sue the lord in his own court. The ultimate feudal lord was the king. By the end of the twelfth century, the king's courts had become the pre-eminent providers of dispute-resolution services for the whole country (although more in relation to serious crimes and property disputes than 'delictual and contractual obligations').[2] The king, of course, could not be sued in his own courts. This is the origin of the doctrine of 'Crown immunity'. However, also by the end of the twelfth century, it was established that the English king was not an absolute monarch, but was subject to 'law' understood metaphysically as a set of norms that bound all the English, including the king. Like the king's subjects amongst themselves, the king had certain obligations of justice towards his subjects. In recognition of such obligations, the Petition of Right was developed as a procedure by which the king could waive his immunity from (could consent to) being sued in his own courts. In contrast to a Petition of Grace, a Petition of Right issued on the basis that a wrong had allegedly been done which, as a matter of justice, deserved a remedy.

The Petition of Right fell out of use in the fifteenth century, but was revived in the middle of the nineteenth in response to the growth of central government brought about by the combination of social and economic problems caused by the Industrial Revolution, and the rise of utilitarian, collectivist social philosophy and policy.[3] The growth of central administration at this time had two main drivers: transfer from local government (notably Justices of the Peace) to central government of regulatory and welfare functions, and the assumption of new central functions in areas such as health and safety at work. As a result of these changes, ordinary people started interacting more frequently and more directly than previously with central government, and became much more prone to suffering physical and economic harm as a result of central government activities.

Two other developments around this time are crucial to our story. The first was the process, which began after the Glorious Revolution, by which the executive became more and more independent of the monarch, leading eventually to the creation of the doctrines of collective and individual ministerial responsibility to Parliament. The second was the development of conceptual legal categories, such as contract and tort, in the wake of the demise of the formulary system of pleading in the nineteenth century. The Petition of Right procedure was reformed in 1860[4] to make it more user-friendly; but around the same time, it was held that the

[2] C Donahue Jr, 'Private Law Without the State and During its Formation' (2008) 56 *American Journal of Comparative Law* 541, 550. Donahue dates the emergence of a more developed common law of obligations to the sixteenth century (555).

[3] JB Brebner, 'Laissez Faire and State Intervention in Nineteenth-Century Britain' (1948) 8 (Supplement) *Journal of Economic History* 59.

[4] Petitions of Right Act 1860.

procedure was not available in relation to tort claims (as opposed to contract and intellectual property claims, for instance).[5] The significance of this holding was greatly increased by the fact that the beneficiary of the immunity from tort claims was no longer the monarch but the executive government, which now answered for the exercise of administrative power not to the monarch, but to Parliament. In other words, Crown immunity had become Executive immunity.

The best functional explanation for the different treatment of tort and contract is probably that all governments rely, to a greater or lesser extent, on third parties for the provision of goods and services for governmental consumption. They need a sound reputation as reliable contracting parties and so have a strong economic incentive to submit contract claims against them to third-party resolution. By contrast, governments have less to lose by refusing to submit to tort claims, and the incentives for submission tend to be political rather than economic.

At an early stage, the immunity of the Crown from being sued in its own courts led to the development of the personal liability of Crown officials in tort. Such liability bore directly on officials because one effect of Crown immunity was that the Crown could not be sued vicariously for wrongs committed by its officers. Moreover, most personal 'tort' claims were made against local officials, central government officials in the medieval period having little direct contact with ordinary citizens. By the seventeenth century, personal damages liability of Crown officials was coming to be seen as inefficient and unfair, prompting the common-law courts (notably King's/Queen's Bench) to develop the prerogative writs (which had originally served essentially administrative purposes) as a means of controlling the activities of local officials operating in a 'judicial' mode.[6] Alongside the common-law courts, from the mid-sixteenth century the conciliar courts (especially the Court of Star Chamber) played a major role in controlling local administration; but they were abolished in 1641, leaving a gap that would not be effectively addressed for more than 200 years.

It seems that the first reaction of the common-law courts in the nineteenth century to tort claims against central government agencies was to adopt a functional public-private distinction as a basis for limiting the scope of the liability (to public functions). By mid-century, however, this functional approach had given way to an institutional approach that distinguished between the Crown and its agents and officials on the one hand, and other governmental agencies (both central and local), according immunity from actions in tort to the former, but not to the latter.

[5] *Viscount Canterbury v Attorney-General* (1843) 12 LJ Ch 281; *Tobin v The Queen* (1864) 12 CBNS 310; 143 ER 1148; *Feather v The Queen* (1865) 6 B&S 257; 122 ER 1191; J McLean, *Searching for the State in British Legal Thought: Competing Conceptions of the Public Sphere* (Cambridge, Cambridge University Press, 2012) 214–23.

[6] EG Henderson, *Foundations of English Administrative Law: Certiorari and Mandamus in the Seventeenth Century* (Cambridge, Mass, Harvard University Press, 1963) 34–5. With the development of the administrative state, the use of the writs was extended to activity in an administrative mode.

This put a premium on drawing the line between the Crown and non-Crown public agencies, the former benefitting from a principle of immunity that did not apply to the latter.[7]

Moves to reform the principle of Crown tort immunity began in earnest in the 1920s but did not bear fruit until the enactment of the Crown Proceedings Act in 1947. The most important provision made the Crown amenable to being sued vicariously for (certain) torts of its agents, officials and employees.[8] Other provisions of the 1947 Act imposed direct (ie personal, as opposed to vicarious) liability on the Crown for breach of employers' and occupiers' duties, and breach of statutory duties that were also imposed on individuals and non-Crown entities. Outside these areas, direct Crown liability is rare,[9] and immunity effectively survives only in cases where no responsible officer can be identified for whose tortious conduct the Crown is vicariously liable. The significance of vicarious liability is well illustrated by contrasting English with US law. In US federal law there remain significant areas of sovereign immunity from both direct and vicarious liability. As a result, personal liability of government officials plays a much larger part, both theoretical and practical, than in English law. At the other extreme, in Australia general direct (and vicarious) liability was imposed on government by statute as early as the mid-nineteenth century, and there is even some doubt about whether Crown immunity from liability was ever part of Australian common law.[10] Certainly, the Commonwealth Government has never enjoyed immunity from suit, or from tort liability.

We might say, then, that while the starting point of US law is 'sovereign' immunity,[11] the starting point of Australian law is 'sovereign liability'. The formal starting point of English law is Crown immunity, but the effect of the waiver of immunity from vicarious liability is to instal Crown liability as the default rule. This difference of starting points affects the way in which the public/private distinction plays out in liability law (by which, for present purposes, I mean the law relating to monetary liability, especially liability for damages). In Australian law and, typically in English law, substantive rules of tort law (relating, for instance, to duty and standard of care), as opposed to immunity rules, are used to justify treating 'public defendants' differently from 'private defendants' when and to the extent that this is considered appropriate. By contrast, in US law, rules about the scope of sovereign immunity from direct and vicarious liability, and the personal liability of government officials, agents and employees, still play significant parts in operationalising the public/private distinction in the law of government liability.

[7] S Anderson, 'Central Executive: The Legal Structure of State Institutions' in *The Oxford History of the Laws of England, Volume 11, 1821–1914* (Oxford, Oxford University Press, 2010) 366–84.

[8] Not only was the Crown itself immune from vicarious liability, superior Crown officials were also immune from vicarious liability for the wrongs of inferior officials: McLean (n 5) 221–22.

[9] See, eg, *Morgan v Ministry of Justice* [2010] EWHC 2248.

[10] *Commonwealth v Mewett* (1997) 191 CLR 471, 542–45 (Gummow and Kirby JJ).

[11] Sovereign immunity is the US version of Crown immunity.

III. The Birth of a Public Law of Tort

In 1873 the French *Tribunal des Conflits* decided that jurisdiction to entertain actions against the state for monetary compensation for harm caused by public employees belonged to the administrative courts (headed by the *Conseil d'Etat*), not the 'ordinary' courts.[12] 'The rules of administrative liability were held to be of a distinct and special character. The need to balance the exercise of private rights with the general public interest required certain limits to be placed upon the regime of state liability.'[13] The basis of the decision was a statute of 1790 that prohibited the ('ordinary') courts from adjudicating claims against the government.[14] Before the Revolution, the '*parlements*' (the predecessors of the 'ordinary', civil courts) had long been obstructive of government reform programs, and the revolutionaries wanted to protect the revolution from judicial reaction. The *Conseil d'Etat* was established to hear complaints against the government against the background of a general principle of sovereign immunity. By 1872, what had started out as a sort of internal complaints office had gained independence as what we would call an administrative tribunal. Just as the institutional divide between the English common-law and Chancery courts led to formal, adjectival and substantive distinctions between common law and equity, so the existence of the administrative courts in France alongside the ordinary courts bred formal, adjectival and substantive distinctions between private law, including the private law of delict, and public law, including the law of government non-contractual liability. The English common law/equity divide resulted from the separation of the 'common law courts' from the royal council against the background of the continuing right of citizens to complain to the monarch (in person or via the Chancellor) about the conduct of royal officials, including the judges. The French public/private divide was the eventual result of a political manoeuvre by the revolutionary government, legitimised by a particular understanding of the constitutional desideratum of separating executive and judicial power,[15] and re-interpreted to address the growing power of government in the face of industrialisation.

So here we have a first possible explanation of why common law systems developed no public law of tort: because tort claims against the government are

[12] L Brown and J Bell, *French Administrative Law*, 5th edn (Oxford, Clarendon Press, 1998) 184–85.

[13] D Fairgrieve, *State Liability in Tort: A Comparative Law Study* (Oxford, Oxford University Press, 2003) 13.

[14] C Harlow, *State Liability: Tort Law and Beyond* (Oxford, Oxford University Press, 2004) 134–41. 'Whereas the French revolution used [statute] as a governmental bulwark to protect the people from a corrupt judiciary, the objective in the common-law world was to protect the people through the courts from a corrupt government': N Jansen and R Michaels, 'Private Law and the State: Comparative Perceptions and Historical Observations' (2007) 71 *Rabels Zeitschrift für Auslandisches und Internationals Privatrecht* 345, 385.

[15] Executive and judicial powers are also sharply separated in Australian law. However, the aim here is to protect the judicial power and the authority of the courts from contamination by executive power rather than (as in France) to protect the executive from interference by the judiciary.

adjudicated by the same courts as handle tort claims between citizens. In this context, it is worth noting that in the US, since the middle of the nineteenth century, contract claims against the US government have been adjudicated by a special contracts tribunal, with the result that US law has a more developed concept of 'government contract' than either English or Australian law. Similarly, in the last 40 years, English law has developed a much sharper distinction between private law and public law, partly on the back of procedural reforms that culminated in 2001 with the establishment of the Administrative Court as a distinct element of the High Court of Justice. Other significant factors in the development of the public/private divide in English law have been Britain's accession to the European Union in 1972 and the enactment of the Human Rights Act 1998, giving greater domestic effect to the European Convention on Human Rights and the European Court of Human Rights.[16]

AV Dicey was famously opposed to the sort of institutional divide adopted in France and the concomitant allocation of claims against the government to the executive rather than the judicial branch. His opposition seems to have been based on an assumption that recognition of a separate public law of liability would inevitably privilege the government at the expense of citizens.[17] But before we consider Dicey's position in more detail, we need to go back in history to set the scene. Although the public law/private law distinction can be traced back to Roman law,[18] its modern manifestation is usually associated with a process, typically referred to as the development of 'the state', in the late medieval and early modern periods.[19] In England, the beginning of the formation of the state is usually associated with the assumption by Henry VIII of the headship of the English Church and the subsequent disestablishment of religious houses. Under feudalism, there is no clear distinction between public and private because economic, social and political relations all depend on ties of status between individuals, including the monarch. Ernst Kantorowicz famously argued that the medieval English kings had two bodies, one personal and the other official; but nevertheless, both bodies were manifestations of a real person and neither was the sort of metaphysical entity that was later to become associated with the state in European political thought.

[16] Merryman argues that civil lawyers put more 'emphasis on, and confidence in, the validity and utility of formal definitions and distinctions' and 'treat the matter of division of the law in more normative terms', whereas common lawyers 'tend to think of the division of the law as conventional, i.e., as the product of some mixture of history, convenience, and habit': J Merryman and R Perez-Perdomo, *The Civil Law Tradition: An Introduction to the Legal Systems of Europe and Latin America*, 3rd edn (Stanford, CA: Stanford University Press, 2007), 91. See also J Allison, *A Continental Distinction in the Common Law: A Historical and Comparative Perspective on English Public Law* (Oxford: Clarendon Press, 1996), ch 6.

[17] Discussing the public law/private law divide in civilian systems, Merryman says that, '[i]n public legal relations the state … as representative of the public interest (and successor to the prince) … was a party superior to the private individual': Merryman and Perez-Perdomo (n 16) 94.

[18] Jansen and Michaels (n 14).

[19] See, eg, Q Skinner, 'The State' in T Ball, J Farr and R Hanson (eds), *Political Innovation and Conceptual Change* (Cambridge, Cambridge University Press, 1989).

Indeed, Janet McLean argues that Kantorowicz's purpose was to 'humanize [the state] after its deification by the German nationalists'.[20] In a feudal context, a distinction between public law and private law makes no sense.[21] There is just one body of law and it applies to everyone—even the monarch, as the 800th anniversary of Magna Carta in 2015 reminded us.

In early-modern English political thought, the greatest theorist of the state was Thomas Hobbes. Significantly, he, too, conceptualised the state in terms of an 'artificial man',[22] a (personalised) 'sovereign'—a way of thinking developed into a theory of 'law' (not 'the state') by John Austin in the nineteenth century and only effectively displaced by HLA Hart in *The Concept of Law* in the mid-twentieth. Even so, what Hart substituted for the personalised sovereign was not a metaphorical state entity, but rules that confer power on the various officials and groups of officials (institutions) that constitute the government. There is an important sense in which Hart's quintessentially English approach yields a theory of law without a state.[23]

The point here is that 'state'-building in England in the sixteenth and seventeenth centuries did not yield a de-personalised, metaphysical state entity.[24] England's flirtation with republicanism was brief and (like its US imitator) quasi-monarchical. The English Revolution changed only the powers and political status of the monarchy, not its nature. The monarch remained (and remains) a person, and the successor of the monarch's official body, the Crown, is (according to Lord Diplock),[25] the collection of individuals (ministers) who, by the late nineteenth century, had become answerable to the House of Commons (and thence, notionally at least, to the people whom MPs represent) rather than to the monarch. It is no accident that 'responsibility' for the conduct of public affairs is not borne by 'the government' but by ministers, individually and collectively. There is, then, an important sense in which the English system of government was (in the late nineteenth century) and perhaps still is (in the twenty-first) monarchical and feudal; and for that reason poor soil for a thriving public law/private law distinction.

Dicey was one of the great theorists of the nineteenth-century English constitution. By inventing a normative theory of the rule of law that resonated deeply with the essentially personalised nature of the English governmental system, he made a constitutional virtue of political reality. He provided an argument and a justification for the absence of a public law/private law distinction by enunciating the principle that all the English, from the highest to the lowest, should (as Magna Carta claimed) be subject to the same 'ordinary law', establishing the 'rights of the

[20] McLean (n 5) 5.

[21] J Merryman, 'The Public Law-Private Law Distinction in European and American Law' (1968) 17 *Journal of Public Law* 3, 6–7; Jansen and Michaels (n 14) 390.

[22] Skinner (n 19) 121.

[23] P Cane, 'Public Law in *The Concept of Law*' (2013) 33 *OJLS* 649, 660–62.

[24] KHF Dyson, *The State Tradition in Western Europe: A Study of an Institution and an Idea* (Oxford, Martin Robertson, 1980) 36–44.

[25] *Town Investments v Department of the Environment* [1978] AC 359, 380–81.

English' and administered by one body of (royal) justices, because having one law for the ruled and another for the rulers was, in his mind, a formula for privilege and impunity of the governors vis-à-vis the governed.

Here we have a second possible reason for the absence of a public law of tort in English (and Australian) law: the essentially personalised, feudal understanding of English government survived the Glorious Revolution, was progressively democratised over the next 200 years, and was championed by a theorist whose deep understanding of history, brilliant clarity of vision and exposition, and overpowering strength of conviction made the development of a separate law of governmental liability all but inconceivable. Not only did the common law develop no public law of government liability, but neither did statute: the technique of the Crown Proceedings Act is to treat the Crown as an ordinary individual.

The US story is somewhat different.[26] English monarchical government was alive and well, even if more-than-previously constrained, for much of the eighteenth century. Moreover, the institutional structure of the new polity established by the US Constitution bore more than a passing resemblance to that of England at the time. Even so, there were significant differences. Most importantly for our purposes, Congress was given much more control over taxing and spending than the English Parliament had (or has). Colonial American legislatures had assumed such power in the eighteenth century, as a result of the greater degree of democratisation in America as compared with England and the association of the executive with the colonial power. As an element of this control over finances, colonial legislatures also assumed responsibility for handling monetary claims against colonial governments, as did Congress, vis-à-vis the federal government, almost as soon as it was established.

Against this background, sovereign immunity can be understood as a mechanism for enabling Congress to control the involvement of the courts in handling claims against the government. As noted earlier, in the 1850s Congress first established a court to handle contract and related claims against the federal government, but no such body has ever been set up to handle tort claims. Over the years, Congress has selectively handed over tort claims to the ordinary courts by waiving sovereign immunity, and the courts have independently developed constitutional heads of tort-like liability. Dicey's common-law, rule-of-law theory of government tort liability never took hold in the US, probably because it was so deeply rooted in an understanding of the nature of government (i.e., concentrated rather than diffused) that did not obtain in the US.

I have not been able to discover any clear explanation of why Congress set up a separate tribunal to handle government contract claims, but has left tort claims to the ordinary courts. However, I have a theory. As noted earlier, governments need

[26] At a theoretical level, the difference can be traced to the influence of Locke on the founders of the new polity. In contrast to Hobbes, (who conceptualised public power as derived from an ultimate, sovereign source), Locke understood government as a trust and public power as delegated by the people to the governors.

a good reputation as reliable contractors. We may also speculate that in financial terms, contract litigation is generally of more significance to governments than tort litigation. When the federal contracts court was first established, its only role was to conduct a trial of the facts and to advise Congress on how the claim should be resolved. Congress would then make the final decision. In this way, Congress was able to maintain close control over contract claims. Although Congress eventually gave the court more power, the history of the court has been dogged by uncertainty about whether it has the power of final decision or is merely advisory, this distinction being of constitutional significance.[27] It may be that Congress has never seen the need to control government tort litigation in the same way, or to the same extent, as government contract litigation.

Interestingly, Stuart Anderson explains the lack of development of a system of public law liability in the late nineteenth century in terms that echo the US experience. He shows (as noted earlier) that, before about 1860, the courts were developing a distinction between public and private functions and applying different (liability) rules depending on the nature of the function which gave rise to the claim. Subsequently, however, they reconfigured liability law by distinguishing between the Crown and other public bodies, extending immunity to the former, but subjecting the latter to 'the ordinary law of tort'. By thus splitting governmental institutions into two groups, the judges disabled themselves from developing principles of liability for the whole of the public sector. Anderson detects in this process 'a pattern of judicial unwillingness to order central government to pay money… Judges saw financial control through Parliament and the Treasury as constitutionally vital, and as reasons why they should not themselves impose liabilities in the absence of the clearest statutory authority.'[28] This explanation is not implausible. However, certain contrasts between Anderson's analysis of the English situation and my earlier analysis of the US position are worth noting.

One is that Parliament, as such, has much less control over government finances than Congress. In fact, like Congress, after the Glorious Revolution the English Parliament briefly adopted the practice of handling monetary claims against the government, but soon instituted the rule that any and all proposals for expenditure had to originate from the executive. Because the executive typically controls Parliament, Anderson's reference to 'financial control through Parliament' may mislead because effective control rests with the government.

A second contrast is related to the first. The US Congress is independent of the President in a way and to an extent that Parliament is not independent of the Executive. For this reason, as observed earlier, statutory waiver of sovereign immunity in the US system can be seen as *Congress* ceding to a court the power to handle government liability claims. The underlying issue is not whether redress will be available against the government, but from whom—Congress or the courts. By contrast, when the English Executive (through Parliament) waives its immunity,

[27] Under the Constitution, federal courts may not exercise purely advisory functions.
[28] Anderson (n 7) 384.

it subjects itself to control by an independent third party—the courts—which it cannot control (at least not in the same way, or to the same extent, as it can control Parliament) and gives up the option of dealing with claims against itself purely as a matter of grace and favour.

This latter contrast has important implications, or so I would argue. In particular, although there is no separate general public law of government torts in the US, there is a sense in which tort liability imposed by courts can be understood as a functional equivalent of a positive Congressional response to a petition for relief, and in which waiver of sovereign immunity can be understood as the substitution of one form of (legal) relief for another. This may help to explain the initially surprising fact that in US law, the basic principle of sovereign immunity applies as much to judicial review applications as to liability claims. In the US context, judicial review, legal liability and supervision by Congress can all be seen as public accountability mechanisms. By contrast, in the English and, more importantly, the Australian context, waiver of immunity is understood as submission by the government to legal liability (in the 'ordinary' law of tort) and a unilateral readjustment of the relationship between the executive and the judiciary.

This conjecture, in turn, may help to explain another significant difference between US law and Australian law. In Australian law, there can be no damages liability for breach of the Constitution (or of judge-made public law rules). This is pure Diceyanism: the law of (tort) liability that applies to everyone is 'ordinary' (private) tort law.[29] The only exception is liability for misfeasance in public office which, by definition, only applies to public officials (but in England not, apparently, directly to the Crown, since this tort is not mentioned in the Crown Proceedings Act). By contrast, US law recognises a category of 'constitutional torts'—liability for breach of the Constitution. Because Congress has not waived immunity in respect of such liability, it falls exclusively on individual government officials. However, the willingness of US courts to invent such liability suggests that damages liability is understood as one of a suite of accountability mechanisms available against government, rather than as an application of private law to the government (which is its character in both Australian and English law.) In this sense, US law recognises what we might call a public law of tort that supplements private law while English and Australian law (excepting the law of misfeasance in public office) recognise only one (private) law of torts that may, nevertheless, apply differently to the governors on the one hand and the governed, on the other.

[29] Perhaps underlying this approach is a conception of private law as independent of political power: Jansen and Michaels (n 14) 348, 359–60, 385–86. This conception (in which the only function of government is to recognise and enforce private law) also underpins, for instance, Hayek's distinction between law that develops organically from custom and precedent, and law deliberately made by a legislator: FA Hayek, *Law, Liberty and Legislation* (London: Routledge and Kegan Paul, 1982), 85–91. Related are Ernest Weinrib's formalistic, corrective justice account of private law (E Weinrib, *The Idea of Private Law* (Cambridge, Mass, Harvard University Press, 1995)) and the claim that the legislature should generally leave private law to the (politically independent) judges (P Cane, 'Courts, Legislatures and the Reform of Tort Law' (2005) 25 *OJLS* 393, 395–96.

To summarise so far: there are various plausible (and mutually consistent) explanations of why English (and Australian) law did not develop a public tort law alongside private tort law in the nineteenth century. The various explanations have some application to the US. But the nature and theory of government tort liability in US law is affected by the fact that the institutional structure and dynamics of the US system of government are different from those of the English and Australian systems. We might say that although US law has no public tort law, as such, the orientation of the US law of government liability is more 'public' than that of English and Australian law while being less public than that of French law. Another way of putting this point may be to say that in the US system, more than in the English system, law is (in Kenneth Dyson's striking phrase) an 'interpreter of the pattern of politics'.[30] In systems, such as the French, that have a strong concept of a metaphysical 'state', law (says Dyson) may be seen as '*the great* interpreter of the pattern of politics'.[31] In England, by contrast, law has traditionally played a relatively minor role in constituting public power and framing its exercise.

IV. The Character of a Public Tort Law

What might a common law version of a public law of non-contractual liability have looked like, had it developed? One way of structuring speculation about the possibilities is in terms of three models of damages liability, which I shall call respectively the 'responsibility' model, the 'corrective' model and the 'accountability' model.

A. A Responsibility Model of Public Liability Law

A basic characteristic of this model is that it is founded on general principles of liability, rather than specific 'torts' or 'delicts'. I use the term 'responsibility' because the paradigm example of such a model is the French system. In the *Blanco* case, which first announced the existence of a law of government liability separate from the 'ordinary' law of liability set out in the *Code Civil*, the *Tribunal des Conflits* described the new scheme of public law liability in terms of 'the responsibility of the state'.[32] The main elements of the system are:[33]

(i) A principle of liability for 'fault' understood in terms of 'illegality'. A distinction is drawn between 'ordinary' fault and 'gross fault' (*faute lourde*).

[30] Dyson (n 24) 41.
[31] ibid (emphasis added).
[32] Harlow (n 14) 136.
[33] Useful accounts include: Fairgrieve (n 13); Brown and Bell (n 12) 182–202; BS Markesinis, J-B Auby, D Coester-Waltjen and SF Deakin, *Tortious Liability of Statutory Bodies: A Comparative and Economic Analysis of Five English Cases* (Oxford, Hart Publishing, 1999) 15–20.

In certain cases, the potential scope of public law liability is limited by the requirement that it will be attracted only by gross fault.

(ii) A principle of strict liability for creation of risk.

(iii) A principle of 'equality' in the face of public burdens (*egalite devant les charges publiques*).

(iv) An understanding of public law liability as attaching directly to the state rather than to individuals by whose agency the state acts. Conduct of individual agents may attract liability in respect of things done on behalf of the state, but such liability is not public law liability in the sense that this term describes the liability of the state in respect of the individual's conduct.

The last of these elements is theoretically the most important because it underpins each of the other three. It explains the equation of fault with illegality in the first principle, the willingness to impose strict liability under the second principle, and the concept of 'equality' in the third principle. In English law, direct liability of the state (or perhaps, more accurately, 'the Crown' or 'the Government') is relatively rare. Much more common is vicarious liability of the state for the tortious conduct of one of its servants or agents who is, in turn, personally liable. In French law, direct liability of the state and personal liability of the agent may exist together. However, the direct liability of the state is primary, whereas vicarious liability is secondary. In the English way of thinking, the state is liable if, and because, its agent is liable. Relatively rarely does English law impose liability on the state independently of the liability of some individual, whereas in French law the liability of the individual is, as it were, additional to that of the state. These patterns of liability reflect the distinction between the corporatist (French) and individualist (English) conceptions of 'the state'.

The concept of 'equality' deserves particular attention. The so-called 'equality principle' attributed to Dicey is, of course, a foundational principle of the English law of governmental liability. However, 'equality' has a quite different reference in English law than in French law. In English law it refers to the relationship between citizens and the government whereas in French law it refers to the relationship between citizens. The equality principle in English law requires that government be treated in the same way as citizens—equality 'before the law', we might say. On the other hand, the equality principle of French law requires that all citizens be treated in the same way when it comes to distribution of the burdens of citizenship—equality in sharing the costs of living in a society. The French principle of equality of citizens is based on a principle of *inequality* of citizens and the state. It goes along with a preference for, or at least a tolerance of, strong government and concentrated public power. Whereas the Glorious Revolution diffused power, formerly concentrated in the monarchy, between the monarch, Parliament and the courts, the French Revolution transferred highly concentrated power from the monarchy to 'the people' embodied in 'the state'.

By the end of the nineteenth century in England, governmental power had once again become much more concentrated as a result of broadening of the franchise and development of ministerial responsibility to Parliament, effectively integrating executive and legislative power. In France, power was further concentrated by an interpretation of separation of powers, according to which control of the executive should be the responsibility of the executive itself, not the courts. In England, by contrast, the Revolution had secured for the courts structural independence from the executive. Indeed, Blackstone emphasised independence of the judiciary as being the core of the English version of separation of powers.[34] Dicey's aim and great achievement—as he saw it, anyway—was to champion independence of the judiciary (the 'ordinary' courts and their 'ordinary' law) in the face of concentration of executive and legislative power implicit in responsible, democratic government and the dramatic growth of a new 'law of the administration'.

As is well known, there was a strong reaction against Dicey, particularly in the 1920s and 1930s. Leading critics were William Robson[35] and Sir Ivor Jennings.[36] Robson, in particular, favoured the creation of a system of administrative courts to handle claims against the government. There was a significant ideological element in this reaction: Dicey made no secret of his laissez-faire politics and his dislike of the welfare state. His opponents, by contrast, wanted to facilitate and promote strong government, and communitarian as opposed to individualist values, unhindered by traditional common-law principles of freedom of contract and security of private property. So far as tort liability was concerned, a general, French-like, principle of government 'responsibility' was championed by Harold Laski.[37] He argued that the appropriate response to the growth of what he called 'positive' (as opposed to 'negative') government functions was a principle to the effect that 'when the action of the state entails a special burden upon some individual or class of men, the public funds should normally compensate for the damage suffered'.[38] Curiously, like Dicey, Laski understood the state in individualist rather than corporatist terms: '[t]he business of the state … has become so much like private business that, as Professor Dicey has emphasized, its officials need "that freedom of action necessarily possessed by every private person in the management of his own personal concerns"'.[39] This suggests that the association between a broad, public-law principle of government liability and a corporatist view of the state is contingent, and that the fact that the English understanding of the state is individualist rather than corporatist need not have stood in the way of adoption of a responsibility model of public-law liability.

The leading contemporary champion of the Diceyan equality principle is Carol Harlow.[40] However, her approach is significantly different both from Dicey's, and

[34] P Cane, *Administrative Tribunals and Adjudication* (Oxford: Hart Publishing, 2009), 29.

[35] W Robson, *Justice and Administrative Law: A Study of the British Constitution* (London, Macmillan, 1928).

[36] I Jennings, *The Law and the Constitution* (London, Hodder and Stoughton, 1933).

[37] H Laski, 'The Responsibility of the State in England' (1919) 32 *Harvard Law Review* 447.

[38] ibid, 452.

[39] ibid, 462 (footnote omitted).

[40] See, most recently, Harlow (n 14).

from Laski's Diceyanism. Dicey proposed the equality principle because he thought of it as pro-liability. He strategically ignored the many anti-liability features of the English law of his day and rejected what he understood as the French approach on the basis of what he saw as its anti-liability bias. Laski shared Dicey's pro-liability ideology, but thought that a general principle of state responsibility, administered by the ordinary courts, would better serve that ideology than the common law of tort. In this respect, Dicey's opponents, such as Robson, Jennings and JDB Mitchell, agreed with Laski, and on that basis objected to equation of the Crown with an ordinary person in the Crown Proceedings Act 1947.[41]

Harlow, by contrast, is less enamoured of a regime of extensive government legal liability administered by courts, and generally favours administrative schemes of reparation for harm caused to citizens by government, over judicial schemes. It is often said that compared with government liability in English law, the scope of liability under the French responsibility principle is not as wide in practice as it is in theory. It is pointed out that liability in French law is narrowed by varying the standard of care and requiring gross fault in some cases, by adopting a strict requirement of causation, and by flexibility in calculating the quantum of damages. Nevertheless, after an initial rush of blood to the head in the 1970s, English courts—much more than Australian courts—have become very wary of imposing tort liability on public authorities. The equality principle is now interpreted as restrictive of public authority liability. Whereas Dicey stressed that public officials should be subject to the same liabilities as private individuals without special privileges or immunities, modern judges and scholars typically argue that public authorities should be subject to no more liabilities than private individuals. We may explain this change by remembering that until late in his career, Dicey was in denial about what Laski called the shift from the negative state to the positive state. For Dicey, the danger was that, even though the state did nothing particularly distinctive,[42] it would claim privileges and immunities that did not benefit private individuals. Now that it is impossible to ignore the positive, welfare, regulatory and entrepreneurial state, the more common worry is that liability will unduly hinder the government from acting in the public interest. This explains, for example, why the empirically unsubstantiated fear of provoking defensive behaviour on the part of public authorities has become so palpable.

We might explain the somewhat greater willingness of Australian courts (compared with English courts) to impose tort liability on public authorities by the fact that Australian colonial governments moved from a negative to a positive mode of governance significantly earlier than old-world governments in England and the US. On the other hand, for reasons particular to the Australian brand of federalism, the High Court of Australia has adopted an extremely narrow understanding

[41] McLean (n 5) 184–85.

[42] Recall that unlike Blackstone, Dicey understood the prerogative not in terms of powers peculiar to the executive, but in much more general terms of ('residual') powers derived from the common law rather than from statute: HWR Wade, *Constitutional Fundamentals* (London: Stevens, 1980), 46–49.

of judicial power and the judicial function. According to this understanding, while it is part of the role of the courts to hold government to compliance with tort law (understood narrowly as the law of non-contractual liability developed by the English superior courts in the eighteenth and nineteenth centuries), creating a broader principle of government responsibility would take courts well beyond their proper sphere, thus contaminating judicial power with executive power by requiring them to balance public and private interests in an unstructured way.

In this context, it is worth considering important recent developments in the understanding of executive power in Australian constitutional law.[43] Unlike the US Constitution, the Australian Constitution did not (purport to) provide a new foundation for the authority of the freshly created Australian state. Rather, it was contained in a statute of the British Parliament and was superimposed on the existing British constitution, which it modified only selectively. From an early stage, the High Court adopted an interpretive theory that treated the Constitution as an ordinary statute. Sir Owen Dixon, considered by many to be the greatest Australian judge of the twentieth century, argued that the Constitution was the 'creature of' the common law,[44] upon which it may perhaps best be regarded as a gloss. The enactment of the Australia Acts 1986 severed the last links between the Australian and English common laws by abolishing all remaining avenues of appeal from Australian courts to the Privy Council. Although the Australian Constitution remains embedded within a UK statute, the High Court has used the opportunity presented by the Australia Acts to reconceptualise the relationship between the Constitution and the common law.

According to the common law, the source of authority of the Constitution was the sovereignty of the Parliament that enacted the Constitution-making statute. The High Court at first attempted to re-ground the Constitution in the sovereignty of the Australian people. More recently, however, it has moved towards treating fundamental principles of the institutional design of the Australian polity—notably representative and responsible government—as informing interpretation of the Constitution. In support of this project, the court increasingly determines public law questions by reference to 'statutory intention' rather than the common law. As part of the project, the Court has begun a process of abandoning the traditional, English approach according to which the non-statutory powers of the executive are derived from 'the prerogative' or 'the common law', and finding their source in the Constitution itself. The Court has rejected the doctrine that the contracting power of the executive, being derived from the common law, is essentially the same as the contracting power of private individuals. It has done this partly on the ground that the requirements of representative and responsible government on which the Constitution is based necessarily affect the characteristics of the executive's contracting power compared with the contracting power of

[43] C Saunders, '*The Concept of the Crown*' (2015) 38 *Melbourne Law Review* 873.

[44] O Dixon, 'The Law and the Constitution' (1935) 51 *LQR* 590.

'natural persons'. In making this move (as in focusing earlier on the sovereignty of the people), the Court might be seen as moving away from a personalised understanding of the State to a more metaphysical, corporatised concept, and from a traditional private-law understanding of the nature of government contracting to a more public-law idea.

If this interpretation of the Court's relevant decisions is plausible, it has implications for the analysis in this chapter. Put crudely, it might perhaps be argued that if the Court can be seen as moving toward a 'public law of executive contracting', it might also be inclined to contemplate a 'public law of executive tort liability'. The received doctrine in Australia is that, even if the executives of the colonial governments originally enjoyed sovereign immunity from tort liability, the Constitution[45] ensured that the Commonwealth executive never did. On the other hand, the legislation that defines the nature and characteristics of that liability provides that 'in any suit to which the Commonwealth or a State is a party, the rights of parties shall as nearly as possible be the same, and judgment may be given and costs awarded on either side, as in a suit between subject and subject'.[46] By the same legislation, the High Court is given jurisdiction to hear claims against the Commonwealth 'whether in contract or in tort' (s 56). We might conclude that, while there is no Constitutional impediment to the development of a public law of tort, and even though such a development would be consistent with the High Court's current approach to the Constitution, this could not be achieved without statutory intervention to amend the Judiciary Act. Given that, even under the present law, the High Court is inclined to be more pro-liability than English or US courts, a move to an even more pro-liability public law of tort might not be inconceivable. But on the assumption that turkeys do not normally vote for Christmas, legislative action to this end seems unlikely.

The position in the US is different again from the English and Australian. In the US system, I argued earlier, the prime issue is not the scope of government liability and judicial control but rather how the power to impose liability on the executive should be distributed between the legislature and the courts. This explains another significant feature of the US position, namely that from the 1790s, Congress distributed the handling of claims against the government between itself and the executive. Under the US equivalent of the Crown Proceedings Act, the Federal Tort Claims Act 1946, most damages claims against the federal government are resolved administratively, rather than through the courts. Moreover, not only has the Supreme Court consistently refused to narrow the scope of sovereign immunity but, on the contrary, in recent years it has cut back on government liability in various other ways as well. In this environment, it seems unlikely that a general principle of government responsibility would be adopted either by Congress or the Supreme Court.

[45] The Parliament may 'make laws conferring rights to proceed against the Commonwealth or a state in respect of matters within the limits of the judicial power' (s 78).

[46] Judiciary Act 1903, s 64.

There was a time in England in the 1920s and 1930s, while reform of Crown immunity was being discussed, when a broad principle of government liability might have found favour in certain quarters and been adopted as the basis for change.[47] In fact, however, the CPA followed the model adopted much earlier in Australia, and at about the same time in the US, of equating government and citizen, and retaining the common-law framework of liability. This outcome is less surprising in the Australian case because the basic pattern was established much earlier, before the full emergence of public law and the positive state. Moreover, the basic pattern came to be seen as a better fit with the Australian understanding of the role of courts in the system of government. By contrast, by the late 1940s in England, the experience of two world wars and a financial depression had irrevocably changed understandings of the relationship between citizen and state in a way that made a shift in the French direction at least conceivable. However, ideological shifts in the past 40 years have made what was conceivable then, more-or-less unimaginable now.

B. A Corrective Model of Public Liability Law

Partly in response to the development of the positive state and partly in response to these more recent ideological shifts, scholars have elaborated what have become known as 'corrective (justice) theories of tort law' and, indeed, of private law more generally. The development of tort law in general, and the law of negligence in particular, in the late nineteenth century and the first half of the twentieth century was significantly informed by utilitarian social philosophy. Perhaps the most important theoretical manifestation of utilitarianism in legal theory was American legal realism. The apotheosis of realism was arguably the economic analysis of law developed by scholars such as Richard Posner and Guido Calabresi in the 1960s and 1970s. Substantively, thinkers such as Jules Coleman[48] and, more recently, Robert Stevens,[49] have countered by emphasising the rights and duties granted and imposed by tort law at the expense of consideration of law's consequences. Methodologically, the likes of Ernest Weinrib[50] and Allan Beever[51] have renounced functionalism in favour of formalism. The substantive and methodological moves are related, of course, because formalism focuses on law's constitutive characteristics rather than its goals, purposes or outcomes.

An equality principle lies at the base of much theorising in this vein. The corrective principle of equality is akin to its Diceyan cousin in the sense that it understands tort law as an expression of the normative equality in tort law of duty-bearers and

[47] McLean (n 5) 184–85.
[48] J Coleman, *Risks and Wrongs* (Cambridge, Cambridge University Press, 1992).
[49] R Stevens, *Torts and Rights* (Oxford, Oxford University Press, 2007).
[50] Weinrib (n 29).
[51] A Beever, *Rediscovering the Law of Negligence* (Oxford, Hart Publishing, 2007).

rights-bearers, doers and sufferers of harm, defendants and plaintiffs. On the other hand, Dicey's principle was normative, whereas the corrective principle of equality purports to be descriptive or interpretive rather than normative. However, it can be portrayed in this way only by treating both those burdened and those benefited by tort duties as private individuals. In fact, of course, private individuals are not all 'equal' but differ in many ways that the law chooses to ignore.[52] This is why Justice is blindfolded. The law, we might say, treats individuals as 'juridical equals'. By contrast, at least since the early-modern period, English law has not treated private citizens and public officials (the Crown in particular) as juridical equals, despite the fact that it is based on a personalised understanding of the state. This historical fact explains why Dicey invented the potent concept of 'the rule of law' to ground and justify the equality principle, the second element of his three-part account of that concept. How, then, can theorists propound corrective justice as the best description or interpretation of tort law when tort law does not treat citizen and state as juridical equals?

Faced with this difficulty, corrective justice theorists might be tempted to classify the law governing the liability of public authorities as not being 'tort law' because it is not concerned with relations between juridical equals; and however much its functions might be similar to those of tort law, formalistically tort law and public-authority liability law must be very different.[53] If they took this path, such theorists might be inclined to say that properly understood, and contrary to what most lawyers think, English law already has a body of public-law liability rules distinct from the body of private-law liability rules that we call tort law. In fact, this is not the direction that theorists take. Amongst those who give the topic any systematic consideration at all, some (those who identify themselves to be theorists of private law, not public law) merely accept that public authorities can be subject to tort duties even though those duties may not be precisely the same as the duties imposed by tort law on private individuals.

Theorists who are more alert to the relationship between public law and private law, but who find the corrective justice/rights-based approach to tort law intuitively appealing, seek to reconcile tort law's wariness of imposing positive duties (in other words, of making nonfeasance tortious and imposing liability for pure omission) with the development of the positive state. There are at least two different ways of doing this. One is to pare down the scope of public-authority tort liability for nonfeasance by insisting that it is (as a matter of description or interpretation, as opposed to prescription) essentially the same as that of a private citizen.[54] A contrasting strategy is to accommodate public authority liability for

[52] I am reminded of a *New Yorker* cartoon in which the judge on the bench asks the court clerk to hand up 'the law for the rich'.

[53] For more extensive discussion see P Cane, 'Tort Law and Public Functions' in J Oberdiek (ed), *Philosophical Foundations of the Law of Torts* (Oxford, Oxford University Press, 2014).

[54] This, essentially, is the strategy adopted by Hanna Wilberg (discussed by Cane ibid 156).

nonfeasance, wider than the tort liability for nonfeasance of ordinary persons, by hiving it off into a different legal category, such as human rights law.[55]

All these approaches share the basic characteristic of understanding and interpreting tort law in particular, and private law more generally, as concerned with personal responsibility (as opposed to the French concept of state responsibility) for causing harm and interfering with entitlements, and with the allocation of rights and duties amongst legal subjects. All aim to provide, more or less explicitly, an account of tort law and its traditional conceptual structure that takes account of the development of the administrative state.

C. An Instrumental/Functional Model of Public Liability Law

In contrast to such approaches are those that are more concerned with the 'social value and economic effectiveness'[56] of tort law than with its internal, conceptual structure and nature.[57] One early functionalist account was Allan Linden's understanding of tort law as a sort of 'ombudsman'.[58] However, Linden was not solely, or even primarily, concerned with the tort liability of public authorities, and he thought of tort law in terms of liability rather than regulation. By contrast, economic analysts of tort law put regulation, in the form of deterrence, at the forefront, and reparation in the background as merely a regulatory tool. At the same time, most economic analysts, like the corrective justice theorists, focus on the impact of tort law on relations between juridical equals rather than juridical unequals. An exception is David Cohen,[59] who speculates that tort law typically overdeters public authorities and recommends, in effect, that it be replaced by a system of 'program-sensitive adjustment policies' that provide compensation selectively for 'administratively caused losses'. William Bishop also argues against expanding the tort liability of public authorities on the basis that this would discourage citizens from desirable self-protection, and also on the ground that there are other techniques available (which he refers to as 'validity review', by which he seems to mean judicial review)[60] for regulating harm-causing activity by public actors.

Functionalists who are more alert to the distinction between liability and regulation are more likely to see them not as alternative but as supplementary tools

[55] This is Francois du Bois's approach (discussed by Cane ibid 156–57). See also D Nolan, 'Negligence and Human Rights Law: The Case for Separate Development' (2013) 76 *MLR* 286. The reverse strategy is to argue, in effect, that breaches of human rights should be understood as torts: J Varuhas, 'A Tort-Based Approach to Damages under the Human Rights Act 1998' (2009) 72 *MLR* 750. One difference between the two approaches is that the former tends to focus on tort law as a protector against harm whereas the latter tends to emphasise its role in protecting rights.

[56] Harlow (n 14) 7.

[57] M Loughlin, *Public Law and Political Theory* (Oxford, Clarendon Press, 1992) distinguishes between 'normativism' and 'functionalism' as styles of public law scholarship.

[58] A Linden, 'Tort Law as Ombudsman' (1973) 51 *Canadian Bar Review* 155.

[59] Cane (n 53) 159–60.

[60] ibid, 160.

of control.[61] Harlow (a long-time observer of the civilian approach) resists the expansion of liability that a move in the French direction would represent by arguing, instead, for greater systematisation and use of discretionary, '*ex gratia*', administrative or ombudsman-based compensation schemes. She[62] also resists the 'tortification' of principles of State liability under EU and human rights law. For her, tort law is and should remain a vehicle of corrective justice, leaving other functions of monetary recompense to more public-spirited regimes. Harlow is a staunch supporter of Dicey's equality principle partly because of the symbolism Dicey vested in it by grounding it in the rule of law; but also, somewhat ironically, because she thinks that the personal-responsibility-based conceptual framework of tort law, which Dicey embraced, provides an unsuitable foundation for government liability in the age of the positive state, which Dicey ignored or denied but which she fully acknowledges and, in important respects, embraces.

In a significant sense, functionalists propose a public law of monetary reparation, but not a public law of tort or liability more generally. For them, tort law is best confined to its traditional territory and supplemented by reparative mechanisms with different characteristics. This solution is a sort of halfway house between an entirely public law of public liability, as in France, and the traditional Diceyan approach. It does not involve inventing anything new, but only working into a coherent system an already-existing suite of regimes: tort law, state liability under EU and ECHR law, and *ex gratia* compensation schemes.

The US system also represents a sort of hybrid, but for a quite different reason. Surprisingly (as noted earlier), the US rule of sovereign immunity is the starting point not only of government liability in tort, but also of judicial review law. It was not until 1976 that Congress enacted a general waiver of immunity from judicial review.[63] Like the similar treatment of tort law, this approach to judicial review reflects the diffusion of power in the US system of government. As in the case of immunity from tort liability, the underlying constitutional issue is not whether the executive will be subject to (civil regulatory) control, but by which branch. By virtue of its law-making primacy, Congress can legislate to allocate the power of control between itself and the courts. Congress cannot technically divide one and the same sort of power between itself and the courts; but what it can do is to increase the amount of judicial control at the expense of legislative control, or vice versa. This way of approaching the matter is congenial to the generally functionalist approach of US courts and scholars compared with their English counterparts, who tend to view law more as a quasi-autonomous normative system rather than as a means to social ends. Here, as in US tort law generally, monetary remedies have a distinctly functionalist, regulatory cast. In this respect, US law may also

[61] Carol Harlow (n 14) leads the pack. See also D Priel, 'A Public Role for the Intentional Torts' in K Barker and D Jensen (eds), *Private Law: Key Encounters with Public Law* (Cambridge, Cambridge University Press, 2013).

[62] Like Nolan and du Bois. See n 55 above.

[63] 5 USC § 702.

be contrasted with French law. Like the English law of torts as it applies to public authorities, French public tort law is responsibility based. The difference between the two lies in their respective concepts of responsibility. The French concept of state responsibility takes full account of the juridical inequality between citizen and government. The French public law of tort is distinct from the private law. By contrast, in English law, the law governing the non-contractual liability of public authorities is seen as an extension or adaptation of personal responsibility principles of ordinary tort law rather than a *sui generis*, juridical category.

At the same time, because public power is so diffused in the US system, it seems even less likely that it could move in the direction of the French system than that the English system could. Congress is likely to want to retain control of the system of handling claims against the government and not hand it over either to the courts, or to an executive tribunal, let alone leave it to the executive to handle claims on a discretionary basis. Because public power is highly concentrated in both the French and English systems, either could have structurally accommodated the approach of the other. Because power is so much more diffused in the US system than in either the French system of the English system, it could not easily accommodate the approach of either.

V. Conclusion

In this chapter, I have offered several explanations of why English law, like US and Australian law, did not develop a public law of tort of the sort developed by the *Conseil d'Etat* in France. I have also speculated about what sort of public law of tort might have developed in each of these systems. My explanations and speculations have been based not on analyses of legal values in each of the systems, but rather on the historical development and structural features of the three system respectively. In this way and to this extent, the discussion has been 'external' rather than 'internal' to the various systems examined. The two modes of analysis and explanation (external and internal) are not inconsistent. However, my general view is that history and structure can tell us a great deal about legal values that looking at the values in isolation cannot.[64]

[64] See generally Cane (n 1).

Part 3

Doctrines, Institutions and Process

5

Property and Power: The Judicial Redistribution of Proprietary Rights

CRAIG ROTHERHAM

I. Property and the Limits of Judicial Power

One of the particularities of the common law is that it vests in the courts the power to alter the law. The existence of this power can be viewed as something of an embarrassment, given that common law jurisdictions tend to pride themselves on being liberal democracies. Judicial powers of this kind conflict with the understanding that law making should be the province of elected legislators and that laws should not have retrospective effect.

This power was not always a source of anxiety for the legal community—largely because its existence was not acknowledged. In his *Commentaries*, Blackstone depicted the common law as recognising customary norms developed at a time beyond the reach of memory. Judges were the 'oracles of the law', pronouncing rather than creating norms.[1] In contrast, Parliamentary modifications of the common law were regarded as ill-conceived attempts to improve on ancient wisdom that were apt to produce disastrous consequences.[2]

The appeal to custom lost some of its lustre with the greater faith in, and commitment to, legislative democracy that was a feature of the Enlightenment. Moreover, the claim that the common law was grounded in some 'ancient constitution' appeared less plausible in the light of several developments. The courts of chancery sought to constrain their discretionary powers in a framework of principle.[3] The common law moved beyond its focus on procedure associated with the forms of action and traditional pleading.[4] In addition, the decline in the use of juries in

[1] WH Blackstone, *Commentaries on the Laws of England* 4 vols (Chicago, Chicago University Press, 1979) vol 1, 69–71.

[2] ibid, vol 1, 10. See D Lieberman, *The Province of Legislation Determined: Legal Theory in Eighteenth Century Britain* (Cambridge, Cambridge University Press, 1989).

[3] J Baker, *An Introduction to English Legal History* 4th edn (London, Butterworths, 2002) 110–11.

[4] The forms of action were abolished and provision made for the simplification of rules of pleading in The Common Law Procedure Act 1852. Baker ibid 90.

private law litigation resulted in more issues being treated as ones for the judge that might be appealed as being wrong at law rather than matters for the jury, whose verdicts could not be reviewed.[5] These developments laid the ground for the emergence of systematic bodies of substantive law. The latter part of the nineteenth century also saw the implementation of the modern system of law reports,[6] and this, along with a tendency of the courts to provide more fully reasoned judgments, made the manner in which judge-made law developed more transparent. As a result, the bodies of substantive law created in this new era could not be legitimated by the claim that they dated to a time out of mind.

Some new basis was required to justify the quasi-legislative powers of the judiciary as they became more apparent. Judicial rhetoric became focused less on the denial of the existence of these powers and more on offering an account of principles that constrained their use. One approach was to continue to emphasise tradition by a slavish respect for precedent. This reached its apogee in a period of what Robert Stevens characterised as 'substantive formalism',[7] when for a century the House of Lords held to the view that they did not have the authority to overrule their own decisions.[8] This could never have been a complete answer. Even if the courts resisted the temptation to overturn present authorities, they would inevitably be required to determine how they should develop existing doctrine to deal with novel issues and the basis of the legitimacy for undertaking this role of interstitial law making would have remained in question. In any event, the highest court became increasingly less comfortable with the notion that it was obliged to follow decisions that might have been revealed in practice to be inadequate or might reflect values that had come to be out of step with contemporary mores.[9]

An alternative approach to legitimating judicial law making involves the identification of some quasi-constitutional principles that could serve to provide the basis for the delimitation of the respective roles of the courts and the legislature. Notions for private property have performed an important function in this regard. The courts and commentators have often promoted the view that the courts' powers to shape the common law are constrained by notions of property. This is apparent in the observation of Blackstone that,

[5] The Common Law Procedure Act 1854 permitted civil trials to proceed without a jury with the consent of the court. Since The Administration of Justice (Miscellaneous Provisions) Act 1933 the court's permission is required to have a jury in a civil trial (with the exception of certain matters, such as fraud and libel): Baker (n 3) 92.

[6] Baker (n 3) 184.

[7] R Stevens, *Law and Politics: The House of Lords as a Judicial Body, 1900–1976* (London, Weidenfeld and Nicolson, 1979). See also A Paterson, *The Law Lords* (London, Macmillan, 1982); P Atiyah, *The Rise and Fall of Freedom of Contract* (Oxford, Clarendon Press, 1979) 660–71.

[8] The rule was suggested by Lord Campbell in *Bright v Hutton* (1851) 3 HLC 341 and became widely accepted when Lord Halsbury announced that it had been established law for some centuries in *London Street Tramways Co Ltd v London CC* [1898] AC 375.

[9] The rule was abandoned in 1966 in a Practice Statement delivered by Lord Gardiner LC in the House of Lords: [1966] 1 WLR 1234.

> So great moreover is the regard of the law for private property, that it will not authorize the least violation of it; no, not even for the general good of the whole community. … In vain may it be urged, that the good of the individual ought to yield to that of the community; for it would be dangerous to allow any private man, or even any public tribunal, to be the judge of this common good, and to decide whether it be expedient or no. … [T]he legislature alone can, and indeed frequently does, interpose, and compel the individual to acquiesce. … [However it provides] him a full indemnification and equivalent for the injury thereby sustained. All that the legislature does is to oblige the owner to alienate his possessions for a reasonable price; and even this is an exertion of power, which the legislature indulges with caution, and which nothing but the legislature can perform.[10]

Not any understanding of property can perform this function. It might, to the contrary, be assumed that property performs no work in legal argumentation and that, instead, the courts approach questions of resource entitlement from the 'bottom up', so that disputes are determined simply by reference to precedent with disputes not covered by existing authority being determined as ad hoc questions of policy. Property will only serve a quasi-constitutional role if it is accepted that some high order conception of property plays a role in determining hard cases with the result that it shapes the concrete rules of entitlement to resources. More particularly, perspective of property that imbue it with a quasi-constitutional status share a particular vision of property as a pre-legal and immutable conception involving the exclusive and inviolable ownership of discrete things within defined boundaries. Such an absolutist conception is suggested by Blackstone's description in the *Commentaries* of property rights as providing owners with a 'sole and despotic dominion'.[11]

According to this conception, property is not simply a product of judicial decision making—rather, it places fundamental limitations on it. This suggests a conception of the private law whereby the courts should intervene only to protect individuals' property rights, their rights to personal security and dignity and to enforce freely chosen bargains. This understanding provides that the judiciary has no power to redistribute property. Property rights are regarded as inviolable, save by legislative intervention, and only then with due compensation. Understood in this way, the courts act within constraints that severely limit the extent to which they might have regard to the public good. This ensures that a line is drawn between the work of the courts in shaping the common law and the legislative realm of policy.

In the United States, the jurisprudence of the *Lochner*-era Supreme Court was founded upon such an understanding: state power to regulate property was interpreted as being limited to the prevention of 'noxious use';[12] and 'liberty of

[10] Blackstone (n 1) vol 1, 135.

[11] ibid, vol 2, 2.

[12] See, eg, *Commonwealth v Alger* 7 Cush 53, 86 (Mass, 1851); *Ohio v Amber Realty Co* 272 US 365 (1926); *Miller v Schoene* 276 US 272 (1928), 276 US 272 (1928).

contract' was held to be constitutionally protected, thereby invalidating state efforts to regulate conditions of employment.[13] This understanding was subjected to criticism from scholars[14] and some judges.[15] It did not survive the New Deal and the coming of the modern regulatory state as the Supreme Court renounced its vision of substantive due process and property came to be understood in less absolute terms.[16]

The legal realists emphasised that appeals to absolutist notions of property were anything but politically neutral. This shift in perspective was aided by Hohfeld's analysis of property as a bundle of discrete legal relationships between people regarding to particular resources.[17] Others built on Hohfeld's insight that the interests collectively known as 'ownership' were separable and that there was no reason why the presence of one interest should imply that of others.[18] It followed that there was no reason to suppose that the protection afforded over a resource should be absolute. This insight revolutionised the received understanding of the nature and proper limits of private power.[19] Notions of 'ownership' came to be regarded with suspicion, with analysis shifting instead to the individual rights in the bundle known as property.[20]

The notion that it is beyond the power of the courts to redistribute property rights surfaces often in the field of proprietary remedies. It is apparent, for example, in decisions on the use of constructive trusts to distribute property on the breakdown of intimate relationships. In refusing to alter property rights where the parties had not bargained for it, the English courts have adopted a more restrictive approach than that found in other major common law jurisdictions.[21] As Lord Morris put it, '[a]ny power to alter ownership must be found in statutory

[13] *Lochner v New York* 198 US 45 (1905). In *LochnerAdkins v Children's Hospital* 261 US 525 (1923) 2nd ed (Oxford, Oxford University Press, 1992) 101–18; M Horwitz, *The Transformation of American Law II: 1870–1960* (Oxford, Oxford University Press, 1992) 145–51.

[14] R Pound, 'Liberty of Contract' (1909) 18 *Yale Law Journal* 454; M Cohen, 'Property and Sovereignty' (1927) 13 *Cornell Law Quarterly* 8.

[15] The most celebrated example being Holmes' dissent in *Lochner v New York* 198 US 45, 75 (1905), where he observed that: 'This case is decided upon an economic theory which a large part of the country does not entertain.'

[16] *West Coast Hotel Co v Parish* 300 US 379 (1937).

[17] W Hohfeld, 'Some Fundamental Legal Conceptions As Applied in Judicial Reasoning' (1913) 23 *Yale Law Journal* 16; and (1917) 26 *Yale Law Journal* 710.

[18] Horwitz (n 13) 145–67.

[19] See, eg, Hale, 'Rate Making and the Revision of the Property Concept' (1922) *Columbia Law Review* 209; A Berle and G Means, *The Modern Corporation and Private Property* (New York, Commerce Clearing House, 1932) 333–39.

[20] B Ackerman, *Private Property and the Constitution* (New Haven, Yale University Press, 1977) 26.

[21] See, for example, the liberal doctrines developed in *Pettkus v Becker* (1980) 117 DLR (3d) 251 (Canada); *Baumgartner v Baumgartner* (1987) 164 CLR 137 (Australia); *Pasi v Kamana* [1986] 1 NZLR 603 (New Zealand). See S Gardner, 'Rethinking Family Property' (1993) 109 *LQR* 263; J Mee, *The Property Rights of Cohabitees: An Analysis of Equity's Response in Five Common Law Jurisdictions* (Oxford, Hart Publishing, 1999).

enactment'.[22] Similarly, this understanding of property explains the hostility expressed toward the notion of the 'remedial constructive trust' in English law. Thus, in *Re Polly Peck International plc (in administration) (No 2)*,[23] the Court of Appeal rejected the concept in part because it countenanced the redistribution of property rights. In Nourse LJ's view: 'You cannot grant a proprietary right to A who has not had it beforehand without taking some proprietary right away from B. No English Court has ever had the power to do that, except with the authority of Parliament.'[24]

There are signs that this strategy is losing its attraction for the judiciary. This essay examines the jurisprudence on the exercise of the judicial discretion to grant damages in lieu of an injunction. There is a long tradition of strictly limiting the use of this jurisdiction on the grounds that it would amount to the expropriation of private property rights. While the Supreme Court has recently signalled an inclination to take a more flexible approach, it has struggled to elucidate any principles to guide the use of this power.

II. Judicially Sanctioned Private Takings: Damages in Lieu of Injunctions

A. Lord Cairns' Act and *Shelfer*

(i) The jurisdiction to grant damages in lieu of an injunction

The Chancery Amendment Act 1858,[25] more commonly referred to as Lord Cairns' Act, was designed to deal with procedural shortcomings resulting from the separation of the administration of law and equity by permitting the courts of chancery to grant damages where they had 'jurisdiction to entertain an application for an injunction … or specific performance'.[26] The intention of the reform appeared to be essentially procedural, by allowing the courts of chancery to award claimants damages where such relief would have been available at common law so that those claimants did not have to initiate a separate suit at law to pursue such a remedy. However, the courts' application of the Act soon resulted in substantive changes. In particular, the courts appropriated for themselves a power unavailable

[22] Lord Morris in *Gissing v Gissing* [1971] AC 886, 898. For similar remarks, see *Pettitt v Pettitt* [1970] AC 777, 805 (Lord Morris), 811 (Lord Hodson) and 817 (Lord Upjohn). For a recent affirmation of this position, see *Lloyds Bank plc v Rossett* [1990] AC 107.

[23] [1998] 3 All ER 812.

[24] ibid, 831.

[25] 21 & 22 Vict c 27. For a thorough account of the Act and its effect, see P McDermott, *Equitable Damages* (Sydney, Butterworths, 1994).

[26] ibid, s 2.

at common law to award damages for future loss in lieu of an injunction.[27] The assertion of such a discretion raised the question as to how readily the courts might allow a defendant to continue to breach the claimant's rights in return for paying damages.

(ii) Early case law on the use of the discretion

The view that the use of the jurisdiction to grant future damages in lieu of an injunction would amount to the judiciary sanctioning a private taking of property was soon expressed. It was raised, for example, in *Isenberg v East India Company*,[28] which concerned a defendant who had accelerated the construction of a development after the plaintiff complained that the completed building would interfere with his light. The counsel for the plaintiff asserted that, 'if the Court in this case sanctions the principle that all they have to fear is the payment of damages, the rights of individuals are practically at an end'.[29]

While it was quickly suggested that the discretion must be constrained to some extent, in a series of cases on 'ancient lights' in which mandatory injunctions were sought, the approach to the discretion varied considerably from case to case. Some judges expressed considerable reluctance when asked to exercise the jurisdiction to grant a mandatory injunction.[30] In *Isenberg*, for example, Westbury LC remarked that: 'The exercise of that power is one that must be attended with the greatest possible caution'.[31] His Lordship noted, in an often-cited dictum, that granting a mandatory injunction when the hardship that would result to the defendant was out of all proportion to the harm complained of by the plaintiff would, 'deliver over the Defendants to the Plaintiff bound hand and foot, in order to be made subject to any extortionate demand that he may by possibility make'.[32]

On other occasions, in contrast, courts suggested that such relief was available virtually as of right.[33] Thus, in *Senior v Pawson*,[34] in weighing a request for a mandatory injunction that would have required the defendant to dismantle buildings that interfered with the plaintiff's right to light, Sir W Page Wood VC remarked:

> It is only in very exceptional cases indeed, that Defendants, who have erected buildings of this description, obstructing the light and air enjoyed by other people, will be considered as entitled, as it were, to a compulsory sale of a Plaintiff's property without any Act analogous to the *Lands Clauses Consolidation Act,* under which, damages can be properly ascertained by means of a jury, and thus become purchasers of property to which otherwise they would, have no right.[35]

[27] *Eastwood v Lever* (1863) 4 De GJ & S 114.
[28] (1863) 3 De GJ & Sm 263.
[29] ibid, 271.
[30] See, eg, *Durrell v Pritchard* (1865) LR 1 Ch 244.
[31] (1863) 3 De GJ & Sm 263, 272.
[32] ibid, 273.
[33] See, eg, *Greenwood v Hornsey* (1886) 33 Ch D 47; *Scott v Pape* (1886) 31 Ch D 54.
[34] (1866–67) LR 3 Eq 330.
[35] ibid, 330.

Sir George Jessel MR considered the issue in *Aynsley v Glover*,[36] where he suggested that the discretion had been conferred in order to prevent plaintiffs using their position to 'obtain a very large sum of money from defendants'.[37] Nonetheless, he concluded that it would be only appropriate to award damages in lieu of an injunction where the plaintiff's injury was 'very slight' and the hardship that would be visited upon the defendant as a result of imposing the injunction considerable. This approach appears to foreshadow the strict attitude favoured by the Court of Appeal two decades later in *Shelfer*.[38]

At times the courts steered a course between these extremes. Thus in *Curriers' Company v Corbett*,[39] Sir RT Kindersley VC observed that:

> The Defendant's new buildings are of considerable magnitude and importance, while the two houses of the Plaintiffs are comparatively of small value and importance; and it has been decided that in such a case the Court will not, as a matter of course, order the Defendant to pull down his new buildings, but will give to the party injured by the erection of those buildings compensation in damages.[40]

When, in *Smith v Smith*,[41] Sir George Jessel MR revisited the issue a year after giving his judgment *Aynsley*, his Lordship offered a more nuanced analysis. While he stated that the 'materiality of the injury to the Plaintiff' was a consideration, he did not suggest that it was available only where the injury was comparatively trivial. Jessel MR noted that, equally, the 'amount which has been laid out by the Defendant' had to be taken into account.[42] In addition, he emphasised that it was necessary to consider the quality of the defendant's behaviour, remarking that:

> this discretion must be a judicial discretion, exercised according to something like a settled rule, and in such a way as to prevent the Defendant doing a wrongful act, and thinking that he could pay damages for it … [I]t is of great importance to see if the Defendant knew he was doing wrong, and was taking his chance about being disturbed in doing it.[43]

(iii) Shelfer

The litigation in *Shelfer* v *City of London Electric Lighting Co*[44] arose out of a complaint of nuisance resulting from vibrations caused by the defendant's electricity-generating operation. At first instance, Kekewich J found that the defendant's

[36] (1874) LR 18 Eq 544.

[37] ibid, 555. Jessel MR remarked, 'I do not like to use the word extort', thereby conveying the impression that he had something of the kind in mind.

[38] Indeed, subsequently in *Slack v Leeds Industrial Co-operative Society* (1924) 2 Ch 475, 487, Pollock MR remarked that, 'The rules that are laid down in *Shelfer* … are also to be found in *Aynsley v Glover*, if not in the same terms, at any rate in words to much the same effect …'

[39] (1865)2 Dr & Sm 355.

[40] ibid, 361.

[41] (1875) LR 20 Eq 500.

[42] ibid, 505. Jessel MR concluded that these considerations weighed in favour of granting a mandatory injunction.

[43] ibid, 505.

[44] (1895) 1 Ch 287.

activities did indeed amount to an actionable nuisance and that the Electric Lighting Acts 1882 and 1888,[45] which authorised the undertaking, did not allow it to be conducted in a manner that amounted to a nuisance.[46] However, instead of issuing an injunction curtailing its operation, Kekewich J was prepared to grant damages under Lord Cairns' Act. In upholding the plaintiffs' appeal, the Court of Appeal was unanimous in concluding that they were entitled to an injunction.

AL Smith LJ observed that:

> a person by committing a wrongful act (whether it be a public company for public purposes or a private individual) is not thereby entitled to ask the court to sanction his doing so by purchasing his neighbor's rights, by assessing damages in that behalf, leaving his neighbour with the nuisance, or his lights dimmed, as the case may be.[47]

His Lordship then formulated his 'good working rule', which was to cast a long shadow over the law on this issue for the next one hundred and twenty years. In his view, damages should be awarded in lieu of an injunction only:

> (1) If the injury to the plaintiff's legal rights is small, (2) And is one which is capable of being estimated in money, (3) And is one which can be adequately compensated by a small money payment, (4) And the case is one in which it would be oppressive to the defendant to grant an injunction ...[48]

The most succinct statement of the philosophy underlying the approach of the Court in *Shelfer* came from Lindley LJ. He remarked that,

> ever since Lord Cairns' Act was passed the Court of Chancery has repudiated the notion that the Legislature intended to turn that Court into a tribunal for legalizing wrongful acts; or in other words, the Court has always protested against the notion that it ought to allow a wrong to continue simply because the wrongdoer is able and willing to pay for the injury he may inflict. Neither has the circumstance that the wrongdoer is in some sense a public benefactor ... ever been considered a sufficient reason for refusing to protect by injunction an individual whose rights are being persistently infringed. Expropriation, even for a money consideration, is only justifiable when Parliament has sanctioned it. Courts of Justice are not like Parliament, which considers whether proposed works will be so beneficial to the public as to justify exceptional legislation, and the deprivation of people of their rights with or without compensation. Lord Cairns' Act was not passed in order to supersede legislation for public purposes, but to enable the Court of Chancery to administer justice between litigants more effectually than it could before the Act.[49]

(iv) Judicial scepticism towards the 'Good Working Rule'

While some courts applied the approach in *Shelfer* without demur, others bridled at its constraints. In *Colls Home and Colonial Store*,[50] a right to light case, Lord Mac-

[45] 45 & 46 Vict c 56 and 51 & 52 Vict c 12.
[46] [1895] 1 Ch 287, 294.
[47] ibid, 322.
[48] ibid, 322–23.
[49] ibid, 315–16.
[50] [1904] AC 179.

naghten doubted that 'the amount of damages which may be supposed to be recoverable at law offers a satisfactory test' for determining whether the courts should make a monetary award in lieu of an injunction. Instead, his Lordship suggested that the issue should turn in large part on the quality of the defendant's behaviour, with it being proper to issue an injunction in cases of calculated breaches 'in order to do justice to the plaintiff and as a warning to others'. However, he concluded,

> if there really is a question as to whether the obstruction is legal or not, and if the defendant has acted fairly and not in an unneighbourly spirit, I am disposed to think that the Court ought to incline to damages rather than an injunction.[51]

His Lordship then paid lip service to the quasi-constitutional principle invoked by Lindley LJ in *Shelfer* in remarking, 'It is quite true that a man ought not to be compelled to part with his property against his will, or to have the value of his property diminished, without an Act of Parliament.'[52] However, he continued, 'On the other hand, the Court ought to be very careful not to allow an action for the protection of ancient lights to be used as a means of extorting money.'[53] The difficulty is that these two statements cannot easily be reconciled. The courts cannot totally exclude the possibility of owner's rights being subject to compulsory purchase and, at the same time, ensure that owners do not selfishly exploit this privilege.

Even Lord Lindley, as he now was, did not, when giving his judgment in *Colls*, appear inclined to maintain a position quite as absolutist as that which he had favoured in *Shelfer* 15 years earlier. He stated:

> I am convinced that even if the plaintiffs have a cause of action, the damages which could properly be awarded them would be very small, and to grant a mandatory injunction in such a case as this would be unduly oppressive and not in accordance with the principles on which equitable relief has been usually granted.[54]

Lord Lindley appeared to have retreated somewhat from the position he favoured in *Shelfer*, favouring a stance similar to that advanced by AL Smith LJ in that case, whereby the availability of damages in lieu of an injunction is largely dependent on the degree of interference caused by the nuisance.

Resistance to *Shelfer* was also apparent in the Court of Appeal's decision in *Kine v Jolly*.[55] The defendant had built a house which interfered with the plaintiff's right to light, substantially diminishing the value of the plaintiff's property. At first instance, after finding that the interference amounted to a nuisance, Kekewich J granted an injunction. The Court of Appeal reversed the decision on the choice of remedy. Cozens-Hardy LJ observed that

> I think it is impossible to doubt that the tendency of the speeches in the House of Lords in *Colls* … is to go a little further than was done in *Shelfer* …, and to indicate that as a

[51] ibid, 193.
[52] ibid.
[53] ibid.
[54] ibid, 212.
[55] [1905] 1 Ch 480.

general rule the Court ought to be less free in granting mandatory injunctions than it was in years gone by.[56]

It would certainly be difficult to disagree with the conclusion that Lord Macnaghten's approach in *Colls* is considerably more open to the award of damages in substitution of an injunction than was true of the judgments in *Shelfer*.[57] On the other hand, Lord Lindley's approach appears to go no further than AL Smith LJ's 'good working rule'. Moreover, Lord Macnaghten's account is plainly *obiter*, as all members of the Court in *Colls* were in agreement that there was no actionable nuisance.[58]

In giving his judgment in *Kine v Jolly*, Vaughan Williams LJ also applied the approach advocated by Lord Macnaghten in *Colls*, concluding that the defendant had done nothing to disentitle himself from benefiting from the Court's jurisdiction to grant damages in lieu of an injunction. Equally, however, he suggested that there was nothing in AL Smith LJ's formula in *Shelfer* that dictated that the Court should grant a mandatory injunction.[59] While his Lordship gave no reasons for this conclusion, it is difficult to accept the view that the facts in *Kine v Jolly* would have satisfied AL Smith LJ's rule. Given that rights to light are qualified in that an actionable nuisance arises only when the interference is so significant that it renders the premises 'substantially less comfortable and convenient',[60] it is unclear that any such breach can be said to satisfy the first of AL Smith LJ's tests, whereby it must be demonstrated that 'the injury to the plaintiff's legal rights is small'.[61] Moreover, given that a majority of the Court of Appeal accepted Kekewich J's finding that the value of the premises had been 'substantially diminished', it is difficult to understand how the breach could satisfy the AL Smith LJ's third test that the injury 'is one which can be adequately compensated by a small money payment'.[62]

Subsequently, in *Leeds Industrial Cooperative v Slack*,[63] the House of Lords concluded that the courts had the jurisdiction to grant damages in lieu of a *quia timet* injunction. The plaintiff had halted the defendant's building development by obtaining an interim injunction and thereby prevented the threatened breach of a right to light occurring. The willingness of the Court to authorise the use of

[56] ibid, 504.

[57] Cozens-Hardy LJ's observation could be read either as suggesting that there is a clear distinction to be made between mandatory and prohibitory injunctions or simply as concluding that, in light of *Colls*, it was apparent that a relatively flexible approach was to be taken in the context of mandatory injunctions without expressing a view on the position to be taken in relation to prohibitory injunctions. His Lordship would have been on safer ground in taking the latter view, as Lord Macnaghten had not explicitly indicated that his approach was applicable to mandatory injunctions alone and such a distinction had been previously rejected by the Court of Appeal in *Shelfer*.

[58] Although Sir Ernest Pollock MR subsequently noted in *Slack v Leeds Industrial Cooperative* [1924] 2 Ch 475, 487 that 'Those words no doubt are *obiter*, but every lawyer will desire to pay respect to observations made by so great a judge.'

[59] ibid, 496.

[60] *Colls Home and Colonial Store* [1904] AC 179, 187 (Lord Macnaghten).

[61] [1895] 1 Ch 287, 322.

[62] ibid.

[63] [1924] AC 851.

the jurisdiction not only to permit continuing nuisances but to authorise future transgressions of the plaintiff's rights is starkly at odds with the absolutist property rhetoric employed by Lindley LJ in *Shelfer*. When the case was sent back to the Court of Appeal to consider the issue on its merits, Sir Ernest Pollock MR treated Lord Macnaghten's formulation in *Colls* as essentially a gloss on AL Smith LJ's 'good working rule', a reflection on what the latter had meant in relation to the requirement that an injury to the plaintiff's rights be 'small'.[64] This interpretation is hardly credible; it is apparent that Lord Macnaghten's analysis represents a rejection of that criterion.

The retreat from *Shelfer* continued in *Fishenden v Higgs & Hill*,[65] when the Court of Appeal once again overturned a refusal of the Court at first instance to award damages in lieu of an injunction. Lord Hanworth MR (as Sir Ernest Pollock had become) went further than he had in *Slack* by suggesting that his analysis in the earlier case should not be taken as endorsing AL Smith LJ's rule.[66] Instead, he stated that 'we ought to incline against an injunction if possible'.[67] Romer LJ suggested that, while he was sure that an injunction would be refused if all of the criteria in *Shelfer* were fulfilled, AL Smith LJ could not be taken to have asserted that an injunction would invariably be denied if any of them were not satisfied.[68] Consistently with Lord Macnaghten's approach in *Colls*, Lord Hanworth MR and Romer LJ justified overturning the decision of the Court below in large part because the defendants had acted in good faith.[69] Both Maugham LJ and Lord Hanworth MR sought to restrict *Shelfer* to its facts by emphasising that it was a case in which the nuisance physically damaged the plaintiff's property.[70] In contrast, Maugham LJ concluded, AL Smith LJ's approach did not offer 'a universal or even a sound rule in all cases of injury to light'.[71]

Perhaps the celebrated departure from AL Smith LJ's rule came in *Miller v Jackson*,[72] where the Court of Appeal declined to award an injunction to prevent a cricket club from playing on a village green backing on to the plaintiff's residence. Lord Denning MR was inclined to deny relief altogether, largely because cricket had been played on the green long before an adjacent field was converted into a housing estate. In explaining his decision to part from nineteenth century precedent that treated as irrelevant any argument that the plaintiff had 'come to the nuisance', his Lordship remarked that the authority in question dated from 'the days where rights of property were in the ascendant'.[73] While Cumming-Bruce LJ, in

[64] [1924] 2 Ch 475, 486–87.
[65] (1935) 153 LT 128.
[66] ibid, 139.
[67] ibid.
[68] ibid, 141.
[69] ibid, 139 (Lord Hanworth MR) and 141 (Romer LJ).
[70] ibid, 138 (Lord Hanworth MR) and 144 (Maugham LJ).
[71] ibid, 144.
[72] [1977] QB 966.
[73] ibid, 981.

contrast, found that the defendant's activity constituted a nuisance, he concluded that the plaintiff should be limited to damages.[74]

Those who have sought to avoid a strict application of *Shelfer* have tended to assert the view that Lord Cairns' Act vests the courts with a discretion that, as such, cannot be reduced to a formula. Thus, in *Fishenden*, Romer LJ argued that AL Smith LJ 'could not have intended to have fettered the discretion imposed on the courts by the Lord Cairns' Act'.[75] In that case Lord Hanworth MR, with a hint of reproach, described AL Smith LJ's formula as 'the high water mark of what might be called definite rules'.[76]

Equally it has been suggested that, because equitable remedies are discretionary, it cannot be assumed that, in the absence of the jurisdiction conferred by Lord Cairns' Act, the claimant would have been entitled an injunction as of right on proof of an actionable nuisance.[77] It would follow that it could not necessarily be said that the claimant is having a right expropriated when damages are granted. This Conclusion is apparent in Millett LJ's analysis in *Jaggard v Sawyer*,[78] where he had little time for absolutist notions of property. He remarked that he thought that:

> references to the 'expropriation' of the plaintiff's property are somewhat overdone, not because that is not the practical effect of withholding an injunction, but because the grant of an injunction, like all equitable remedies, is discretionary.... If he wants to be protected he must seek equitable relief, and he has no absolute right to that. In many cases, it is true, an injunction will be granted almost as of course; but this is not always the case, and it will never be granted if this would cause injustice to the defendant...[79]

Despite the notion that equitable remedies are discretionary, the understanding that prohibitory injunctions, like that sought in *Jaggard*, are available 'as of course' pre-dates the judicial practice of using Lord Cairns' Act to award future damages in lieu of an injunction.[80] This suggests that it is in fact quite reasonable to regard the effect of awarding a release fee in substitution of a mandatory injunction in *Jaggard* as expropriating the plaintiff's rights. Whether it follows that this outcome is objectionable is another matter. Moreover, the final claim is unsupportable. There are plainly cases in which an injunction has been granted despite the fact that it was oppressive.[81]

[74] ibid, 988–99. The other member of the court, Geoffrey Lane LJ concluded that the plaintiffs were entitled to an injunction because 'damages cannot be said to provide an adequate form of relief' (ibid, 987).

[75] (1935) 153 LT 128, 141.

[76] ibid, 138.

[77] In *Redland Bricks v Morris* [1970] AC 652, 665, Lord Upjohn makes this claim with regard to mandatory injunctions, while accepting that prohibitory injunctions are available 'as of course'.

[78] [1995] 1 WLR 269.

[79] ibid, 287.

[80] *Imperial Gas Light and Coke Company* v *Broadbent* (1859) 7 HLC 600, 612 (Lord Kingsdown).

[81] For an outstanding example, see *Trenberth Ltd v National Westminster Bank Ltd* (1980) 39 P & CR 104, discussed below text accompanying nn 97–100.

(v) *Release fee awards under Lord Cairns' Act*

Lord Cairns' Act has been applied not only to grant damages for anticipated future loss but equally to award relief representing a sum that reasonable people in the parties' circumstances might have negotiated as a fee for the relaxation of the claimant's rights. The possibility of making a release-fee award in lieu of an injunction was first recognised in *Wrotham Park Estate Co Ltd v Parkside Homes Ltd.*[82] The case concerned a housing development built in breach of a restrictive covenant, an infringement which resulted in no diminution in value to the properties affected. Brightman J concluded that awarding a mandatory injunction requiring the destruction of the development would have been an 'unpardonable waste'[83] and concluded that, using its jurisdiction under Lord Cairns' Act, the Court could award the claimant a sum calculated on the basis of a hypothetical bargain. Perhaps surprisingly, counsel for the claimant did not raise the question as to whether the constraints upon the exercise of that jurisdiction by the Court of Appeal in *Shelfer* applied to release-fee relief. Instead, Brightman J relied upon earlier authorities that suggested that the courts should be especially cautious when asked to award mandatory injunctions, a view that was rejected in *Shelfer.*[84]

In principle at least, a release-fee award ought to be available in response to a nuisance. In practice, difficulties may arise in applying such relief to certain nuisances. However, there would seem little practical difficulty awarding such relief in the case of nuisances in the form of breaches of rights to light, where the extent of an interference with individual claimants' rights can be relatively easily determined. Support for the view that such relief should be available in this context was provided in a series of cases involving breaches of rights to light. In *Carr-Saunders v Dick McNeil Associates Ltd*,[85] in which the claimant sought a monetary award after abandoning a claim for a mandatory injunction, Millett J suggested that a claimant was entitled to a monetary award representing what would have amounted to a reasonable fee to have charged for the relaxation of the right.[86] This approach was subsequently followed in the High Court in *Tamares Ltd v Fairpoint Properties Ltd (No 2).*[87] Finally, the Court of Appeal in *Regan v Paul Properties DPF No 1*[88] also assumed that release-fee relief could be awarded in the event that a mandatory injunction was refused.

[82] [1974] 1 WLR 798 (Ch).

[83] ibid, 811.

[84] Thus, AL Smith LJ stated that his good working rule applied 'whether the case be for a mandatory injunction or to restrain a continuing nuisance' ([1895] 1 Ch 287, 322).

[85] [1986] 1 WLR 922.

[86] ibid, 931.

[87] [2007] 1 WLR 2167 (Ch D), [2007] EWHC 212 (Ch). See D Fox, 'Remedies for Interference with a Prescriptive Right to Light' [2007] *CLJ* 267.

[88] [2006] EWCA Civ 1391, [2007] Ch 135.

Nonetheless, the notion that release-fee relief might be appropriate in the context of nuisance was doubted by Patten J in the Court of Appeal in *Forsyth-Grant v Allen.*[89] The Court rejected the suggestion that the claimant might be awarded an account of the defendant's profits resulting from building in breach of the claimant's right to light. In addition, Patten J remarked that

> nuisance does not involve the misappropriation of the claimant's rights in the same way, even as in a case of trespass, let alone as in a case of conversion or copyright or trademark infringement. … [T]his should not entitle the claimant, in my judgment, to more than compensation for the loss which she has actually suffered…[90]

This is an odd view. For one thing, it is not clear that any categorical distinction between trespasses and nuisances should determine that gain-based relief should be available for one but not the other. Given that the claimant was denied a mandatory injunction to put an end to the breach, *Forsyth-Grant* is exactly the sort of case in which the claimant could be said to have been deprived of a proprietary right. Moreover, the defendant in *Forsyth-Grant* had been prepared to pay a reasonable fee for the relaxation of the claimant's right to light.[91] Would we really prefer a state of affairs where the defendant need not have bothered to negotiate? And would Patten J really have suggested that a reasonable fee was not appropriate for an interference with a right to light if he had been faced by a defendant who had proceeded to build in the face of a claimant's protestations? His Lordship grudgingly acknowledged that the law as it stands entitles claimants in this context to release-fee relief 'in appropriate cases'.[92]

The provision of release-fee relief appeared to offer a way of using the jurisdiction conferred by Lord Cairns' Act without the court being prey to the accusation that it was allowing defendants to expropriate claimants' rights in return for paying for their loss. At least, such relief requires defendants to pay a reasonable price in return for allowing them to override claimants' rights.

(vi) Lord Cairns' Act and trespass

In dealing with trespass to land, one might expect the courts to have adopted a similar approach to their discretion to grant damages in lieu of an injunction as that favoured in relation to the tort of nuisance. The reality, however, is that the courts have been even stricter in exercising the jurisdiction in cases of trespass. Thus, in *Woollerton and Wilson v Richard Costain Ltd*,[93] the Court considered trespasses of airspace by the jib of a crane more than fifty feet above the roof level of the claimant's land. Stamp J concluded that, because trespass is actionable *per se*,

[89] [2008] EWCA Civ 505, [2008] 2 EGLR 16.
[90] [2008] 2 EGLR 16 [32].
[91] His efforts to negotiate were rebuffed by the claimant who refused to communicate.
[92] [2008] 2 EGLR 16 [32].
[93] [1970] 1 WLR 411.

the claimant was entitled to an injunction as of right even if the conditions in *Shelfer* were satisfied. His Lordship remarked:

> Indeed, the very fact that no harm is done is a reason for rather than against the granting of an injunction: for if there is no damage done the damages recovered in the action will be nominal and if the injunction is refused the result will be no more nor less than a licence to continue the tort of trespass in return for a nominal fee.[94]

Influenced, however, by the fact that the defendants' breach was inadvertent and that they had offered to pay a release fee, the Court suspended the operation of the injunction to allow them to finish the work in question. Stamp J noted that, if the defendants had committed the trespass intentionally, no appeal to the importance of the work in question would have enabled them to escape an injunction with immediate effect.

More recently, however, the courts have been prepared to resort to their jurisdiction under Lord Cairns' Act in order to provide release-fee relief in circumstances where the defendant has suffered no apparent loss from the breach. This was the case in *Bracewell v Appleby*.[95] The defendant, enjoyed a right of way over a private road that provided the only access to his and other houses in a *cul-de-sac*. He purchased and built a new home upon an adjoining plot of land that could only be accessed via the private road and his first plot of land. Two of the other owners of homes in the *cul-de-sac* sued in trespass. At trial, it was found that the right of way did not confer upon the defendant the privilege to access the new property and that any use of the private road for that purpose therefore amounted to a trespass. Graham J awarded monetary relief in lieu of a prohibitory injunction that would have left the defendant's new house uninhabitable, rejecting the contention by the counsel for the claimants that, 'there is no place in a case involving trespass for the application of the approach adopted in *Wrotham Park*'.[96] The relief awarded was calculated, not according to actual loss suffered by the other owners (which was presumably negligible), but, instead, pursuant to what the claimants might have demanded as a reasonable fee in return for relaxing their rights.[97] This approach to relief has the advantage of circumventing the objection made in earlier cases that, where the claimant was entitled only to nominal damages, such relief could not be regarded as an adequate remedy and, therefore, an injunction must be awarded.

Bracewell v Appleby might have been thought to have signaled a greater willingness by the courts to refuse an injunction in the context of a trespass. However, a few years later in *John Trenberth Ltd v National Westminster Bank Ltd*,[98] Walton J appeared to advance on the basis that an injunction was available regardless of how oppressive its effect might be. The defendant, whose building had

[94] ibid, 413.
[95] [1975] Ch 408.
[96] ibid, 411.
[97] For a discussion of relief award on a release-fee basis, see above text to nn 82–84 and below text to nn 112–23.
[98] (1980) 39 P & CR 104.

fallen into such a state of disrepair that it was dangerous to the public, sought to effect the necessary repairs but this would have required the temporary erection of scaffolding on the plaintiff's neighbouring premises. The defendant sought permission but the plaintiff refused. The defendant went ahead with the work, thereby committing a trespass and the plaintiff responded by seeking an injunction. Walton J concluded that the plaintiff was entitled to the remedy as of right and, moreover, suggested that Stamp J had been wrong in *Woollerton* to suspend the operation of such relief.[99]

The result in *Trenberth* was so unreasonable that it encouraged the Law Commission to consider the issue,[100] leading eventually to the enactment of the Access to Neighbouring Land Act 1992, allowing the courts to grant orders overriding landowners' powers of exclusion in such cases. This course of events is consistent with the notion that it is for the courts to enforce property rights and for Parliament alone to alter those rights. Yet, it is odd to treat as absolutely out of the question the notion that the courts might limit the availability of injunctive relief within carefully subscribed limits.[101]

The question of awarding damages in lieu of a prohibitory injunction subsequently arose in *Anchor Brewhouse Developments Ltd v Berkley House (Docklands Developments) Ltd*,[102] another case involving cranes, the jibs of which had to be left free to swing in the wind when not in use and which on occasion entered into airspace owned by the plaintiff. Scott J, citing *Trenberth*, had little trouble in reaching the view that the plaintiff was entitled to an injunction as of right. Moreover, his Lordship announced that he had 'some difficulty' with the case of *Bracewell v Appleby*,[103]

> mainly because, as it seems to me, the learned judge regarded the damages he was awarding as a once and for all payment. But it was, as I see it, not within the power of the judge to produce that result. Whether or not an injunction were granted, the defendant's use of the right of way would, after the judgment as well as before, represent trespass unless and until he were granted a right of way. The judge could not by an award of damages put the defendant in the position of a person entitled to an easement of way.[104]

Scott J is right to suggest that it is difficult to reconcile the approach in *Bracewell v Appleby*, and indeed any case in which damages are granted in lieu of a permanent injunction, with an absolute commitment to the protection of property. The awarding of such relief in *Wrotham Park*, for example, effectively eliminated the plaintiff's restrictive covenant and, in *Bracewell v Appleby*, the result effectively conferred the defendant with an easement. Despite Scott J's instinct that such an outcome is unthinkable, it is plain that the courts have allowed themselves the

[99] ibid, 108.

[100] *Rights of Access to Neighbouring Land* (Cmnd 9692, 1985).

[101] See E Waring, *Aspects of Property: The Impact of Private Takings*, PhD Thesis (Cambridge University, 2009).

[102] [1987] EGLR 172.

[103] [1975] Ch 408.

[104] [1987] EGLR 172, 177.

power to redistribute property rights in this fashion. Wherever the court grants damages in lieu of an injunction in the context of a nuisance, for example, it effectively confers upon the defendant a positive easement to pursue an activity that would otherwise amount to an actionable nuisance.

A few years later, in *Jaggard v Sawyer*,[105] the Court of Appeal considered a dispute broadly similar to that arising in *Bracewell v Appleby*. Sir Thomas Bingham MR briefly discussed the decisions in *Trenberth* and *Anchor Brewhouse Developments* and their Lordships unanimously agreed that it was appropriate to award a release fee in lieu of an injunction. Bigham MR noted but gave short shrift to Scott J's criticism of *Bracewell v Appelby* in the latter case, plainly preferring the approach taken by Graham J in *Bracewell* to that adopted in the earlier decisions.

(vii) A return to the strict application of Shelfer in nuisance

Despite attempts to reject or reinterpret AL Smith LJ's rule in order to loosen the constraints on the jurisdiction to grant damages in lieu of an injunction, there are equally instances where the courts have strictly applied *Shelfer*. Thus, in *Kennaway v Thompson*,[106] the Court of Appeal declined to have regard to the public interest in refusing to limit the plaintiff to damages. Lawton LJ remarked that, 'The principles enunciated in *Shelfer's* case, which is binding on us, have been applied time and time again during the past 85 years.'[107] His Lordship asserted that *Miller v Jackson* was the only case that 'raises a doubt about the application of the *Shelfer* principles to all cases',[108] a remark that suggests that the Court did not benefit from having had all the relevant authorities cited to it.

More recently, in *Regan v Paul Properties DPF No 1*[109] the Court of Appeal manifested a determination to apply *Shelfer* strictly even in cases in which the plaintiff sought a mandatory injunction. The defendant had proceeded with a building development after having been advised by an expert that any interference with the claimant's right to light that would result would be minor. The claimant sought a mandatory injunction but at first instance was limited to damages on the basis that it had failed to demonstrate that a monetary award would be inadequate. Applying *Shelfer*, the Court of Appeal overturned the decision to deny an injunction. Mummery LJ suggested that Lord Macnaghten's remarks in *Coll* had been treated as carrying an authority that he had never intended them to have.[110] This strict approach was soon after endorsed by a differently constituted Court of Appeal in *Watson v Croft Promosport*,[111] where again the court upheld an appeal against the decision at first instance to award damages in lieu of an injunction.

105 [1995] 1 WLR 269.
106 [1981] 1 QB 88.
107 ibid, 93.
108 ibid.
109 [2006] EWCA Civ 1391, [2007] Ch 135.
110 ibid, [39].
111 [2009] EWCA Civ 15, [2009] 3 All ER 249.

(viii) Release-fee awards and Shelfer

It was noted that *Shelfer* was not cited in *Wrotham Park*, the seminal decision providing for release-fee relief in lieu of an injunction.[112] Nonetheless, the 'good working rule' has assumed importance in this context since, more than 20 years later, it was applied in *Jaggard v Sawyer*.[113] The Court of Appeal upheld the award of a release fee in preference to granting an injunction that would have denied the defendant access via a private road to a newly built house. The judge in the County Court hearing the case at first instance had applied *Shelfer* in awarding damages in lieu of an injunction (concluding that the 'good working rule' was satisfied). On appeal, *Shelfer* was discussed at some length by both Sir Thomas Bingham MR and Millett LJ.[114] Their Lordships did not refer to the fact that *Shelfer* had not previously been applied in the context of release-fee relief. They accepted the conclusion reached at first instance that the award calculated by reference to a reasonable fee was small enough to meet the strictures of AL Smith LJ's rule. It might be asked, however, whether a more generous fee, such as that awarded in *Wrotham Park* (where Brightman J suggested that the claimant was entitled to receive 5 percent of the profits of the development)[115] could really be characterised as 'small'.[116] It might be doubted that, given that claimants in such cases have apparently suffered no loss, the size of the fee that might have been negotiated between the parties should be relevant in determining the availability of an injunction. However, in *Jaggard v Sawyer*, both Bingham MR and Millett LJ expressed the view that an award calculated in this manner was in essence compensation for loss.[117] This suggests that the sum awarded reflected an 'injury' suffered by the claimant, which would explain why their Lordships considered whether it conformed with the first part of AL Smith LJ's rule.

Later decisions saw the courts applying *Shelfer* to release-fee relief in the context of nuisances in the form of breaches of rights to light. In *Regan v Paul Properties DPF No 1 Ltd*[118] without quantifying the release-fee award to which the claimant would have been entitled, Mummery LJ found that such relief would not have

[112] Above nn 82–84.

[113] [1995] 1 WLR 269.

[114] Kennedy LJ concurred with Bingham MR.

[115] [1974] 1 WLR 798 (Ch) 816. See above 93–94.

[116] Indeed, in *Tamares Ltd v Fairpoint Properties Ltd* [2006] EWHC 3589 (Ch), [2007] 1 WLR 2148, Gabriel Moss QC, sitting as a deputy High Court judge, concluded that the good working rule was satisfied in respect of a breach for which his Lordship, in a separate hearing, eventually granted relief in the form of a release fee for £50,000 (*Tamares Ltd v Fairpoint Properties Ltd (No 2)* [2007] EWHC 212 (Ch), [2007] 1 WLR 2167 (Ch D). While it is not entirely clear from his analysis, Moss QC would seem to have had in mind the injury in the form of the diminution in the value of the property (which was at the most £3030).

[117] *Jaggard* (n 113) 281–82 (Bingham MR), 291 (Millett LJ). See C Rotherham, "Wrotham Park Damages' and Accounts of Profits: Compensation or Restitution?' [2008] *Lloyd's Maritime and Commercial Law Quarterly* 25.

[118] [2006] EWCA Civ 1391, [2007] Ch 135.

been small for the purposes of AL Smith LJ's rule.[119] In a subsequent right to light case, *HKRUK II v Heaney*,[120] Judge Langlan QC suggested that the claimant would have been entitled to a substantial release fee in the context of a breach of a right to light and considered whether the claimant might be limited to such relief in lieu of an injunction. He proceeded on the basis that, in applying the 'good working rule', the object of the inquiry for the purposes of determining whether any 'injury to the plaintiff's legal rights is small' was the diminution in value of the claimant's property as a result of the interference rather than the more substantial release fee that would have resulted from the hypothetical bargain method. While it might be argued that this is contrary to the approach taken by the Court of Appeal in *Jaggard v Sawyer*, this conclusion did not greatly assist the defendant as Judge Langlan QC took the view that the diminution in the value of the claimant's property by 2 per-cent (amounting to £80,000) was not a small injury for the purposes of the first part of AL Smith LJ's rule. In any event, he held that the prospective release fee, which was calculated at £225,000, was relevant to the determination of whether the injury could be 'be adequately compensated by a small money payment' in terms of the third part of that rule.[121] Unsurprisingly, he concluded that this award was not small for these purposes. Judge Langlan QC's approach is illogical. The first and third limbs of AL Smith LJ's rule are clearly linked; if a release fee is not indicative of an 'injury' for the purposes of the first limb, it cannot be regarded as compensating that injury for purpose of the third limb.

The net effect of the return to a stringent application of AL Smith LJ's rule and the application of that rule to release-fee relief was to return the law to a position more severe than that taken in *Shelfer* at the height of the Victorian age. The result in the context of rights to light was to create considerable anxiety amongst developers.[122] The strict enforcement of rights to light in the fashion contemplated in *Regan* and *Heaney* presented a considerable obstacle for developers. It might be responded that developers should have to obtain the consent of those who would be affected by their schemes. Large developments are, however, likely to compromise the rights of numerous landowners and, not only are the transaction costs involved in seeking consent likely to be substantial, but there is also a real prospect of some landowners 'holding out' in order to solicit pay-offs that greatly exceed their own valuations of their entitlements. This is precisely the kind of situation in which law and economics scholars have suggested that damages should be preferred to an injunction because strategic behavior from landowners is likely to mean that parties would generally fail to reach a bargain even where this result would be in the interests of all involved.[123]

[119] ibid, [72].

[120] [2010] EWHC 2245 (Ch), [2010] EGLR 15.

[121] See above text to n 48.

[122] See *Rights to Light* (2014) Law Com No 356 [1.8] and [8.28]–[8.69].

[123] G Calabresi and D Melamed, 'Property Rules, Liability Rules and Inalienability: One View of the Cathedral' (1972) 85 *Harvard Law Review* 1089.

B. The Retreat from *Shelfer*

(i) *Lawrence v Fen Tigers Ltd*

The Supreme Court had the opportunity to reconsider whether *Shelfer* was good law in *Lawrence v Fen Tigers Ltd.*[124] The claimants complained that their right to the quiet enjoyment of an isolated bungalow that they had purchased in 2006 was breached as a result of activities conducted at a stadium that had been used for various of types of motor sports since 1975. The court at first instance had found that the defendants' activities amounted to an actionable nuisance and granted an injunction. The Court of Appeal upheld the appeal on the ground that the defendants' use of the land did not constitute a nuisance.

The Supreme Court upheld the defendants' appeal on the question of liability, finding that the activities conducted at the stadium did indeed give rise to a nuisance. Nonetheless, the court favoured an approach that allowed it to give greater weight to the interests of the defendant and the public. For one thing, it held that an activity might give rise to a prescriptive easement if carried on for a period of 20 years during which it amounted to a nuisance. In addition, it showed a greater willingness to have regard to the interest of the defendant in cases where the claimant has 'come to the nuisance'. In this regard, Lord Neuberger concluded that the defendant's use of the land could be taken into account in order to determine the nature of the locality in question for the purposes of deciding the reasonableness of the defendant's activity but only to the extent that the activity did not amount to a nuisance.[125]

Most striking, however, was the Court's reappraisal of the judicial discretion to award damages in lieu of an injunction. Inevitably, this raised the question as to the status of AL Smith LJ's 'good working rule'. The matter as to whether the claimant ought to have been limited to damages had not been raised at first instance, and Lord Neuberger concluded that, in consequence, the court had no findings upon which to base a determination as to how the discretion should be exercised. His Lordship concluded that the defendant should be invited take advantage of a provision in the judgment of Seymour QC at first instance that gave the parties permission to apply for the discharge of the injunction. This would allow the judge to consider the issue fully in light of their Lordships' guidelines on the matter.[126]

There was agreement amongst their Lordships that the exercise of the jurisdiction to grant damages in lieu of an injunction should no longer be constrained

[124] [2014] UKSC 13, [2014] AC 822.

[125] ibid, [65]–[72]. While acknowledging the issue, his Lordship appeared to underestimate the logical paradox that was created by requiring that the court decide whether the activity amounted to nuisance in order to determine the extent to which it shaped the character of the neighbourhood, given that a conclusion on this latter question was necessary for resolving whether the activity amounted to a nuisance.

[126] ibid, [151].

by a strict application of AL Smith LJ's rule from *Shelfer*. Lord Neuberger remarked that,

> Given that we are changing the practice of the courts, it is inevitable that, in so far as there can be clearer or more precise principles, they will have to be worked out in the way familiar to the common law, namely on a case by case basis.[127]

It is apparent, however, that their Lordships' different judgments betray quite contrasting views as to how the exercise of the discretion should be approached. This lack of consensus places any lower court required to perform this task in an invidious position.

(ii) Guidelines on the use of the discretion: The 'Good Working Rule' and the onus of proof

Lord Neuberger gave much the longest judgment and his analysis is likely to have the most influence on the development of guidelines in future cases. He suggested that, *prima facie*, a claimant should be entitled to an injunction on proof of a nuisance and that the burden lay on the defendant to persuade the court that damages should be granted instead.[128] However, the effect of his Lordship's approach was to greatly lower the obstacles that would lay in a defendant's path to discharging that burden.

Lord Neuberger, echoing Romer LJ's analysis in *Fishenden*,[129] favoured an approach that effectively inverts AL Smith LJ's rule by making satisfaction of the four criteria a sufficient rather than necessary condition for awarding damages in lieu of an injunction. On this view, if the tests listed by AL Smith LJ are all met, a court should deny an injunction and grant damages; if they are not all fulfilled, however, the court might still exercise its discretion in the defendant's favour.[130] Lord Neuberger endorsed Lord Macnaghten's dictum from *Colls* as a basis for deciding whether to award damages instead of an injunction in cases where AL Smith LJ's rule was not satisfied, emphasising the importance of the parties' conduct.[131]

Lord Sumption suggested that the law might go even further, proposing that the award of damages should be the default position.[132] In his view, 'There is much to be said for the view that damages are ordinarily an adequate remedy for nuisance…'. His Lordship remarked that

> the *Shelfer* principle was based mainly on the court's objection to sanctioning a wrong by allowing the defendant to pay for the right to go on doing it. This seems to be an unduly

[127] ibid, [132].
[128] ibid, [121].
[129] (1935) 153 LT 128. See above text to nn 65–71.
[130] [2014] UKSC 13, [2014] AC 822, [123].
[131] ibid, [121].
[132] ibid, [161].

moralistic approach to disputes, and if taken at face value would justify the grant of an injunction in all cases, which is plainly not the law.[133]

It is difficult to see that there is any escaping a 'moralistic' position in this context. It is simply the case that Lord Sumption would prefer a position that was more utilitarian or communitarian than the libertarian stance favoured by the court in *Shelfer*.

It is unlikely that Lord Sumption's suggestion that the court should start from a presumption that damages should be awarded will gain acceptance. Indicating that he preferred Lord Neuberger's 'nuanced approach',[134] Lord Mance remarked that

the right to enjoy one's home without disturbance is one which I believe that many, indeed most, people value for reasons largely if not entirely independent of money … I would not therefore presently be persuaded by a view that 'damages are ordinarily an adequate remedy for a nuisance …[135]

Lord Clarke preferred to reserve the question as to who should bear that burden of proof, while Lord Carnwarth did not address the issue.

(iii) The relevance of the public interest

Lord Neuberger took a dim view of the 'unsatisfactory way in which it seems that the public interest is to be taken into account when considering the issue whether to grant an injunction or award damages'.[136] He remarked further that, 'I find it hard see how there could be any circumstances in which it arose and could not, as a matter of law, be a relevant factor'.[137] It is apparent then that Lord Neuberger envisioned an approach to the discretion that departed from *Shelfer*, not only by considering the quality of the parties' behaviour and the hardship that would result from granting an injunction (following Lord Macnaghten in *Colls*), but also by having regard to the interests of the wider community. Other members of the Court agreed that the judiciary might take account of the public interest in choosing between remedies.

It is less clear how a court is supposed to approach the exercise of identifying the public interest and what significance the fact that the land use causing a nuisance has received planning permission might have.[138] The issue receives its starkest treatment in the judgment of Lord Sumption, who remarked:

The main question, as it seems to me, is not whether the judge in deciding on the appropriate remedy should take account of the public interest or, more generally, of interests

[133] ibid, [160].
[134] ibid, [168].
[135] ibid, quoting Lord Sumption ibid [161].
[136] ibid, [118].
[137] ibid, [123].
[138] See M Lee, 'The Public Interest in Private Nuisance: Collectives and Communities in Tort' [2015] *CLJ* 329 for an account of the complexities raised by the issue.

> which are not before the court. He will usually lack the information to do so effectively, and is in danger of stepping outside his main function of deciding the issue between the parties. The main question is whether the current principles of law governing the availability of injunctions are consistent with the public interest reflected in the successive and increasingly elaborate legislative schemes of development control which have existed in England since 1947.[139]

Thus, in Lord Sumption's view, the planning system already ensures that an assessment of whether the use in question is in public interest is made by a body empowered by the legislature to undertake such an inquiry. According to this analysis, the courts lack the institutional competence and/or legitimacy to second-guess such an evaluation of the public interest. Thus, Lord Sumption suggested 'it may well be that an injunction should as a matter of principle not be granted in a case where a use of land to which objection is taken requires and has received planning permission'.[140]

Lord Neuberger was not prepared to go so far. He argued that evidence that the public benefit of the use had been considered in a planning process in which a defendant had gained planning permission may support the argument that the use in question is in the public benefit. However, he concluded that, even where it was evident that the planning authority had been influenced by its perception of the public benefit of the use, this would be only one factor to weigh in deciding whether it would be appropriate to award damages in lieu of an injunction.[141] Lord Mance and Lord Carnwarth took the view that the fact that planning permission had been granted should not give rise to presumption that an injunction should not be awarded.[142]

While the Supreme Court in *Lawrence* made it clear that the public good was a factor to be taken into account in choosing between remedies, the decision does not clarify just how much weight it should have. It appears implicit in Lord Sumption's suggestion that, 'an injunction should not usually be granted in a case where it is likely that conflicting interests are engaged other than the parties' interests'[143] that his Lordship treats the public interest as paramount. Lord Mance, in contrast, characterised this conclusion as 'putting the significance of planning permission and public benefit too high'.[144] The other Lords would seem to be closer to Lord Mance's than Lord Sumption's view on the subject. Nonetheless, there is no real indication in any of their judgments how readily the public interest might outweigh private rights. Historically, the approach of the courts was to have limited regard to this consideration in determining liability in nuisance[145] and to disregard

[139] [2014] UKSC 13, [2014] AC 822, [158].
[140] ibid, [161].
[141] ibid, [125].
[142] ibid, [167] (Lord Mance), [246] (Lord Carnwath).
[143] ibid, [161].
[144] ibid, [168].
[145] See, eg, *AG v Birmingham BC* (1859) K & J 528 (refusal to deny injunction on the basis of the public interest—decided prior to the courts' recognising possibility of using Lord Cairns' Act to grant

it altogether in choosing between remedies.[146] Is the mere fact that an activity is socially expedient now sufficient to justify the courts sanctioning private takings of property rights? The fact that the majority of their Lordships indicated that it would be appropriate to have a presumption in favour of issuing an injunction suggests this was not what they had in mind. It is likely that the courts will develop a norm that permits this result only where the weight of the public interest in an activity continuing significantly outweighs the interests of the claimant.

(iv) The celebration of discretion

One explanation of the failure of the Supreme Court in *Lawrence* to give an adequate account of how the public interest and private rights are to be balanced is that their Lordships treat the fact that the power conferred by Lord Cairns' Act is discretionary thus relieving them of the responsibility of providing any such guidelines. This begs the question as to the extent to which this discretion should be constrained.

Noting the 'more open-minded approach adopted in *Colls, Kine* and *Fishenden*', Lord Neuberger suggested that the court's discretion should not be 'fettered'.[147] Nonetheless, Lord Macnaghten's approach in *Colls*, which was favoured in those later cases, did not leave the discretion to grant damages in lieu of an injunction unconstrained. For his part, Lord Neuberger suggested that

> it is only right to acknowledge that this does not prevent the courts from laying down rules as to what factors can, and cannot be taken into account by a judge when deciding whether to exercise his discretion to award damages in lieu. Indeed, it is appropriate to give as much guidance as possible so as to ensure that, while the discretion is not fettered, its manner of exercise is as predictable as possible.

The notion that a discretion might be subject to 'rules' limiting the factors that can be considered and to 'guidance' ensuring predictability of the 'manner of the exercise' of the discretion but that neither would result in that discretion being 'fettered' suggests distinctions that are best opaque and at worst nonexistent. To characterise particular constraints as 'fettering' a discretion is simply to provide a pejorative description of norms of which one does not approve. Lord Neuberger's willingness to provide guidance as to when an injunction should be denied suggests that his real objection was as to the extent of the constraints placed on the discretion in *Shelfer* rather than on the fact that the power might be constrained *per se*.

damages for future loss); *St Helens v Tipping* (1865) 11 HL Cas 642 (liability automatically followed proof of physical damage). See B Pontin, *Nuisance Law and Environmental Protection: A Study of Nuisance Injunctions in Practice* (Witney, Lawtext, 2013).

[146] See, eg, *Shelfer v City of London Electric Lighting Co* (1895) 1 Ch 287, 315 (Lindley LJ); *Kennaway v Thompson* [1981] 1 QB 88, 93 (Lawton LJ).

[147] [2014] UKSC 13, [2014] AC 822, [117].

Lord Clarke agreed with Lord Neuberger's suggestion that the discretion in question 'should not as a matter of principle be fettered'.[148] He was content to state that 'the general principle is or should be that equitable relief will be granted where it is appropriate and not otherwise and that, where damages are an adequate remedy, it is inappropriate to grant equitable relief'.[149] This is unhelpful. For one thing, notions of appropriateness and adequacy in themselves simply restate the question. Moreover, it might be argued that, if the criterion of 'adequacy' of damages were treated in much the same way as it is in the context of specific performance, claimants asserting their right to quietly enjoy their land would always be entitled to an injunction. Equally, it is clear that Lord Macnaghten's approach in *Colls* is not tied to the issue of whether damages are an adequate remedy but rather to questions of the quality of the parties' behaviour and the relative hardship imposed by the remedies. In addition, it is apparent that, to the extent to which the members of the Supreme Court in *Lawrence* were emphasising that the public interest should be a factor in the exercise of the discretion, this has nothing to do with whether damages are adequate from perspective of the claimant but rather whether, in certain circumstances, it might be appropriate to limit the rights of the individual claimant in the name of the public good.

There appears to be a tendency to hide behind a discretion in this context in the belief that it might somehow absolve the courts from offering meaningful guidelines on how the power in question should be exercised. It might be thought that leaving the courts' power to expropriate private rights 'unfettered' allows them to avoid the controversy that would come with guidelines that clarified the weight that a judge should give to the public interest. Yet the notion of an unstructured and therefore virtually unreviewable discretion accords badly with the aversion to 'palm tree justice' that has often been expressed from the English bench.[150] Indeed, it is out of step with Lord Neuberger's extra-judicial claim that 'the discretionary remedial constructive trust offends against the fundamental principle that property rights are a matter of strict law not discretion'.[151]

(v) *Gain-based relief*

As already suggested, the use of gain-based relief can overcome some of the objections to the denial of injunctions. Resort to such relief ensures that, if the defendants are in some sense permitted to expropriate claimants' rights, at least they must pay a fair price for it. If the courts are going to permit the defendant to override the claimant's rights, they should in return share some of the gain that the defendant stands to make from the infringement.

[148] ibid, [169]–[170].

[149] ibid, [171].

[150] See *Muscat v Smith* [2003] EWCA Civ 962, [2003] 1 WLR 2853, [45] (Buxton LJ); *National Provincial Bank v Ainsworth* [1965] AC 1175, 1219 (Lord Hodson); *Gissing v Gissing* [1969] 2 Ch 85, 95 (Edmund Davies LJ) and *Cassell & Co Ltd v Broome* [1972] AC 1027, 1087 (Lord Reid).

[151] Lord Neuberger, 'The Remedial Constructive Trust—Fact or Fiction', Lecture at the Banking Services and Finance Law Association Conference, Queenstown, New Zealand, 10 August 2014.

There are several objections to limiting monetary awards given in substitution of an injunction to the actual loss suffered by the claimant. First, and most obviously, it would be unfair to permit defendants to profit from an on-going breach in return for merely compensating claimants for their loss. Secondly, if the breach is potentially profitable for the defendant, limiting a claimant to relief for loss would tend to leave the defendant with little incentive to bargain for permission to pursue the course of action in question, given that claimants will invariably demand a release-fee that exceeds the burden of the breach. Thirdly, such a restriction would equally reduce claimants' incentive to sue in response to such a breach. Finally, there is a concern that loss-based damages are systematically liable to undercompensate claimants because they do not take account of the subjectivity of claimants' valuation of their entitlements.[152]

An advantage of release-fee relief is its flexibility, with the court's view as to what is 'reasonable' dependent in part on the quality of the parties' behaviour. As a result, a judge might respond to egregious breaches by awarding the claimant a large share of the gain.[153]

It is perhaps surprising then that the Supreme Court, while radically reforming the judicial approach to the exercise of the jurisdiction to award damages in lieu of an injunction, showed some reticence toward the notion that relief might be tailored in some way to the defendant's gain. Drawing on *Jaggard v Sawyer* for support,[154] Lord Neuberger expressed the view that it was 'at least arguable' that, where damages were awarded in lieu of an injunction, they might well 'also include the loss of the claimant's ability to enforce her rights, which may often be assessed by reference to the benefit to the defendant of not suffering an injunction'.[155] His Lordship's characterisation of the issue has the disadvantage of blurring the line between compensation for loss and gain-based relief. Lord Neuberger noted that Lord Carnwath had pointed to 'factors which support the contention that damages in a nuisance case should never, or only rarely, be assessed by reference to the benefit to the defendant in no injunction being granted'.[156] For this reason, and because the Court had not heard argument on the point, he concluded that it would be inappropriate to decide whether such relief should be available in this context.[157]

[152] See C Rotherham, 'Deterrence as a Justification for Awarding Accounts of Profits' (2012) *OJLS* 1, 18.

[153] In *Stadium Capital Holdings (No 2) Ltd v St Marylebone Property Co Plc* [2010] EWCA Civ 952, [13], Peter Smith J (sitting in the Court of Appeal) in the course of directing that the case be sent back to the High Court to determine an appropriate release fee, suggested that 'in an appropriate case it is possibly arguable that the measure of damages can represent 100% [of the defendant's profit]'. Patten LJ suggested that relief calculated on this basis 'by definition, will not produce a figure equal to 100% of the profits of the unlawful venture' (ibid [17]).

[154] [1995] 1 WLR 269. See above text to nn 78–105.

[155] [2014] UKSC 13, [2014] AC 822, [128].

[156] ibid, [131].

[157] ibid.

Lord Carnwath indicated that he was 'reluctant to open up the possibility of assessment of damages on the basis of a share of the benefit to the defendants'.[158] It is not clear, however, how compelling the concerns that his Lordship raised really are. He suggested that particular problems arise in relation to nuisance because 'the injury is less specific' compared with other wrongs.[159] This would hardly appear any more fatal than it is for the quantification of compensatory damages. Moreover, the fact that the extent of the interference is only one factor that is relevant to the quantification of a release fee means that the courts might be less concerned with determining the claimant's loss with exactitude than they are when awarding compensation based on actual harm. His Lordship equally noted that particular problems would be faced 'where the nuisance affects a large number of people'.[160] Perhaps the problem is not so much with the number of defendants *per se*; after all, a number of cases involving trespasses and breaches of restrictive covenants involve multiple defendants.[161] One concern may be uncertainty as to whether everyone with a potential claim can be identified. If this cannot be done, it would not be possible to determine the appropriate release-fee that should be awarded to those claimants who are identified. In addition, different defendants in a nuisance case are liable to suffer to varying degrees, a consideration which should be reflected in their awards but which is liable to considerably complicate the quantification of such relief. However, these problems do not invariably arise in nuisance cases. Thus, it is difficult to see any objection to the use of gain-based relief on these grounds in rights to light cases. Given this, there seems no good reason to totally exclude such relief in all cases of nuisance.

Lord Carnwarth also suggested that providing relief in the form of a release fee 'seems to represent a radical departure from the normal basis regarded by Parliament as fair and appropriate in relation to injurious affection suffered as a result of activities carried out under statutory authority'.[162] The remark is curious. Release-fee relief is radically different from awards that provide compensation for actual harm, precisely because the former type of relief is gain based and the latter loss based. Moreover, it is entirely appropriate that relief provided in response to judicially sanctioned private takings is categorically different from compensation given for harms resulting from statutorily authorised activities.

Lord Clarke, in contrast, while leaving the question open was not convinced that there was any compelling reason for not awarding release-fee relief in cases of nuisance. Citing *Jaggard v Sawyer*, his Lordship remarked, 'If it can be done in trespass I do not at present see why it should not in principle be done in nuisance in a case like this…'[163]

[158] ibid, [248].
[159] ibid.
[160] ibid.
[161] See, eg, *Jaggard v Sawyer* [1995] 1 WLR 269; *Wrotham Park v Parkside Homes* [1974] 1 WLR 798 (Ch).
[162] [2014] UKSC 13, [2014] AC 822, [248].
[163] ibid, [173].

It is unfortunate that the Court in *Lawrence* did not more clearly recognise the role that gain-based relief can play in balancing the interests of the parties. Individuals' rights should not be lightly sacrificed on the altar of public convenience let alone overridden simply because the defendant's economic interest in the matter outweighs that of the claimant. However, permitting one party to expropriate the rights of another is less objectionable if the defendant is required to pay a fair price that reflects the benefit that the defendant will derive from the opportunity. Moreover, it should be borne in mind that the judicial willingness to award injunctive relief had a significant deterrent effect in some contexts and that this is liable to have been considerably reduced following the decision in *Lawrence* to overrule *Shelfer*.[164] The availability of gain-based relief could mitigate this state of affairs. Indeed, in exceptional cases involving egregious breaches of rights, if the courts are reluctant to order mandatory injunctions on the grounds that to do so might be economically wasteful or because an offending development has already been sold by the defendant, they might make use of accounts of profits to strip defendants of their entire gain.[165]

(vi) Is nuisance a special case?

One thing which remains to be seen is whether nuisance may be viewed as a special case in which the court might legitimately exercise the jurisdiction provided under Lord Cairns' Act, while it declines to do so in response to other wrongs. It is unclear whether, following *Lawrence*, the courts will be more willing to award damages in lieu of an injunction in cases involving trespasses. Despite the absolutism apparent in some trespasses decisions on the issue,[166] it is difficult to see that after *Lawrence* the courts can meaningfully maintain that they have no power to interfere with property rights. It might be hoped that the possibility of awarding substantial release fees or even accounts of profits should encourage the judiciary to take a more flexible approach to the exercise of the jurisdiction to grant damages in substitution of an injunction in cases of trespass.

III. Conclusion

Property has served as a symbol of the limits of judicial power. Private property has been presented as providing a quasi-constitutional constraint on judicial action. It is apparent, however, that the courts have shifted from the view that they

164 Rotherham (n 152).

165 On the question of the availability of accounts of profit for torts, see *Forsyth-Grant v Allen* [2008] EWCA Civ 505, [2008] 2 EGLR 16; *Devenish Nutrition Ltd v Sanofi-Aventis SA* [2008] EWCA Civ 1086, [2009] 3 All ER 27. See C Rotherham, 'Gain-Based Relief in Tort after *Attorney General v Blake*' (2010) 126 *LQR* 102.

166 See text to nn 93–104.

have no power to redistribute proprietary entitlements. The anxiety surrounding the judiciary overriding private property rights appears to have substantially dissipated. Equally, the disquiet with judicial engagement in considerations of public policy also seems largely to have vanished. What is less clear is whether the courts will be able to articulate satisfactory guidelines constraining the judicial power to sanction private takings of proprietary rights.

6

Trustees' Powers and Social Justice

MATTHEW HARDING*

I. Introduction

I have two aims in this chapter. First, I want to consider what trusts law has to say about when trustees of express trusts may exercise their administrative and dispositive powers in order to pursue social justice.[1] Secondly, I want to consider whether the trusts law position on trustees' powers and social justice is defensible. I pursue the first aim in Part 2; there, I argue that trusts law permits trustees to exercise administrative and dispositive powers for social justice ends only to the extent that this is within their mandate as trustees. I pursue the second aim in Parts 3 and 4. There, I consider the trusts law position on trustees' powers and social justice from the perspective of political philosophy. At first glance, this perspective might seem an odd one when thinking about trusts law. However, it is far from an odd perspective when thinking about the pursuit of social justice; moreover, much work has been done on the place of private law in political philosophy, and this chapter aims in a modest way to contribute to that wider project. In Part 3, then, I consider the trusts law position on trustees' powers and social justice in light of the work of John Rawls, undoubtedly one of the leading thinkers on social justice in the liberal tradition of political philosophy. I argue that the trusts law position makes broad sense when considered in light of the Rawlsian view of the subject matter of social justice. In Part 4, I consider some arguments for and against the Rawlsian view, arguments which inform a considered response to

* Versions of this chapter were presented at the Modern Studies in the Law of Trusts and Wealth Management conference held in Singapore in July 2015, and of course at the Private Law and Power colloquium held in Brisbane in September 2015. I am grateful to participants in both events, and especially to Paul Finn, for thoughtful and challenging comments. My thanks are also due to Patrick Emerton for detailed and helpful comments on a draft, David Pollard for hugely helpful advice, and Joseph Huntley for outstanding research assistance.

[1] By 'social justice', I have chiefly in mind the object of improving the economic position of the poor or those who lack welfare in other ways. I do not intend this conception of social justice to be controversial; nonetheless, readers who disagree with it should be able to follow the arguments of this chapter in light of their own conceptions of social justice.

the trusts law position from the perspective of political philosophy. I suggest that arguments against the Rawlsian view may remain unanswered, and that we may have to depart from the Rawlsian view if we are to defend the trusts law position from the perspective of political philosophy.

II. The Trusts Law Position

In this part of the chapter, I consider the trusts law position on trustees' powers and social justice. I argue that the trusts law position is that trustees are permitted to exercise administrative and dispositive powers for social justice ends only to the extent that they are authorised to do so by their mandate.[2] A trustee's mandate is to be gleaned largely from the terms of the relevant trust instrument, expressing the specific intentions of the settlor.[3] However, a trustee's mandate also takes shape according to the general purpose of the trust; trustees must exercise administrative and dispositive powers for that purpose, as well as in accordance with the specific intentions of the settlor.[4] In cases of trusts for charitable purposes, the general purpose of the trust takes the form of its constitutive purpose (relief of poverty, advancement of education, etc). In cases of trusts for defined beneficiary classes, the general purpose of the trust emerges from reflection on the overall character or nature of the arrangement that the settlor has put in place, although courts have not said much about how exactly the general purpose of such a trust may be ascertained.[5] In developing the argument that trustees are constrained in the pursuit of social justice by their mandate in light of the general purpose of their trust, I consider first the law on administrative powers, and then the law on dispositive powers.

A. Administrative Powers

The question whether trustees may exercise administrative powers in order to pursue social justice is part of the larger question whether trustees may exercise

[2] On the concept of a trustee's mandate, see also P Miller and A Gold, 'Fiduciary Governance' (2015) 57 *William and Mary Law Review* 513. My analysis may differ from Miller and Gold's insofar as I emphasise that what they call 'service' mandates invariably entail some element of fidelity to purpose.

[3] For ease of expression I use the term 'settlor' even when I have in mind testamentary trusts, trusts created by more than one person and trusts implementing non-donative arrangements (eg pension or superannuation trusts).

[4] See *Balls v Strutt* (1841) 1 Hare 146; 66 ER 984, 149 (Sir James Wigram V-C); *Duke of Portland v Topham* (1864) 11 HL Cas 32; 11 ER 1242, 54 (Lord Hatherley); *Cowan v Scargill* [1985] 1 Ch 270, 288 (Megarry V-C); *Harries v Church Commissioners* [1992] 1 WLR 1241, 1246 (Nicholls V-C); *Re Merchant Navy Ratings Pension Fund* [2015] All ER (D) 298, [228]–[229] (Asplin J).

[5] For some thoughts as to how the general purpose of a pension trust might be discerned: D Pollard, *The Law of Pension Trusts* (Oxford, Oxford University Press, 2013), ch 9.

such powers in order to pursue ethical or social objectives more generally. The administrative powers that are usually in view when this larger question is under consideration are powers of investment. Where the terms of a trust instrument specifically authorise trustees to exercise powers of investment for ethical or social ends, trustees may undoubtedly do so; to this extent, trustees may have scope, within their mandate, to pursue social justice. And, of course, the terms of many trust instruments provide trustees with just such authorisation: so-called 'ethical', 'sustainable' or 'socially responsible' investment products and practices have proven popular and increasingly so. Matters are more complicated where the terms of a trust instrument do not specifically authorise trustees to exercise investment powers in order to meet ethical or social objectives. In those cases, trusts law has proven much more sceptical of the proposition that trustees may have regard to such objectives. At the same time, however, trusts law permits trustees to pursue ethical or social goals where the general purpose of the trust shows that the trustee's mandate extends to the exercise of investment powers in the service of ethical or social goals, even if the terms of the trust instrument do not specifically authorise the exercise of investment powers in such a way.

To substantiate these claims, let me turn first to the well-known case of *Cowan v Scargill*, in which the ten trustees of the British Mineworkers' Pension Scheme had reached deadlock over whether to sign off on an investment plan.[6] Five of the trustees, who had been appointed by the National Union of Mineworkers, refused to sign off on the plan because it contemplated investments in industries that might compete with British coal, and such investments were inconsistent with Union policy. The objectives of the Union trustees seem to have been complex, but it is at least plausible to suggest that among those objectives was a social justice goal: the goal of improving the economic position of British mineworkers.[7] With more confidence it can be said that the Union-appointed trustees sought, in the exercise of their investment powers, to implement ethical and social ends that had been adopted as a matter of Union policy.[8] *Cowan v Scargill* therefore raises the question squarely whether trustees may exercise administrative powers for ethical or social ends.

In responding to this question, Megarry V-C had this to say:[9]

> When the purpose of the trust is to provide financial benefits for the beneficiaries, as is usually the case, the best interests of the beneficiaries are normally their best financial interests. In the case of a power of investment, as in the present case, the power must be exercised so as to yield the best return for the beneficiaries, judged in relation to the risks of the investments in question; and the prospects of the yield of income and capital appreciation both have to be considered in judging the return from the investment.

[6] *Cowan* (n 4).
[7] ibid, 295–96.
[8] ibid, 279.
[9] ibid, 287.

And this:[10]

> In considering what investments to make trustees must put to one side their own personal interests and views. Trustees may have strongly held social or political views … In the conduct of their own affairs, of course, they are free to abstain from making … investments [at odds with their views]. Yet under a trust, if investments of this type would be more beneficial to the beneficiaries than other investments, the trustees must not refrain from making the investments by reason of the views that they hold.

For Megarry V-C, in light of these principles it was simply not open to the Union trustees to exclude a range of investments on ethical or social grounds without regard to likely financial returns.

Cowan v Scargill shows that the trusts law position is that trustees may not pursue ethical or social ends to the extent that their mandate is to produce financial returns for beneficiaries.[11] And, as Megarry V-C noted, in cases where trustees are entrusted with the management of funds on behalf of beneficiaries, their likely mandate is to produce financial returns for those beneficiaries, unless the terms of the trust instrument specifically provide otherwise. This may not preclude trustees from having regard to ethical and social considerations when working out how best to produce financial returns for beneficiaries; indeed, in its 2014 report, *Fiduciary Duties of Investment Intermediaries*, the Law Commission of England and Wales expressed the view that trustees and other institutional investors might, in certain circumstances, be best placed to choose investments on financial grounds precisely by taking into account certain ethical and social considerations (such as the long-term sustainability of a particular industry, for example).[12] Nonetheless, the trusts law position, as reflected in *Cowan v Scargill*, is that such regard to ethical and social considerations must always remain subsidiary or ancillary to the main purpose of producing financial returns in cases where a trustee's mandate is

[10] ibid, 287–88.

[11] There is an exception, in the trusts law of Manitoba. According to s 79.1 of the Trustee Act CCSM T160, 'A trustee who uses a non-financial criterion to formulate an investment policy or to make an investment decision does not thereby commit a breach of trust if, in relation to the investment policy or investment decision, the trustee exercises the judgment and care that a person of prudence, discretion and intelligence would exercise in administering the property of others.'

[12] Law Commission (England and Wales), *Fiduciary Duties of Investment Intermediaries* (Law Com No 350, 2014), ch 6. Note also the United Nations Environment Programme Finance Initiative's Principles for Responsible Investment, which, at the time of writing, had 1,380 signatories managing some US$59 trillion (www.unpri.org/about-pri/about-pri). In this movement, two reports have proven influential in identifying ways in which institutional investors, including trustees, may pursue ethical and social objectives consistent with an overarching purpose of generating financial returns: Freshfields Bruckhaus Deringer, *A Legal Framework for the Integration of Environmental, Social and Governance Issues into Institutional Investment* (Report for the UNEP FI, October 2005); Asset Management Working Group of the UNEP FI, *Fiduciary Responsibility: Legal and Practical Aspects of Integrating Environmental, Social and Governance Issues into Institutional Investment* (July 2009). A third report takes the view that fiduciary duties require decision makers to take ethical and social objectives into account when making investment decisions, and urges policymakers and regulators to act accordingly: UNEP FI et al, *Fiduciary Duty in the 21st Century* (September 2015).

to produce financial returns.[13] And some commentators go so far as to argue that, given the strictures of modern portfolio theory, a mandate to produce financial returns is necessarily at odds with trustees taking into account ethical or social considerations even in an ancillary way.[14]

I now want to consider cases in which the general purpose of a trust is not to produce financial returns for beneficiaries. In these cases—and again assuming that the terms of the trust instrument do not specifically authorise trustees to exercise investment powers for ethical or social ends—the question whether trustees may make choices about investments in order to pursue such ends is more complicated. *Harries v Church Commissioners* illustrates some of the complications.[15] There, the Commissioners were administering trusts for various charitable purposes entailing the provision of economic support to Church of England clergy. The investment strategy of the Commissioners was called into question by the Bishop of Oxford and others on the basis that certain investments contemplated by the strategy were at odds with Christian belief and practice.[16] Nicholls V-C recognised that the case before him differed from *Cowan v Scargill* insofar as the general purpose of the trusts before him was not to produce financial returns for a defined beneficiary class.[17] At the same time, however, Nicholls V-C recognised that the mandate of trustees of a trust the general purpose of which is not to produce financial returns will usually nonetheless require those trustees to exercise investment powers so as to produce financial returns; after all, producing financial returns is typically both consistent with and an effective way of supporting the pursuit of another purpose.[18] In other words, the absence of a general purpose of producing financial returns is far from a sure indicator that a trustee's mandate authorises her to exercise investment powers for ethical or social ends.

That said, in *Harries v Church Commissioners*, Nicholls V-C recognised that the general purpose of a trust might occasionally be such that trustees are permitted to exercise investment powers for ethical or social ends, even though the terms of the trust instrument do not specifically authorise this.[19] The Vice-Chancellor gave as examples trustees of temperance charities refusing to invest in brewing, and trustees of Quaker charities refusing to invest in arms manufacturing.[20] In cases like these, where contemplated exercises of investment powers would directly

[13] See, eg, S Daykin, 'Pension Scheme Investment: Is It Always Just About the Money?' (2014) 28 *Trust Law International* 165, discussing Law Commission, *Fiduciary Duties* (n 12).

[14] R Thornton, 'Ethical Investments: A Case of Disjointed Thinking' (2008) 67 *CLJ* 396, but see Lord Nicholls of Birkenhead, 'Trustees in their Broader Community: Where Duty, Morality and Ethics Converge' (1996) 70 *Australian Law Journal* 205.

[15] *Harries* (n 4).

[16] The precise relief sought is set out at ibid, 1242–43.

[17] ibid, 1248–49. It must be said, in connection with this aspect of Nicholls V-C's judgment, that the distinction between a purpose of producing financial returns for a defined beneficiary class and a purpose of providing economic support to a group of a particular description is a fine one.

[18] ibid, 1246.

[19] ibid.

[20] ibid.

contradict the constitutive purpose of a charitable trust, Nicholls V-C appears to have thought that a trustee's mandate is likely to authorise her to decline the contradictory investments on ethical or social grounds related to the trust's purpose.[21] Moreover, and perhaps more controversially, in cases where choosing certain investments might, for ethical or social reasons, alienate potential donors and beneficiaries of a charitable trust, Nicholls V-C seems to have thought that trustees may reject those investments for those reasons.[22] To alienate stakeholders in a charitable trust may, over time, frustrate the pursuit of the constitutive purpose of that trust; thus, trustees whose mandate is to carry out that constitutive purpose may in some circumstances be permitted to decline to exercise investment powers in ways that will undermine the purpose even indirectly.

Applying these principles to the case before him, Nicholls V-C noted that the Commissioners' investment strategy did rule out certain types of investments on ethical grounds; for example, the Commissioners did not invest in gambling, alcohol or tobacco.[23] However, Nicholls V-C was also satisfied that the Commissioners pursued ethical objectives within a general framework of producing financial returns for the trust.[24] The Vice-Chancellor considered that, in having regard to ethical considerations in this limited way, the Commissioners were acting within their mandate, given that their general purpose, to provide economic support to Anglican clergy, was best served by seeking to produce financial returns. The Vice-Chancellor refused to endorse the more radical ethical investment strategy urged by the Bishop of Oxford and others, stating that 'the circumstances in which charity trustees are bound or entitled to make a financially disadvantageous investment decision for ethical reasons are extremely limited'.[25] Thus, *Harries v Church Commissioners* reveals an application of the principle that trustees may take into account ethical or social considerations only to the extent authorised by their mandate, even if the case also shows that a mandate might be more accommodating of such considerations in cases of trusts for charitable purposes with ethical or social elements.

In its report on *Social Investment by Charities*, the Law Commission of England and Wales arguably expressed a more robust view than Nicholls V-C about the circumstances in which charity trustees may take into account ethical and social

[21] In *Cowan* (n 4) 288–89, Megarry V-C referred to the possibility that a class of beneficiaries might all hold strong beliefs on ethical or social questions, in which case trustees might be free to reflect those beliefs in exercising their investment powers. To my mind, we might understand this scenario in one of two ways: (a) as a rare case where the general purpose of a trust for a class of beneficiaries (as opposed to a charitable purpose) is not to produce financial returns for those beneficiaries; or (b) as an implication of the rule in *Saunders v Vautier* (1841) Cr & Ph 240; 41 ER 482. For present purposes, I am content to leave open the question of which is the better understanding.

[22] *Harries* (n 4) 1247. The Vice-Chancellor also discussed the difficulties of ascertaining whether stakeholders have one or another ethical or social view, and stated that trustees should not seek to reflect stakeholder views where there is no clear consensus among stakeholders: see 1247–48.

[23] ibid, 1250.

[24] ibid.

[25] ibid.

considerations when exercising investment powers. According to the Law Commission, charity trustees may, consistent with their mandate, make 'social investments', viz, investments that aim both to produce financial returns and to further a charity's constitutive purpose. When making such investments, according to the Law Commission, charity trustees 'are not under a duty to seek the best financial return …, but may consider the overall return, comprising both the financial return and the furtherance of the charity's purposes'.[26] Clearly, on this view, charity trustees have considerable scope to take ethical and social considerations into account when exercising investment powers, so long as these ethical and social considerations relate to the constitutive purpose of their trust. Even though the Law Commission thought that the mandate of charity trustees entailed this freedom of action even under current law, it nonetheless recommended a change to statute law to put the matter beyond doubt.[27] This recommendation is now reflected in section 15 of the Charities (Protection and Social Investment) Bill 2015–2016, before the House of Commons at the time of writing.

B. Dispositive Powers

The case law reveals that, as in the case of administrative powers like investment powers, trustees may exercise their dispositive powers to achieve social justice ends only to the extent that this is authorised by their mandate.[28] In some cases, a trustee's mandate will clearly extend to the exercise of dispositive powers for social justice ends, such as in the case of a trustee of a charitable trust for the relief of poverty who is specifically authorised by the trust instrument to apply trust funds for that purpose. In other cases, the extent to which a trustee's mandate extends to the exercise of dispositive powers for social justice ends may require closer scrutiny. Take, for example, a discretionary trust with a beneficiary class composed of employees and ex-employees of a particular group of companies, along with relatives and dependents of such persons. Such a trust has been recognised as valid and enforceable in law since the landmark case of *McPhail v Doulton* was decided in the early 1970s.[29] The beneficiary class of such a trust might well span the wealthy and the poor, the able-bodied and the disabled, the healthy and the sick, the young and the elderly, and so forth. In other words, trustees exercising dispositive

[26] Law Commission, *Social Investment by Charities: The Law Commission's Recommendations* (September 2014), [1.14].

[27] ibid, [1.35].

[28] By 'dispositive powers', I mean powers of appointment and trust powers given to trustees as such, along with powers given to charitable trustees to apply trust assets for the constitutive purpose of their trust. That said, much of what I say in the text also applies to powers of appointment whose donees are not trustees.

[29] [1971] AC 424. See also, in relation to powers of appointment, *In re Gestetner Settlement* [1953] 1 Ch 672; *In re Gulbenkian's Settlements* [1970] AC 508.

powers in relation to this beneficiary class might be presented, in a localised way, with circumstances that seem to call for the application of some sort of principles of social justice. A fortiori where the beneficiary class is very large, numbering, say, in the tens or even hundreds of thousands.[30] But can such trustees seek to pursue social justice ends when exercising their dispositive powers?

In *McPhail v Doulton* itself, Lord Wilberforce issued some dicta about the duties of trustees exercising dispositive powers under a discretionary trust in respect of a class like the one I have just described:[31]

> [A] trustee with a duty to distribute, particularly among a very large class, would … examine the field, by class and category; might indeed make diligent and careful inquiries, depending on how much money he had to give away and the means at this disposal, as to the composition and needs of particular categories and of individuals within them; decide upon certain priorities or proportions, and then select individuals according to their needs and qualifications.

The duties that Lord Wilberforce described in this passage are duties of justice; they are duties that call for the development and application of allocative principles in respect of competing claims to the assets of the trust.[32] They therefore do not preclude the pursuit of social justice in the exercise of dispositive powers, at least in cases where the terms of the trust instrument do not specifically provide otherwise.[33] But whether or not they permit the pursuit of social justice depends on the general purpose of the trust to which they relate. In the case of *McPhail v Doulton* itself, the arrangement put in place by the settlor was described by one judge as a 'forward-thinking' one for 'furthering the welfare of the employees and those connected with them'.[34] Given that the trust had a general purpose of establishing a scheme for furthering the welfare of the beneficiary class, and given that the trustees were almost certainly presented with circumstances calling for the

[30] Dicta from Lord Wilberforce in *McPhail* ibid, 457 suggest that in some cases, a very large beneficiary class might, in and of itself, render a trust invalid; and see also *R v District Auditor, ex p West Yorkshire Metropolitan County Council* [1986] RVR 24. However, other cases have suggested that a very large beneficiary class will only be problematic where, in light of the size of the class, trustees are unable sensibly to discern their mandate: *In re Manisty's Settlements* [1974] 1 Ch 17, 26, 29 (Templeman J); *In re Hay's Settlement Trusts* [1982] 1 WLR 202, 212 (Megarry V-C).

[31] *McPhail* (n 29) 449.

[32] Recognition that the principled allocation of resources in response to competing claims is a matter of justice is as old as Aristotle: *Nichomachean Ethics* (D Ross trans, Oxford, Oxford University Press, 1925), bk V.

[33] They do preclude the application of certain principles of justice, such as the principle of equal division: *McPhail* (n 29) 451, 457. The circumstances in which the execution of a discretionary trust might call for equal division have been much traversed by judges over the centuries: see, eg, *Moseley v Moseley* (1673) Rep Temp Finch 53; 23 ER 28; *Clarke v Turner* (1694) 2 Freeman 198; 22 ER 1158; *Warburton v Warburton* (1702) IV Brown 1; 2 ER 1; *Harding v Glyn* (1739) 1 Atk 469, 26 ER 299; *Gower v Mainwaring* (1750) 2 Ves Sen 87, 28 ER 527; *Kemp v Kemp* (1801) 5 Ves Jun 849, 31 ER 891. Equal division is not necessarily inconsistent with the pursuit of social justice, but neither is it a promising way to achieve it in circumstances where claimants are differently situated prior to allocative decisions being made.

[34] *In re Baden's Deed Trusts (No 2)* [1973] Ch 9, 17 (Sachs LJ).

application of principles of social justice because of the character of the beneficiary class, it seems plausible to suggest that the trustees' mandate in *McPhail v Doulton* permitted them to have regard to social justice considerations in exercising their dispositive powers consistent with their duties. That said, in other circumstances the general purpose of a settlor in creating a discretionary trust with a beneficiary class like the one in *McPhail v Doulton* might be inconsistent with trustees seeking to achieve social justice in exercising their dispositive powers. This might be the case where, for example, the settlor has put in place a scheme for rewarding service or merit as opposed to providing welfare.[35]

Now consider a discretionary trust whose beneficiary class is limited to members of a particular family. The general purpose of such a trust is likely to entail nothing more sophisticated than the provision of material benefits, typically in the form of income or capital, to members of the beneficiary class. In this sort of trust, the mandate of trustees seems not to authorise the exercise of dispositive powers for social justice objectives, except, as always, where the terms of the trust instrument provide otherwise. So, for example, the trustees of such a trust may not exercise dispositive powers so as to ensure that the beneficiaries pay a just amount of income tax, or with an eye to breaking up concentrated wealth. The wide-ranging duties of justice described by Lord Wilberforce in relation to a beneficiary class like the one in *McPhail v Doulton* seem obviously inapplicable to a typical family trust;[36] nonetheless, the trustees of any discretionary trust, no matter what the beneficiary class, owe duties to the beneficiaries to exercise their dispositive powers carefully, to have regard when doing so to the claims of beneficiaries,[37] and, above all else, to exercise their powers consistently with the general purpose of the trust. These duties rule out any exercise of dispositive powers inconsistent with the purpose of providing material benefits to beneficiaries and, as a result, seem to leave no room for social justice considerations.

One consequence of the trusts law position is that where trustees exercise a dispositive power in favour of a particular beneficiary because they consider this the best way to achieve a social justice objective, the disposition in question is liable to be declared invalid as a 'fraud on the power'.[38] The case of *X v A* illustrates the point.[39] There, the trustees of a family discretionary trust sought directions as to whether they could exercise a dispositive power in favour of a particular beneficiary so as to pay to her a 'very substantial part' of the capital of the trust.[40]

[35] Similarly, where a charitable trust for the advancement of education funds scholarships based on merit or potential, rather than need, the scope for trustees to take into account social justice considerations in selecting scholars may be limited.

[36] Thus, James Penner asserts that where a court is called on to execute a family discretionary trust with a small beneficiary class, equal distribution is required: J Penner, *The Law of Trusts*, 8th edn, (Oxford, Oxford University Press, 2014) [3.57].

[37] See generally *Gartside v Inland Revenue Commissioners* [1968] AC 553 (HL).

[38] For the principles governing frauds on a power: *Vatcher v Paull* [1915] AC 372, 378 (Lord Parker); *Wong v Burt* [2005] 1 NZLR 91; *Kain v Hutton* [2008] 3 NZLR 589, [46]–[54] (Tipping J).

[39] [2005] EWHC 2706.

[40] ibid, [1].

The beneficiary in question, who was the wife of the settlor and had his full support, wanted to donate the capital to a charity, and the evidence suggested strongly that the beneficiary's plan was to pursue social justice objectives by making that donation.[41] Justice Hart endorsed the proposition that, in a trust whose general purpose is the provision of material benefits to beneficiaries, where a dispositive power is exercised in favour of a beneficiary, it must be so as to generate a material benefit for that beneficiary; and he found that on the facts before him that demand was not satisfied. The beneficiary would not benefit materially by giving away to charity practically her whole interest under the trust, even though she felt herself under a moral obligation to do so.[42] Thus, Hart J recognised that where trustees exercise a dispositive power in favour of a beneficiary because they, together with that beneficiary, share a social justice objective, or even because they wish to enable a beneficiary to pursue a social justice objective, the trustees' action is liable to be declared invalid as a fraud on the power. Such trustees exceed their mandate, as disclosed by the terms of the trust instrument and the general purpose for which the trust was created.

At first glance, Hart J's decision in *X v A* seems at odds with the decision of Pennycuick J in the earlier case of *In re Clore's Settlement Trusts*.[43] In that case, Pennycuick J upheld the exercise of a power of advancement to pay to a charity a sum of money that a beneficiary felt morally bound to donate to that charity. On a wide reading, Pennycuick J's reasoning suggests that a beneficiary may derive material benefit simply by having his moral obligation discharged;[44] on a narrower reading, the reasoning suggests that such material benefit is ascertainable where trustees, by exercising a dispositive power, relieve a beneficiary from discharging a felt moral obligation from other resources.[45] In *X v A*, Hart J noted that the proposed capital distribution exceeded by far the beneficiary's other resources; thus, Hart J thought that the distribution would not improve the beneficiary's material situation because the beneficiary was not in a position to make the donation except with the capital of the trust.[46] This reasoning seems deficient; it fails to account for the possibility of a partial discharge of felt moral obligation or the financial burdens associated with it. Moreover, on a wide reading, the reasoning of Pennycuick J in *In re Clore's Settlement Trusts* seems difficult to accept in the case of a trust whose general purpose is the provision of material benefits to beneficiaries; how can the discharge of a moral obligation ever count as a material benefit? But for present purposes, these points are not germane. More important is the fact that neither

[41] ibid, [17], [20]. The beneficiary and the settlor also seemed to have the aim of ensuring that their children and grandchildren would not be corrupted by significant inherited wealth: ibid, [46]. For Hart J, the trustees were not free to take that consideration into account when exercising their dispositive powers: ibid, [47].

[42] ibid, [34], [42]–[43].

[43] [1966] 1 WLR 955.

[44] ibid, 959.

[45] ibid.

[46] [2005] EWHC 2706, [42].

In re Clore's Settlement Trusts nor *X v A* supports the proposition that, in the case of a trust the general purpose of which is to provide material benefits to beneficiaries, a dispositive power can be exercised to pursue a social justice objective. Both cases stand for the proposition that such an exercise of power is permissible only where the social justice objective is ancillary or coincidental to the purpose of generating material benefits for beneficiaries, even if the two cases differ on the question of what counts as such a material benefit.

III. The Trusts Law Position and the Rawlsian View

John Rawls's great contribution to moral and political philosophy is his theory of social justice.[47] For Rawls, the content of social justice is given by two general principles, according to which, broadly speaking: (a) certain civil and political liberties are to be secured for all; and (b) social and economic inequalities are to be arranged so that they redound to the greatest benefit of the worst off in the community and are attached to offices and positions open to all under conditions of fair equality of opportunity.[48] Much has been written about Rawls's principles of social justice, and about his theoretical derivation of the principles, but those aspects of Rawls's work are not my primary concern in what follows; as I mentioned at the outset, I am content for present purposes to work with a provisional sense of social justice as centrally oriented at improving the position of the poor or those who lack welfare in other ways. Instead, I want to focus on Rawls's account of the subject matter of social justice, ie, his account of the social and economic affairs to which principles of social justice, whatever they might be, apply.

Rawls's account of the subject matter of social justice is developed with reference to what he calls the 'basic structure' of society.[49] For Rawls, social, political and economic arrangements that are within the basic structure are subject to principles of social justice and must be organised so as to serve those principles; in contrast, arrangements that are not within the basic structure may be organised, consistent with the demands of social justice, on bases other than social justice. Key, then, to Rawls's account of the subject matter of social justice is his understanding of the basic structure. As interpreters of Rawls's work have often pointed out, his understanding of the basic structure is not easy to discern from his writings. In his most sustained treatment of the topic, Rawls identifies as within the basic structure: 'the political constitution'; 'the legally recognized forms of property'; 'the organization of the economy'; 'the nature of the family'; 'such operations as income and inheritance taxation designed to even out the ownership of property'; 'rules that govern

[47] J Rawls, *A Theory of Justice*, revd edn (Oxford, Oxford University Press, 1999).
[48] ibid, 266.
[49] The idea of the basic structure is first introduced by Rawls in ibid, 6.

the transactions and agreements between individuals and associations (the law of contract and so on)'; and 'rules relating to fraud and duress'.[50] But this laundry list of institutions does not take us far in understanding precisely how the basic structure is constituted, and what is and is not within it, because it gives us no clear sense of the role of the basic structure in a political community and it is only with such a sense that we may grasp why, for Rawls, the basic structure is of special interest from the perspective of social justice.

More guidance can be obtained by reflecting on Rawls's famous 'division of labour' argument. According to this argument, the role of the basic structure is 'to secure just background conditions against which the actions of individuals and associations take place'.[51] For Rawls, once we appreciate that the basic structure performs this role, we are in a position to see why it is important that the basic structure conform to principles of social justice; if we care about social justice, and if individual and associational action within the basic structure is apt, over time, to produce social injustice, then we have reason to want the basic structure to keep this tendency in check and to correct it where necessary. Rawls spells this out in an important passage:[52]

> [W]e arrive at the idea of a division of labor between two kinds of social rules, and the different institutional forms in which these rules are realized. The basic structure comprises first the institutions that define the social background and includes as well those operations that continually adjust and compensate for the inevitable tendencies away from background fairness … [These rules] are framed to leave individuals and associations free to act effectively in pursuit of their ends and without excessive constraints … What we look for, in effect, is an institutional division of labor between the basic structure and the rules applying directly to individuals and associations and to be followed by them in particular transactions. If this division of labor can be established, individuals and associations are then left free to advance their ends more effectively within the framework of the basic structure, secure in the knowledge that elsewhere in the social system the necessary corrections to preserve background justice are being made.

In light of the division of labour argument, institutions like property, contract and the family are within the basic structure insofar as they establish parameters within which 'post-institutional' individual and associational action takes place.[53] To the extent that these institutions establish such parameters, they must be reconciled

[50] J Rawls, *Political Liberalism* (New York, Columbia University Press, 1996), 258, 268.

[51] ibid, 266.

[52] ibid, 268–69. See also at 282–84; J Rawls, *Justice as Fairness: A Restatement* (E Kelly ed, Cambridge Mass, Belknap Press, 2001), 10, 53–54.

[53] This paragraph, and my understanding of the implications of the division of labour argument more generally, owe much to K Kordana and D Tabachnik, 'Rawls and Contract Law' (2005) 73 *George Washington Law Review* 598; K Kordana and D Tabachnik, 'The Rawlsian View of Private Ordering' (2008) 25 *Social Philosophy and Policy* 288; S Scheffler, 'Distributive Justice, the Basic Structure and the Place of Private Law' (2015) 35 *OJLS* 213; P Emerton and K James, 'The Justice of the Tax Base and the Case for Income Tax' in M Bhandari (ed), *Philosophical Foundations of Tax Law* (Oxford, Oxford University Press, forthcoming). The phrase 'post-institutional' I borrow from Kordana and Tabachnik.

with the demands of social justice on the Rawlsian view. In contrast, the norms to which post-institutional action within institutional settings is susceptible will vary from institution to institution, but such norms will typically derive their content from the purpose to which actors in a particular institutional setting are oriented by virtue of being in that setting.[54] A similar, albeit broader, idea may be found in Rawls's early essay, 'Two Concepts of Rules'.[55] There, Rawls distinguishes between practices constituted by some system of rules on the one hand, and action within practices so defined on the other hand, and he argues that the justification of action within a practice is a matter of appealing to the practice itself, and not a matter of appealing to the considerations that go to justifying the system of rules constituting the practice. Rawls's general position on the justification of practices and of action within practices helps to inform our understanding of his conception of the basic structure and the sense in which he argues that the institutions within it are susceptible to social justice considerations.[56]

To reinforce these points, consider the family. There is no doubt that Rawls considers the family to be within the basic structure and to that extent within the range of subject matter of social justice. However, as Rawls makes clear in his later work, the family is within the basic structure only in a particular sense.[57] He recognises that action within the family is post-institutional action of the type about which social justice has nothing to say; thus, for Rawls, parents are not subject to principles of social justice in making decisions about how to allocate family resources among their children.[58] Rather, Rawls's view is that it is rules and practices establishing the family as a framework for individual and associational action that are within the basic structure. For Rawls, it is these constitutive rules and practices—for example, the legal understanding of marriage or the rules governing the availability and consequences of separation and divorce—that should be reconciled with the demands of social justice.[59]

What are the implications of this Rawlsian view of the subject matter of social justice for trusts law? One implication would seem to be that those rules of trusts law that give shape to the institution of the trust as a framework for individual and associational action are within the basic structure and therefore should be organised in accordance with principles of social justice. It is sometimes assumed that

[54] Rawls, *Political Liberalism* (n 50) 259, 262; Rawls, *Justice as Fairness* (n 52) 10–11.

[55] J Rawls, 'Two Concepts of Rules' (1955) in S Freeman (ed), *John Rawls: Collected Papers* (Cambridge Mass, Harvard University Press, 1999) 20.

[56] 'The crucial point, then, is that Rawls focuses on the fundamental "rules of the game" and not on what moves players are morally free or constrained to make within a particular game in progress. To stay with the metaphor for a moment, the question is not whether in an ongoing poker game those who have won a great deal shouldn't (be made to) give some of their winnings to those who have lost nearly all they had. The question is whether we ought not rather play some other game that does not, time and again, produce destitute losers': T Pogge, *Realizing Rawls* (Ithaca, Cornell University Press, 1989), [1.5].

[57] Rawls, *Justice as Fairness* (n 52) 162–68.

[58] ibid, 10 n 8.

[59] See especially ibid, 167.

Rawls's theory of justice has implications only for public law including the tax and transfer system, and not for private law. This is clearly not the case if Rawls's division of labour argument is understood in the way I have set out above. Indeed, as Anthony Kronman has pointed out, the legal regulation of private law institutions might, depending on circumstances, be a particularly effective way to respond to the demands of social justice.[60] Kronman has in mind contractual regulation via such mechanisms as minimum wage laws, but his general point applies just as much to the regulation of trusts as frameworks for individual and associational action as it does to contracts.

The question of what trusts law might look like if it were appropriately responsive to social justice demands is not easily answered from a Rawlsian perspective because, from that perspective, what social justice requires of one institution within the basic structure cannot be known with certainty except in conjunction with knowledge of what social justice requires of the basic structure as a whole.[61] In the absence of such a holistic inquiry, the implications of social justice for trusts law can only be approached as a matter of conjecture. That said, some design features of trusts law present as likely candidates for inspection from the Rawlsian viewpoint, simply because they seem readily to demand evaluation in light of social goals.[62] One example would seem to be the law of perpetuities. It seems plausible to assert that, all else being equal, social justice is not served by a legal framework that permits large holdings of wealth to be maintained and augmented by families across generations, especially if, as a result of such practices, the wealth is shielded from tax.[63] Of course, trusts enable families to preserve their holdings in just this way, and historically this has been one of their primary attractions.[64] To the extent that the law of perpetuities requires such holdings to be broken up,

[60] A Kronman, 'Contract Law and Distributive Justice' (1980) 89 *Yale Law Journal* 472. Louis Kaplow and Steven Shavell argue that the regulation of private law institutions is less economically efficient than a tax and transfer scheme as a method of redistributing income for social justice ends: 'Why the Legal System is Less Efficient than the Income Tax in Redistributing Income' (1994) 23 *Journal of Legal Studies* 667. But as Kordana and Tabachnik point out, social justice, at least on a Rawlsian view, is about more than income redistribution; among other things it is about the allocation of the 'social bases of self-respect' and this good might be more efficiently redistributed to the worst off where legal rules prevent others from treating them unjustly than where such rules permit the unjust treatment and then tax those who mete it out: 'Rawls and Contract Law' (n 53) 617–18.

[61] See L Sugin, 'Theories of Distributive Justice and Limitations on Taxation: What Rawls Demands from Tax Systems' (2004) 72 *Fordham Law Review* 1991.

[62] For some reflections on social dimensions of the trust: see MW Lau, *The Economic Structure of Trusts* (Oxford, Oxford University Press, 2011), 156–58, discussing P Lepaulle, 'An Outsider's View Point of the Nature of Trusts' (1928) 14 *Cornell Law Review* 52.

[63] Thus Rawls's preference for what he calls a 'property-owning democracy': *Justice as Fairness* (n 52) 135–48.

[64] See M Chesterman, 'Family Settlements on Trust: Landowners and the Rising Bourgeoisie' in G Rubin and D Sugarman (eds), *Law, Economy and Society, 1750–1914: Essays in the History of English Law* (Abingdon, Professional Books Ltd, 1984) 124, 143–44, arguing that the use of strict settlements by landed families in the 18th and 19th centuries had significant distributive implications for society as a whole and may have frustrated the development of industrial capitalism in Britain.

and possibly subjected to tax, every now and again, it would seem to be the sort of design feature that is apt to render trusts law consistent with social justice. However, developments in the law of perpetuities in the United States, as a result of which family holdings may be maintained and augmented in perpetuity within a trust structure, are to be viewed with suspicion in light of the Rawlsian view.[65]

For present purposes, what is of most interest is how we should understand trustees' exercises of their administrative and dispositive powers, given the Rawlsian view of the subject matter of social justice. What are the implications of the Rawlsian view for such exercises of trustees' powers? Here, it is helpful to draw a distinction between: (a) the rules empowering settlors to confer administrative and dispositive powers on trustees and the rules imposing duties on trustees in the exercise of those powers; and (b) exercises of administrative and dispositive powers themselves. On the Rawlsian view, the rules described at (a) help to constitute the trust as a framework for individual and associational action; they are, to that extent, within the basic structure and should, in conjunction with everything else in the basic structure, serve principles of social justice. Thus, from a Rawlsian perspective, it might be open to argue that settlors should be precluded from empowering trustees in ways that are likely to generate patterns of social injustice when taken in aggregate across time; it might also be open to argue that trusts law should contain a default rule imposing duties on trustees that, if discharged, would tend to produce outcomes conducive to social justice. If restricting the options available to settlors or imposing certain duties on trustees were the best way to ensure that the basic structure conformed to principles of social justice, then the Rawlsian would see no reason not to reform trusts law accordingly.[66]

In contrast with the rules conferring and circumscribing trustees' administrative and dispositive powers, on a Rawlsian view the exercise by trustees of such powers amounts to post-institutional action of the type about which social justice has nothing to say. In other words, the justification of the exercise of trustees' powers is not a matter of conformity with principles of social justice; it is, rather, a matter of the conformity of such exercise with norms entailed in the institutional framework of the trust. Earlier we saw that, on a Rawlsian view, the norms

[65] See also I Goodwin, 'How the Rich Stay Rich: Using a Family Trust Company to Secure a Family Fortune' (2010) 40 *Seton Hall Law Review* 467; A Hofri-Winogradow, 'The Stripping of the Trust: From Evolutionary Scripts to Distributive Results' (2014) 75 *Ohio State Law Journal* 529; J Soled and M Gans, 'Asset Preservation and the Evolving Role of Trusts in the Twenty-First Century' (2015) 72 *Washington and Lee Law Review* 257. Compare A Hofri-Winogradow, 'How Harmful is Trust Proliferation?' (SSRN, posted 10 July 2015), presenting empirical findings that suggest that at least some perpetual and long-term trusts may not in fact endure for their legally permitted lifespan.

[66] It might be objected that reforming trusts law in these ways would interfere too greatly with a settlor's freedom to choose the terms of her trust. But from a Rawlsian perspective 'freedom of trust', just like freedom of contract, only makes sense as post-institutional; in other words, for a Rawlsian it makes no sense to be concerned about freedom of trust except within an institutional scheme that is justified in accordance with the demands of social justice. See Kordana and Tabachnik, 'Rawls and Contract Law' (n 53) 616–17 and, more generally, L Murphy and T Nagel, *The Myth of Ownership: Taxes and Justice* (Oxford, Oxford University Press, 2002).

that guide post-institutional action within an institutional setting will typically derive their content, not from principles of social justice, but rather from the purposes to which the institution in question is directed. And when we look to the norms guiding the post-institutional action of trustees, we find that the content of those norms is derived in just this way. Although the precise content of a trustee's mandate varies from case to case depending on the terms of the trust instrument and the general purpose of the trust, the justification of the general requirement that trustees act within mandate, perhaps the key post-institutional norm guiding the action of trustees, is best understood with reference to the various purposes towards which trusts are oriented. Thus, the emphasis in trusts law on not permitting trustees to exceed their mandates is hardly surprising from the Rawlsian perspective, even though this means that in most circumstances trustees may not pursue the social justice that is the primary concern of Rawls's theory. Rather, this general strategy, the strategy characteristic of the trusts law position on trustees' powers and social justice, makes broad sense when considered in light of the vision of social ordering that emerges from Rawls's division of labour argument and his early work in 'Two Concepts of Rules', viz, the vision of the basic structure as the site of concern about social justice, establishing institutional frameworks and arrangements within which individual and associational action may be carried out in pursuit of a range of other purposes.

IV. Challenges to the Rawlsian View and the Trusts Law Position

I hope to have said enough to show that the trusts law position on trustees' powers and social justice makes broad sense in light of what I have called the Rawlsian view. That the trusts law position is sensible to the Rawlsian in this way suggests that the trusts law position might turn out to be defensible from the perspective of Rawlsian political philosophy. And yet at the same time it seems counterintuitive that a theory that describes justice as the 'first virtue'[67] of social institutions could remain unmoved by the fact that trustees who seek to pursue social justice may not do so except to the extent permitted by their mandates. GA Cohen, for example, argues in his influential critique of Rawls's account of the subject matter of social justice that it makes no sense to care about the justice of the basic structure but not at the same time care about the justice of post-institutional action within institutional settings delivered by the basic structure.[68] As Cohen points out, such post-institutional action has just the sorts of distributive consequences

[67] Rawls, *A Theory of Justice* (n 47) 3.

[68] G Cohen, *If You're An Egalitarian, How Come You're So Rich?* (Cambridge Mass, Harvard University Press, 2000), 136–42.

that are of interest from the perspective of social justice; this is, after all, why Rawls thinks that the justice of the basic structure is something to worry over and maintain. Given that post-institutional action has these consequences, Cohen argues, a theory that seeks to spell out what must obtain if a just society is to be achieved should have something to say about post-institutional action as well as the basic structure. Thus, on Cohen's account, Rawls's division of labour argument restricts the scope of his theory in ways that cannot be justified given the concern for social justice that motivates the theory.[69]

Cohen's argument suggests that it is not enough, at least for liberals who care about social justice, simply to assume that trustees, when exercising administrative and dispositive powers, should not be part of the project of pursuing social justice. Instead, questions should be asked about how trustees exercise their powers in light of distributive patterns of interest from the perspective of social justice, as well as questions about how trustees, by exercising their powers in different ways, might do better from a social justice perspective in light of those distributive patterns. Imagine that it could be shown that, as a general proposition, trustees by exercising their dispositive powers in certain ways were minimising the tax liabilities of the wealthy and thereby contributing to distributive consequences of concern given the demands of social justice. In light of Cohen's argument, it would be insufficient to point out that, because such exercises of dispositive power were not part of the basic structure, they stood to be justified, not in accordance with the demands of social justice, but rather in accordance with the norms entailed in the trust as a framework for post-institutional action. Similarly in the case where trustees of large pension or superannuation trusts could, if they invested trust funds in a coordinated fashion, solve certain problems associated with social injustice.[70] On Cohen's view, to say that such trustees should not be responsible for bringing about those social justice goals because social justice is a matter for the basic structure is indefensible.

Cohen's argument is a serious challenge both to the Rawlsian view of the subject matter of social justice and to the trusts law position insofar as that position is consistent with the Rawlsian view. If Cohen's argument is accepted, we should probably start thinking about the reform of trusts law so that, for example, it contains a default rule at least permitting and perhaps even requiring trustees to have regard to social justice considerations when exercising their administrative and dispositive powers, even in cases where their mandates do not authorise this.[71] To endorse such a rule would be to collapse the distinction between the basic structure and

[69] Cohen is careful to explain that his argument about the subject matter of social justice does not entail any particular conclusion about the content of principles of social justice that should apply to post-institutional action: ibid, 141–42.

[70] See the example of Finland, discussed in O Kangas, *Pensions and Pension Funds in the Making of a Nation State and a National Economy: The Case of Finland* (United Nations Research Institute for Social Development Social Policy and Development Working Paper No 25, March 2006).

[71] In this regard, we might view the trusts law of Manitoba as a model: see (n 11).

post-institutional action within its parameters that is critical to the Rawlsian view and, to that extent, it would represent an abandonment of that view.[72] So what reasons might be offered for maintaining the Rawlsian view, and a commitment to the trusts law position, in the face of Cohen's argument?

One reason, offered by Rawls himself, is that the achievement of social justice is a goal of a type that is just too complex for people to strive for in any meaningful way in their individual and associational lives. Partly because social justice questions only make sense, on the Rawlsian view, when asked in relation to the basic structure as a whole, and partly because achieving social justice across time depends on a range of predictions and counterfactuals that are beyond the capacity of most people to attempt, Rawls thinks that to expect individuals and associations to pursue social justice in the post-institutional setting is to impose on them an 'excessive if not impossible burden'.[73] The state, on the other hand, with its vast apparatus for information gathering and management and production of expert knowledge, particularly on economic questions, is well placed to assess the demands of social justice across the basic structure.

This argument seems strongest when considering post-institutional action on a small scale. The example Rawls gives when articulating the argument is of land being passed from one generation of a family to the next.[74] It seems highly plausible to assert that landowners, making decisions about what will happen to their land when they die, are typically poorly placed to consider the sorts of society-wide distributive questions that are raised by an inquiry into social justice. And given the widespread use of trusts in family and small business settings, Rawls's argument about lack of expertise and resources seems to have something to offer by way of a justification of the trusts law position on trustees' powers and social justice, at least some of the time. That said, many trusts entail post-institutional action on a grand scale. Large pension or superannuation trusts are among the clearest examples, as are large charitable trusts. In at least some such trusts, considerable expertise and resources are available, say within an investment strategy unit or through teams of advisers, to undertake just the sorts of predictive and counterfactual investigations that are required where the demands of social justice are in view.[75] Moreover, a vast amount of information on such questions, produced by government, academics and others, is available in the public domain. Where resources allow, this information can be gathered, reviewed, analysed and used. In the case of such large, well-resourced trusts, Rawls's argument seems to lose much of its force.[76]

[72] See L Murphy, 'Institutions and the Demands of Justice' (1999) 27 *Philosophy and Public Affairs* 251, 261–62.

[73] Rawls, *Political Liberalism* (n 50) 266–67, (the quotation is on 266).

[74] ibid, 267.

[75] For example the Wellcome Trust has an investments team of 37 staff and an investments committee with 14 members: www.wellcome.ac.uk/Investments/Investment-team/index.htm.

[76] If large, well-resourced trusts are better able to discern the demands of social justice, then, all else being equal, there may be an argument for settlors minded to pursue social justice objectives to donate

Perhaps, then, we should be looking for another reason for thinking that working to achieve social justice is an inappropriate burden to place on trustees, at least in the case of trustees with considerable expertise and resources at their disposal. Thomas Pogge offers such a reason in his book, *Realizing Rawls*.[77] It is sometimes argued that the generality of Rawls's theory of justice—the fact that the subject matter of the theory is the basic structure taken as a whole—is a weakness of the theory because it makes difficult the task of drawing on the theory to generate meaningful prescriptions to be applied in law reform and public policy debates.[78] However, Pogge suggests that the generality of Rawls's theory of justice is in fact a strength of that theory. For Pogge, Rawls recognises that in a complex, post-industrial economy whose institutions are inter-related in various ways, some aspects of social justice can be meaningfully addressed only by taking a society-wide view.[79] Moreover, Pogge says, all of the citizens of a political community characterised by such complexity and inter-relatedness have a special sort of moral responsibility to take on, through their representative institutions, the business of striving for social justice. In other words, because of its society-wide dimensions, social justice is properly pursued as a society-wide project.[80] If Pogge's thoughts are sound, then it is inappropriate for trustees to shoulder the burden of pursuing social justice in the exercise of their powers, not—or not only—because they lack the expertise or resources to do so effectively, but rather because morally that burden should not be outsourced to them.

Pogge's thoughts seem to offer a promising line of argument for those minded to defend the trusts law position on trustees' powers and social justice in light of the Rawlsian view. That said, we should be careful not to make too much of them. For one thing, there seems no reason to conclude, from the fact that citizens have a collective moral responsibility to pursue social justice as a society-wide project, that they have no individual moral responsibility to pursue social justice in their post-institutional action as well, at least some of the time. Pogge himself has argued in other work that people have post-institutional duties to change institutions in ways that serve social justice.[81] Moreover, once it is accepted that people have post-institutional duties to make institutions more just, it is difficult to resist the further conclusion that people have post-institutional duties to pursue social justice even where this pursuit is not directed at institutional change.[82] And Cohen has argued that the society-wide pursuit of social justice may depend in critical ways

or 'buy in' to such trusts rather than seeking to implement their social justice goals via more modest arrangements.

[77] Pogge (n 56) [1.6].

[78] See, eg, B Rothstein, *Just Institutions Matter: The Moral and Political Logic of the Universal Welfare State* (Cambridge, Cambridge University Press, 1988), ch 1.

[79] Pogge (n 56) [9].

[80] ibid, [1.6].

[81] T Pogge, *World Poverty and Human Rights*, 2nd edn (Cambridge, Polity, 2008) ch 1. Rawls, too, talks of a duty to support just institutions: Rawls, *A Theory of Justice* (n 47) 293–95.

[82] See generally Murphy (n 72).

on a certain ethos or culture which is likely to flourish only where citizens take an active interest in social justice in their day-to-day lives.[83] It seems difficult, then, to move from Pogge's intuitively attractive thoughts, about citizens' collective moral responsibility to pursue social justice as a society-wide project, to the proposition that it is inappropriate for citizens to pursue social justice post-institutionally in ways not directed at institutions. It is also worth pointing out, although this point is not a philosophical objection, that if the society-wide pursuit of social justice in relation to the basic structure rules out the post-institutional pursuit of social justice, then this includes the post-institutional pursuit of social justice by settlors of trusts as well as trustees. And this seems to mean that settlors who wish to empower or require trustees to pursue social justice, within the mandate that they give to those trustees, should refrain from doing so. The implications for social and ethical investment options, as well as for charitable trusts whose constitutive purposes are oriented at social justice goals, would be significant.[84]

Another sort of reason for endorsing the trusts law position on trustees' powers and social justice might point to the distinction Rawls draws in 'Two Concepts of Rules' between the justification of a practice and the justification of action pursuant to that practice. Earlier we saw that this distinction helps to illuminate Rawls's division of labour argument and how, in light of the distinction and the division of labour argument, the justification of trusts law as a framework for individual and associational action is properly viewed as a matter of social justice, while the justification of trustees' exercises of administrative and dispositive powers within the framework of trusts law is properly viewed as a matter of post-institutional norms generated pursuant to that framework. The overarching post-institutional norm of relevance for present purposes is the requirement that trustees adhere to their mandate. Thus, it might be argued, the trustee who seeks to pursue social justice even though this is not authorised by her mandate is overreaching, appealing to a pre-institutional justification for her post-institutional action. And, in a sense, by appealing to such a pre-institutional justification, such a trustee ceases to act as a trustee, because to act as a trustee just is to act pursuant to a role circumscribed and defined by post-institutional norms like the requirement to adhere to mandate.

As a matter of law, the fact that a trustee ceases to act as a trustee and appeals to pre-institutional norms as a basis for her (in)action does not, in and of itself, justify ordering that trustee to discharge her mandate. For example, there is some evidence that in some jurisdictions, trustees of charitable trusts to fund educational scholarships have refused to exercise their administrative and dispositive powers on the basis that the terms of their trusts have explicitly discriminated against historically disadvantaged groups. These trustees have not been authorised by their mandates to refuse to act in this way; instead they have appealed

[83] Cohen (n 68) 123–28.

[84] For some further thoughts on the general question whether social justice is better pursued by the charity sector or the state, see D Halliday and M Harding, 'Keeping Justice in its Place: On the Division of Labour Between Charitable Organisations and the State', unpublished manuscript on file with the author.

to pre-institutional norms as justifications for their actions.[85] Nonetheless, in several cases courts have not only refused to order such trustees to carry out their mandates, but have also made orders varying the terms of the trusts in question to remove the discriminatory conditions.[86] The effect of these orders has been to deliver to trustees a new mandate consistent with the pre-institutional norms to which the trustees have appealed in refusing to discharge the mandate they were originally given. Indeed, even in *Cowan v Scargill*, where the Union trustees had clearly overreached as a matter of law in refusing to sign off on an investment strategy for social and ethical reasons,[87] Megarry V-C refused to make orders against those trustees and instead urged them to adhere to their mandate in light of his declaration of the correct law.[88]

Putting the legal position to one side, the more pressing question for present purposes is why, as a matter of moral and political philosophy, we might be bothered that the occupant of a post-institutional role steps outside that role by appealing to a pre-institutional justification for post-institutional action. Patrick Emerton and Kathryn James have suggested that, on a Rawlsian view, it may make no sense even to speak of a pre-institutional justification for post-institutional action. Emerton and James point out that, for Rawls, if a constitution is adopted in accordance with the demands of social justice, and a legislative scheme is adopted in accordance with that constitution, and an institutional scheme is adopted in accordance with that legislative scheme, then the demands of social justice are fully met by adherence to the norms of the institutional scheme in question. To appeal to those demands as grounds for stepping outside roles generated by that institutional scheme is to do the impossible.[89] Of course, Emerton and James's argument depends on the existence of a just constitution and on legislative and institutional schemes that are procedurally just in the right ways. None of this can be assumed except in ideal theory, and so their arguments leave open the question of whether trustees can and should appeal to social justice considerations when acting in a post-institutional setting that is less than just.[90] Moreover, even if a just institutional scheme can be presupposed when considering post-institutional action, Emerton and James's argument seems to leave room for trusts law to

[85] The norms in question have been constitutional anti-discrimination norms. In Rawlsian theory, anti-discrimination norms form part of the content of social justice (Rawls, *A Theory of Justice* (n 47) 57–65) and so the constitutional norms to which charity trustees have appealed in these cases are, from a Rawlsian perspective, norms of social justice.

[86] See, eg, *In re Canada Trust Co v Ontario Human Rights Commission* (1990) 69 DLR (4th) 321 (although there the trustees were for a long time reluctant to eschew their mandate and approached the court for directions only after sustained public pressure); *Curators Ad Litem to Certain Beneficiaries of Emma Smith Educational Fund v The University of KwaZulu-Natal* 2010 (6) SA 518.

[87] See *Cowan* (n 4) 293 ('there are some who are temperamentally unsuited to being trustees, and are more fitted for campaigning for changes in the law. This, of course, they are free to do; but if they choose to become trustees they must accept it that the rules of equity will bind them in all that they do as trustees').

[88] ibid, 296–97.

[89] Emerton and James (n 53).

[90] That the basic structure in most and perhaps all societies is, to one or another degree, unjust seems a plausible proposition.

incorporate a default rule, adopted in a procedurally just way, specifying that trustees may or even must have regard to social justice considerations when exercising their administrative or dispositive powers. To that extent, their argument seems unmoved by the division of labour between the basic structure and post-institutional action being collapsed; instead, Emerton and James seem committed to the view that such a collapse is consistent with Rawlsian demands of social justice notwithstanding Rawls's division of labour argument.[91]

Cohen's argument—the argument that for liberals who care about social justice, there is no reason to be interested only in the justice of the basic structure and not in the justice of post-institutional action within the basic structure—seems to present a challenge to the Rawlsian view that has not yet been fully met. To the extent that the trusts law position is consistent with the Rawlsian view, Cohen's argument therefore seems also to present a challenge to the trusts law position. Perhaps in the end the only way to defend the trusts law position in light of Cohen's challenge to the Rawlsian view is to depart from the Rawlsian view and find reasons for maintaining the trusts law position that do not appeal to social justice at all. Such reasons might point to the values that are served by maintaining a social role or office of trusteeship the central norm of which is that trustees must adhere to their mandate.[92] They might point to the detrimental implications for citizens' pursuit of various conceptions of the good life of a world in which the single-minded pursuit of social justice is the dominant type of post-institutional action.[93] In light of such reasons, arguments might be crafted to the effect that trustees, when exercising administrative and dispositive powers, should refrain from pursuing social justice objectives, never mind how such objectives are pursued in the design of trusts law as a framework for individual and associational action. Such arguments would be inconsistent with the Rawlsian view, because their starting point would not be a concern for social justice per se, but rather a concern for values and modes of interaction that can only be understood in opposition to social justice.[94] Thus, it might turn out that the trusts law position is defensible from the perspective of political philosophy only once we turn away from the Rawlsian view that, at first glance, seems in striking ways to reflect it.

[91] In this regard, it seems significant that when considering the prospect of a rule requiring citizens to have regard to social justice considerations in their post-institutional action, Emerton and James appeal not to their argument from procedural justice but rather to the argument that post-institutional actors lack the expertise and resources to make the predictions and counterfactual judgments necessary if social justice is to be pursued: n 53.

[92] As Paul Finn has pointed out to me, courts may find it difficult to control trustees' exercises of discretionary power where such exercises of power are purportedly in the service of social justice ends. Such control, and judicial strategies directed against trustee overreaching and fraud more generally, may be necessary if citizens are to maintain confidence in the trust as a facilitative institution.

[93] See also M Harding, *Charity Law and the Liberal State* (Cambridge, Cambridge University Press, 2014), ch 4; Halliday and Harding (n 84).

[94] That such arguments would not be consistent with Rawlsian commitments becomes even clearer once we appreciate that their visions of ideal social ordering might well fail to be consistent with the demands of Rawlsian social justice. Rawls's own views on the matter are stated unequivocally in *A Theory of Justice* (n 47) 3: 'laws and institutions no matter how efficient and well-arranged must be reformed or abolished if they are unjust'.

7

Undue Influence and the Spiritual Economy

SIMONE DEGELING*

Choosing what to believe, and exercising the right to hold that belief, are of as much concern today as they were when Miss Allcard entered the sisterhood of which Miss Skinner was the lady superior.[1] In addition to the resurgence of traditional organised religion[2] there is a proliferation of personal development courses or so called large group awareness training courses (referred to in this chapter as a 'LGAT').[3] These appear to offer in an apparently of a secular setting some kind of spiritual experience. They involve a search for meaning, an identification of values and some kind of prescription which if followed promises a better life. One such course, The Turning Point, came into broader view after a participant Rebekah Lawrence committed suicide after taking part in that course.[4]

This chapter uses the case of Rebekah Lawrence as a starting point for analysis. It deals with three questions. First, it argues that LGAT cases, if they are not already, ought to be caught by the spiritual advisor category of presumed undue influence. Second, the analysis offers some insights into the normative accounts of undue influence. Scholars disagree as to whether undue influence is best seen as some type of (equitable) wrongdoing or an example of unjust enrichment, or

* I am grateful for the helpful comments and criticisms of colleagues at the Faculty of Law, University of Melbourne and participants at a symposium held at the Faculty of Law, University of Sydney at which earlier versions of this chapter were presented. Kit Barker, Pieter Degeling, Arthur Glass, Jessica Hudson and Keith Mason were also generous in their discussions with me. I am also grateful to Ian Wilkinson for his research assistance. The usual disclaimers apply.

[1] *Allcard v Skinner* (1887) LR 36 Ch D 145 (CA) ('*Allcard*'). Accepted in *Johnson v Buttress* (1936) 56 CLR 113 (HCA) and *Geffen v Goodman Estate* 81 DLR (4th) 211; [1991] 2 SCR 353 (SCC).

[2] See generally J Micklethwait, and A Wooldridge, *God is Back. How the Global Rise of Faith is Changing the World* (London, Allen Lane, 2009).

[3] For example the Turning Point Course run by People Know How. See www.peopleknowhow.com.au, accessed 4 March 2010. Turning Point (and its website) no longer exists.

[4] She '… stepped off a ledge of the second floor window at her workplace to fall to her death'. Report by the Coroners Court of New South Wales into the death of Rebekah Anne Lawrence dated 8 December 2009, Deputy State Coroner M MacPherson ('Coroner's Report') [1].

perhaps both. This chapter concludes that a dual analysis must be possible, but offers a more nuanced way of understanding the wrong. Finally, to the extent that undue influence is properly to be regarded as part of the law of unjust enrichment, the chapter offers some tentative conclusions as to the normative basis of that category. On the assumption that Professor Weinrib's corrective justice account of unjust enrichment is correct, or is at least a working hypothesis,[5] it is argued that undue influence, or at least this species of undue influence (spiritual advisor category) cannot be understood sensibly within a Kantian framework.

I. Rebekah Lawrence and The Turning Point

Rebekah Lawrence died on 20 December 2005. As is recorded in the Coroner's findings, she had attended a self-development course described as a '… journey to the core of the human spirit, developing emotional maturity, intelligence, soulfulness that deepens the quality of life through recollection and the practice of self-mastery'.[6] Her suicide followed immediately on her completion of this course. The expert evidence of a consultant psychiatrist was that Rebekah was suffering a psychosis at the time of her death[7] and that this psychosis was as a result of an 'environmental stress', specifically her participation in the course run by People Know How.[8]

Rebekah was married and was in conflict with her husband about her desire to have a child. Her husband did not share this desire, and there was some talk of separation. She attended eight therapy sessions with a psychotherapist to help clarify these issues and following the positive experience of friends, decided to enrol in The Turning Point course.[9] There was clear evidence accepted by the Coroner that Rebekah suffered no pre-existing psychiatric illness or disturbance, but rather that prior to her participation Rebekah psychologically was a reasonably healthy person.[10] Further, the consultant psychiatrist gave evidence that he had treated other individuals who had attended The Turning Point and other similar courses. Rebekah's response, whilst dramatic, was not unique.[11]

[5] Professor McInnes deftly describes this ambivalence when he notes that '[d]espite occasional dissent, it is generally agreed that the principle of unjust enrichment is *informed by the logic of corrective justice…*' (emphasis added) irrespective which account of corrective justice is employed. M McInnes, 'Resisting Temptations to Justice' in R Chambers, C Mitchell and J Penner, *Philosophical Foundations of the Law of Unjust Enrichment* (Oxford, Oxford University Press, 2009) 112.

[6] Coroner's Report (n 4) citing The Turning Point promotional material [14].

[7] Coroner's Report (n 4) [46].

[8] ibid, [46]–[47].

[9] It turned out that her therapist had also attended The Turning Point Course, both as a participant and as a member of the 'service team', ibid, [10].

[10] ibid, [59].

[11] ibid, [64].

The purpose of the course, according to the Coroner's Report, was to achieve some kind of inner transformation and self- development. It was run over a number of days and was conducted with a 'high degree of intensity',[12] the sessions being described as 'a pressure cooker'.[13] Participants had little time for sleep and a significant component of the course involved '... personal confrontation with past events and difficulties'.[14] The leaders of The Turning Point Course were not trained in therapy or analysis. The techniques they adopted were designed to break down inner psychological defences and participants were warned that they should take the day after the course off from work (Monday 19th December), which Rebekah did.[15] That night Rebekah made several attempts to contact staff from People Know How, described by the Coroner as a '... call for help'[16] but that sadly the staff were simply not equipped to know that this was 'a serious situation and that Rebekah needed urgent medical (or at least psychological) intervention'.[17]

Rebekah returned to work on the morning of Tuesday 20 December and reported that she had '... had a wonderful life-changing weekend'.[18] Having been uncharacteristic in her behaviour all day, by 5.30pm she was acting in a childlike manner. As recorded by the Coroner, '[f]inally, Rebekah was naked repeatedly ranting "I love you David, I love you David." Then she was heard singing as she climbed onto the windowsill and jumped out the window'.[19] Rebekah later died in hospital.

The sad facts of this case obviously raise issues for the legislature in terms of what is defined as constituting therapy, who is entitled to call themselves a 'therapist' (the Coroner recorded that as at the date of verdict, there were no legal restrictions in Australia for practising under the title 'psychotherapist' or 'counsellor' and therefore no public safeguards against untrained or incompetent practitioners in this field)[20] and the regulation of practitioners 'offering services for self-development in order to protect vulnerable members of the public'.[21] Such important questions are beyond the scope of this analysis. In addition, it should be noted that the Coroner did not recommend that charges be laid against the principals of The Turning Point, calling instead for legislative change regulating the self-development industry. Further, the facts could raise questions of liability in negligence and possibly breach of contract. Such issues will not be considered here.

Rather, this analysis seeks to extrapolate beyond the facts of this case to other similar courses where, in addition to potentially suffering the physical and

[12] ibid, [13].
[13] ibid, [21].
[14] ibid, [23].
[15] ibid, [30].
[16] ibid, [33].
[17] ibid, [33].
[18] ibid, [34].
[19] ibid, [37].
[20] ibid, [71].
[21] ibid, [70].

psychological injuries suffered by Rebekah Lawrence, participants transfer value to the organisation, in the form of course fees and the often substantial value of their labour. Typically, participants are encouraged to enrol in a seemingly endless progression of courses which offer the promise of personal happiness and transformation. In addition to the mounting financial costs of these courses, participants are strongly encouraged to 'volunteer' for the organisation—participation in running the organisation itself being held out as a development opportunity and a chance to 'be the person that you want to be'. This chapter looks at such cases through the prism of undue influence.

II. Undue Influence

At the outset, it is necessary to state that the law allows a person to dispose of their property as they wish. Neither the law, nor this analysis, makes any value judgment about these individual choices, or the belief systems which lie behind them.[22] Undue influence as a legal category is concerned to determine '... whether at the time when [the plaintiff] executed the transfer she was under such influences as to prevent the gift being considered as that of one free to determine what should be done with her property'.[23] The doctrine is '...not to save people from the consequences of their own folly but to save them from being victimised by other people'.[24]

The first point for this analysis is therefore to argue that undue influence should presumptively apply to the relationship between participants in LGATs and the organisation conducting this 'training'. Arguably this should be through recognition via the spiritual advisor category. As we know, equity presumes that transactions between those standing in certain relationships with one another will be presumed to be tainted by undue influence (so called category 2A undue influence)[25] unless and until the contrary is shown, and the presumption of influence is discharged. The categories include solicitor and client, trustee and beneficiary, doctor and patient, guardian and ward, parent and child and, relevantly,

[22] Although exceptions can always be found. For example, the remarks of Sir G M Giffard VC in relation to spiritualist beliefs: '... the system, as presented by the evidence, is mischievous nonsense, well calculated, on the one hand, to delude the vain, the weak and the foolish and the superstitious ...'. *Lyon v Home* (1868) LR 6 Eq 655, 682.

[23] *Allcard* (n 1) 173 (Cotton LJ).

[24] *Geffen v Goodman Estate* 81 DLR (4th) 211; [1991] 2 SCR 353, [24] (Wilson J), quoting Lindley LJ in *Allcard*.

[25] Outside England and Wales, the traditional Commonwealth position is that undue influence is described as class 1 (actual) undue influence and class 2 (presumed) undue influence. In 2001 the House of Lords in *Royal Bank of Scotland plc v Etridge (No 2)* [2002] 2 AC 773 ('*Etridge*') emphasised that there was only one unitary category of undue influence, which could be proved in two ways, see [93] and [210]–[228] (Lord Clyde).

spiritual adviser and adherent.[26] Modern cases continue to apply the spiritual advisor category.[27]

The onus of rebutting the influence lies with the defendant who, in order to keep the transfer of value, must demonstrate that the plaintiff is emancipated from the influence. Justice Young et al make the point that it is not always necessary to show independent advice to rebut the presumption, but practically speaking it will often be difficult for a religious body to support the transaction where there has been no independent advice.[28] In *Allcard* itself, it will be recalled that the most persuasive elements of the story were that the rules of the sisterhood forbade communication with 'externs', thus effectively preventing the plaintiff from seeking independent advice. As stated by Sir J Douglas Hazen CJ in *Austin v McCaskill*[29] '… the transfer without having independent advice, there is no doubt that the law regards with suspicion transfers that are made … by practically anyone to some person who has authority or control over him, … [including members of a congregational church to the pastor.]' Similarly, in *McCulloch v Fern*, the plaintiff who was a member of the Church Universal and Triumphant lived in the church community on a rural and isolated property: '… She was isolated from her husband; she was not permitted free communication with her children or anyone else inside or outside the small community of Mrs Fern's followers living on the property … Mrs McCulloch did not have the benefit of legal advice.'[30] Palmer J relied on the unrebutted presumption to find undue influence, although in the alternative found actual undue influence.

[26] *Allcard* (n 1); *Norton v Relly* (1764) 2 Eden 286, 28 ER 908; *Huguenin v Basely* (1807) 14 Vesey Jnr 273, 33 ER 526; *Nottidge v Pince* (1860) 2 Giffard 246, 66 ER 103.

[27] Australia: *Hartigan v International Society for Krishna Consciousness* [2002] NSWSC 810 ('*Hartigan*'); *Khan v Khan* [2004] NSWSC 1189 (was a Mufti who gave advice, but case succeeded as actual undue influence; there was no reliance on any presumption. Refer to [31] and [41]); *Luffram v Australia and New Zealand Banking Group Ltd* (1986) ASC 55–483 (Funds were provided to a spiritual advisor on security of a guarantee/mortgage given by the adherent as security for the debt. Security discharged in part as having been procured under undue influence, but no discussion of substantive equitable doctrine); *McCulloch v Fern* [2001] NSWSC 406; *Quek v Beggs* (unreported decision of McLelland J, Supreme Court of New South Wales, 7 December 1990). Canada: *Austin v McCaskill* (1922) 49 NBR 236, 70 DLR 819; *Gill v Darbar* (2002) BCSC 969; *Harris v Cohen* [1994] WDFL 1597 (religious advisor category undue influence not established on evidence); *Lehman v Kester* (1909) 13 OWR 1205 (undue influence not established on the evidence). England/Wales: *Lyon v Home* (1868) LR 6 Eq 655; *Morley v Loughnan* [1893] 1 Ch 736 (although involving a religious advisor from the Plymouth Brethren, the action succeeded as an actual undue influence case); *Azaz v Denton* [2009] EWHC 1759 (QB) (claim failed due to laches); *Roche v Sherrington* [1982] 1 WLR 599 (claim failed for procedural reasons; defendant was Opus Dei, an unincorporated association); *Tufton v Sperni* [1952] 2 *The Times LR* August 29, 1952. There are also Scottish examples: *Anderson v The Beacon Fellowship* (1992) SLT 111 (Outer House).

[28] P Young, C Croft, and M Smith, *On Equity* (Sydney, Lawbook Co, 2009) 317. See the empirical work of Ridge in the practice of the New South Wales Synod of the Uniting Church in Australia in receiving benefits: P Ridge, 'Legal and Ethical Matters Relevant to the Receipt of Financial Benefits by Ministers of Religion and Churches' (2003) 12 *Griffith Law Review* 91.

[29] (1922) 49 NBR 236, 70 DLR 819, [9].

[30] *McCulloch v Fern* [2001] NSWSC 406, [62] (Palmer J).

There has been at least one case in which we might attempt to make the link between the spiritual advisor category of presumed undue influence and LGATs, or at least to the Church of Scientology, which shares some characteristics with LGATs (although it identifies itself as a religion). *Catt v The Church of Scientology*[31] concerned two former members of the Church of Scientology who sued for the return of money which they claimed had been transferred by them under the force of undue influence to two Scientology-based organisations. The only report of the case that research could locate deals with an interlocutory matter, the claimants seeking (and failing to obtain) disclosure and inspection of documents containing confidential information revealed in so called 'auditing' or counselling sessions in which the claimants participated. The substantive law of undue influence and its application to the case was not discussed by the Court.

The concern for the vulnerable which drives the policy of the law[32] in the spiritual advisor case arguably also exists in the relationship between participant and the LGAT. Such courses promise a system of beliefs and values, a way to a better life, and in addition are explicitly concerned with transformation, spiritual growth and inner change. Participants reveal deeply personal information and experiences, and place deep levels of trust in the facilitators and the LGAT course. Recall the Coroner's description of The Turning Point Course in which '[p]articipants were encouraged to deal with personal issues relating to ego, emotions, body, anger, sadness, sex and stages of consciousness from child to adult; high states of consciousness and what was described as ego defences'.[33] As Kirby P (as he then was) remarked in *Stivactas v Michaletos [No 2]*:

> … the categories of relationship giving rise to a presumption of undue influence are not closed. … it would be unrealistic nowadays to apply the rule to 'religious and spiritual advisers' but not to a social worker having a particular relationship of ascendancy analogous to that which, in earlier times, would have been performed by a religious adviser.[34]

Some difficulty may be caused by the fact that, typically, there is not one identifiable adviser, or leader. LGAT courses are run by a 'leader' and a team of 'volunteers'. However, the recipient of any value transferred by the participant in an LGAT is likely to have some corporate form.[35] There is no suggestion in the cases that there must be one adviser and that it must be the adviser who personally benefits from

[31] *Catt v Church of Scientology* [2001] CP Rep 41.

[32] *Allcard* (n 1) 171 (Cotton LJ).

[33] Coroner's Report (n 4) [17]-[18].

[34] Unreported decision of the NSW Supreme Court of Appeal, 31 August 1993, BC9301874, 4.

[35] Notwithstanding the difficulties experienced by the plaintiff in *Roche v Sherrington* [1982] 1 WLR 599 in suing Opus Dei, an unincorporated association. The plaintiff was a member of Opus Dei who was instructed by the sect to go to Kenya to teach and whilst there his entire salary was either paid to Opus Dei or loaned to an Opus Dei charity. He sought a declaration setting aside these gifts as having been procured by undue influence and an order for repayment. Sherrington and Farrell were chosen as representative defendants. Despite Slade J holding (at 608) that as a 'matter of principle, a transaction between an individual and an unincorporated association may give rise to a presumption of undue influence on the part of the members of the association' and that there was an arguable case of undue

the transfer. For example in *Allcard* itself, although the claim ultimately failed due to Miss Skinner's tardiness in seeking rescission, there was no suggestion that the lady superior benefitted personally from the gifts.[36] Similarly, in *Hartigan*, the plaintiff transferred to the International Society for Krishna Consciousness (ISKCON) title to her rural property. She did not have a spiritual master, who stood in a direct relationship to her, although she did have particular confidence in two, named individuals.[37] Rather, she had read literature and taken some counselling and instruction, both formal and informal, in Krishna Consciousness beliefs.[38] She succeeded in her claim for the realised value of the property transferred to ISKCON.[39]

On many fact patterns, it would of course be possible to fit the LGAT example into the second category of presumed undue influence (category 2B), in which the presumption is raised by the facts, rather than the status of the parties, or indeed into actual undue influence. The point is to realise that the protections offered by the rebuttable presumption of influence ought to be available in the LGAT example. Any advice which might operate to emancipate the LGAT course participant from influence would have to take account of the fact that transfers of value are likely to be small but many over a long period of time.

III. Doctrinal and Normative Foundations of Undue Influence

Scholars disagree about the foundations of undue influence. Broadly speaking, commentary is around two axes: a wrongs analysis and an unjust enrichment analysis. There is also a variant which accommodates the mixed nature of the evidence by arguing that there is *both* a wrong and an unjust enrichment phenomenon. The wrongs analysis posits that liability is a function of some type of breach of duty, for example a duty not to exploit or abuse a position of influence.[40] A different

influence, the claim failed for procedural reasons. The members of Opus Dei represented in the action included many who were not members on the date(s) the plaintiff's salary had been transferred. The requirement of 'same or common interest in the proceedings' was therefore not satisfied. By contrast, The Turning Point was conducted by Zoeros Pty Ltd, trading under the name People Know How, Coroner's Report (n 4) [69].

36 *Allcard* (n 1) 179 (Lindley LJ).

37 *Hartigan* (n 27) [92]–[93] (Bryson J).

38 ibid, [91]. Ironically her gift was a mistaken gift, predicated on her flawed understanding of the requirements of Krishna Consciousness.

39 See also *Tufton v Sperni* (1952) 2 Times Law Reports 516.

40 R Bigwood, 'Undue Influence: 'Impaired Consent' or 'Wicked Exploitation'' (1996) 16 *OJLS* 503; R Bigwood, 'From *Morgan* to *Etridge*: Tracing the (Dis)Integration of Undue Influence in the United Kingdom' in J Neyers et al (eds), *Exploring Contract Law* (Oxford, Hart Publishing, 2009) 379. The wrongs analysis is also discussed in P Birks, 'Undue Influence as Wrongful Exploitation' (2004) 120

model is proposed by Professor Chen-Wishart, described as a 'relational theory'.[41] Under this approach, the 'subtle and complex dynamics of trusting relationships'[42] are accommodated, such that a defendant who violates the substantive or procedural norms implicit in a particular relationship may not be able to enforce any bargain and/or will have to return any benefit obtained. The unjust enrichment analysis, most famously championed by Professors Birks and Chin[43] looks to the weakness of the plaintiff and the effect of the undue or excessive influence on the plaintiff's decision or intention to transfer wealth.

This chapter does not seek to engage, other than in passing, with the debate as to which of the above characterisations is correct. In view of the mixed evidence presented in the cases, it seems likely that offering both unjust enrichment and some type of wrongs-based analysis is required. In a case such as Rebekah Lawrence, where the harms potentially constituted psychological and physical injury, a wrongs analysis may open the door for a claim for some type of equitable compensation in relation to these injuries.[44] There is also the difficult issue of the relationship between any wrong of undue influence and the equitable wrong of unconscionability. It would be very easy to identify vulnerability in the fact of the plaintiff's desire for personal and spiritual growth, this vulnerability being that which is exploited by the conduct of the defendant.

Rather, this discussion makes two points. First, in relation to the wrongs analysis, it suggests that part of the difficulty we have in accepting this view is that we are locked into a version of wrongdoing that is too blunt. Similar arguments have also been made by Chen-Wishart in her search for an account of undue influence that brings into the ledger the motivation and conduct of both plaintiff and

LQR 34, 34–37; J Edelman and E Bant, *Unjust Enrichment in Australia* (Melbourne, Oxford University Press, 2006), ch 10, esp 237–39; P Ridge, 'The Equitable Doctrine of Undue Influence Considered in the Context of Spiritual Influence and Religious Faith: *Allcard v Skinner* revisited in Australia' (2003) 26 *University of New South Wales Law Journal* 66.

[41] M Chen-Wishart, 'Undue Influence: *Beyond* Impaired Consent and Wrongdoing towards a Relational Analysis' in A Burrows and Lord Rodger of Earlsferry (eds), *Mapping the Law Essays in Memory of Peter Birks* (Oxford, Oxford University Press, 2006) 201; 'Undue Influence: Vindicating Relationships of Influence' (2006) 59 *Current Legal Problems* 231; 'Legal Transplant and Undue Influence: Lost in Translation or a Working Misunderstanding' (2013) 62 *International and Comparative Law Quarterly* 1.

[42] M Chen-Wishart, 'Undue Influence: *Beyond* Impaired Consent and Wrongdoing towards a Relational Analysis' in A Burrows and Lord Rodger of Earlsferry (eds), *Mapping the Law Essays in Memory of Peter Birks* (Oxford, Oxford University Press, 2006) 203.

[43] P Birks and N Y Chin 'On the Nature of Undue Influence' in J Beatson J and D Friedmann (eds), *Good Faith and Fault in Contract Law* (Oxford, Clarendon Press, 1995) 57. See also J Edelman and E Bant, *Unjust Enrichment in Australia* (Melbourne, Oxford University Press, 2006) ch 10. Alternatively, it might be possible to view undue influence as a policy motivated unjust factor, where the policy of the law is to protect the vulnerable from such transactions (I am grateful to Professor Bryan for this suggestion). There are of course inherent difficulties in any proliferation of policy-motivated unjust factors.

[44] See generally N Skead, 'Undue Influence and the Remedial Constructive Trust' (2008) 2 *Journal of Equity* 143. Skead documents cases where courts have responded to actual or presumed undue influence other than by way of rescission.

defendant, as well as the outcome of the impugned transaction.[45] Secondly, in relation to the unjust enrichment analysis, to the extent that Professor Weinrib's analysis of the normative basis of unjust enrichment law is correct, this chapter questions the extent to which undue influence can be sensibly understood within a Kantian framework.

A. Wrongs Analysis

Professor Bigwood[46] seeks to account for undue influence as a form of wrongdoing which takes a prophylactic stance in presuming wrongdoing and shifting the burden of proving the fairness of the transaction to the ascendant party. Bigwood is not necessarily looking for positive actions on the part of the defendant. Rather he speaks of manipulative capacity which can be 'passively exploited' to constitute a wrong.[47] This manipulative capacity has its source in a power imbalance which exists between plaintiff and defendant, this imbalance having an interpersonal relational quality. He asserts that '... power, however great, is inert in itself ... to possess power is not necessarily to use it'.[48] I contest this proposition below. However, I note Bigwood does later concede that it might be '... unrealistic to suppose that a person can be so much in another's power as to keep his or her interactions free from even the gentlest influences which result from that power'.[49]

In later work following the House of Lords decision in *Etridge*[50] Bigwood develops his explanation more explicitly to take account of the interpersonal dynamics between the parties.[51] Drawing on the work of Flannigan,[52] and linking relational or so called class 2A and 2B undue influence cases to a principle of fiduciary accountability, he points to the so called 'trust' quality in relationships of influence, trust in this sense being either vigilant trust or deferential trust.[53] Deferential trust exists in 'the sense that the trusting person will defer to the judgment of the trusted person'.[54] Bigwood identifies deferential trust in relationships which are traditionally thought of as presumed categories of influence includ-

[45] Describing dominant accounts as 'one-dimensional': Chen-Wishart (n 42), 203; 'Undue Influence: Vindicating Relationships of Influence' (2006) 59 *Current Legal Problems* 231, 266.

[46] Bigwood, 'Undue Influence' (n 40).

[47] ibid, 508, 512–513.

[48] ibid, 506.

[49] ibid, 507.

[50] *Etridge* (n 25) as a result of which England and Wales have now only one class of undue influence which may be proved through either the route of proving overt pressure on the plaintiff or an evidential presumption of undue influence satisfied via the elements of the existence of a relationship of influence and a transaction calling for explanation.

[51] Bigwood, 'From *Morgan* to *Etridge*' (n 40) 379.

[52] See especially R Flannigan, 'The Fiduciary Obligation' (1989) 9 *OJLS* 285.

[53] Bigwood, 'From *Morgan* to *Etridge*' (n 40) 403.

[54] Flannigan (n 52) 286.

ing guardians and spiritual advisors.[55] By contrast, in situations of vigilant trust '[t]here is typically no deference or vulnerability involved. It is the kind of trust that employers have in their [employees].'[56] A relationship may contain both vigilant and deferential trust.[57] Bigwood contemplates that vigilant trust may be breached 'in many and varied ways, all of which are generally unappreciated by the trusting party or difficult to detect. The law accordingly holds the vigilantly trusted party strictly liable …'.[58] An obvious example of this phenomenon is the liability of the fiduciary where there is a possibility of a conflict of duties, or duty and self-interest.[59] However, of greater relevance is the approach described by Bigwood on infringement of deferential trust. Despite acknowledging the role of deference and the potential for hidden dynamics to be at work in these relationships, breach is apparently modelled as exploitation by the defendant. Even using the language of deferential trust, this account rests on an 'exercise by the fiduciary of … influence over the subordinate party for the fiduciary's own ends'.[60]

Wrongdoing can be understood in different senses. At its simplest, the argument that undue influence is about an equitable wrong being committed by the defendant says that the wrong is absent, in the words of Lindley LJ, when:[61] '… no deception was practiced [on Miss Allcard]; that no unfair advantage was taken [of Miss Allcard]; that none of her money was obtained or applied for any purpose other than the legitimate objects of the sisterhood'. Positive action is required. Bigwood on the other hand constructs wrongdoing to include 'passive exploitation' which exists whenever an ascendant party receives in circumstances where he '… failed to ensure that the plaintiff was emancipated from the dependence or excessive reliance in him'.[62] Unless the presumption of undue influence is rebutted, '… the law raises a presumption of wrongdoing whenever a commercial transaction … takes place between the parties'.[63] Thus, also though not explicitly stated, Bigwood seems to suggest that simply to receive may constitute a wrong. Positive action is not required. However, the model of liability and the language employed by Bigwood, and his view of the relational power balance between the parties, is nonetheless cast in terms of purposiveness in the conduct of the defendant. Passive exploitation is still exploitation. This thread carries through to his later work,

[55] Bigwood, 'From *Morgan* to *Etridge*' (n 40) 412.

[56] Flannigan (n 52) 287.

[57] ibid, 287 and 294.

[58] Bigwood, 'From *Morgan* to *Etridge*' (n 40) 403.

[59] *Commonwealth Bank of Australia v Smith* (1991) 42 FCR 390, 392 (The Court); *Breen v Williams* (1996) 186 CLR 71, 135 (Gummow J); *Birtchnell v Equity Trustees and Agency Co Ltd* (1929) 42 CLR 384, 408 (Dixon J); *Boardman v Phipps* [1967] 2 AC 46, 124 (Lord Upjohn).

[60] Bigwood 'From *Morgan* to *Etridge*' (n 40) 403. See also the discussion of 'passive' exploitation or by 'omission only' at 414.

[61] *Allcard* (n 1) 179 (Lindley LJ).

[62] Bigwood 'Undue Influence' (n 40) 513 quoting P Birks, *An Introduction to the Law of Restitution* (1985) 184.

[63] Bigwood 'Undue Influence' (n 40) 514.

which uses the deferential trust idea, and in which breach of that trust is modelled as a type of exploitation[64] or wrongdoing.[65]

Arguably, this conception of wrongdoing as the defendant's exploitative conduct (whether passive or active) does not easily fit with the presumed undue influence cases. In particular, because relationships of presumed undue influence may be rational and perhaps even constituted by the actions of the plaintiff. In addition, accounts of the defendant's conduct must accommodate the fact that the defendant may in reality do very little except receive the value in question. Part of the difficulty is perhaps that undue influence analysis is cast in terms of power, when a more helpful concept may, in fact, be authority. As is explained below, one understanding (albeit a non-legal understanding) of authority is that authority is power whose exercise is seen as legitimate by the object of that power. Political scientists and sociologists are concerned with understanding power as a phenomenon. Professor Steven Lukes, as is well known, writes about his 'radical' view of power, in which he describes three dimensions of power.[66] As will be seen, the third dimension of power resonates strongly with presumed undue influence. The first dimension is overt power. We know that power is at work because in a situation of conflict of subjective interests in decision-making, one party is seen to win and one to lose. One prevails over the other.[67] The second dimension of power is covert power, the power to control the agenda, the menu of options for decision. By ignoring or sidelining grievances such that they are not up for discussion, and by shaping the options apparently available for discussion and action, power is present. This dimension is about decision-making and non-decision-making.[68] The third dimension of power is very difficult to detect. It is arguably present even when there is an absence of conflict; indeed, it is the very absence of conflict or grievance which hints at its presence. This dimension of power is the ability to influence desires and thoughts; the ability to make individuals want what objectively speaking is not in their best interest and operates to paralyse an awareness of self-interest by 'shaping [the weaker party's] perceptions, cognitions and preferences'.[69] Relationships of authority can typify this third dimension of power. The weaker party does not question the legitimacy of the relationship. Rather, whether it be because of the 'rightfulness' of the defendant's position (for example, in presumed undue influence terms, because she is a spiritual advisor, doctor, parent guardian etc), or because, for example, of great personal charisma, it is the plaintiff or weaker party who clothes the ascendant party with authority. In this way, apparent consensus is produced between the ascendant and the weaker party.

[64] Bigwood, 'From *Morgan* to *Etridge*' (n 40) 429.
[65] ibid, 430.
[66] S Lukes, *Power: A Radical View* 2nd edn (London, Palgrave Macmillan, 2005).
[67] ibid, 19.
[68] ibid, 25.
[69] ibid, 28.

This is arguably precisely what occurs in presumed undue influence cases such as the spiritual advisor and adherent. To speak about the adherent clothing the advisor with authority recognises the adherent's agency in the relationship, in a way which is simply not present when we speak about wrongfulness arising from exploitation. Authority as a concept is sympathetic to the fervour and genuine wish of the plaintiff to transfer value. Indeed, one thing which characterises these cases is the depth of the plaintiff's desire to transfer value. Recall Miss Allcard about whom it was doubted that even advice may not have shaken her desire to gift her fortune to the sisterhood. Similarly the plaintiff in *Gill v Darbar* who transferred her whole estate to her Sikh spiritual advisor:

> For the last century of her life, [the plaintiff] had been in the thrall of Amar Singh. He was the most influential person in her life. She believed he had powers which might be regarded as supernatural: she believed he was a Sant [saint].[70]

If we think about the presumed undue influence relationship in these terms, it is possible to suggest that the wrongfulness lies not in exploitation, or even passive exploitation, but simply in receiving value under the guise of authority. The defendant must remove or dispel his or her authority and act to put the transfer of value beyond it. The wrong lies in receiving value without dispelling authority. In this third dimension of power, it is simply not possible to speak, as Bigwood appears to, of possessing power without exercising it. There is no space in the relationship that is not covered by the power that derives from the authority vested in the defendant recipient by the plaintiff. It is the plaintiff who confers authority on the defendant and all the defendant can do is to attempt to remove or neutralise it. Paradoxically, whether it be by receiving value without removing the authority, or by the very action designed to remove authority, the recipient is exercising power. If we cast the wrongful conduct in this way, the analysis is capable of swallowing even the cases where the recipient is described as being without fault.

B. Unjust Enrichment

As has been said, the other paradigmatic view of undue influence is that it is an example of unjust enrichment. The discussion which follows accepts that view as tenable, and instead queries the extent to which the normative account of unjust enrichment which draws on the work of Professor Weinrib is capable of accommodating undue influence. As will be seen, it will be argued that undue influence sits uncomfortably with Kantian ideas about law. Undue influence may be another instance where non-Kantian ideas about law have a role to play.[71]

[70] *Gill v Darbar* [2002] BCSC 969, [150].

[71] Professor Smith has in relation to policy motivated unjust factors identified instances where non Kantian norms inform the conclusion that a transfer of value violates corrective justice and is therefore unjust. For example, the public law norms which are in play when restitution is given of payments made to public authorities pursuant to an ultra vires demand (*Woolwich Equitable Building Society*

In *The Idea of Private Law*[72] and subsequent, specific work dealing with unjust enrichment[73] Professor Weinrib has attempted to demonstrate how a theory of corrective justice might be used to explain the law of unjust enrichment. Drawing on Aristotlean notions of corrective justice, Weinrib identifies that the parties must be returned to their pre-transactional equality. Aristotle didn't elucidate the nature of this equality, argues Weinrib. Assuming that it cannot be taken to mean equality of material or other wealth, Weinrib imported Kantian notions of right such that before the disequilibrium the parties are equal as self-determining agents: '[t]he equality of corrective justice … [is] … the equality of free wills in their impingement of one another'.[74] Prior to the disruption, the plaintiff and the defendant are equally voluntary, autonomous and self-willed. The actions of either can impair the self-determining agency in the other, thus disturbing their pre transactionally equal state. Corrective justice will be satisfied when the parties are returned to their pre transactional positions as free-willed, self-determining agents.

There have been scholarly and tightly-reasoned critiques of Weinrib's analysis in relation to unjust enrichment.[75] This discussion will not revisit these critiques. Rather, two points will be made. First, to notice that even on his revised unjust enrichment analysis, Professor Weinrib requires wrongdoing by the defendant. This obviously has relevance for the normative account of undue influence. Secondly, to observe that equity (or at least undue influence) is informed by normative concerns which are not easily accommodated in a Kantian analysis. At the outset, it must also be said that this analysis accepts the reading of Aristotle and Kant given by Professor Weinrib in his work.[76]

Turning first to wrongs, even on his revised unjust enrichment analysis, Weinrib insists that some form of wrongdoing by the defendant is required. He explains

v IRC [1993] AC 70) and the forces of distributive justice which inform redistribution of benefits and burdens in a contribution/reimbursement claim. L Smith, 'Restitution: The Heart of Corrective Justice' (2001) 79 *Texas Law Review* 2115, 2144–45. See also S Degeling, 'Understanding Policy Motivated Unjust Factors' in C Rickett and R Grantham (eds), *Structure and Justification in Private Law* (Oxford, Hart Publishing, 2008) 267.

[72] E Weinrib, *The Idea of Private Law* (Cambridge Massachusetts, Harvard University Press, 1995).

[73] E Weinrib, 'Restoring Restitution' (2005) 91 *Virginina Law Review* 861; 'The Normative Structure of Unjust Enrichment' in Rickett and Grantham (n 71) 21; 'Correctively Unjust Enrichment' in R Chambers, C Mitchell, and J Penner, *Philosophical Foundations of the Law of Unjust Enrichment* (Oxford, Oxford University Press, 2009) 31.

[74] Weinrib (n 72) 84.

[75] These include: K Barker '*Theorising Unjust Enrichment Law* Being Realist(ic)' (2006) 26 *OJLS* 609; K Barker, 'The Nature of Responsibility for Gain: Gain, Harm and Keeping the Lid on Pandora's Box' in R Chambers, C Mitchell and J Penner, *Philosophical Foundations of the Law of Unjust Enrichment* (Oxford, Oxford University Press, 2009), 162–80; M Doyle 'Corrective Justice and Unjust Enrichment' (2012) 62 *University of Toronto Law Journal* 229; M McInnes, 'Unjust Enrichment: A Reply to Professor Weinrib' [2001] 9 *Restitution Law Review* 29; M McInnes, 'Resisting Temptations to 'Justice" in Chambers, Mitchell and Penner above 100; L Smith, 'Restitution: The Heart of Corrective Justice' (2001) 79 *Texas Law Review* 2115.

[76] McInnes, 'Unjust Enrichment' (n 75) 30–31.

that '... the law construes as normatively defective a transfer of value in which the transferor did not intend to give something for nothing and in which the transferee accepted what was transferred as not having been given for nothing'.[77] Based on the public (juridical) meaning of the parties' interactions the defendant accepts the benefit when he does not '... take the opportunity to reject a benefit that [he] knows to be (or takes the risk of being) non-gratuitously provided'.[78] In this model, the defendant therefore is only liable when he accepts a benefit as having been given non-gratuitously. This development is designed to meet the criticism, based on the pattern of strict liability in unjust enrichment, that a passive recipient, one who has committed no wrong, may be liable.[79] In the sense that Weinrib is thereby constructing a breach of duty or engaging the conscience of the recipient, wrongdoing is present.

It is possible to map onto this account of the normative defect in the transfer of wealth, transfers of value in relationships which raise the presumption of undue influence. The presumption of influence and the steps equity requires the recipient to take in order to keep the value, usually via emancipating the plaintiff from that influence, could, with relative ease, be cast as the actions required to ensure that the defendant is not taking the risk on a transfer of value, such that their acceptance of the benefit is not an 'obligation-creating condition'.[80] As was discussed above, much turns on how wrongdoing is constructed. If we subscribe to the view that undue influence can be said to be a function of wrongdoing (irrespective of Weinrib's account of unjust enrichment), it sits more easily within the Weinrib scheme. However, to the extent that Weinrib's analysis is still at odds with the liability model in unjust enrichment, the known tensions between that analysis and unjust enrichment continue to play out *if* we regard undue influence as part of the law of unjust enrichment.[81]

In addition to the demonstrated tensions between the Weinrib analysis and the unjust enrichment liability model, it is possible to notice additional difficulties which perhaps arise from the equitable foundations of undue influence. Other work has been done which highlights the particular concerns of equity.[82] The discussion which follows suggests tentatively that, at least to the extent that notions of Kantian right are imported into the normative account of unjust enrichment, undue influence does not sit easily in this framework. To the extent that this corrective justice account of unjust enrichment delegates the normative inquiry of what is 'unjust', non-Kantian ideas about law arguably inform this inquiry when it occurs in equity. Two themes will briefly be discussed: paternalism and prophylaxis.

[77] Weinrib, 'Correctively Unjust Enrichment' in Chambers, Mitchell, and Penner (n 75) 52.
[78] ibid, 43.
[79] ibid, 32.
[80] ibid, 42.
[81] See generally n 75.
[82] For example: L Smith, 'The Motive Not the Deed' in J Getzler (ed), *Rationalising Property, Equity and Trusts: Essays in Honour of Edward Burn* (London, Butterworths, 2003) 53; 'Fusion and Tradition' in S Degeling and J Edelman, *Equity in Commercial Law* (Sydney, Thomson Lawbook Co, 2005) 19.

Kant's Universal Principle of right states that 'any action is right if it coexist with everyone's freedom in accordance with a universal law, or if on its maxim the freedom of choice of each can coexist with everyone's freedom in accordance with a universal law.'[83] As explained by Ripstein,[84] Kant conceives of (equal) freedom as '… one in which each person is free to use his or her own powers, individually or cooperatively, to set his or her own purposes, and no one is allowed to compel others to use their powers in a way designed to advance or accommodate any other person's purposes'. Within a system of reciprocal limits, each person is sovereign.

Each person is free to use their own abilities to identify and then decide to pursue their own purposes or objectives consistent with the freedom of others to do the same. In this model, wrongdoing consists of domination: 'It is not that somebody does something that causes something bad to happen to you; it is that somebody does something to you.'[85] The wrongdoer makes the victim subject to another person's choices, uses their means to advance purposes that they have not identified for themselves, impairs their independence. This system of limits on freedom recognises the right of each person to their own purposiveness, but does not go so far as to require one person to promote the ends of the other. Autonomy in this legal context is very specific and means that we are the authors of our own destiny; we are sovereign and within the system of reciprocal limits, are expected to look after ourselves. This theme is illustrated by an example given by Kant in *The Metaphysics of Morals* when he discusses freedom as an innate right (independence from being constrained by another's choice). He explains (emphasis in the original) that it is acceptable to tell another a lie or promise something insincerely, since it is up to the other to decide whether or not to believe. Consistently with the notion that each person is sovereign, each is free to accept or reject the statement:

> This principle of innate freedom already involves the following authorizations, which are not really distinct from it (as if they were members of the division of some higher concept of a right): innate *equality*, that is, independence from being bound by others to more than one can in turn bind them; hence a man's quality of being *his own master (sui iuiris)*, as well as being a man *beyond reproach (iusti)* since before he performs any act affecting rights he has done no wrong to anyone; and finally, is being authorized to do to others anything that does not diminish what is theirs, so long as they do not want to accept it—such things as merely communicating his thoughts to them, telling or promising them something, whether what he says is true and sincere or untrue and insincere (*veriloquium aut falsiloqiuim*); for it is entirely up to them whether they want to believe him or not.[86]

[83] M Gregor, *Immanuel Kant The Metaphysics of Morals* (Cambridge, Cambridge University Press, 1991) 56.

[84] A Ripstein, *Force and Freedom. Kant's Legal and Political Philosophy* (Cambridge Massachusetts, Harvard University Press, 2009) 33.

[85] ibid, 42.

[86] Gregor (n 83) 63, [238] in the original text.

This commitment to self-reliance and legal self-responsibility is at odds with the paternalistic quality of undue influence. Recall the statements at the commencement of this chapter, which record equity's concern to ensure that the plaintiff is not victimised by another, to ensure that the process by which the decision to transfer wealth is unaffected by undue influence. Arguably, the value being protected in equity does not align with the Kantian model of legal autonomy. Equity often requires the defendant to have regard for the welfare of the plaintiff. On this account of Kantian autonomy, there is no such legal requirement.

The other striking feature of undue influence law, irrespective of whether we subscribe to the wrongs account or the unjust enrichment account, is that equity has prophylactic purposes. The presumption of undue influence operates to prevent harm. In addition to relieving the burden on the plaintiff of showing that a particular transfer is a result of excessive influence, it also operates to call into question others which 'might have been' so influenced. For example, as demonstrated by Ridge, religious organisations which are caught by the spiritual advisor category of presumed undue influence have developed compliance mechanisms to ensure that the donors of those gifts do not do so under any influence.[87] Prophylaxis as a value similarly has tensions with autonomy. However, perhaps to the extent that the role of law is to hinder hindrances to autonomy, prophylaxis can sit within a Kantian framework.[88]

IV. Conclusion

The spiritual advisor category of presumed undue influence remains highly relevant. This analysis suggests that in today's society, spiritual guidance and development occurs in a variety of forms, including through the medium of LGAT training courses. The spiritual economy and its attendant transfers of value continue to require equity's oversight.

There is a debate whether undue influence should be regarded as either or both an equitable wrong and part of the law of unjust enrichment, and important consequences flow from this characterisation. For example, to the extent that it might be regarded as a wrong, the psychological and physical injuries suffered by a claimant such as Rebekah Lawrence would be recoverable, in addition to any transfer of value. As has been said, much in this analysis turns on the way in which the wrong is understood. Scholars including Chen-Wishart and Bigwood have done much

[87] See Ridge (n 28).
[88] See Ripstein (n 84) ch 2.

work to further our understanding of the cases. This chapter has argued for a different and potentially more sophisticated notion of wrongdoing which recognises, for example, the mere receipt of a benefit in a relationship of presumed undue influence and in which we are able to disaggregate this wrongful character from any notion of exploitation by the defendant. Such analysis may be enhanced by a more sophisticated representation of how power over willing subjects is secured.

To the extent that undue influence is properly to be regarded as part of the law of unjust enrichment, Professor Weinrib's account of unjust enrichment comes into view. Research has demonstrated that ideas not compatible with Kantian framework are relevant for the determination of 'injustice' in that model. This chapter suggests that equity is a site for other non-Kantian ideas. At the minimum, this must represent another limitation on Professor Weinrib's account of unjust enrichment.

8

A Public Law Tort: Understanding Misfeasance in Public Office

DONAL NOLAN*

I. Introduction

Although the antecedents of the tort of misfeasance in public office go back at least as far as the early eighteenth century,[1] the cause of action itself is of relatively recent vintage, and can be traced back to *Farrington v Thomson*,[2] a 1959 decision of the Supreme Court of Victoria.[3] The misfeasance tort only really started to gain traction in the mid-1980s,[4] however, and the subsequent proliferation of the cause of action across the Commonwealth culminated in central questions pertaining to the scope of the tort being settled by what has been described as a 'quartet'[5] of leading cases decided between 1995 and 2003 in Australia,[6] New Zealand,[7]

* I am grateful to Mark Aronson, Kit Barker, Peter Cane and Paul Finn for their comments on an earlier draft, and for pointing me in the direction of useful sources. The usual caveat applies.

[1] See in particular *Ashby v White* (1703) 2 Ld Raym 938, 92 ER 126. In the words of Paul Finn, '[f]rom relatively early times, the law of torts, distantly mirroring the criminal law, provided a variety of actions on the case to the citizen injured by misconduct in public office. The modern legacy of this has been the recreation of the tort in misfeasance in public office': P Finn, 'The Forgotten "Trust": The People and the State' in M Cope (ed), *Equity: Issues and Trends* (Annandale, Federation Press, 1995) 144.

[2] *Farrington v Thompson and Bridgland* [1959] VR 286.

[3] In the same year, the Supreme Court of Canada handed down *Roncarelli v Duplessis* (1959) 16 DLR (2d) 689, a case which (although decided under Quebec's civil law regime) also recognised a form of misfeasance liability.

[4] The key decision was that of the English Court of Appeal in *Bourgoin SA v Ministry of Agriculture* [1986] QB 716. Four years previously, academic commentators in Australia had said tentatively that '[a] new tort [of misfeasance in a public office] seems to be emerging', but that the 'very existence of the new tort cannot yet be taken to have been established beyond doubt': M Aronson and H Whitmore, *Public Torts and Contracts* (Sydney, Law Book Co, 1982) 120, 121. *Bourgoin* resolved any such doubts.

[5] See M Aronson, 'Misfeasance in Public Office: A Very Peculiar Tort' (2011) 35 *Melbourne University Law Review* 1, 4.

[6] *Northern Territory v Mengel* (1995) 185 CLR 307 (HCA).

[7] *Garrett v Attorney-General (NZ)* [1997] 2 NZLR 332.

England[8] and Canada.[9] The current vitality of the tort is attested to by the frequency with which it now appears in the law reports of these countries, and by the spirited opposition which met a (subsequently abandoned) proposal by the Law Commission of England and Wales that the cause of action be abolished.[10]

Although some ambiguities remain, the quartet of leading cases significantly clarified the scope and the elements of the cause of action for misfeasance. Nevertheless, recent academic commentary demonstrates that the underlying nature of the tort remains highly contested.[11] In this chapter, I argue that misfeasance in public office is best understood as a distinctively public law tort, put forward a public law rationale for its recognition, and consider some analogous legal doctrines. I also critique two rival conceptions of the cause of action, which I call the 'tort law' conception and the 'private law' conception. Finally, I consider some practical implications of my analysis for the future development of the tort.

Two preliminary points are in order. The first is that, although the recent development of the misfeasance tort has been a superb example of how judges and scholars can learn from and build on the work carried out in other Commonwealth countries, the law in the various jurisdictions to which reference is made may not be entirely uniform, and to the limited extent that differences exist, the descriptive claims made in this chapter concern English law. And the second preliminary point is that the central thesis of the paper is premised on the assumption that a viable distinction can be drawn between private law and public law. Although the difficulties in drawing a clear line between the 'private' and 'public' spheres are well-known, the claim that such a line can usefully be drawn between private *law* and public *law* seems less controversial, and indeed it would be difficult to make much sense of the modern common law without recognising such a distinction.[12] Quite how we should draw this line is a question that we will come to shortly.

II. Misfeasance in Outline

Various attempts have been made to capture the essence of the misfeasance tort, though doing so is not altogether straightforward. The first instance judge in

[8] *Three Rivers District Council v Bank of England (No 3)* [2003] 2 AC 1 (HL).

[9] *Odhavji v Woodhouse* [2003] 3 SCR 263 (SCC).

[10] See Law Commission (England and Wales), *Administrative Redress: Public Bodies and the Citizen* (Law Com No 322, 2010) [3.65]–[3.72]. According to the Commission (at para 3.66) many of those who responded to its Consultation Paper recommending abolition of the tort 'stated that misfeasance still played a necessary role as a marker for particularly opprobrious action by public officials'.

[11] '[T]he very rationale of the tort is uncertain': M Aronson, 'Misfeasance in Public Office: Some Unfinished Business' (2016) 132 LQR 427, 429.

[12] For an overview of the issues, see P Cane, 'Public Law and Private Law: A Study of the Analysis and Use of a Legal Concept' in J Eekelaar and J Bell (eds), *Oxford Essays in Jurisprudence (Third Series)*

the leading English case, *Three Rivers District Council v Bank of England (No 3)* described it as 'a deliberate and dishonest wrongful abuse of the powers given to a public officer',[13] while in other cases it has been defined in terms of 'the abuse of public office',[14] or the 'abuse of a public function'.[15] However, none of these formulations captures the relational aspect of the tort, as reflected in the requirement that either the abuse of power, office or function be targeted at the claimant, or that the defendant realise that it will probably cause the claimant loss. Perhaps the most effective encapsulation of the essence of the tort came in the leading Canadian case, *Odhavji v Woodhouse*, where Iacobucci J defined the tort in terms of a public officer intentionally injuring a member of the public 'through deliberate and unlawful conduct in the exercise of public functions'.[16]

This composite definition embraces what are generally considered to be two distinct limbs of the tort. The first (the 'targeted malice' limb) covers situations where the exercise of public power or authority is specifically intended to injure the claimant. This limb of the tort is exemplified by the decision in *Roncarelli v Duplessis*,[17] where the then Prime Minister and Attorney General of Quebec was held liable for revoking the plaintiff's restaurant licence as revenge for his support of the Jehovah's Witnesses, against whom the Provincial government had been conducting a campaign. The second limb of the tort (the 'illegality' limb) covers situations where a public officer acts in the knowledge that he or she has no power to do the act complained of, and that the act will probably cause loss to the claimant. A classic example of the operation of this limb of the tort is the *Farrington* case, where the defendant police officers were held liable for ordering the plaintiff to shut his hotel after his conviction for a licensing offence, since they knew that they had no right to do this under the relevant legislation.

In both types of case the defendant can be said to have acted in bad faith.[18] The targeted malice limb involves bad faith in the sense of acting for an improper or

(Oxford, Clarendon Press, 1987). For a critique of the distinction, see C Harlow, "Public' and 'Private' Law: Definition Without Distinction' (1980) 43 *MLR* 241. *Cf* G Samuel, 'Public and Private Law: A Private Lawyer's Response' (1983) 46 *MLR* 558, 558 ('the distinction is really very fundamental to Western legal thought'); N Bamforth, 'Hohfeldian Rights and Public Law' in M Kramer (ed), *Rights, Wrongs and Responsibilities* (Basingstoke, Palgrave, 2001) 12–13 (without the distinction 'it becomes very difficult to impose any clarity or ordering on the law'). And note that even Harlow finds it necessary to employ the distinction (see, eg, n 29 below).

13 *Three Rivers District Council v Bank of England (No 3)* [1996] 3 All ER 558, 582 (Clarke J). See also, eg, *Kuddus v Chief Constable of Leicestershire Constabulary* [2001] UKHL 29, [2002] 2 AC 122 [90] (Lord Hutton).

14 *Elguzouli-Daf v Metropolitan Police Comr* [1995] QB 335, 347 (Steyn LJ). See also, eg, J McBride, 'Damages as a Remedy for Unlawful Administrative Action' [1979] *CLJ* 323, 326.

15 *Crawford Adjusters (Cayman) Ltd v Sagicor General Insurance (Cayman) Ltd* [2013] UKPC 17, [2014] AC 366 [134] (Lord Sumption).

16 *Odhavji* (n 9) [30].

17 n 3.

18 '[B]ad faith is the constant': Aronson (n 11) 434.

ulterior motive. The illegality limb involves bad faith in that the defendant does not have an honest belief that his or her act is lawful. This focus on bad faith is exemplified by the fact that, although reckless indifference as to the illegality and its probable consequences is sufficient to ground the tort in its second form, this recklessness must be subjective.[19] It follows that the claimant must establish that the defendant knew that his or her conduct was unlawful, or that he or she wilfully disregarded the risk that it was, and that he or she knew that it would probably cause the claimant loss, or wilfully disregarded the risk that it would do so. The use of these 'narrow and high level mental elements'[20] means that a sharp contrast can be drawn between the conduct that gives rise to misfeasance liability and lesser instances of maladministration, such as mere delay, the making of good faith mistakes, or the taking of good faith decisions on an erroneous or incomplete factual basis.[21] Put simply, the misfeasance tort does not encompass incompetence, however gross.[22]

The centrality of bad faith to the misfeasance tort also allows us to draw a sharp contrast between this cause of action and negligence,[23] where of course bad faith is not required (and rarely present). This contrast is accentuated by the fact that it is not a precondition of misfeasance liability that the defendant owed the claimant any particular duty,[24] and by the fact that, in the *Three Rivers* case, the House of Lords rebuffed an attempt to introduce the proximity concept into the misfeasance tort, reasoning that the requirement that the defendant must have acted in bad faith and in the knowledge that his or her conduct would probably cause harm was sufficient to ensure that the tort was kept within reasonable bounds.[25]

Two other features of the cause of action should be mentioned at this stage. The first is that the defendant in a misfeasance action must be the holder of a public office, a concept that has been said in this context to encompass any person who exercises governmental power, in other words 'the power to interfere with the way

[19] As held in *Mengel*, *Garrett* and *Three Rivers*.

[20] A Doecke, 'Misfeasance in Public Office: Foreseen or Foreseeable Harm' (2014) 22 *Torts Law Journal* 20, 33.

[21] *B v Home Office* [2012] EWHC 226 (QB), [2012] 4 All ER 276 [130] (Richard Salter QC).

[22] *Three Rivers* (n 13) 578 (Clarke J). See also *Pyrenees Shire Council v Day* [1998] HCA 3, (1998) 192 CLR 330, 376 (Gummow J). Note that in Australia there is conflicting authority as to the mental element required with regard to the consequences of the defendant's actions under the second limb of the tort, with some courts taking the view that the harm to the plaintiff need only be a *foreseeable* result of the defendant's action, at least where the defendant actually knows that he or she is acting unlawfully: see K Barker et al, *The Law of Torts in Australia*, 5th edn (Melbourne, Oxford University Press, 2012) 301.

[23] *Three Rivers* (n 13) 582 (Clarke J).

[24] *Mengel* (n 6) 357 (Brennan J); *Three Rivers* (n 13) 584 (Clarke J) (approved by Lord Steyn on appeal to the House of Lords: [2003] 2 AC 1, 193). *Cf* S Dench, 'The Tort of Misfeasance in a Public Office' (1981) 4 *Auckland University Law Review* 182, 201. See further on this point, T Cockburn and M Thomas, 'Personal Liability of Public Officers in the Tort of Misfeasance in Public Office: Part 2' (2001) 9 *Torts Law Journal* 245, 246–49; Aronson (n 5) 25–30.

[25] [2003] 2 AC 1, 193 (Lord Steyn), 228 (Lord Hutton).

in which other citizens wish to conduct their affairs'.[26] And the second is that the act or omission in respect of which a misfeasance action is brought must have been a purported performance of the functions of that office.[27] These two limitations will be considered in more detail later on.[28]

III. Why a *Public Law* Tort?

In this section of the chapter, I present a conception of the misfeasance tort as a distinctively public law cause of action. There is nothing original about the claim that misfeasance is a public law tort. Indeed, this claim is one that is frequently made by commentators.[29] However, I want to look behind this recurrent claim to consider in what sense or senses misfeasance is properly analysed as part of public law.

Naturally, the claim that misfeasance is a public law tort must depend on a conception of public law into which the tort fits. Perhaps the most pervasive such conception rests on the supposition that (in Peter Cane's words) whereas 'private law is concerned primarily with relations between citizens', 'public law deals primarily with the public sector and with relations between citizens and the bureaucracy'.[30] As Cane points out, this way of distinguishing between private law and public law has two dimensions: an institutional dimension and a functional dimension. The institutional dimension refers to the distinction between public agencies and officials on the one hand, and private citizens on the other. And the functional

[26] *Society of Lloyd's v Henderson* [2007] EWCA Civ 930, [2008] 1 WLR 2255 [25] (Buxton LJ). See also *Cannon v Tahche* [2002] VSCA 84, 5 VR 317 [49] (Winneke P, Charles and Chernov JJA) ('an office cannot be characterised as a public office for the purposes of the tort if no relevant power is attached to it'); *Three Rivers* (n 8) 229 (Lord Hobhouse) (public officers are 'those vested with governmental authority and the exercise of executive powers'). See generally on the concept of a public officer, P Finn, 'Public Officers: Some Personal Liabilities' (1977) 51 *Australian Law Journal* 313.

[27] *Mengel* (n 6) 355 (Brennan J).

[28] See below, text following n 145.

[29] See, eg, B Gould, 'Damages as a Remedy in Administrative Law' (1972) 5 *New Zealand Universities Law Review* 105, 122 (writing of the need to establish the misfeasance tort 'in order to fill a substantial gap in our administrative law'); Dench (n 24) 182; R Evans, 'Damages for Unlawful Administrative Action: The Remedy for Misfeasance in Public Office' (1982) 31 *ICLQ* 640, 640 ('an administrative tort'); P Hogg, *Liability of the Crown*, 2nd edn (Scarborough, Carswell Press, 1989) 112; S Arrowsmith, *Civil Liability and Public Authorities* (Humberside, Earlsgate Press, 1992) 226; R Sadler, 'Liability for Misfeasance in a Public Office' (1992) 14 *Sydney Law Review* 137, 138; M Andenas and D Fairgrieve 'Misfeasance in Public Office, Governmental Liability and European Influences' (2002) 51 *ICLQ* 757, 761; C Harlow, *State Liability: Tort Law and Beyond* (Oxford, Oxford University Press, 2004) 130; C Booth and D Squires, *The Negligence Liability of Public Authorities* (Oxford, Oxford University Press, 2006) [6.02]; P Cane, *Administrative Law*, 5th edn (Oxford, Oxford University Press, 2011) 218; Aronson (n 5) 2. See also *Pyrenees Shire Council* (n 22) 376 (Gummow J).

[30] Cane (n 29) 4. Note that Cane qualifies this formulation of the distinction with the words '[i]n rough terms'.

dimension refers to the distinction between public functions and private activities. Seen in these terms, then, public law 'is concerned with public institutions and their relations with private citizens, and with the performance of public functions', while private law 'is concerned with private activities and relations between private citizens'.[31]

If we buy into this classical conception of public law, then the classification of misfeasance in public office as a public law doctrine is relatively straightforward. The institutional dimension gives us a particularly clear answer, since we have seen that it is only public officers who can be liable under this cause of action. Here also the contrast with private law seems especially sharp, since a distinguishing feature of private law is its universality—private law duties are potentially owed by everyone to everyone else, whether they be individuals, corporations, or state agencies.[32] It therefore comes as no surprise to see that an institutional understanding of the private law/public law distinction seems to underlie many of the claims to the effect that misfeasance is a public law tort.[33]

The functional dimension of the distinction between public law and private law is also consistent with the classification of misfeasance within public law, though here a caveat is necessary. We have seen that only conduct that amounts to a purported performance of the functions of the defendant's office can give rise to misfeasance liability, so that, for example, a malicious act done by a public officer solely in his or her capacity as a private individual would fall outside the ambit of the cause of action.[34] The link with the functions of the relevant public office is therefore not in doubt, and naturally many of those functions are likely to count as public functions on any plausible account of that concept. The need for a caveat arises, however, because there is some authority in favour of the view that the misfeasance tort extends to all the functions of the public office in question,[35] and yet not *all* of those functions are rightly conceived as public functions. On the other hand, it will be argued below that the ambit of the tort should be limited to the exercise of peculiarly public functions,[36] and, if this were to be done, then no mismatch between the scope of the cause of action and this functional conception of public law could arise.

In any case, any ambiguity arising out of this kind of functional analysis of public law can be resolved by adopting an alternative such analysis, which focuses not on the functions performed by the relevant public officer, but on the function or

[31] ibid.

[32] On this way of conceptualising the distinction between public law and private law, see R Barnett, 'Foreword: Four Senses of the Public Law-Private Law Distinction' (1986) 9 *Harvard Journal of Law and Public Policy* 267, 270–71.

[33] See, eg, Sadler (n 29) 138; Booth and Squires (n 29) [6.02]; Aronson (n 5) 2.

[34] Aronson (n 11) 441 (giving the example of a uniformed and on duty police officer 'who punches his domestic partner during an argument').

[35] See below, text following n 161.

[36] See below, text following n 162.

functions performed by public law itself. Consideration of the tort of misfeasance in public office in this light requires us to turn our attention to the specific role that the cause of action might be playing within the broader normative system of public law.

In investigating that question, I take as a starting point Martin Loughlin's observation that public power is generated by the loyalty of individuals to the system, such that it may be said 'ultimately to rest on opinion and belief'.[37] It follows that:

> [The capacity of public power] depends on strengthening the bonds of allegiance between governors and governed. Although this can be achieved in a number of ways, one of the most effective is to impose checks on the exercise of governmental power. Such constraints, which ensure that public power is wielded only for public purposes, bolster the confidence of the people in the integrity of government and this greatly enhances the capacity of public power.[38]

This idea of public law as a means of building and maintaining trust between government and citizenry resonates with one of the most powerful judicial rationalisations of the misfeasance tort, which was given by Nourse LJ in the English Court of Appeal in *Jones v Swansea CC* when he said that:

> The assumptions of honour and disinterest on which the tort of misfeasance in a public office is founded are deeply rooted in the polity of a free society … It ought to be unthinkable that the holder of an office of government in this country would exercise a power thus vested in him with the object of injuring a member of that public *by whose trust alone the office is enjoyed*.[39]

If we try to tie this rhetoric down a little, it seems to me that we arrive at a conception of the misfeasance tort as a public demonstration of the fact that deliberate abuse of public office is intolerable behaviour for which an official will be held to account by the courts.[40] The element of betrayal of public trust means that there is something *especially reprehensible* about malice or dishonesty in the performance of a public servant's duties,[41] which 'attracts particular public censure'[42] and demands judicial denunciation.

Conceiving of the misfeasance tort in these terms would locate the cause of action firmly within a broader set of legal doctrines that find their raison d'être in the need to protect and enhance public trust in those exercising governmental power and authority. Some other tort doctrines—such as the availability of

[37] M Loughlin, *The Idea of Public Law* (Oxford, Oxford University Press, 2003) 78.

[38] ibid, 85.

[39] *Jones v Swansea CC* [1990] 1 WLR 54, 85 (emphasis added).

[40] See also Mark Aronson's suggestion that the award of damages in *Roncarelli* (n 3) served to 'denounce the defendant's conduct' ('Some Australian Reflections on *Roncarelli v Duplessis*' (2010) 55 *McGill Law Journal* 615, 630).

[41] This point is made by Aronson (ibid, 631). See also Aronson and Whitmore (n 4) 121 ('there is a special sense of outrage when a public official wilfully abuses power').

[42] *Three Rivers* (n 8) 139 (Auld LJ). See also Sadler (n 29, 139) ('Malicious or wilful abuse of official power is socially intolerable').

exemplary damages against public wrongdoers—are, for example, best understood in these terms.[43] Similarly, a public trust rationale has long been thought to underscore the parallel criminal offence of misconduct in public office.[44] And another example of such a doctrine is the rule that a councillor who, through wilful misconduct, is found to have caused loss to a local authority, is liable to make good the loss.[45] In one of the leading cases on this rule, *Porter v Magill*, Lord Bingham reiterated that it was an important principle of public law that public powers were conferred 'as if upon trust', and said that it followed from this principle that 'those who exercise powers in a manner inconsistent with the public purpose for which the powers were conferred betray that trust and so misconduct themselves'.[46]

Although, for various reasons that I will come to, I find a public trust rationale along these lines to be the most appealing explanation of the misfeasance tort, we should note that an alternative public law rationale of the cause of action conceives of the tort as a means of *deterring* official misconduct, in order to improve standards of public administration. According to Stephen Todd, for example, the tort 'is predicated upon the absolute need to prevent the abuse of power by public officers charged with the exercise of public functions'.[47] Famously, a deterrence rationale for the imposition of tort liability (coupled with a clearly punitive damages award) was at the forefront of Holt CJ's judgment in the seminal case of *Ashby v White*:

> If public officers will infringe men's rights, they ought to pay greater damages than other men, to deter and hinder other officers from the like offences ... To allow this action will make public officers more careful to observe the constitution of cities and boroughs, and not to be so partial as they commonly are in all elections, which is indeed a great and growing mischief, and tends to the prejudice of the peace of the nation.[48]

In due course, we shall see that the choice between these rival public law conceptions of the misfeasance tort may have doctrinal implications, but for now it will suffice to note that both fit comfortably within Loughlin's account of public law as 'a form of political reasoning driven by prudential considerations',[49] the difference

[43] See below, text following n 78.

[44] See below, text to n 64.

[45] *Porter v Magill* [2001] UKHL 67, [2002] 2 AC 357 [19] (Lord Bingham) and authorities there cited.

[46] ibid.

[47] S Todd, 'Liability in Tort of Public Bodies' in N Mullany and A Linden (eds), *Torts Tomorrow: A Tribute to John Fleming* (North Ryde, LBC Information Services, 1996) 37.

[48] *Ashby* (n 1) 956, 167. Similarly, in the English Court of Appeal in the *Three Rivers* case, Auld LJ said that '[t]he clear public policy behind the tort is to achieve an honest and fair public administration, by encouraging public officers not to abuse their position and to compensate those who suffer if they do' (*Three Rivers* (n 8) 143). See also *Garrett* (n 7) 350 (Blanchard J); H Wruck, 'The Continuing Evolution of the Tort of Misfeasance in Public Office' (2008) 41 *University of British Columbia Law Review* 69, 74–75. For a general discussion of a deterrence rationale for the tort, see E Chamberlain, 'Misfeasance in a Public Office: A Justifiable Anomaly within the Rights-Based Approach?' in D Nolan and A Robertson (eds), *Rights and Private Law* (Oxford, Hart Publishing, 2012) 576–78.

[49] Loughlin (n 37) 163.

being only the prudential consideration said to drive the recognition of the cause of action. Nor of course should we ignore the possibility that both considerations are in play, so that the tort is premised on the need publicly to denounce official misconduct *and* the need to deter such misconduct in the first place. On this view, more than one public law aim is served by a misfeasance tort conceived in more general terms as a mechanism for 'disciplining arbitrary public behaviour'.[50]

Central features of the misfeasance tort are explicable in terms of a public law rationale along the lines I have outlined. As mere incompetence or thoughtlessness involves no betrayal of public trust (at least in a strong sense), the scope of the cause of action is limited to bad faith conduct that, by definition, amounts to an abuse of the defendant's position.[51] This limitation also ties in with the public law principle that litigation should not 'unduly hamper the governmental process',[52] by helping to ensure that officials are 'able to make bona fide decisions without the constant worry of being sued for alleged misuse of their statutory powers'.[53] As Brennan J said in response to the plaintiffs' argument in *Mengel* that the mental element of the tort should be relaxed to include constructive knowledge of illegality:

> If liability were imposed upon public officers who, though honestly assuming the availability of powers to perform their functions, were found to fall short of curial standards of reasonable care in ascertaining the existence of those powers, there would be a chilling effect on the performance of their functions ....[54]

Furthermore, the public law rationale for the tort favoured here explains the restriction of liability to *public officers*, defined as those persons who exercise governmental power,[55] since it is precisely by conferring special powers on such persons through the offices that they hold[56] that the public places its trust in them.[57] A public employee who does not hold an office to which such powers attach cannot, by definition, betray the public's trust; nor of course can an individual or corporation wielding only private (or economic) power. Such persons are not therefore answerable to the public in the same way that a public officer is.[58]

[50] Aronson (n 40) 629.

[51] *Mengel* (n 6) 357 (Brennan J).

[52] P Craig, *Administrative Law*, 7th edn (London, Sweet & Maxwell, 2012) 864.

[53] *Takaro Properties Ltd v Rowling* [1976] 2 NZLR 657, 672 (Beattie J). See also *Garrett* (n 7) 350 (Blanchard J) (extension of the misfeasance tort could have a 'stultifying effect on governance').

[54] *Mengel* (n 6) 358. For an earlier judicial statement to like effect, see *Cullen v Morris* 2 Stark 576, 587; 171 ER 741, 744 (Abbott LCJ). Concern about the 'chilling effect' of an overly broad misfeasance action is central to the argument Doecke (n 20) makes against extending liability to cases of foreseeable (as opposed to foreseen) harm.

[55] See above, text to n 26.

[56] As Loughlin (n 37) points out (at 79), strictly speaking, 'the power vests not in the individual but in the office itself'.

[57] 'The public is, in the eyes of the law, regarded as reposing "trust and confidence" in [public officers]': Finn (n 26) 315.

[58] *Tampion v Anderson* [1973] VR 321 (counsel instructed to assist a Board of Inquiry not a public officer, although paid out of the public purse, because not answerable to members of the public for the performance of his/her duties).

Finally, there are at least two further features of the cause of action for misfeasance which are consistent with it belonging in public law, rather than private law. One is that in misfeasance cases the Hohfeldian right-duty relation so typical of private law is absent.[59] And the other is that the authorities on misfeasance do not distinguish between positive acts and omissions of public officers,[60] and while this is characteristic of public law doctrine, the act/omission distinction plays a central role in the private law of tort.[61]

To recap, the central argument of this section of the chapter is that the most plausible conception of the cause of action for misfeasance envisages it is a mechanism designed to build and maintain trust between the state and its citizenry, a conception that locates the tort firmly within a system of public law understood as a means of 'strengthening the bonds of allegiance between governors and governed'.[62] Seen in these terms, the claim that misfeasance is a public law tort appears irrefutable.

IV. Why a Public Law *Tort*?

Thus far, I have focused on what I see as being the public law aspect of the cause of action for misfeasance in public office. But misfeasance is of course also a tort, and in this section of the chapter I consider this aspect of the cause of action, and how it might be reconciled with a public law analysis.

A useful starting point here is the broadly co-extensive criminal offence of misconduct in public office, defined by Archbold as a wilful neglect of duty or misconduct by a public officer that amounts to 'an abuse of the public's trust in the office holder'.[63] Consistently with that definition, the object of the offence has been said to be to ensure that 'an official does not, by any wilful act or omission, act contrary

[59] R Stevens, *Torts and Rights* (Oxford, Oxford University Press, 2007) 90. For a refutation of Erika Chamberlain's argument to the contrary, see text following n 116 below. And for a clear implication to the effect that reliance on a Hohfeldian right can usefully serve to distinguish private law from public law claims, see J Beatson, "Public' and 'Private' in English Administrative Law' (1987) 103 *LQR* 34, 56. A careful analysis of the relationship between Hohfeldian rights and public law led Bamforth (n 12, 10) to conclude that none of the senses in which the word 'right' has been used in English judicial review cases seems to be 'strictly Hohfeldian', while Jason Varuhas has argued that in public law *individual* Hohfeldian rights are found only in human rights cases: J Varuhas, 'The Reformation of English Administrative Law?' [2013] *CLJ* 369, 396–412.

[60] See below, n 158 and accompanying text.

[61] Aronson (n 5, 32) draws attention to the distinction between the misfeasance tort and the law of negligence in this regard. For an overview of the relevance of the distinction in negligence law, see P Cane, *Atiyah's Accidents, Compensation and the Law*, 8th edn (Cambridge, Cambridge University Press, 2013) 70–83.

[62] n 38.

[63] *Archbold: Criminal Pleading, Evidence and Practice, 2015* (London, Sweet & Maxwell, 2012). There is extensive discussion of the crime with reference to the tort in Aronson (n 5) 15–18. And see more generally on the offence, PD Finn, 'Official Misconduct' (1978) 2 *Criminal Law Journal* 307.

to the duties of his office' and 'abuse intentionally the trust reposed in him'.[64] The parallel with the public law conception of the tort of misfeasance is clear.

If the rationale of the misfeasance tort is, loosely speaking, to hold those guilty of wilful official misconduct publicly to account, then why not simply do this through the criminal law, as the Law Commission argued in its report on *Administrative Redress*?[65] Why also recognise a form of tortious liability? After all, as Robert Sadler notes, the tort 'took its basic parameters from the crude elements of the crime',[66] and the crime 'will almost invariably have been committed should the tort be proven'.[67]

There seem to me to be three reasons why a tort remedy is justified, despite the existence of the parallel criminal offence and the possibility in some cases of judicial review proceedings to compel a public officer to comply with his or her public law obligations. One is that a disadvantage of relying on the criminal law in this context is that this requires the state authorities to themselves initiate proceedings against one of their own officials, whereas of course claims in tort can be brought by private individuals, thereby empowering members of the public whose trust has allegedly been betrayed to themselves police official misconduct. As Robert Stevens has pointed out (with reference to exemplary damages):

> A crime, like a tort, is a wrong. However, it is a wrong against society. The state brings the action not as private actor, but as a representative of society. The possible difficulty arises where the state itself is a wrongdoer. It may be thought objectionable for the state to police itself by bringing a prosecution, and so the individual claimant is permitted to bring a claim on behalf of society against the state.[68]

In *Roncarelli*, for example, how likely was it that the authorities in Quebec would have called to account the Prime Minister and Attorney General of the Province for his malicious conduct?

A second reason for allowing official misconduct to be challenged via a tort action is that this may ensure that the procedure is better matched to the issue in question.[69] Because the purpose of the tort claim is to hold the defendant to

[64] *DPP v Marks* [2005] VSCA 277 [35], drawing on Lord Mansfield's classic formulation in *R v Bembridge* (1783) 22 State Trials 1, 155. See also *Shum Kwok Sher v HKSAR* (2002) 5 HKCFAR 381 [80]-[81] (Sir Anthony Mason NPJ); *Attorney General's Reference (No 3 of 2003)* [2005] QB 73 [57] (Pill LJ); Finn (n 63) 308; C Davids and M McMahon, 'Police Misconduct as a Breach of Public Trust: The Offence of Misconduct in Public Office' (2014) 19 *Deakin Law Review* 89, 90.

[65] n 10, para 3.71.

[66] Sadler (n 29) 162.

[67] ibid, 160. In *Attorney General's Reference (No 3 of 2003)* (n 64) Pill LJ said (at [48]) that the mental element of the tort appeared also to be appropriate for the criminal offence, although he also made clear (at [46]) that only 'serious' misconduct would suffice for criminal liability, and that the seriousness of the consequences that may follow from the act or omission in question would be a relevant consideration in this regard. There is no equivalent of this 'seriousness' requirement in the tort.

[68] Stevens (n 59) 88.

[69] Beatson (n 59) 43.

account for past misconduct, rather than to challenge the validity of a decision taken by the administration, there is no need for the short time limits associated with judicial review proceedings, the purpose of which is to avoid the relevant authority and third parties being held in suspense for extended periods.[70] Furthermore, the investigation of alleged misconduct (and in particular the state of mind of the defendant official) will generally require the resolution of factual disputes and hence procedural tools—such as discovery and cross-examination—better suited to the ordinary trial procedure than to specialist public law proceedings, where these mechanisms are discouraged because of the delays and additional expense entailed.[71] Finally, the availability of short cuts such as strike-out proceedings and applications for summary judgment (which are widely used in the misfeasance context)[72] provide defendants with a 'screening mechanism' to prevent public authorities being troubled by wholly unmeritorious litigation, just like the permission requirement in judicial review proceedings.[73]

And the third justification for a tort remedy is that it provides a mechanism for compensating members of the public particularly affected by an act of official misconduct, the underlying thinking being that 'deliberate abuse of public office directed at an individual citizen calls for an effective sanction enforceable as of right by that citizen'.[74] This thinking is reflected not only in the tort's standing rule—the requirement that the claimant have suffered some form of adverse consequence as a result of the misconduct—but also in the requirement that the defendant must either have specifically intended to injure the claimant, or, alternatively, realised that his or her unlawful conduct would probably cause the claimant loss. Although falling short of the kind of Hohfeldian right-duty relation found in private law, these relational aspects of the misfeasance tort nevertheless serve to distinguish it from a purely disciplinary sanction that could be imposed in the absence of any particular target or victim of the misconduct.[75] Furthermore, even

[70] *Davy v Spelthorne Borough Council* [1984] 1 AC 262, 274 (Lord Wilberforce).

[71] Craig (n 52) para 27-006.

[72] Aronson (n 11) 432.

[73] On the rationale of permission, see Craig (n 52) para 27-032 (who describes it as a 'screening mechanism').

[74] *Watkins v Secretary of State for the Home Department* [2006] UKHL 17, [2006] 2 AC 395 [75] (Lord Walker). See also Finn (n 1) 147–48: 'The criminal law secured the collective interest of the public in the conduct of its officials. But unless civil liability in damages was also to be imposed in favour of a person actually injured by misconduct, officials would have been relieved of personal responsibility for their action at the very point where the trust principle had its greatest salience for the injured citizen.'

[75] *Garrett* (n 7) 350–51 (Blanchard J). Hence the difficulty of the question that faced the Caribbean Court of Justice in *Marin v Attorney-General* [2011] CCJ 9 (AJ), [2011] 5 LRC 209, which was whether the state should itself be able to bring an action in the misfeasance tort. A majority of the Court held that the Attorney General was entitled to seek damages from ministers of a former government who were accused of corruptly selling off state land at undervalue. However, in a powerful dissenting judgment, de la Bastide P and Saunders J argued that in such cases the state's interests were adequately protected by the possibility of criminal prosecution, and that the tort was designed to protect purely private interests. In their view, the misfeasance tort 'captures an interface between those who

though, on the public law analysis, interpersonal justice is not the raison d'être of the misfeasance tort, the existence of a tort remedy may nevertheless perform a vindicatory function, by enabling victims of abuse of public office to hold the public officer in question publicly to account, and to obtain redress for the loss they have suffered as a result.[76]

Finally, we should remember that there is nothing particularly unusual about using a mechanism (in this case tort liability) that developed in the private law context to achieve public law goals.[77] Declarations and injunctions, for example, are well-established public law remedies that originated within private law. And in many jurisdictions, violations of constitutional or human rights may give rise to damages claims that to some extent mimic tort liability, but are generally classified as a public law remedy.[78] In common law systems at least, the key to the distinction between public law and private law lies not in the choice of remedy, but in the nature of the underlying dispute.

V. Three Analogies

Although an unusual tort in many respects, misfeasance in public office is not the only example of a tort mechanism that serves primarily public law aims. In this section of the chapter, I highlight three other doctrines that are analogous to misfeasance in this respect: malicious prosecution and related causes of action; public nuisance; and exemplary (or punitive) damages.

A. Malicious Prosecution

The essence of the tort of malicious prosecution is that the defendant has, without reasonable cause, maliciously prosecuted the claimant on a criminal charge that was determined in the claimant's favour, and that the claimant has suffered damage as a result. In the leading modern English case on the tort, *Gregory v Portsmouth CC*, Lord Steyn said that a distinctive feature of the cause of action was that

are entrusted with the task of exercising executive or government powers and those who must conduct their affairs subject to the exercise of such powers', and it is 'impossible for the state to situate itself within this paradigm' (at [24]–[25]).

[76] E Chamberlain, 'What is the Role of Misfeasance in a Public Office in Modern Canadian Tort Law?' (2009) 88 *Canadian Bar Review* 575, 599–600. On the concept of 'vindication', see K Barker, 'Private and Public: The Mixed Concept of Vindication in Torts and Private Law' in S Pitel, J Neyers and E Chamberlain (eds), *Tort Law: Challenging Orthodoxy* (Oxford, Hart Publishing, 2013), who argues (at 83) that the purposes that the various forms of vindication serve 'potentially span the divide between public and private ends'.

[77] Samuel (n 12) 562, pointing out that historically the prerogative remedies 'could venture outside the field of public law, just as private law actions could act vice versa'.

[78] See, eg, Human Rights Act 1998 (UK) s 7.

'the defendant has abused the coercive powers of the state',[79] and in a more recent Privy Council decision on malicious prosecution, Lord Sumption said in his dissenting opinion that this tort was an example of a 'limited category of causes of action in which the essence of the tort is the abuse of a public function for some collateral private purposes of the person performing it', of which misfeasance in a public office was the paradigm case.[80] Other examples given by Lord Sumption included maliciously procuring a search warrant, and maliciously procuring the arrest of a ship.[81]

B. Public Nuisance

A public nuisance is a crime that must, by definition, either affect a section of the public, or interfere with a right enjoyed by the public generally, such as the right to use a public highway. Unusually, the commission of this crime may also give rise to liability in tort towards a person who suffers particular damage over and above the inconvenience and injury suffered by the public in general. The similarities between this cause of action and misfeasance in public office are striking. First, while the essence of a public nuisance is some detriment to the interests of the public (or at least a section of the public), the essence of misfeasance is a betrayal of public trust. Secondly, public nuisance is both a tort and a crime, and in substance the same is true of misfeasance in a public office, albeit that the parallel crime of misconduct in public office has a slightly different name and there are some relatively minor differences between the elements of the tort and the equivalent crime. And finally, there is also a connection between the standing rules of the two causes of action, because in the case law on misfeasance we can see echoes of the 'special damage' requirement familiar from the law of public nuisance.[82] This was particularly apparent in Lord Hobhouse's opinion in the *Three Rivers* case, where his description of the standing rule in misfeasance was clearly borrowed from the law of public nuisance:

> [Misfeasance in public office] is not generally actionable by any member of the public. The plaintiff must have suffered special damage in the sense of loss or injury which is specific to him and which is not being suffered in common with the public in general.[83]

[79] [2000] 1 AC 419, 426.

[80] *Crawford Adjusters* (n 15) [134]-[135]. A little later on in his opinion (at [145]), Lord Sumption describes malicious prosecution as 'a form of misfeasance in public office'.

[81] ibid, [143]. See also N McBride and R Bagshaw, *Tort Law*, 5th edn (Basingstoke, Palgrave Macmillan, 2015) 726, who refer to the torts of maliciously and without reasonable and probable cause procuring the issue of an arrest warrant or search warrant.

[82] This is particularly evident in the prototype misfeasance cases. See, eg, *Whitelegg v Richards* (1823) 2 B & C 45, 52; 107 ER 300, 302 (Abbott CJ).

[83] *Three Rivers* (n 8) 231. See also *Marin* (n 75) [84] (Wit J).

Again, the analogy between misfeasance and public nuisance has been previously commented on by others. According to Erika Chamberlain, for example, both torts are 'hybrids of public and private law' that straddle the public/private divide.[84]

C. Exemplary Damages

The final analogy with misfeasance in public office can be found in the law relating to exemplary damages. The connection between official misconduct and exemplary damages was emphasised in the leading case of *Rookes v Barnard*, where Lord Devlin said that one of the two categories of case in which exemplary damages had previously been awarded consisted of 'oppressive, arbitrary or unconstitutional action by servants of the government'.[85] As Aronson observes, the rules governing the award of exemplary damages in English law therefore represent 'an acknowledgement of the special position reserved for claims against public officials for misconduct that is oppressive, arbitrary or unconstitutional'.[86]

Exemplary damages are punitive in nature, and are clearly intended to punish and deter.[87] The rationale of awards of exemplary damages against public defendants has been said to be to curb or discourage the abuse of power by persons purporting to exercise legal or governmental authority conferred on them by virtue of the official status or employment that they hold.[88] In *Kuddus v Chief Constable of Leicestershire Constabulary*, Lord Hutton said that 'the power to award exemplary damages in such cases serves to uphold and vindicate the rule of law because it makes clear that the courts will not tolerate such conduct',[89] and Lord Nicholls expressed a similar view:

> On occasion conscious wrongdoing by a defendant is so outrageous, his disregard of the claimant's rights so contumelious, that something more [than compensatory damages] is needed to show that the law will not tolerate such behaviour.[90]

[84] E Chamberlain, 'The Need for a "Standing" Rule in Misfeasance in a Public Office' (2007) 7 *Oxford University Comparative Law Journal* 215, 236. See also P Vines, 'Misfeasance in Public Office: Old Tort, New Tricks?' in S Degeling, J Edelman and J Goudkamp (eds), *Torts in Commercial Law* (Sydney, Lawbook Co, 2011) 232–33; and J Murphy, 'Misfeasance in a Public Office: A Tort Law Misfit?' (2012) 32 *OJLS* 51, 60. Chamberlain is nevertheless at pains to distinguish the two causes of action (at 236*ff*), though her attempt to do so is not always convincing.

[85] *Rookes v Barnard* [1964] AC 1129, 1226.

[86] Aronson (n 5) 13. This 'special position' is also manifested in the English legal aid rules, which privilege the provision of civil legal services 'in relation to abuse by a public authority of its position or powers': Legal Aid, Sentencing and Punishment of Offenders Act 2012 (UK) sch 1, para 21. For discussion of the meaning of 'abuse of power' in this context, see *Director of Legal Aid Casework v R (Sisangia)* [2016] EWCA Civ 24.

[87] See, eg, *Kuddus* (n 13) [51] (Lord Nicholls).

[88] *Rookes* (n 85) 1223 (Lord Devlin); *Watkins* (n 74) [75] (Lord Walker).

[89] *Kuddus* (n 13) [79].

[90] ibid, [63]. See also *A v Bottrill* [2002] UKPC 44, [2003] 1 AC [20] (Lord Nicholls) (exemplary damages awarded where necessary to demonstrate that defendant's conduct is 'altogether unacceptable

The parallels with the public law analysis of the misfeasance tort I have argued for are clear,[91] and were made explicit by Lord Wilberforce in *Cassell & Co Ltd v Broome*, when he cited Holt CJ's judgment in *Ashby v White*,[92] commented that '[e]xcessive and insolent use of power is certainly something against which citizens require as much protection today', and, in effect, treated 'servant of government' in the exemplary damages context as equivalent to 'public officer' in the misfeasance context.[93]

The parallels between the two doctrines become even clearer when they operate in tandem, and exemplary damages are awarded against a defendant held liable for misfeasance. That exemplary damages are available in misfeasance cases was accepted by the House of Lords in *Kuddus*, and it has been argued that they are peculiarly appropriate in this context.[94] According to Erika Chamberlain, for example, the availability of exemplary damages in misfeasance actions 'is necessary to express a sense of public outrage at the misuse of the powers that were granted to the official to exercise in the public interest', and to deter officials from misusing their powers in the future.[95] On a strictly doctrinal level, misfeasance cases in which targeted malice has been established will almost certainly—if not inevitably—fall within Lord Devlin's first category in *Rookes v Barnard*, and the same is likely to be true of many of the cases within the alternative 'illegality' limb of the tort.[96] On the other hand, in *Kuddus* Lord Scott denied that 'every abuse of power which constitutes the tort of misfeasance' would give rise to an award of exemplary damages.[97] Hence, although there are strong connections between the two doctrines, they have independent spheres of operation, and in English law exemplary damages can of course also be awarded against private defendants in certain (very limited) circumstances.

VI. Two Rival Conceptions

In this section, I identify two conceptions of the misfeasance tort that differ from the public law conception put forward in this chapter, and subject them to critique. This discussion reveals that the favoured conception of the cause of action

to society'); C Harlow, 'A Punitive Role for Tort Law?' in L Pearson, C Harlow and M Taggart (eds), *Administrative Law in a Changing State: Essays in Honour of Mark Aronson* (Oxford, Hart Publishing, 2008) 251.

91 See also Aronson and Whitmore (n 4) 121; Sadler (n 29) 154.
92 n 1.
93 *Cassell & Co Ltd v Broome* [1972] AC 1027, 1120.
94 See, eg, Booth and Squires (n 29) [6.26].
95 Chamberlain (n 48) 577.
96 Sadler (n 29) 155–56.
97 *Kuddus* (n 13) [91].

has implications not only for the scope of misfeasance itself, but also for broader theoretical and taxonomical debates within private law scholarship.

A. The Tort Law Conception

The claimant in *Watkins v Secretary of State for the Home Department*[98] was a convicted prisoner whose legal correspondence had been repeatedly interfered with by prison officers in violation of the Prison Rules (a form of secondary legislation). In an action against the relevant government department and a number of individual prison officers, he sought damages for misfeasance in public office. The trial judge found that three of the officers had breached the rules in bad faith, but the defendants none the less denied that any liability arose, on the ground that damage was a necessary ingredient of the cause of action in misfeasance, and the breaches had caused the claimant no loss. The Court of Appeal rejected this argument, made a nominal award of general damages, and remitted the case to the trial court for determination of whether exemplary damages should be awarded against the three prison officers.[99] However, the defendants' appeal from that decision was allowed by the House of Lords, which held that misfeasance in public office was actionable only on proof of material damage, meaning financial loss, physical injury or mental injury amounting to a recognised psychiatric illness.[100] The reasoning of the House of Lords in *Watkins* reflects a very different conception of the misfeasance tort than the public law conception argued for in this chapter. Unfortunately, the adoption of what we might term a 'tort law' conception of the cause of action led in this case to a serious injustice, and a failure by the UK's highest court to hold the defendants to account for their wilful abuse of their official positions.[101]

Lord Bingham's analysis of the authorities in *Watkins* led him to conclude that special damage had either been expressly recognised as an essential ingredient of the cause of action for misfeasance, or assumed to be one. Although this interpretation of the authorities was surely correct—misfeasance is, after all, an action on the case—the House's failure to recognise the essentially public law nature of the cause of action for misfeasance led it to adopt an unnecessarily narrow approach to this concept. Understood in public law terms, the requirement of

[98] [2006] UKHL 17, [2006] 2 AC 395.

[99] [2004] EWCA Civ 966, [2005] QB 883.

[100] For this definition of material damage, see *Watkins* (n 74) [7] (Lord Bingham). In *Karagozlu v Metropolitan Police Commissioner* [2006] EWCA Civ 1691, [2007] 1 WLR 1881, the English Court of Appeal held that for these purposes 'material damage' also encompassed loss of liberty, including curtailment of the residual freedom of a prisoner.

[101] A tort law conception of misfeasance liability is also evident in the dissenting judgment of de la Bastide P and Saunders J in *Marin* (n 75), when they said that: 'Here we are not concerned with principles of constitutional or public law. We are concerned with tort law' (at [4]). See also the claim by one of the majority judges in the case, Wit J, that the misfeasance tort is 'au fond a private law tort with private law remedies' (at [75]).

special damage is essentially a standing rule, which determines why it is that this particular claimant is entitled to hold a public officer to account for his or her wilful misconduct. However, by not conceiving of misfeasance in these terms, but rather as part of 'tort law', the House was led to a very different notion of damage as a form of material setback to certain core interests (a notion particularly associated with the law of negligence). It followed that, even though the claimant in *Watkins* was surely enough of a victim of the misconduct to satisfy a public law standing rule—Lord Walker described the likely impact of the defendants' actions on him as 'much the same as an actual assault which occasioned no lasting harm, such as a slap in the face'[102]—the absence of such a material setback to his interests robbed him of the ability to bring the defendants to account, with the result that their quite outrageous abuse of their positions went (it would appear)[103] wholly unpunished.

The significance of the House of Lords' conception of misfeasance as part of tort law—as opposed to public law—can be seen throughout a critical passage of Lord Bingham's speech in *Watkins*, in which he gave a number of reasons for maintaining the requirement of material damage in this context. One such reason was that a person in the claimant's position had other remedies open to them: prison officers who broke the rules were amenable to judicial review, and they might also face disciplinary sanctions or prosecution for the crime of misconduct in public office.[104] Misfeasance, in other words, was to be *contrasted* with what Lord Walker called 'these avenues provided by public law'[105] as responses to official misconduct, and not *aligned* with them as another means of holding public malefactors to account. Similarly, Lord Bingham's perception that the claimant's aim in the case was to punish the defendants by means of an award of exemplary damages was seen as a further reason to resist his argument for a remedy, since tort law was concerned not with punishment, but with compensation, as reflected in the general policy of the law to discourage the award of exemplary damages.[106] He concluded:

> [I] would not for my part develop *the law of tort* to make it an instrument of punishment in cases where there is no material damage to compensate.[107]

A similar focus on 'tort law', and its connotations and implications, is apparent in the other opinions in *Watkins*.[108] For example, Lord Hope argued with reference to Scots law that:

[102] *Watkins* (n 74) [68].

[103] See ibid, [69], where Lord Walker pointed out that no disciplinary action had been taken, nor any prosecutions brought, against the officers in question.

[104] ibid, [26]. See also [65] (Lord Rodger). *Cf* [69] (Lord Walker).

[105] ibid, [69].

[106] ibid, [26].

[107] ibid, [26] (emphasis added). See also [9], where Lord Bingham agrees with the claim that 'the primary role of the law of tort is to provide monetary compensation for those who have suffered material damage rather than to vindicate the rights of those who have not'.

[108] See, eg, ibid, [62] and [64] (Lord Rodger).

> The function of *the law of delict* ... is to ensure that if loss is caused by another person's wrongful act the loss will be compensated ... It is not the function of *the law of delict* to exact anything more, and certainly not anything by way of punishment.[109]

Hence, he reasoned, the function of the misfeasance tort was 'to compensate the claimant, not to punish the public officer'.[110]

This conception of misfeasance in public office as part of 'tort law' is also evident in some of the academic writing in this area, and underlies the analysis of the cause of action in John Murphy's article 'Misfeasance in a Public Office: A Tort Law Misfit?'.[111] Murphy describes his article as an exploration of the peculiarities of the misfeasance tort from the perspective of what he terms two popular contemporary theories of *tort law* (namely rights-based theory and corrective justice theory), and identifies four significant problems of fit he believes the cause of action represents for these theories. He goes on to claim—not entirely convincingly—that misfeasance is not as anomalous as the theories in question might lead us to believe. However, although Murphy's account of the misfeasance tort itself is broadly consistent with the public law conception of the cause of action favoured here—he argues that the tort plays a discrete and vital role in holding public officers to account, and serves to 'correct and deter egregious abuses of public power'[112]—and although, at one point, he describes misfeasance as a 'public wrong',[113] Murphy nevertheless chooses to classify misfeasance as part of a category he terms 'tort law', and fails to advert to the possibility that a categorisation in terms of 'public law' might be more appropriate. And yet a cause of action located within public law can hardly be thought to pose a problem for theories that we might more accurately describe, not as theories of 'tort law', but as theories of *private law* (or, if not the whole of private law, at least a substantial slice of it).[114] Classification of the misfeasance tort along the lines argued for in this chapter would

[109] ibid, [31] (emphasis added). See also [81] (Lord Carswell).

[110] ibid, [32].

[111] Murphy (n 84). For another example of the characterisation of misfeasance as part of 'tort law' having an impact on scholarly analysis of the cause of action, see Chamberlain (n 84) 218 ('the development of misfeasance into a compensation for public wrongs is 'unsuited to the fundamental structure of tort law'); 232–33 (arguing that 'in its instrumentalism, the modern analysis [of misfeasance] ignores the normative foundations of tort law'); and 239 (contrasting 'public law remedies' and 'tort law remedies', and claiming that in its current state misfeasance is 'inconsistent with the underlying purpose and structure of tort law').

[112] Murphy (n 84) 74–75.

[113] ibid, 58.

[114] The two works that Murphy particularly focuses on are E Weinrib, *The Idea of Private Law* (Boston, Harvard University Press, 1995); and Stevens (n 59). Although Weinrib's book is primarily concerned with tort liability, the title of the work makes clear that his concern is solely with 'private law', and he says nothing about misfeasance. As for Stevens, although his work is entirely concerned with tort liability, he seems untroubled by misfeasance, which he seems to accept does not fit his rights-based theory, and which he describes (at 242) as 'a genuinely public wrong'. We can presumably surmise from this (and from other passages in his book) that Stevens does not envisage his theory as encompassing anything other than what we might call the 'private law of tort'.

therefore seem completely to undermine Murphy's central argument that the tort poses 'considerable problems of fit'[115] for the theories in question.

B. The Private Law Conception

That takes us neatly to another conception of the misfeasance tort that can be contrasted (this time more directly) with the public law conception put forward in this chapter. The gist of this analysis is that the cause of action for misfeasance can plausibly be accommodated within a rights-based account of private law. Two different accounts along these lines can be found in the scholarly literature.

The first such account is that of Erika Chamberlain, who maintains that misfeasance in public office is a tort that arises out of a Hohfeldian right-duty relation of the orthodox kind.[116] On closer inspection, Chamberlain's argument is essentially a historical one, in that she claims that, originally, the claimant in a misfeasance action was required to establish the violation of an existing legal right (for example, in *Ashby*, the right to vote),[117] and that in recent times the courts have either watered down or simply abandoned this requirement. Although this historical claim seems doubtful,[118] it need not detain us here. The public law conception of the misfeasance tort argued for in this chapter purports to provide an interpretation of the modern tort of misfeasance, and, to the extent that Chamberlain's account does not seek to do this, it does not represent a challenge to that conception. (Indeed, at one point, Chamberlain expressly accepts that the misfeasance tort is now 'a compensation system for public wrongs'.)[119] Nevertheless, it is worth pointing out that Chamberlain's pre-existing right analysis seems to rest on a rather fuzzy concept of rights. She maintains, for example, that the plaintiff in *Roncarelli* 'had a right not to have his liquor licence revoked for reasons irrelevant to the relevant licensing legislation', and that the defendant in the case violated this right.[120] It is uncertain what kind of right Chamberlain has in mind here. If the plaintiff in the case had a traditional private law right of some kind, then it is wholly unclear what it was, and why he did not simply rely on that right, instead of bringing the type of action that he brought. It seems, however, that Chamberlain conceives of the 'right' in question as some kind of administrative/procedural right. At one point, for example, she says that '[s]ome rights are enforceable as a matter of administrative law by *certiorari* or *mandamus*',[121] and in a later paper she says that misfeasance 'has historically protected rights of a more civic or political

[115] Murphy (n 84) 74.

[116] See in particular Chamberlain (n 84) and (n 48). For another critique of Chamberlain's position, see Murphy (n 84) 56–58.

[117] See, eg, Chamberlain (n 84) 219.

[118] Murphy (n 84) 56; and on *Ashby* in particular, see Aronson (n 5) 33.

[119] Chamberlain (n 84) 218.

[120] ibid, 230.

[121] ibid, 220.

nature'.[122] At this point, it becomes doubtful whether Chamberlain is using the language of rights in any meaningful sense. After all, she seems to accept that the right of which she speaks does not fit the Hohfeldian right-duty model typically associated with private law,[123] and yet it is wholly unclear what alternative rights model she thinks is applicable in the public law sphere (where the claim that a holder of a liquor licence has a *right* not to have it revoked for irrelevant reasons would surely raise eyebrows).[124]

Four further points should be made about Chamberlain's account. The first is that Chamberlain argues that, historically, the misfeasance tort was limited to the first, 'targeted malice,' limb; that recognition of the second, 'illegality,' limb dates back only to the 1986 case of *Bourgoin SA v Ministry of Agriculture*;[125] and that this development undermined 'the historical standing rules of misfeasance'.[126] However, these claims are highly dubious, not least because: (1) in legal terms, 'malice' has traditionally extended beyond its popular sense of personal spite to encompass 'conscious violation of the law to the prejudice of another';[127] and (2) the modern incarnation of misfeasance as a tort is traceable to a 1959 decision that exemplifies the illegality limb of the cause of action.[128] The second point is that, in her most recent paper on the subject, Chamberlain posits an alternative rights-based account of the misfeasance tort, according to which it instantiates a right 'not to be foreseeably harmed by a public officer's deliberately unlawful conduct'.[129] Setting aside the difficulties of formulating a right along these lines that encompasses both limbs of the misfeasance tort (Chamberlain's version appears somewhat simplified), both the plausibility and the utility of a rights analysis of the tort along these lines are questionable, and it seems to me that it does not represent a serious challenge to a public law analysis of the tort. The third point is that, in the same paper, Chamberlain hedges her bets somewhat, by putting forward an alternative account of misfeasance as a deterrence mechanism.[130] This account seems perfectly plausible, and is consistent with the public law conception of the tort argued for in this paper. And the final point is that Chamberlain's attempt to provide a private law account of the misfeasance tort in terms of rights can be contrasted

[122] Chamberlain (n 48) 561.

[123] ibid, 562. On the relevance of Hohfeldian rights to the public law/private law distinction, see n 59.

[124] Indeed, Aronson (n 5), a public lawyer, specifically denies (at 629) that the plaintiff in *Roncarelli* had a right to maintain or renew his permit. Naturally, it would be different if on the facts a *human right* of the claimant were engaged.

[125] [1986] QB 716.

[126] Chamberlain (n 84) 223–25.

[127] *Ferguson v Kinnoull* (1842) 9 Cl & F 251, 321; 8 ER 412, 438 (Lord Cottenham). See further Dench (n 24), who says—writing in 1982—that 'there is ample authority for the proposition that an official will be liable in the tort of misfeasance either if he is motivated by ill will or if he acts unlawfully with knowledge of that fact' (at 195).

[128] *Farrington* (n 2).

[129] Chamberlain (n 48) 554. *Cf* the formulation at 567 ('the right not to be injured by the unlawful actions of a public officer'), which is manifestly over-broad.

[130] ibid, 576–78. Note also the marked ambivalence of the conclusion to her paper (at 578–79).

with a number of statements in the case law and literature, which specifically deny that a claim in misfeasance rests on a duty/right relationship, such as Lord Hobhouse's statement in the *Three Rivers* case that the misfeasance tort 'does not, and does not need to, apply where the defendant has invaded a legally protected right of the plaintiff'.[131]

The second account of the misfeasance tort that seeks to locate it within a rights-based system of private law is that of Jason Neyers, who argues that 'much of the modern doctrine of misfeasance in public office can be explained if one accepts' that (as he maintains) 'there exists in English law an implicit doctrine of abuse of rights that prevents persons from acting for the primary purpose of injuring others'.[132]

Neyers' account gives rise to at least two obvious difficulties. The first is that he freely admits that his explanation does not readily encompass the cases falling within the second, 'illegality', limb of the misfeasance tort, where—unlike in the targeted malice cases—the primary purpose of the defendant is not necessarily to injure the claimant. Neyers seeks to explain away many of these cases in two different ways. The first way is by reference to a pre-existing right analysis, which is no more persuasive in his account than it is in Chamberlain's.[133] And the other way is by arguing that some of these cases are abuse of rights cases where the 'abuse has to be proven through a series of derivations'.[134] This second argument is difficult to follow, but seems to amount to a watering down of the 'abuse of rights' idea, such that the desire to injure the claimant need not in fact be the defendant's *primary* purpose, but need only be an incidental by-product of a different goal. This seems to me to be both forced and unconvincing.

The other difficulty with Neyers' abuse of rights rationale is that it is not clear why only public officers are liable for what he calls 'the targeted infliction of gratuitous harm'[135] in the absence of collective action that would amount to the tort of conspiracy. Neyers' attempt to explain this in terms of a 'misguided legal pragmatism' that led the courts to focus first on the most serious abuses of right (namely, those by government officials and in combination) 'until satisfied that a coherent and workable system of liability had been created'[136] again seems forced and unpersuasive, and in any case it is unclear why he assumes that these kinds of abuses *are* more serious than, say, an abuse of overwhelming economic power by a multi-national corporation.[137] All in all, then, Neyers' private law conception of the misfeasance tort is no more convincing than Chamberlain's.

[131] *Three Rivers* (n 8) 229. See also 193 (Lord Steyn); Stevens (n 59) 90; Aronson (n 5) 35; Murphy (n 84) 54–55.

[132] J Neyers, 'Explaining the Inexplicable? Four Manifestations of Abuse of Rights in English Law' in Nolan and Robertson (n 48) 319.

[133] ibid, 320, where again it is unclear what kind of 'right' Neyers thinks is in play.

[134] ibid.

[135] ibid.

[136] ibid, 329.

[137] Note also that the courts have specifically denied that misfeasance can usefully be compared to, or equated with, the so-called 'economic torts' that regulate the use of private economic power: see

VII. Four Implications

Which conception of misfeasance in public office we sign up to has concrete implications for the future development of the cause of action. In this section of the chapter, I identify a number of issues concerning misfeasance where this can be seen, and consider what light the public law conception of the tort can shed on these questions.

A. Standing

The earlier discussion of the *Watkins* case shows that the favoured conception of the misfeasance tort has implications for the question of who should be entitled to bring a claim. In that case, the House of Lords' adoption of the 'tort law' conception of misfeasance caused them to impose a restrictive standing rule, in the form of a material damage requirement reminiscent of negligence. The application of that approach on the facts resulted in a failure to hold the defendant public officers to account for their wilful misconduct, and since this is the primary rationale of the tort on the public law conception of the cause of action, that conception implies a more flexible approach, consistent with the principles governing damages awards in public law more generally.[138]

Issues of 'standing' do not arise as such in private law, where 'entitlement to a remedy and the right to apply for that remedy' are not treated as separate questions.[139] In public law, by contrast, standing is 'seen as a separate preliminary or jurisdictional issue going to the right to apply for a remedy and not to the merits',[140] and is the subject of a voluminous literature.[141] Analysis of standing in the misfeasance context can usefully be illuminated by consideration of that literature, but it also needs to be remembered that (unlike in judicial review proceedings) there is, in this case, no separation of the 'right to complain' and the 'right to a remedy'.[142] Furthermore, the 'tort' element of the misfeasance cause of action is reflected in the requirement of damage, which cannot be ignored.[143]

Sanders v Snell [1998] HCA 64, 196 CLR 329 [37], [39] (Gleeson CJ, Gaudron, Kirby and Hayne JJ); and *Three Rivers* (n 13) 583 (Clarke J).

[138] As to which, see P Cane, 'Damages in Public Law' (1999) 9 *Otago Law Review* 489. According to Cane (at 505), '[i]t is widely accepted that the availability of damages against the state should not be limited to infringement of interests in the traditional catalogue'.

[139] P Cane, 'The Function of Standing Rules in Administrative Law' [1980] *Public Law* 303, 303. See similarly Craig (n 52) 772 ('[i]n private law there is no separation of standing and the merits'). *Cf* Stevens (n 59) ch 8.

[140] Cane (n 139) 303–04.

[141] For an overview of the topic in the English context, see Craig (n 52) ch 25.

[142] Cane (n 139) 306.

[143] This requirement is of course rooted in the ancient distinction between actions in trespass and actions on the case. The latter (of which misfeasance is an example) were almost invariably actionable

The trick, then, is to define damage in terms that serve both to differentiate the claimant from members of the public in general—to 'mark the claimant out', as it were—and to justify an award of compensatory damages, while not unduly compromising the primary aim of holding public officers to account for their wilful misconduct. In my view, the solution to this lies either in a requirement that the claimant must have been 'personally adversely affected' by the misconduct (a test that has been recommended for use in the public law context more generally),[144] or alternatively in the notion of the claimant as a 'victim' of the defendant's misconduct that draws on the standing rules employed in human rights instruments such as the European Convention on Human Rights.[145]

B. Who Can Be Liable

The public law conception of the misfeasance tort also has implications for who should be subject to potential liability. Carol Harlow's proposal that the tort be expanded to give a remedy against private defendants exercising corporate power[146] can, for example, be rejected, as the public law conception of the cause of action rests on the assumption that there is something particularly reprehensible about the misuse of *public* power, and that holding officials publicly to account for wilful misconduct serves to strengthen the bond between the state and its citizens. The misuse of purely *private* power raises very different questions, and is better dealt with in other ways. It is not a matter for public law.[147] Lord Devlin's reasoning when ruling out the possibility of extending exemplary damages to cases of abuse of private power is highly pertinent in this respect:

> When one man is more powerful than another, it is inevitable that he will try to use his power to gain his ends; and if his power is much greater than the other's, he might perhaps be said to be using it oppressively. If he uses his power illegally, he must of course pay for his illegality in the ordinary way; but he is not to be punished simply because he is the more powerful. In the case of the government, it is different, for the servants of

only on proof of damage. But even if we set aside the historical baggage—as recommended in *Watkins* (n 74) by both Lord Walker (at [74]) and Lord Carswell (at 78])—it would not make sense to treat misfeasance as actionable per se. This is because that concept makes sense only where the defendant has violated a right of the claimant but caused no loss, and we have seen that, in misfeasance cases, liability is not based on a right violation of this kind.

144 See, eg, Law Commission (England and Wales), *Administrative Law: Judicial Review and Statutory Appeals* (Law Com No 226, 1994) 41–44. See also Cane (n 138) 505 ('made worse off').

145 *European Convention on Human Rights*, art 34. This latter possibility would echo the requirement that exemplary damages are recoverable only by a 'victim' of the defendant's punishable behaviour: see *Rookes* (n 85) 1227 (Lord Devlin).

146 Harlow (n 29) 130. See also *Bradford Metropolitan CC v Arora* [1991] 3 All ER 545, 552 (Neill LJ) and *Kuddus* (n 13) [66] (Lord Nicholls), where similar points are made in respect of exemplary damages.

147 *R v Disciplinary Committee of the Jockey Club, ex p Aga Khan* [1993] 1 WLR 909, 932 (Hoffmann LJ).

> the government are the servants of the people and the use of their power must always be subordinate to their duty of service.[148]

A more difficult question is which of those persons who work for, or do work for, public entities should be susceptible to misfeasance liability. Singling out those traditionally classed as public officers may serve to exclude public employees with minimal public responsibilities and those who discharge public duties by virtue of having contracted with a public authority.[149] This has caused Aronson to argue that the tort should be restyled as 'abuse of public power' and extended to public employees who are not office-holders and to contractors performing governmental functions that have been outsourced.[150] Again, a functional approach should be adopted, but this does not require any re-styling of the cause of action. Rather, public officers should be simply be defined in a way that meshes with the rationale of the tort. The definition used earlier—that a public officer is a person who exercises governmental power[151]—is ideal, as it is by giving special power to a person that the public reposes trust in him or her, and so only a person with such power is capable of the betrayal of public trust at which both the tort and the parallel crime are directed.[152] And if the concept of a public officer extends to all those 'vested with governmental authority and the exercise of executive powers' (as Lord Hobhouse put it in *Three Rivers*),[153] then it is irrelevant whether or not the defendant is actually employed in the public service.[154]

C. To Which Types of Misconduct Can Liability Attach?

That takes us to a closely related issue,[155] namely the types of misconduct to which misfeasance liability can attach. One possibility would be to limit liability to misconduct that amounts to an exercise of the defendant's power as a public officer (that is to say an exercise of the power the conferral of which on the defendant makes the defendant a public officer). There are two reasons why this possibility must be rejected.[156] The first is that much of the conduct that amounts to

[148] *Rookes* (n 85) 1226.

[149] Finn (n 26) 314.

[150] Aronson (n 5) 44. See also Arrowsmith (n 29) 232 (the misfeasance tort should arguably be extended to nationalised industries and privatised public utilities).

[151] See n 26.

[152] This point is made particularly clearly in *Cannon* (n 26) at [53]. See also *Leerdam v Nouri* [2009] NSWCA 90, 255 ALR 553 [6], [17] (Spigelman CJ).

[153] *Three Rivers* (n 8) 229.

[154] *Crawford Adjusters* (n 15) [134] (Lord Sumption). See also Aronson (n 11) 437 (who draws an analogy with the extension of judicial review to 'private sector actors exercising public power'). The same point was made forcefully in the context of the parallel criminal offence by Lord Millett NPJ in *HKSAR v Kay* (HKCFA FACC No 3 of 2011) at [44].

[155] Indeed, it has been argued in the context of the parallel criminal offence that it is a mistake to separate the two questions out at all: see *HKSAR v Kay* (n 154) [46] (Lord Millett NPJ).

[156] See also *Odhavji* (n 9) [17] (Iacobucci J), denying that the misfeasance tort is limited to cases in which the defendant is 'engaged in the unlawful exercise of a particular statutory or prerogative power'.

misfeasance in public office will be unlawful as a matter of public law, so that by acting in this way the defendant will frequently have exceeded his or her powers.[157] And the other reason is that an omission can clearly amount to misfeasance for the purposes of the tort, and yet it is hard to conceive of a failure to act—for example, a failure by a financial regulator to take measures with respect to a bank in difficulties[158]—as an *exercise of power*.[159] This second objection also rules out a broader version of this test, which overcomes the first objection by extending the test to encompass a 'purported' exercise of public power.[160]

Then again, a rival test, according to which a misfeasance action can lie in respect of 'any act or omission done or made by a public official in purported performance of the functions of his office',[161] seems too broad. Take the case of *Jones v Swansea City Council*, where it was alleged that the defendant council's refusal to allow one of its tenants to change the use of rented commercial property had been motivated by malice. Although the council's decision was not susceptible to judicial review, because the power to refuse permission derived not from statute but from the terms of the lease, the English Court of Appeal held that it could nonetheless be the subject of an action in misfeasance. According to Slade LJ:

> I see no reason why a decision taken by the holder of a public office, in his or its capacity as such holder ... should be incapable of giving rise to an action in tort for misfeasance of public office merely because the decision is taken in the exercise of a power conferred by a contract and in this sense has no public element ... in the present context ... it is not the juridical nature of the relevant power but the nature of the council's office which is the important consideration.[162]

[157] See also ibid, [30] (Iacobucci J). Indeed, this must by definition be true in cases that fall within the second, illegality, limb, of the tort, the whole point of which is that the defendant knew that he or she *lacked* the power to do the act complained of.

[158] This was the basis of the litigation against the Bank of England in *Three Rivers* (n 8), where Lord Hutton specifically said (at 228) that the tort could be constituted by an omission as well as by acts (see also Lord Hobhouse at 230). Both *Garrett* (n 7) (alleged failure properly to investigate rape complaint) and *Odhavji* (n 9) (alleged failure to co-operate with investigation into fatal shooting) were omissions cases. As Aronson points out (n 5, 50), the misfeasance tort 'clearly covers wilful refusals to perform public duties', and the same is true of the parallel crime: see, eg, *R v Dytham* [1979] QB 722 (policeman who failed to help a man beaten to death outside a club guilty of the offence of misconduct in a public office).

[159] See also *Mengel* (n 6) 355 (Brennan J).

[160] For the use of a test along these lines, see *Calveley v Chief Constable of the Merseyside Police* [1989] AC 1228, 1031–32 (Lord Bridge).

[161] *Mengel* (n 6) 355. See also the very broad test favoured by Arrowsmith (n 29) 231 ('all acts done in the course of an authority's business').

[162] [1990] 1 WLR 54, 70–71. See also at 85 (Nourse LJ) ('It is not the nature or origin of the power which matters. Whatever its nature or origin, the power may be exercised only for the public good. It is the office on which everything depends'). The issue did not arise on appeal to the House of Lords, but Lord Lowry said that he was inclined to agree with the reasoning of the Court of Appeal: [1990] 1 WLR 1453, 1458. See also *Calveley* (n 160), where Lord Bridge said (at 1032) that a senior police officer's decision to suspend a subordinate would be capable of attracting misfeasance liability; and *Emanuele v Hedley* (1998) 179 FCR 290, where it was held that a public officer could be liable in misfeasance in respect of an activity no different to that daily undertaken by many in the private sector, namely stimulating interest in a land sale.

The problem with this approach is that it is hard to square with the public law rationale of the tort, which suggests a closer link to the availability of judicial review, and to require that in some sense the public officer was engaged in the act of 'governing' or 'public regulation' when the misconduct occurred, as opposed to employing the merely private, or economic, power of a landlord or employer.[163] After all, only in the former category of case can there be said to be a betrayal of the trust that the public put in the defendant by conferring a *special* power on him or her. For this reason, it is suggested that the ambit of misfeasance liability should be limited to conduct of a public officer 'in the exercise of public functions', as was held by the Supreme Court of Canada in the *Odhavji* case.[164]

D. Vicarious Liability

The final issue is the question of vicarious liability. In English law, it would appear that the general principles of vicarious liability apply in misfeasance cases,[165] but in *Mengel* the High Court of Australia suggested that vicarious liability would arise only exceptionally, where there was de facto authority for the misconduct in question.[166] Quite what was meant by this was left unclear. The ambiguity in the Commonwealth case law on this issue is echoed in the scholarly literature. According to Aronson, there is no reason why vicarious liability should not be imposed in the usual way, and (connectedly) it is perfectly reasonable for the relevant public authority to meet the costs of the litigation and any personal liability imposed on the public officer.[167] Indeed, Cane goes further, and argues that 'it is symbolically important that the government should accept responsibility to citizens even for the acts of rogue functionaries'.[168] However, Chamberlain points out that the fact that damages are typically not paid by the public officer individually 'seriously undermines the deterrent effect of the misfeasance tort', while acknowledging that the possibility that public authorities will discipline wrongdoers and develop

[163] For a similar argument with respect to the scope of the parallel criminal offence, see JR Spencer, 'Policemen Behaving Badly: The Abuse of Misconduct in Office' [2010] *CLJ* 423. And for an illuminating discussion of the same issue in the judicial review context, see Craig (n 52) 854–55.

[164] *Odhavji* (n 9) [30] (Iacobucci J).

[165] *Racz v Home Office* [1994] 2 AC 45; *Three Rivers* (n 8) 191 (Lord Steyn), 230 (Lord Hobhouse). In *Kuddus* (n 13), for example, the defendant was the Chief Constable, rather than the individual police officer accused of misconduct.

[166] *Mengel* (n 6) 347. See also *Emanuele* (n 162), where the Federal Court of Australia held that vicarious liability should not be imposed where a public officer had acted in plain derogation of the duty owed to his employer. Note that the difference between English and Australian law on this question may now be reinforced by differing approaches to the question of when an employee's deliberate wrongdoing falls within the course of his or her employment. The leading cases are *Lister v Hesley Hall Ltd* [2001] UKHL 22, [2002] 1 AC 215 and *New South Wales v Lepore* (2003) 212 CLR 511 (HCA) respectively.

[167] Aronson (n 5) 45–48. Aronson's understanding is that governments do in fact meet these costs in misfeasance cases: ibid, 46.

[168] Cane (n 138) 513.

policies to minimise future misuse of power may still enable the tort to perform a deterrence function.[169]

The ambivalence in respect of vicarious liability reflects the two differing public law conceptions of the misfeasance tort. On the deterrence model, as Chamberlain points out, the imposition of vicarious liability may be seen as problematic, since it could be argued that just as a public officer can be fined or imprisoned for committing the crime of misconduct, so they should foot the bill personally if held liable for the parallel tort. However, on the alternative (and in my view preferable) public law conception of the tort as a mechanism for holding public officers to account for wilful misconduct, the possibility of vicarious liability seems unproblematic. What matters on this view of the tort is that there is a public demonstration of the fact that deliberate abuse of public office is intolerable behaviour for which the relevant official will be held to account by the courts. Who actually foots the bill is neither here nor there.[170]

VIII. Conclusion

I would like to make two final points by way of conclusion. The first is that the continuing debates over the nature of the cause of action for misfeasance in public office reflect the late arrival in common law systems of a clear distinction in substantive terms between public law and private law.[171] Although it has been argued in this chapter that the misfeasance tort is best understood in public law terms, the very fact that it is a tort makes this analysis counter-intuitive and (for some) troublesome. And yet, as Geoffrey Samuel has said—echoing Maine and Maitland—in common law systems 'much "public law" has been secreted in the interstices of private law',[172] and so it should come as no surprise if, in misfeasance cases, the courts have 'tried to craft a certain kind of public outcome with the tools of private law'.[173] Only if we are prepared to look beyond categories like 'tort law' to consider

[169] Chamberlain (n 48) 578.

[170] Tellingly, there is a similar ambivalence when it comes to vicarious liability and exemplary damages. In *Kuddus* (n 13), for example, Lord Scott took the view (at [131]-[137]) that vicarious liability for exemplary damages was contrary to principle, but Lord Hutton said (at [79]) that the power to award exemplary damages where an employing authority was held vicariously liable for official misconduct 'serves to uphold and vindicate the rule of law because it makes clear that the courts will not tolerate such conduct' (though he ultimately chose to leave the matter open, as did Lord Nicholls (at [69]), the question not having been raised on the appeal).

[171] See *O'Reilly v Mackman* [1983] 2 AC 237, 277 (Lord Diplock). See also JWF Allison, 'Variation of View on English Legal Distinctions Between Public and Private' [2007] *CLJ* 698, 705.

[172] G Samuel, 'Governmental Liability in Tort and the Public and Private Law Distinction' (1988) 8 *Legal Studies* 277, 301.

[173] D McKee, 'The Public/Private Distinction in *Roncarelli v Duplessis*' (2010) 55 *McGill Law Journal* 461, 471.

the different substantive roles played by public law and private law can we hope to understand the true nature of the misfeasance action.

And the second point is that, although in this chapter I have emphasised the distinction between public law and private law, it is fitting to end on a more harmonious note, and to point out the intriguing parallels between the public law conception of misfeasance in public office that I have put forward and fiduciary principles found in private law.[174] As Chamberlain points out in her discussion of a possible deterrence rationale for the misfeasance tort:

> A useful analogy can be drawn between fiduciaries and public officials. Both are entrusted with fairly substantial powers, which they are expected to use in the best interests of their beneficiaries or the public, respectively. Given the natural temptation to misuse these powers, it is important to have meaningful consequences for any abuse. The law protects the integrity of both the fiduciary relationship and the rule of law by imposing penalties that are sufficiently severe to deter future misuse of power.[175]

Though one might quibble with the presentation of this parallel in purely deterrence terms, the force of the analogy still hits home. For while, admittedly, the distinction between betrayal of private trust and betrayal of public trust seems fundamental, the fact remains that in both contexts it is the betrayal of trust—trust encapsulated in a conferral of power—which lies at the heart of the relevant law.

[174] Analogies with trustees and fiduciaries are also drawn by Lord Hobhouse in *Three Rivers* (n 8) at 235–36; by Wit J in *Marin* (n 75) at [103]; and by Aronson (n 5) at 8–9. For a more general conception of the relationship between citizenry and state as fiduciary in nature, see Finn (n 1).

[175] Chamberlain (n 48) 578.

9

Public Power, Discretion and the Duty of Care

KIT BARKER*

I. Introduction

One of the key features of a public body—a feature that enables it to perform most of the functions accorded to it—is that it is imbued with statutory powers that private individuals lack. The latter do, of course, have powers of their own—they can create their own personal rights and duties through contract, for example, or create and dispose of property rights. But public powers are obviously far more extensive and all-encompassing than those enjoyed by you, or I. This reflects the need for society to overcome the limitations that inhere in individual, as opposed to collective capacities; and it is legitimised by constitutional checks and balances. Government needs more powers precisely because it is charged with grander social and regulatory tasks of a type that you and I cannot practically undertake alone; and it is legitimate for it have them (only) because they carry the stamp of democracy and because their exercise is subject to careful scrutiny by an independent judiciary with its own significant powers of review.

Just as statutory powers are a key feature of public bodies, so too is discretion a key feature of many of the powers that public bodies have. Discretions pose a challenge for traditional conceptions of the rule of law, but they are also essential in the modern day to the capacity of government to carry out its functions efficiently and effectively. The increased contemporary importance of discretionary public power has credibly been attributed to the broadening of state functions that has occurred since the nineteenth century, the increased technicality of many important regulatory tasks, and the complexity and variability of the types of decision that state officials are nowadays called upon to make.[1] Standardised answers and

* My thanks to Peter Billings, Ross Grantham and Donal Nolan for their helpful comments on an earlier draft. All remaining errors are my own.

[1] D Galligan, *Discretionary Powers A Legal Study of Official Discretion* (Oxford, Clarendon Press, 1986) 64–84.

hard and fast rules are less appropriate in fields of welfare provision than they are, for example, when it comes to fixing property rights, or the terms of commercial contracts. The additional flexibility and efficiency that discretions can bring to modern administrative practice is therefore thought to justify the sacrifice they entail in terms of transparency and predictability of legal standards, provided that they are subject to sufficiently exacting, independent controls.

This is what one might call the public law perspective upon discretionary public powers in the modern day: such powers are viewed as both crucially important to the achievement of our collective ends and yet as potentially dangerous—flexible tools to be embraced, but jealously guarded to ensure their compliance with accepted norms of legality, rationality, procedural fairness and respect for fundamental human rights. There is also, however, an important, private law dimension to discretionary public powers. This relates to the effect that the 'discretionary' quality of such powers has upon determinations of a public body's civil liability—in particular, its liability for negligence. What effect, private law asks, does the existence of 'discretion' in respect of a public power have upon an authority's duty to take care not to harm particular, private interests when exercising it?

This is the question considered in this chapter. It has been central to debates in the law of negligence for many years and has proven particularly controversial and difficult to answer, despite being regularly litigated at the highest appellate level in several jurisdictions[2] and attracting the attention of distinguished jurists,[3]

[2] England and Wales: *Suffolk Rivers Catchment Board v Kent* [1941] AC 74 (HL); *Home Office v Dorset Yacht Co Ltd* [1970] AC 1004 (HL); *Anns v Merton London Borough Council* [1978] AC 728 (HL); *X (Minors) v Bedfordshire County Council* [1995] 2 AC 633 (HL); *Stovin v Wise* [1996] AC 293 (HL); *Barrett v Enfield London Borough Council* [2001] 2 AC 550 (HL); *Phelps v Hillingdon London Borough Council* [2001] 2 AC 619 (HL); *W and Another v Essex County Council* [2001] 2 AC 592 (HL); *Gorringe v Calderdale Metropolitan Borough Council* [2004] UKHL 15; *D v East Berkshire Area Health Authority* [2005] UKHL 23; *Brooks v Commissioner of Police of the Metropolis and Others* [2005] UKHL 24; *Van Colle and Anor v Chief Constable of the Hertfordshire Police* [2008] UKHL 50; *Trent Strategic Health Authority v Jain* [2009] UKHL 4. Australia: *Sutherland Shire Council v Heyman* (1984) 157 CLR 424 (HCA); *Pyrenees Shire Council v Day* (1998) 192 CLR 330 (HCA); *Romeo v Conservation Commission of the Northern Territory* (1998) 192 CLR 431 (HCA); *Crimmins v Stevedoring Industry Finance Committee* (1999) 200 CLR 1 (HCA); *Brodie v Singleton Shire Council* (2001) 206 CLR 512 (HCA); *Sullivan v Moody* (2001) 207 CLR 562 (HCA); *Graham Barclay Oysters Pty Ltd v Ryan* (2002) 211 CLR 540 (HCA); *Stuart v Tania Kirkland-Veenstra & Anor* (2009) 237 CLR 215 (HCA). Canada: *Just v British Columbia* [1989] 2 SCR 1228 (SCC); *Cooper v Hobart* [2001] 3 SCR 537 (SCC); *Edwards v Law Society of Upper Canada* [2001] 3 SCR 562 (SCC); *R v Imperial Tobacco Canada* [2011] 3 SCR 45 (SCC).

[3] See, eg, S Bailey and M Bowman, 'The Policy/Operational Dichotomy—A Cuckoo in the Nest' (1986) 45 *CLJ* 430; B Feldthusen, 'Failure to Confer Discretionary Public Benefits: The Case for Complete Negligence Immunity' (1997) 5 *Tort Law Review* 17; S Bailey & M Bowman, 'Public Authority Negligence Revisited' (2000) 59 *CLJ* 85; D Fairgrieve, *State Liability in Tort* (Oxford: Oxford University Press, 2003) esp chs 1–4; C Harlow, *State Liability* (Oxford, Oxford University Press, 2004); C Booth & D Squires, *The Negligence Liability of Public Authorities* (Oxford, Oxford University Press, 2006) esp ch 2; D Nolan, 'Governmental Liability', ch 17 in K Oliphant (ed), *The Law of Tort* 3rd edn (London, Lexis Nexis Butterworths, 2007); M Aronson, 'Government Liability in Negligence' (2008) 32 *Melbourne University Law Review* 44; P Cane, *Administrative Law* 5th edn (Oxford, Oxford University Press, 2011) ch 8 esp 201–10, 213–18; P Vines, 'Straddling the Public/Private Divide: Tortious Liability of Public Authorities' (2010) 9 *The Judicial Review* 445; B Feldthusen, 'Public Authority Immunity from Negligence Liability: Uncertain, Unnecessary, and Unjustified' (2013) 92 *Canadian Bar Review* 211.

law reform bodies[4] and legislators[5] alike. The existence of 'discretion' in respect of public power is generally understood as weakening private law rights and as militating against, or diluting the content of, duties of care, but its precise effects are still not well understood. Part of the reason for this is that the language of discretion is itself slipperier than a wet fish, so that divining the nature of the problem that the concept of discretion presents is problematic. But there are also larger, normative and empirical forces at work, which are prone to complicate matters and thwart any straightforward accommodation of discretionary power and private law rights. For one thing, public money is now desperately short, which means that hard choices have to be made between using the scarce resources that are available in the public system to compensate the victims of careless, discretionary decision-making, on the one hand, and funding crucial public services, on the other. At the same time, States' human rights obligations have raised public expectations about the levels of protection that citizens are entitled to expect from their governments, particularly in Europe.[6] In the background also, of course, there are continuing and intensifying debates about the proper relationship between private and public law;[7] and about the implications of the rule of law for the way in which private law claims against the state should properly be handled—whether they should be treated in as nearly-as-possible-the-same way as those involving private parties, or be subject to some special regime. Profound insights into the way in which the private liabilities of the state are conceptualised and constructed in different jurisdictions in the light of these controversies were provided by Peter Cane's excellent contribution in Chapter 4 of this volume.

The aim of this chapter is to explore the difficult relationship between public discretion and private law duties of care in the light of recent experience in Australia and the United Kingdom. It seeks to identify the nature and source of courts' concerns about discretion in negligence cases and the precise way in which those concerns have affected legal reasoning regarding the duty question. It also briefly considers the way in which the relationship between discretionary power and private rights has recently been changed in Australia by a series of controversial, legislative reforms.

Part II begins with an examination of the various meanings that the term 'discretion' is accorded in the cases and draws out some of the concerns that courts

[4] Law Commission (England and Wales), *Administrative Redress: Public Bodies and the Citizen* (Consultation Paper No 187, 2008 and subsequent Report No 322, 2010); Ipp D et al, *Review of the Law of Negligence: Final Report* (Commonwealth Treasury of Australia, September 2002) ('Ipp Review').

[5] See Part IV.

[6] This is the story in the UK, where the Human Rights Act 1998 (UK) has resulted in a change of culture in negligence cases against public authorities. In many instances, claims under the Act are now brought in parallel with, or in preference to, claims at common law. Claims under the Act are not considered in this chapter. See generally, D Hoffman (ed), *The Impact of the UK Human Rights Act on Private Law* (Cambridge, Cambridge University Press, 2013).

[7] For an overview of some of these debates and the reasons for their recent intensification, see K Barker, 'Private Law: Key Encounters with Public Law' in K Barker and D Jensen (eds), *Private Law: Key Encounters with Public Law* (Cambridge, Cambridge University Press, 2013) 3.

have about imposing tort liabilities on public powers of a 'discretionary' type. Part III then explores the way in which these concerns affect courts' reasoning about duties of care. Part IV provides an overview of the most controversial features of the Australian legislation.

II. Discretion—A Protean[8] Concept

To understand the way in which concerns about discretion affect courts' decisions about a public body's negligence liability, one must first identify what they mean by the term 'discretion'. Unfortunately, this is a matter about which judges are themselves unclear.

A 'central' sense of the term is usefully provided by Professor Galligan in his seminal work on discretionary powers:

> Discretion, as a way of characterising a type of power in respect of certain courses of action is most at home in referring to power delegated within a system of authority to an official or set of officials, where they have some significant scope for settling the reasons and standards according to which that power is to be exercised, and for applying them in the making of specific decisions.[9]

As Galligan himself accepts, however, the concept of discretion is accorded more than one meaning in the law.[10] In the current context, I suggest that it has been equated with at least four, distinct ideas: (i) the existence of a '*power*' in the hands of a decision-maker (a capacity to change others' legal rights and duties); (ii) an *immunity* from any liability in respect the exercise of the power; (iii) 'freedom of choice' as to how to use the power (what a Hohfeldian[11] might call a '*privilege*' or *liberty* from any duty to use it in one way, rather than another, or to take any particular level of care in its use); and (iv) the exercise by a decision-maker of some *judgement* (as in the phrase—'just use your discretion'). Galligan's own definition references more than one of these ideas, I think, adverting as it does to an official's authority, power, and the existence of some 'scope' for the official to choose his

[8] *Carty v Croydon London Borough Council* [2005] EWCA Civ 19, [25] (Dyson LJ).

[9] Galligan (n 1) 21.

[10] ibid, ch 1. Some of the identified meanings provided by Galligan in the public law context map on to those identified here as being in judicial use in private law.

[11] The basic terms used in this section (power, liability, duty, immunity and privilege) are all derived from Hohfeld's scheme, to which I have sought to adhere as closely as possible throughout the chapter. For the full analytical scheme with its terms, their correlatives and opposites, see W Hohfeld, *Fundamental Conceptions as Applied in Judicial Reasoning*, W Cook ed, (New Haven CT, Yale University Press, 1919). The application of Hohfeldian conceptions of duty and right to the relationship between citizen and state (or public body) remains controversial, but is not unprecedented. For discussion and references, see K Barker, 'Private and Public: The Mixed Concept of Vindication in Torts and Private Law' ch 3 in S Pitel, J Neyers and E Chamberlain (eds), *Tort Law: Challenging Orthodoxy* (Oxford, Hart Publishing, 2013) 59, 65 and fn 19.

or her own reasons and standards, both when it comes to making rules and in determining how to interpret and apply them. The idea of an official having some 'scope to choose' reasons and standards could itself be an allusion to the existence of either a privilege in respect of the decision that is being made (a liberty to choose amongst different options, free of any duty), or an immunity.

A. Discretion as Power

If discretion is understood in the first sense, then the idea of a 'discretionary power' is tautologous: if all one means in describing a statutory power as 'discretionary' is that its possessor has the ability to change others' rights and duties (for example by taking a child into care, a criminal into custody, or by withdrawing a liquor licence from a commercial enterprise), then one is simply restating that which any legal power necessarily entails.[12] One can, of course, loosely engage in this type of talk and sometimes we do. I can say that my fate lies within your 'discretion' and you will probably know that I mean you have the ability to change it for better, or for worse—that my life lies 'in your hands'. But when courts refer to a statutory power as a 'discretionary' one, they must surely be using the term discretion in a different sense than this, unless they are to be regarded as needlessly repeating themselves.

B. Discretion as Immunity ('No Liability')

More often, judges referring to discretionary decisions mean that the decision-maker has a limited domain of immunity in respect of the decision in question.[13] A body has an immunity when it is not *liable* to any legal consequence (i.e. any change in its legal duties) as a result of what it does, or omits to do, because courts have no *power* to impose legal responsibilities upon it. Blanket public body immunities are now rare, but courts have nonetheless often identified 'discretionary'

[12] Assuming, of course, that one follows the definitions of the Hohfeldian scheme, ibid.

[13] See, eg, *Anns* (n 2) 754 (Lord Wilberforce) (identifying 'discretions' with 'policy' decisions which it is 'for the authority or body to make … not … the courts'); *Ross v Secretary of State for Scotland* [1990] SLT 13, 16–18 (Lord Milligan) (aligning discretion with 'policy' decisions' that are not susceptible to judicial scrutiny and which therefore attract 'no liability' and a qualified 'immunity'); *X* (n 2) 736 (Lord Browne-Wilkinson) ('a local authority cannot be *liable* in damages for doing that which Parliament has authorised. … if the decisions complained of fall within the ambit of … statutory discretion they cannot be *actionable* in common law') (my emphasis); *Barrett* (n 2) 561 (Lord Slynn) ('if an authority acts … within its discretion—ie it is doing what Parliament has said it can do … then there can be no *liability*') (my emphasis); *Connor v Surrey County Council* [2010] EWCA Civ 286, [82]–[83] (Laws LJ) (interpreting Lord Browne-Wilkinson, ibid, as identifying statutory discretions with policy choices enjoying 'immunity from suit', which are justified by the statute and the rule of law). For an Australian example of the same use, see *Sutherland Shire Council v Becker* [2006] NSWCA 344, [107] (Bryson JA, Mason P agreeing).

decisions as ones that are 'non-justiciable' by courts and which are therefore 'immune' from liability for constitutional reasons; typically because the decision in question involves the making of legislation or quasi-legislation, or because it relates to matters of social or economic policy properly lying within the remit of elected government, rather than the courts.[14] On this construction, determining whether a decision lies 'within' or 'outside' a public body's 'discretion' entails making a decision about the boundaries of the immunity that has been accorded to it either by the terms of the statute by which it is empowered, or which is a necessary implication of the constitutional law doctrine of the separation of powers.

One difficult aspect of the debate about discretion in this sense, which has divided courts, is whether the existence of a public law immunity in respect of a particular decision necessarily entails an equivalent immunity in the law of negligence. If the function of both areas of the law is to hold public bodies accountable for their actions and regulate their behaviour, then this principle (which I shall call the 'mirror' principle) might be considered desirable, on the basis that otherwise the law as a whole ends up sending mixed messages to public actors. It tells them at one and the same time that their decision is permissible and untouchable in terms of administrative policy and public law, but that making it may nonetheless expose them to serious consequences in terms of legal liability in damages in private law.

The argument for the mirror principle is based on the importance of the law as a whole sending coherent incentive messages to public actors. It has its attractions, but errs in assuming that the functions of public and private law are precisely the same and that it is *only* incentivising public behaviour that is at stake (or important) in either case. In fact, of course, it is *not* the only function of negligence law (if indeed it is a function at all) to incentivise public bodies to adhere to public standards and the rule of law. Private law also has important compensatory and corrective justice functions that public law does not, which could perfectly well justify imposing civil liability for the harmful, careless use of a statutory power, even where the decision in question is 'publicly' unimpeachable. There is therefore no logical contradiction involved in saying that a decision to use a power is both valid and immune from legal consequences (in public law), and negligent (in private law).[15] Any court that reaches such a conclusion is simply expressing the view that doing corrective justice is at least as important a priority for the law of tort as sending coherent, behavioural messages to government officials.

[14] ibid.

[15] This follows from the basic premises of a Hohfeldian, analytical scheme—the absence of any liability on the part of D to public law consequences does not preclude the existence of a private duty to another party. But there are also suggestions that this is acceptable from the point of view of legal policy too: see *Barrett* (n 2) 572 (Lord Slynn) (rejecting 'excess of power' in the administrative law sense as necessary to negligence liability); *Phelps* (n 2) 653 (Lord Slynn). For an analysis of *Phelps*, suggesting that Lords Clyde and Nicholls joined Lord Slynn in rejecting any requirement of ultra vires action as a precondition of tort liability, see Booth & Squires (n 3) [2.43].

Although the mirror principle continues to have its adherents[16] and has undoubtedly impacted historically on the construction of immunities in earlier negligence cases, its popularity has recently declined. It is hence now generally accepted by courts in both England and Australia that a public body's liability in negligence does *not* depend on whether or not a relevant decision was intra or ultra *vires*.[17] In fact, courts have been increasingly keen in recent years to differentiate public and private law immunity concepts, whilst shrinking the ambit of both. In both countries, this accords with the basic, Diceyan view that public and private actors should be treated equally before the law wherever possible.[18]

C. Discretion as Privilege (Liberty—'No Duty')

A public decision-maker has a discretion in the sense of a 'privilege' or liberty when its decision is not attended by any legal duty—whether this be a duty to decide one way or another (what one might call a 'result' duty), or to act in a particular way when deciding (for example to decide rationally, honestly, or with reasonable care). Privileges are distinct and, in practice, less extreme than immunities, because they at least leave open the possibility of courts granting damages in respect of the exercise of a given power. Privileges can attach not just to the exercise of a public body's statutory powers, but also to the performance (or non-performance) of its duties.[19]

Courts now frequently associate public 'discretions' with the absence of any private law duty of care and therefore with privileges in the described sense.[20]

[16] See, eg, P Craig, D Fairgrieve, 'Barrett, Negligence and Discretionary Powers' (1999) *Public Law* 626, 648 (different approaches as between tort and public law 'will not withstand examination' because both public and private law are 'ways of holding a public body to account').

[17] See Part III C (ii).

[18] AV Dicey, *Introduction to the Study of the Law of the Constitution* 7th edn (London, Macmillan, 1908) 189–91, 198–99. For some of the necessary exceptions that finesse the equality principle (including, for example, the whole of modern administrative law), see P Hogg and P Monahan, *Liability of the Crown*, 3rd edn (Scarborough Ontario, Carswell, 2000) [1.2]. For the criticisms of the Diceyan viewpoint and the extent to which it has been varied in the US, where civil liabilities have come to be regarded as one more public accountability mechanism, see Cane, Chapter 4 of this volume, esp, 96–7.

[19] This is sometimes mistakenly thought to be a contradiction in terms, but it is not. The fact that a defendant is under a *public* duty to act is not logically inconsistent with the defendant having no *private* law duty to individual members of the public when acting under the public duty. Indeed, this is the position in most cases involving the breach of statutory duties, save where the statute makes it clear that a private duty is intended. Although 'privilege' and 'duty' are hence logical opposites in a Hohfeldian scheme, a public law duty and a private law privilege (itself correlating to the absence of any private law duty on the part of the authority) can clearly co-exist. For the same reasons there is no logical contradiction between the existence of public law duty and private law immunity: see *Stovin* (n 2) 951–52, 957 (Lord Hoffmann, Lords Goff and Jauncey agreeing).

[20] See, eg, *Crimmins* (n 2) 78 (Kirby J) 'discretions necessarily imply, in some cases at least, … a privilege not to act'); *Phelps* (n 2) 673–74 (Lord Clyde) (aligning discretion with policy matters in respect of which there is less likely to be a duty of care); *Stovin*, 953 (Lord Hoffmann, Lords Goff and Jauncey agreeing) ('In the case of a mere [discretionary] statutory power … the legislature has chosen to confer a discretion *rather than create a duty*') (my emphasis).

Indeed, as we shall see in Part III, although there are probably still some, rare sorts of decision that are accorded an immunity on grounds of their constitutional non-justiciability, in the great majority of cases, courts concerns about 'discretion' are now accommodated either as part of a court's consideration of the question whether or not a duty of care is owed by the defendant on a particular sets of facts, or in considering whether or not the duty has been breached.

Whereas public decision-makers are almost never, for important constitutional reasons, accorded a privilege from their public law duties when exercising their powers (such as the duty to act in accordance with the requirements of legality, or procedural fairness), they are therefore sometimes accorded a privilege from any private law duty of care and the language of 'discretion' has been used to express and justify this result. Unfortunately, saying there is no duty of care because the decision-maker has a statutory 'discretion' in respect of a power does not tell one what sorts of decisions attract the private law privilege, or why. The only way of determining this is to consider the *substance* of the decision itself and the reasons why the imposition of a duty of care in respect of it might be problematic.[21]

D. Discretion as Judgement

A final sense of the word discretion is 'judgement' or 'discernment'.[22] At first sight, it is hard to see why the fact that a public decision involves 'judgement' should militate against the existence of any duty of care. By definition, all human decisions that involve making free choices involve personal judgement. The making of decisions that involve 'discretion' in this sense is therefore not particular to public actors with statutory powers—it is something we all do, every day. As Lord Slynn famously said, there can be discretion (in this sense) even in the hammering-in of a nail,[23] which can hardly be described as a peculiarly public act. Furthermore, whilst some of the choices public actors make undoubtedly require special expertise, or involve decisions that are very sensitive and complex, they are not unique in this regard. It is possible to think of analogous decisions made by private professionals, such as doctors, who also have to operate in discrete, highly specialised fields and who are also required to make difficult, variable, sensitive and carefully co-ordinated choices, including choices about the efficient allocation of scarce resources as between individuals or groups with potentially competing needs.

Although courts therefore sometimes identify the problematic aspect of the exercise of public powers as relating to the fact that they involve 'discretion' in the sense of judgement, the truth is that their real concern is not that personal judgement is involved, but that they do not have the practical *capacity* to be able to *assess* whether or not the exercise of judgement is unreasonable. This is sometimes

[21] *Carty* (n 8) [26] (Dyson LJ).
[22] ibid, [25] (Dyson LJ) ('discretion … connotes the exercise of judgement in making choices').
[23] *Barrett* (n 2) 571.

referred to as the 'practical,' 'pragmatic' or 'competence' aspect of the judicial concern about the justiciability of a public body's decision, which is formally distinct to the concern expressed above about courts intruding upon spheres of immunity or privilege that exist for constitutional reasons.[24] The practical difficulty of assessing decisions regarding statutory powers can stem from the technical, or subjective[25] nature of the statutory standards that an official is called upon to interpret and apply, the variability of the fact patterns concerned (is one decision regarding child welfare ever really like another?), the polycentricity[26] of the decision in question (the idea that the making of the decision may depend on—and itself affect—a network of other decisions being made by the same, or a different public agency), the fact that the parameters of a decision may be constrained by limited resources, the informational constraints that attend the private law system in its current form, or the court's own lack of expertise in the field of public resourcing and budgetary allocation.[27] Where the type of decision being made has no obvious analogy in the private sphere, courts have hence indicated that it is especially difficult (although not always impossible),[28] for a court to judge the public body's behaviour.

There is clear evidence that 'practical' considerations of this kind have been thought to justify granting public bodies a privilege from any duty of care and the language of practical 'incapacity' or 'incompetence' to judge 'discretionary' decisions is now regularly deployed to this effect.[29] Indeed, if the Australian experience of recent years is at all representative, the practical concern is far more often relied upon as a basis for according the public body a privilege, than any constitutional concern they entertain about overstepping their constitutional role in relation to decisions of a political type. This is surprising, because the practical difficulty of

[24] For the practical concern, which now seems to dominate, see, eg, *Dorset Yacht* (n 2) 1067 (Lord Diplock) ('there is no criterion by which a court can assess where the balance lies'); *Barrett* (n 2) 580–81, 583 (Lord Hutton); *Connor* (n 13) [92] (Laws LJ) (identifying a new 'pragmatic approach' in which the 'competence' of the court rather than the 'authority of the legislature' governs the justiciability of discretionary decisions). In Australia, see, eg, *Heyman* (n 2) 468–69 (Mason J); *Brodie* (n 2) 628 (Hayne J); *Crimmins* (n 2) 13 (Gleeson CJ); *Barclay* (n 2) 555 (Gleeson CJ); *Newcastle City Council v Shortland Management Services* [2003] NSWCA 156 [79]–[82] (Spigelman CJ, Mason P and Sheller JA agreeing).

[25] For statutory duties contingent on the interpretation and application of subjective standards, see, eg, *X* (n 2) (Children and Young Persons Act 1969 (UK), s 2(2)); *Shortland* (n 24) (Local Government Act 1993 (NSW), s 114). For an example of statutory powers of this type, see *Stuart* (n 2) (Mental Health Act 1986 (Vic), s 10).

[26] On which, see, L Fuller, 'The Forms and Limits of Adjudication' (1978) 92 *Harvard Law Review* 353, 393–401. For possible examples of 'polycentric' decision, see the decisions in *X* (n 2) regarding child protection, where multiple agencies are involved as part of a network of interconnected, protective choices.

[27] *Dorset Yacht* (n 2) 1067 (Lord Diplock).

[28] *Road and Traffic Authority of New South Wales v Refrigerated Roadways Pty Ltd* [2009] NSWCA 263, [272] (Campbell JA, McColl JA and Sackville AJA agreeing).

[29] See, eg, *Crimmins* (n 2) 13 (Gleeson CJ); *Barclay* (n 2) 555 (Gleeson CJ) ('What is the content of the duty owed …? If it is not possible to answer that question with reasonable clarity, that may cast doubt on the existence of the duty'); *Shortland* (n 24) [82] (Spigelman CJ, Mason P and Sheller JA agreeing).

deciding whether a body has breached its duty is no reason to deny that the duty exists. I do not cease to owe my son a moral duty of kindness, just because it may be difficult for you to decide, on a given set of facts, whether I have been kind, or unkind to him. The same is true regarding legal duties: a public authority deciding whether or not to detain a psychiatric patient does not cease to owe the patient a duty of care simply because it may be difficult to tell whether its decision was reasonable or unreasonable, given the sensitivities of the situation and the competing public and private interests involved. A more logical conclusion is simply that where such difficult, 'discretionary' judgements are involved, the plaintiff is less likely to be able to discharge the onus of proving any breach of duty on the facts.[30] In fact, cases regularly fail on this basis, not least because courts are happy to take account of the resources available to an authority in determining the standard of care that it is expected to observe.[31]

In one, recent case, the New South Wales Court of Appeal said that such problems relating to the assessment of relevant standards in public body cases will indeed, most often, affect a plaintiff's ability to prove breach, but that they can also sometimes negate any duty of care, where it can be predicted that decisions about the use of a given power will *always* be so impossible to judge that it is simply not worth putting the defendant to the obligation to adduce evidence at trial.[32]

The idea here is presumably that, although courts ought in principle (any immunities aside) to be trying to assess the reasonableness or otherwise of a public defendant's conduct on the facts of every, individual case, there are some categories of power, the exercise of which will be universally impossible for courts to judge for one of the reasons identified above; and that this justifies them not wasting public time and money in trying to do so. They may then choose to send a clear message to plaintiffs to not bother litigating decisions about the use of the power in question, by deploying a broad 'no duty' rule.

Examples of statutory powers, the exercise of which will *always* be practically impossible for a courts to judge will surely be rare, so it seems unlikely that judicial difficulties of this sort will provide a reason for them to rule out any duty of care in most instances. Moreover, the strategy of negating duty on account of such difficulties directly contradicts the approach normally deployed in private law[33] and is therefore decidedly questionable from the Diceyan point of view. The usual approach of civil courts toward specialised forms of decision-making is, after all,

[30] An approach favoured by Gibbs CJ (Wilson J agreeing) in *Heyman* (n 2) 448. See also *Barrett* (n 2) 591 (Lord Hutton) ('the standard of care … will have to be determined against the background that [the defendant] … is given discretions to exercise by statute in a sphere involving difficult decisions in relation to the welfare of children'); *Gorringe* (n 2) [5] (Lord Steyn, citing P Craig, *Administrative Law* 5th edn (2003) 898); *Refrigerated Roadways* (n 28); Bailey & Bowman (n 3); Nolan (n 3) [17.11].

[31] *Refrigerated Roadways* (n 28). This principle is now recognised in most Australian states and territories under recent legislation. See, eg, Civil Liability Act 2003 (Qld), s 35(a).

[32] ibid, [280] (Campbell JA, McColl JA and Sackville AJA agreeing). See also *Brodie* (n 2) 628 (Hayne J).

[33] *Stovin* (n 2) 938–39 (Lord Nicholls, dissenting).

simply to abandon difficult breach questions to the contest of expert evidence and, in especially sensitive cases, to accord the benefit of any residual doubt about the matter to the decision-maker, provided that his or her conduct is supported by a respectable body of expert opinion for which there is a rational, evidential basis. That approach applies in both the United Kingdom[34] and Australia[35] to most forms of professional decision and there seems no reason in principle why it could not also be extended to certain, difficult types of public decision, if courts are genuinely struggling with the question whether or not the decision was made with reasonable care.[36] This seems a more rational and defensible approach than throwing one's hands in the air and declaring the relevant sphere of decision to be a duty-free zone.

The upshot of this, initial inquiry into the way judges understand the particular problems of 'discretionary power' is that they use the term 'discretion' to mean very different things, so that the labelling of a public decision as 'discretionary' is likely to be unhelpful as an indicator of whether or not a duty of care will attach to its use.[37] If all we mean by saying that a public actor with a power has a discretion is that he or she has the ability and authority to affect others' rights and duties (in the first sense), then we are stating the obvious without advancing the debate. If we mean that he or she has a potentially difficult, subjective, or specialised judgement to make with finite resources (the fourth sense), then that does nothing *in itself* to distinguish him or her from you or me, or at least from other specialised, expert, private decision-makers. It also does not follow as a matter of either logic, or law, that a duty of care will not be owed, because in many instances the sole effect of the practical difficulty about determining the proper standard will be that it is harder for a plaintiff to prove unreasonable conduct amounting to a breach of duty.[38] If what we mean is that the public actor's decision is attended by an immunity from any private law liability (the second sense), or that he or she

[34] *Bolam v Friern Hospital Management Committee* [1957] 1 WLR 583, 587 (McNair J); *Bolitho v City and Hackney Health Authority* [1998] AC 232 (HL). There is an exception regarding a doctor's informational duties regarding clinical risk: *Montgomery v Lanarkshire Health Board* [2015] UKSC 11 [85]–[88].

[35] The issue is now governed in most States and Territories by statutory equivalents of the *Bolam* standard, with similar exceptions for doctors' informational duties: eg Civil Liability Act 2003 (Qld), s 22; Civil Liability Act 2002 (NSW), s 5O.

[36] J Bell-James and K Barker, 'Negligence Liability in the Wake of Ipp: Sceptical Reflections on the 'Policy Defence' (2016) 40 *Melbourne University Law Review* 1; Bailey & Bowman, 'Policy/Operational Dichotomy' (n 3) 435–36. Bailey & Bowman, 'Negligence Revisited' (n 3) 130 interestingly suggest that this approach is in fact to be found in the judgments of Lords Slynn and Hutton in *Barrett* (n 2) at 98–99 and 115–16 respectively. For a helpful examination of the way in which the technique of varying standards of care could be used more generally, see D Nolan, 'Varying the Standard of Care in Negligence' (2013) 72 *CLJ* 651.

[37] *Barrett* (n 2) 571 (Lord Slynn); *Carty* (n 8) [25] (Dyson LJ): 'the question whether the careless performance of a statutory function can give rise to a negligence claim is not necessarily determined by whether the label "discretion" can be applied to the function'.

[38] See n 30.

has a privilege (the third), then we have at least started to express important and meaningful legal conclusions that have clear repercussions for the existence of a duty of care, but the language of discretion itself tells us nothing about the reasons for drawing those conclusions, or indeed about the circumstances in which they ought to be drawn. For this information, we still have to look elsewhere.

The more we persist in according definitive legal significance in private law to the idea that a public power is 'discretionary,' the more confusion is likely to result. For example, it becomes too easy to slip into the error of thinking that, because a decision is discretionary in one sense of the word, it is also discretionary in another, different, legally significant sense. We might, for example, falsely conclude that the mere fact that a decision of a public body relates to the exercise or non-exercise of a power (the first sense of discretion), or involves a degree of expert or sensitive judgement (the fourth sense) necessarily means that that public body has an immunity from liability (sense two) or enjoys a privilege from any legal duty of care (sense three). Lord Romer fell into precisely this type of error in the *East Suffolk* case, when he assumed that a public authority that has a discretion in the sense of a 'mere statutory power' cannot owe a common law duty to exercise the power,[39] thus automatically enjoying a privilege. This does not follow logically and Lord Romer's assumption has since been proven wrong as a matter of law.[40] Furthermore, whilst one might think that one could reduce the risk of confusion caused by the language of discretion by downgrading its legal status and using it instead merely as a loose 'guide' to the actionability of public decisions in negligence,[41] this does not really help: it is hard to see how a concept can serve usefully even as a 'guide' to the duty question if its underlying meaning is indeterminate. In these circumstances, it seems advisable to look past the language of discretion altogether and identify alternative legal concepts that more precisely map courts' concerns about imposing liability in cases involving statutory powers and the types of decision to which these concerns apply.

III. Discretion, Justiciability and the Duty of Care

To the extent that the above analysis reveals the nature of judicial concerns about imposing duties of care on public parties exercising 'discretionary' public powers,

[39] *East Suffolk* (n 2), 97–98.

[40] It was doubted from an early stage in *Anns* (n 2) 754–55 (Lord Wilberforce) and rejected in *Crimmins* (n 2). There are admittedly signs of reluctance in *Gorringe* (n 2) to impose duties of care on road authorities in circumstances where no statutory duty to maintain the highway exists (I am grateful to Donal Nolan for this point), but the requirement of a statutory duty to act before common liability can arise is not, I suggest, an absolute rule even in English law and the approach was clearly rejected by the High Court of Australia in *Brodie* (n 2).

[41] An approach favoured by Lord Slynn in *Barrett* (n 2) 571 ('the wider the area of discretion accorded, the more likely it is that the matter is not justiciable').

they appear to relate to courts' doubts as to whether they have either the constitutional authority (power) or the practical capacity to judge decisions of a particular type, or types. Such concerns are commonly collectively referred to as concerns about the 'justiciability' of public decisions, but the use of that that umbrella term tends to obscure the fact that the two arguments are fundamentally distinct.[42] They could, after all, apply to completely different sorts of decision: some public decisions may be perfectly easy to adjudge unreasonable (because they are so blatantly ridiculous that anyone—even a non-expert—can tell this to be the case) but nonetheless lie within a domain of immunity that courts refuse to enter upon for constitutional reasons.[43] Conversely, they might raise no constitutional concerns at all (and therefore be, in principle, appropriate for judicial resolution from the political point of view), but simply present hard choices about sensitive matters that a court will struggle to assess, owing to the difficulty and specialised nature of the question at issue.[44]

This section explores the various ways in which courts' concerns about the justiciability of 'discretionary' decisions affect their reasoning about duty, focusing in particular on their vain attempts to develop criteria for distinguishing between cases that are—and are not—justiciable in the constitutional sense. Since the position to which I committed above is that arguments about the practical justiciability of a decision are—or should be—irrelevant to the existence of any immunity or privilege, I focus here solely on the constitutional dimension of the concern, whilst recognising that courts have in practice tended to merge the two arguments in their discussion. The picture that emerges is that courts have become ever more ready in recent years to scrutinise public decisions in the social policy sphere on a case-by-case basis. They have also come to approach these cases in as-nearly-as-possible-the-same way as they would cases involving private parties, rejecting special public law criteria for duty along the way. Both of these are welcome developments from the point of view of the rule of law and the achievement of the aims of corrective justice. On the downside, however, it is still very difficult to identify any clear criterion by which the justiciability of a public decision can be predicted in advance. I shall suggest that this residual uncertainty is likely to prove inescapable, at least as long as the doctrine of justiciability is tied to unstable, judicial conventions regarding the separation of powers.

A. Discretion is Not the Only Concern

Before detailing the criteria which courts have suggested as tests of the constitutional justiciability of public decisions, it is important to acknowledge the fact that

[42] *Refrigerated Roadways* (n 28) [266]–[267] (Campbell J A, Mc Coll JA and Sackville AJA agreeing).

[43] A fictional example might be a decision to cancel all health care services in order to focus on increasing resources for the collection of parking fines.

[44] For example, a decision whether or not to exercise powers to compulsorily detain a person suspected of being a suicide risk, as in *Stuart* (n 2).

the 'discretionary' nature of such decisions is not the only—nor even probably the most important—concern influencing courts' reasoning about duty in such cases. In fact, there are a host of policy factors that operate to limit the scope of any duty of care in public body cases. These include: (i) the fact that the body's liability is very often one for a pure omission to prevent harm that has been more immediately caused by third parties (criminals, builders, employers, careless drivers, for example), or by natural events;[45] (ii) the worry that imposing a duty will cause defensive practices that will deleteriously affect standards of public service provision in the longer term;[46] (iii) the concern that a duty may place the decision-maker in an impossible position of legal or ethical conflict between competing responsibilities owed to different individuals or groups;[47] (iv) the concern that imposing a duty may be incompatible with the 'scheme,' 'intentions' or 'purposes' of the empowering legislation;[48] (v) the perception that 'indeterminate' or 'massive' liabilities could result from a single, wrong, regulatory decision, to the detriment of the public purse (a concern that is especially prevalent where losses are purely economic);[49] (vi) the fear that imposing a duty might result in *incoherence* between the law of negligence and other legal principles (including other domains or principles of private law, but also public law processes for the review of decisions through statutory appeals and judicial review);[50] and (vii) a concern—increasingly loudly voiced by the High Court of Australia in recent years—that an appropriate balance should be struck between the responsibility of public agencies to protect individuals and the latter's duty[51] to look out for themselves[52] (which nowadays manifests itself in the form of a debate about a plaintiff's 'vulnerability').

[45] This is the key issue in many, big cases: eg *Heyman* (n 2); *Barclay* (n 2); *Stuart* (n 2); *Mitchell v Glasgow City Council* [2009] UKHL 11 (all of which failed for lack of the normal relationships of control, assumption of responsibility, specific reliance, or 'creation of risk' that trigger positive duties to act).

[46] See, eg, *Stovin* (n 2) 958 (Lord Hoffmann, Lords Goff and Jauncey agreeing); *Brooks* (n 2); *Van Colle* (n 2).

[47] See, eg, *D v East Berkshire* (n 2); *Lawrence v Pembrokeshire County Council* [2007] EWCA Civ 446; *Jain* (n 2); *Sullivan* (n 2); *X v South Australia* [2005] SASC 150; *Precision Products (NSW) Ltd v Hawkesbury City Council* [2008] NSWCA 278 [114] (Allsop P); *Dansar Pty Ltd v Byron Shire Council* [2014] NSWCA 364 [161], [181] (Meagher JA, Leeming JA agreeing).

[48] See Part III D.

[49] See, eg, *Barclay* (n 2) 665 (Callinan J); *Amaca Pty Ltd v New South Wales* [2004] NSWCA 124 [157] (Ipp JA) (a case of physical injury); *Makawe Pty Ltd v Randwick City Counci*l [2009] NSWCA 412 [93] (Hodgson JA); *Electro Optic Systems Pty Ltd v State of New South Wales* [2014] ACTCA 45 [353] (Jagot J), [733] (Katzmann J).

[50] *X* (n 2) (duty of care inconsistent with statutory consultation and appeals schemes in educational welfare cases; and with the multi-disciplinary framework of child-protection measures); *Sullivan* (n 2) (imposition of duty incompatible with the law of defamation). See also *Precision Products* (n 46) [113], [116]–[119] (Allsop P) (duty incompatible with both administrative law and statutory appeal mechanisms regarding environmental notices).

[51] Or sometimes, their liberty—see, eg, *Stuart* (n 2) where a duty on the part of the police to detain a person contemplating suicide was considered inconsistent with the latter's freedom of choice.

[52] See, eg, *Amaca* (n 49) [156] (Ipp JA); *Makawe* (n 49) [17], [21]–[22] (Hodgson JA).

None of these concerns is peculiar to cases involving public bodies. Concerns about omissions liability, defensive practice, conflicting duties, incompatibility with statutory purposes, indeterminate liability, systemic incoherence and vulnerability are hence widespread in modern debates about the duty of care in cases dealing with the liability of private individuals, or businesses, for both physical harm and economic loss.[53] The concern about omissions liability is especially prominent in the case law and explains a good number of the most important instances in which plaintiffs have failed.[54] Whilst all of these arguments may, therefore, surface with particular regularity in cases involving public bodies, none of them concerns the defendant's public status per se; and a high proportion of decisions about duty are decided on traditional private law grounds that have nothing to do with public 'discretion' at all. This will be reassuring to those who support the Diceyan point of view.

B. Justiciability—Immunity or Privilege?

In the UK, judges at one time sought to accommodate concerns about the constitutional justiciability of 'discretionary' public body decisions at a logically distinct, separate stage of negligence proceedings, prior to considering whether or not the body owed any duty of care on the facts.[55] If the hurdle was passed, then—and only then—would they deliberate upon the duty question, which is now governed by the three-stage approach in *Caparo Industries plc v Dickman*.[56] This effectively granted public bodies an immunity in cases raising justiciability problems of a constitutional type, which was, I suggested above, eminently logical, because if a court is genuinely *incapable* of judging a matter on such grounds, it lacks even the *power* to impose legal obligations on a defendant in respect of the decision in question. Whether or not a duty of care exists on the facts is simply not something the court can even consider.[57] In recent years, however, some courts in the United

[53] Defensive practice arguments are hence also strong in claims against private doctors and influence 'development risks' defences in product liability cases; conflicting ethical and legal duty arguments feature in cases against private advisors/litigators, whose primary responsibility is always to their client; courts are wary of contradicting statutory intentions across the board in private law; indeterminate liability arguments feature strongly in cases involving claims against private parties for negligent misstatement, or relational economic loss; arguments about coherence between negligence law and the law of defamation surface in respect of references provided by private employers, not just in respect of statements made by public parties (see, eg, *Spring v Guardian Assurance plc* [1995] 2 AC 296 (HL)); and vulnerability arguments are now common in Australia in respect of claims against private builders for defective work, as well as many other cases of pure economic loss. For consideration of most of these factors in the context of a claim between purely private parties see *Caltex Refineries (Qld) Pty Ltd v Stavar* (2009) NSWCA 258 [102]–[105] (Allsop P).

[54] See n 45 and text.

[55] *Anns* (n 2) 755 (Lord Wilberforce) (indicating that where discretion is involved, a plaintiff must show that the defendant is acting outside that discretion 'before he can begin to rely upon a duty of care'. See also (more cautiously) *X* (n 2) 737–38 (Lord Browne-Wilkinson).

[56] [1990] 2 AC 605 (HL).

[57] Booth & Squires (n 3) [2.01] and fn 1.

Kingdom have tended to treat justiciability questions simply as *part of* the duty of care inquiry conducted on individual sets of facts, not as a prior 'in/out' question, which construes justiciability arguments instead as relevant to the grant of fact-specific privileges, not immunities. This allows more cases to proceed to a full trial of the facts and evidence. The same tendency is even more evident in Australia, where courts often regard the justiciability of a decision as just one 'factor' within the High Court's multifactorial approach to duty in novel cases.[58]

There are two possible explanations for this apparent shift of thinking from immunity to fact-specific privilege. The first is that, in most cases in which justiciability has been cited as merely a duty factor, it has been the practical, not the constitutional version of the argument that has been in play. This is not to say that the practical argument actually justifies a privilege,[59] but this explanation at least leaves some residual scope for the operation of genuine immunities based on constitutional justiciability arguments in a small number of cases.[60]

The second explanation is simply that courts have become much more proactive and no longer regard themselves as lacking the constitutional power to judge discretionary public body decisions in the vast majority of cases. In the United Kingdom, there is certainly evidence that courts are now especially wary of granting tort immunities in the wake of the Human Rights Act 1998.[61] The same hands-on attitude has also been expressed on occasion in Australia, despite the absence of equivalent human rights norms in that jurisdiction. In a notorious passage in the *Brodie* case, which clearly sent something of a wave of panic through governments and their insurers at the time, Gaudron, McHugh and Gummow JJ said:

> Appeals also were made to preserve the 'political choice' in matters involving shifts in 'resource allocation'. However [C]itizens, corporations, governments and public authorities generally are obliged to order their affairs so as to meet the requirements of the rule of law in Australian civil society. Thus, it is no answer to a claim in tort against the Commonwealth under s 75(iii) of the Constitution that its wrongful acts or omissions were the product of a 'policy decision' taken by the Executive Government; still less that the action is 'non-justiciable' because a verdict against the Commonwealth will be adverse to that 'policy decision'. Local authorities are in no preferred position.[62]

[58] See, eg, *Crimmins* (n 2) 33–34, 39–40 (McHugh J); *Electro Optic* (n 49) [209]–[210] (Jagot J) (but seeming to reserve the possibility of prior immunity in very rare cases for justiciability concerns of a constitutional, rather than practical nature). For a recent account of the multifactorial approach and the various factors affecting determinations in public body cases, see Bell-James and Barker (n 36).

[59] See Part II D.

[60] *Electro Optic* (n 49) [210] (Jagot J). See also, perhaps, *Meshlawn P/L and Anor v State of Qld and Anor* [2010] QCA 181 [70]–[72] (Chesterman J).

[61] *Barrett* (n 2) (although the domestic act was not in issue in that case). The source of the move was really the concern about 'immunities' and Art 6 of the European Convention on Human Rights stemming from *Osman v United Kingdom* [1998] EHRR 101. The concern was diffused to some extent in *Z v United Kingdom* (2001) 34 E HRR 3.

[62] *Brodie* (n 2) 560.

The reaction of Australian governments to local authorities' concerns about these comments was, as we shall see in Part IV, to swiftly introduce statutory immunities for public bodies in respect of all decisions regarding 'general allocations of resources', alongside a battery of other provisions purporting to reduce public body exposure to civil liability. At common law, however, although courts do sometimes still favour considering justiciability questions at a logically prior stage of reasoning, so as to grant genuine immunities, the predominant approach is simply to consider such questions flexibly at trial, when considering the duty question.

C. The Search for Justiciability Criteria—Harvesting the Fruitless Tree

Whether constitutional justiciability goes to immunity or privilege, it is fair to say that courts have struggled to articulate clear criteria by which the justiciability of a decision can be predicted. One reason for this may be that that there are very few, if any, cases in either the United Kingdom or Australia in recent years in which negligence claims against public authorities have failed on the constitutional ground, so that there is simply a lack of clear and authoritative criteria of 'non-justiciability'. But the main reason is likely to be that, because the source of privilege (or immunity) is traditionally thought to lie in courts' conceptions of their relationship to government—in the doctrine of the separation of powers—there are no very clear norms for them to apply. This relationship is conceived of in the United Kingdom in terms of unwritten conventions, not rules; and even if written constitutional rules apply (as in Australia),[63] they are stated in such abstract terms as to offer little guidance to judges as to when they should intervene in a public body's decision in any particular case. Judicial culture on these matters shifts and conventions are hard to calibrate.

(i) Policy, or Operation

The best-known attempt at a criterion of legal justiciability consists in the distinction between matters of 'policy' and operation drawn by Lord Wilberforce in *Anns*.[64] This has also been deployed, on occasion, in Australian courts.[65] Lord Wilberforce expressly aligned the term 'policy' with matters in respect of which there exists a delegated 'discretion,' by which he almost certainly meant an implied

[63] *Commonwealth Constitution* Chapters 1–3.

[64] *Anns* (n 2) 754.

[65] See, eg, *Heyman* (n 2) 442 (Gibbs CJ), 500 (Deane J) (it is generally the implied intention of the statute to preclude liability for policy as opposed to operational decisions), 468–69 (Mason J); *Pyrenees* (n 2) 358–59 (Toohey J), 425–26 (Kirby J).

immunity in the second sense identified above.[66] By contrast, he thought that 'operational' matters (which he described expressly as actions taken in the 'practical execution' of policy decisions)[67] generally attract no such immunity and can be subject to negligence duties in the ordinary way.

Even Lord Wilberforce recognised that the distinction between policy and operation is not a failsafe guide to justiciability, since some acts of execution can also attract immunity, when they are dictated by a policy.[68] Political scientists have highlighted the absence in practice of any clear line between policy-formulation (deciding) and administration (executing)[69] and courts are now generally cautious about the distinction, without having gone so far as to fully reject it.[70] One reason why it continues to be regarded as 'of some use'[71] may be that 'deciding' policy clearly involves the making of a quasi-expert *judgement* of some sort, whereas 'implementing' a policy decision need not, so that matters of 'implementation' are more likely both to be easy for courts to assess without special expertise, and less likely to raise constitutional concerns. If a public authority has been clear about what it itself thinks ought generally to be done in respect of the use of a power, by stating this in a 'policy,' then it is much easier and less politically controversial for a court to conclude that a particular officer who has departed from that approach was at fault. But it is not, of course, *all* 'decisions' that Lord Wilberforce thought raise justiciability concerns and command immunities—only certain *sorts* of decision: those he refers to as 'policy' decisions. The distinction between policy and operation as his Lordship framed it (decision/execution) does not therefore tell us how to determine which 'decisions' are amenable to scrutiny and which are not. We have to look deeper for some substantive characterisation of this subset of 'decisions' that is sufficiently problematic to command a privilege or immunity. The word 'policy' does not really help in this determination. It is either indeterminate in meaning, or—if taken simply to mean those decisions that command immunity, as it sometimes is[72]—self-referential and conclusory. Further specification is required.

[66] *Anns* (n 2) 754 ('the decision is one for the authority to make … not the courts').

[67] ibid.

[68] ibid, 755. If, for example, the limited time devoted by an inspector to a particular building inspection was a consequence of a council decision to allocate more resources to health care or road maintenance, then a plaintiff's claim might still require the questioning of the latter decision and fail on the ground that it was non-justiciable

[69] P Wilenski, *Public Power and Public Administration* (Sydney, Hale & Ironmonger, 1986) 51–54.

[70] In the UK see, *Rowling v Takaro Properties Ltd* [1988] AC 473 (PC) 501 (Lord Keith); *Stovin* (n 2) 951–52 (Lord Hoffmann, Lords Goff and Jauncey agreeing), 938–39 (Lord Nicholls); *Barrett* (n 2) 571–72 (Lord Slynn), 583 (Lord Hutton); *Phelps* (n 2) 658 (Lord Slynn), 665 (Lord Nicholls), 973–74 (Lord Clyde). In Australia, see *Crimmins* (n 2) 50 (McHugh J), 101 (Hayne J); *Barclay* (n 2) 556 (Gleeson CJ); *Refrigerated Roadways* (n 28) [259] (Campbell JA).

[71] *Refrigerated Roadways* (n 28) [259] (Campbell JA).

[72] Some judges and distinguished writers (see, eg Cane (n 3) 213 fn 56) understand Lord Wilberforce to use the term 'policy' in this way and are accordingly critical for the reason stated in the text. But this interpretation does not actually square with the contrast his Lordship draws between policy decisions, on the one hand, and their execution on the other. It seems that His Lordship was actually

The uncertainty generated by the porous nature of the distinction between policy and operation has caused some commentators to suggest that courts should harden it up by making the distinction a formal, not a substantive one. Booth and Squires hence proffer an alternative approach:

> The alternative approach, we suggest, is to shift the focus of the court from whether a decision is one of policy, as a matter of substance, to whether it is a policy as a matter of form ... Under an approach focusing on form, if a decision was formulated or approved at a senior level, following internal discussions and external consultation, and was applied in other cases and intended to guide future practice, it can be regarded as a 'policy' and unsuitable for judicial scrutiny. If the decision was made on an ad hoc basis, at a low level in an organization, and by a person actually delivering a service, and if it was applied only to the facts of a particular case, it is more likely to be 'operational'.[73]

This approach is advocated on the basis that it is easier to apply—courts simply look to the way in which the decision was taken and the level of seniority of those involved in making it, and grant a privilege wherever the necessary formalities have been met and consultations carried out. It is also supported on the basis that, wherever these formalities have been observed, it is likely that internal checks will have operated and sufficient publicity will have attached to the decision in question to enable it to be changed, if it turns out to be wrong.[74]

A weak version of this, more formal approach has been embraced by some governments in Australia.[75] However, although it might have some advantages in terms of increasing certainty, it is hard to accept its democratic legitimacy. It provides a license to public bodies to immunise their own careless decisions by formalising them in advance at a sufficiently senior level. This is not only questionable from the constitutional point of view, but also prone to promote harmful administrative hubris and reduce standards of public service. Unless there is some express or implied statutory immunity, or privilege, granted to an authority under its empowering legislation, the judicial grant of privileges or immunities to practices that it has formalised seems quite inappropriate. It grants the authority the power to legislate its own protections without the express or implied authority of Parliament.

making two distinctions—one between deciding and executing (acts of execution do not usually attract immunity) and the other between decisions that attract immunities and decisions that don't (decisions of a policy type do attract immunity and other decisions generally do not).

[73] Booth & Squires (n 3) [2.80].

[74] ibid, [2.83].

[75] See n 121 and Part IV. The provisions allow authorities to rely on their compliance with their (own) general procedures ... 'as evidence of the proper exercise of [their] functions'. If 'evidence' here means 'irrebuttable' evidence, then this is tantamount to allowing the authority to write its own immunities, but it is unlikely that this is the provisions' effect: *Transpacific Cleanaway Ltd v South East Water Limited* [2008] VCAT 1798 [71] (Macnamara DP).

(ii) Within, or Outside Power

Another approach that is mixed in with Lord Wilberforce's first approach in *Anns* and which gained some popularity at one time in English Courts, is one that metes out privilege for decisions according to whether or not the decision fell 'within' or 'outside' the public body's 'powers' in the public law sense.[76] Courts sometimes, alternatively, talk in terms of whether or not the decision fell 'within', or 'outside discretion'. Lord Wilberforce hence went on to suggest in the judgment cited above that some policy decisions might be subject to a duty of care if they are 'outside the ambit of the power' or 'not within the limits of a discretion bona fide exercised'.[77] The approach derives from passages in the judgments of Lords Reid, Diplock and Morris in *Home Office v Dorset Yacht*,[78] Lord Reid in that case indicating that 'discretionary' decisions might fall outside any tort immunity where 'the discretion is exercised so carelessly or unreasonably that there has been no real exercise of the discretion'.[79] The same sort of approach was deployed by Lord Browne-Wilkinson in *X (Minors) v Bedfordshire County Council* as a supplement to the 'policy' test.[80] It was echoed by Lord Hoffmann's suggestion in *Stovin v Wise* (since retracted)[81] that private entitlements to compensation might attend the 'irrational' exercise of discretionary public powers.[82] It is also finds some resonance in Scotland, where emphasis has been placed on the need to prove bad faith on the part of the authority before any duty of care can attach to a public decision of a discretionary type;[83] and in the *Barrett* case, where Lord Slynn suggested that an authority with powers will not normally be liable for their exercise unless it acts in a 'wholly unreasonable way', so as to have gone 'outside' them.[84]

It is a notable and potentially puzzling feature of Lord Browne-Wilkinson's judgment in *X*, that he clearly thought that the question whether or not a decision lies 'within discretion' in the relevant sense is both a matter to be gauged *independently* of public law criteria,[85] and a question that is *distinct* from the issue whether or not the decision is justiciable by a court.[86] Both propositions are confusing at

[76] *Dorset Yacht* (n 2) 1031 (Lord Reid) ('abuse or excess of power'), 1037 (Lord Morris) (not acting 'within ... powers'), 1065 (Lord Diplock); ('ultra vires'); *Anns* (n 2) 758 (Lord Wilberforce) ('outside the ambit of the power'); *Barrett* (n 2) 570 (Lord Slynn) ('outside its discretion ... outside the power').

[77] *Anns* (n 2) 755, 758. See also *Heyman* (n 2) 442 (Gibbs CJ).

[78] See n 76.

[79] *Dorset Yacht* (n 2) 1031.

[80] *X* (n 2) 736 (so unreasonable as to be 'outside the ambit of the discretion'), 738 ('outside the statutory discretion').

[81] *Gorringe* (n 2) [26].

[82] *Stovin* (n 2) 953 (Lords Goff and Jauncey agreeing).

[83] *Ross* (n 13) 19 (Lord Milligan).

[84] *Barrett* (n 2) 570 (Lord Slynn).

[85] *X* (n 2) 736 ('I do not believe ... it is either helpful or necessary to introduce public law concepts ... into the question of liability at common law for negligence'). His Lordship was at pains to distinguish Lord Diplock's approach in *Dorset Yacht* in this respect from the other judgments in that case, which did not mention the concept of 'ultra vires'.

[86] ibid, 736–67 (where the issues of 'discretion' and 'justiciability' are considered under distinct headings).

first glance—how else would one judge whether or not a decision lay 'within or outside power', other than by reference to administrative law criteria? And how is this question different to the question whether or not a court has the constitutional power to judge the decision?

In fact, his judgment may well, I suggest, contain two valuable intuitions that have since been validated. The first is the idea that the criteria of privilege and immunity can be different in tort and public law. We saw in Part II that this point has a solid, logical basis and it is now increasingly widely accepted as a matter of legal policy: since *Stovin v Wise*,[87] there has been a general retreat by English judges from the use of public law criteria as litmus-tests for duty in negligence cases, which acknowledges some of the distinct functions and purposes of public and private law.[88] In Australia, the confusion never really existed in the first place and public law criteria have never seriously taken off as a litmus test of duty at common law.[89]

The second idea is that there are at work, in courts' reasoning about duty, two, different principles. One is that courts should grant a public body a privilege, or immunity, from duty where this represents the express or implied intention of Parliament, as derived from the terms of the relevant statute (where, as Lord Browne-Wilkinson says, the relevant act is 'authorised' by the statute).[90] The other is that—independently of any expressed statutory intention—courts should not judge certain types of decision, simply as a matter of deference to the constitutional doctrine of the separation of powers.

If this construction of Lord Browne-Wilkinson's judgment is correct, then it becomes more obvious why he thought that the question whether a decision was 'within or outside power' has nothing to do with the public law criteria that customarily feature in cases of judicial review. In fact, the question is a straightforward question about whether or not Parliament expressed an intention in the empowering legislation to grant a privilege from duty to the decision-maker. That is not a question that requires resort to criteria of Wednesbury unreasonableness, or public law irrationality. Rather, it is question to be decided in accordance with the normal rules of statutory interpretation, with which private law courts are already perfectly familiar in cases involving individuals and corporations.

My suggestion, therefore, is that the question whether or not a given decision was 'within or outside power (or discretion)' is now meaningless as a separate

[87] *Stovin* (n 2).

[88] *X* (n 2) 736–37 (Lord Browne-Wilkinson); *Barrett* (n 2) 572 (Lord Slynn), 586 (Lord Hutton, Lords Steyn and Nolan agreeing) (but note the reservation of Hutton at 586 that the ratio of *Stovin* may still apply in cases involving failure to exercise a power); *Phelps* (n 2) 653 (Lord Slynn); *Gorringe* (n 2) [4]–[6] (Lord Steyn).

[89] The use of public law criteria was doubted from an early stage, being rejected the majority of the High Court in *Pyrenees* (n 2) (but *cf* Brennan CJ at [22]) and in *Crimmins* (n 2) 35–36 (McHugh J), 78–9 (Kirby J). Note however, that recent legislative interventions have modelled themselves around public law approaches: Part IV.

[90] *X* (n 2) 736.

indicator of whether or not a duty of care was owed in respect of it; and that the use of this criterion should be entirely abandoned. The public law construction of the idea (intra/ultra vires) is inappropriate, given the different question that it at stake in private law litigation, and has been rejected by the courts; and the question whether Parliament intended to grant an immunity, or privilege, is one that is best considered in its own terms.

(iii) Justiciability Unmediated

The perception that the criteria mentioned above are either inconclusive, or inappropriate, has resulted in courts reverting to an atomistic approach that considers the question of constitutional justiciability in its own terms on the facts of each case,[91] without reference to any further proxy. This is the undoubtedly the most pragmatic strategy, but it will always be subject to instability and uncertainty for the reasons earlier identified: conventions of judicial deference to the executive are not prescribed by clear rules and standards and the way they are interpreted and applied is bound to vary. The best that can be done is to compile a list of the sorts of decision that judges say they are unwilling to judge, but the precedential value of these statements for future cases is itself likely to be fairly weak, since all instances will turn on their own facts. Examples of decisions that have been said not to be justiciable hence include: decisions about primary legislation;[92] quasi-legislative decisions regarding the passing of zoning prescriptions, inter-governmental dealings, by-laws, orders, health and safety regulations and commercial regulations;[93] 'political' decisions regarding the weighing of competing 'public interests';[94] and decisions regarding the raising of revenue, or the allocation of resources (financial or otherwise) to different social priorities.[95] Importantly, the mere fact that a decision is 'financial' or 'budgetary' does not necessarily mean that it will be regarded as raising constitutional concerns,[96] although it may make the decision more complex, so as to trigger judicial anxieties about its 'practical' justiciability, or about the plaintiff's ability to prove that the defendant breached its duty of care.[97]

[91] *Barrett* (n 2) 571 (Lord Slynn) ('the ultimate question is whether a particular issue is justiciable or whether the court should accept that it has no role to play').

[92] *Barclay* (n 2) 553–54 (Gleeson CJ).

[93] *Pyrenees* (n 2) 394 (Gummow J); *Crimmins* (n 2) 21 (Gaudron J), 37 (McHugh J), 62 (Gummow J), 100–01 (Hayne J); *Barclay* (n 2) 553–54 (Gleeson CJ); *Brodie* (n 2) 559–60 (Gaudron, McHugh and Gummow JJ).

[94] *Carty* (n 8) [25] (Dyson LJ).

[95] *Anns* (n 2) 754 (Lord Wilberforce) (decisions about the 'scale of resources … [a council] can make available to carry out its functions'… matters of 'efficiency and thrift'); *Heyman* (n 2) 469 (Mason J) (decisions 'dictated by financial [or] economic factors'… 'allocation[s] of resources'); *Barclay* (n 2) 553–54 (Gleeson CJ); *Phelps* (n 2) 653 (Lord Slynn) ('weighing of competing public interests').

[96] *Barclay* (n 2) 557 (Gleeson CJ). See also *Brodie* (n 2) 559 (Gaudron, McHugh and Gummow JJ) (such considerations can simply be considered at the breach stage); *Crimmins* 50 (McHugh J); *Romeo* (n 2) 484 (Kirby J).

[97] See, eg, *Brodie* (n 2) 559 (Gaudron, McHugh and Gummow JJ); *Romeo* (n 2) 484 (Kirby J).

Some judges take the view that it is mainly decisions relating to a body's legislative and quasi-legislative functions that are non-justiciable.[98] This produces a relatively clear and defensible line. However, others take a deferential approach toward a wider range of decisions that are unrelated to the making of binding rules. A popular view, derived from Mason J's judgment in *Heyman*, is that courts should steer clear of all decisions that are dictated by 'financial, economic, social or political factors or constraints'.[99] In Australia, most governments have now legislated so as to immunise all decisions bearing on 'general allocations of resources', as we shall see in Part IV. This immunity now supplements the justiciability protections at common law and has added to their uncertainty and complication. The question whether a decision involves a 'general,' or 'specific' resource allocation seems fated to run into exactly the same difficulties as the common law distinction between decisions of 'policy' and matters of 'operation'.[100]

These problems are unlikely to resolve themselves easily and one may simply have to accept that the parameters of constitutional immunity and privilege that attend public body decision-making will always be inexact, as well as specific to the judicial culture of different jurisdictions. This might be thought unproblematic, given the small number of cases in which the issue now tends to arise in practice. Alternatively, one might try to achieve greater certainty in other ways. One might, for example, draw the line of constitutional non-justiciability conservatively around legislative functions (the definition of which is pretty clear); or (much more radically) simply abandon the doctrine of constitutional non-justiciability altogether, so as to open the door for courts to scrutinise all forms of public decision. Neither of these options is likely to commend itself to governments, or indeed to courts. The political strain currently being placed on constitutional justiciability doctrine may, however, be relieved somewhat by an alternative approach to the grant of privileges that has been developed by courts in recent years.

D. An Alternative Approach—Compatibility with Parliamentary Intentions

A possible way of bypassing some—probably only some—of the inherent instability and uncertainty of arguments about the constitutional justiciability of a public decision is to determine the existence of tort privileges instead by reference to the intentions of the legislator, as they are revealed by the legislation under which the public body is accorded its powers. A significant range of existing decisions

[98] See, eg, Crimmins (n 2) 21 (Gaudron J), 62 (Gummow J), 100–01 (Hayne J); *Barclay* (n 2) 557 (Gleeson CJ), 606–07 (Gummow & Hayne JJ, Gaudron J agreeing).

[99] *Heyman* (n 2) 469. This formulation proved popular with the Ipp Committee, although decisions of this type were not to be accorded a full immunity—see Part IV.

[100] *New South Wales v Ball* [2007] NSWCA 71; *Refrigerated Roadways* (n 28) [405] (Campbell JA).

expressly consider parliamentary intentions and purposes as being crucially relevant to the existence of a duty of care[101] and it is an observable feature of recent case law that judges far more often rule out duties on this basis, than they do by reverting to constitutional justiciability arguments. This approach is subtly distinct from normal justiciability doctrine, although courts often, understandably, connect the two ideas. The importance of separating them was, I believe, at the heart of Lord Browne-Wilkinson's judgment in *X*, to which I adverted above.[102] Whereas justiciability doctrine determines immunities and privileges by reference to a judiciary's own conventions regarding the separation of powers, the approach based on parliamentary intentions makes them depend on legislative will as expressed by the specific piece of legislation from which a public body derives its statutory powers. On many sets of facts, the two approaches will generate the same outcome, but, whereas the former is conducted on the basis of judicial convention, the latter applies standard rules of statutory interpretation.

Parliamentary intentions have been thought to be relevant to duty questions in two, very different ways. Some judges have taken the view that the existence of a duty of care is dependent on the express or implied expression of a *positive* intention that a private law right should arise from exercise of the powers the statute grants. This is the eccentric view of Lord Hoffmann in *Stovin v Wise*[103] and of Brennan J in *Sutherland Shire Council v Heyman*.[104] It was rightly rejected by Gummow and Hayne JJ in the *Barclay Oysters* case[105] and by Lord Steyn in *Gorringe*.[106] It falsely assimilates duty criteria at common law with the rules that apply to actions for the breach of statutory duty. However, the second view, which is now adopted by most courts, is that statutory intentions are relevant only in potentially negating a duty of care that a court might otherwise impose.[107] On this view, negligence duties in such cases are created at common law by courts for reasons of justice and the protection of private rights, but all such duties can be prevented or removed by Parliament for public reasons. Parliamentary intention thus works negatively to remove rights at common law and to accord privileges, not to create these rights in the first place. Gaudron J in *Crimmins* thought that

[101] See, eg, *X* (n 2) 730 (Lord Browne-Wilkinson); *Pyrenees* (n 2) 347 (Brennan CJ); *Crimmins* (n 2) 39–40 (McHugh J); 72–76 (Kirby J); *Barclay* (n 2) 596–98 (Gummow and Hayne JJ); *Stuart* (n 2) 239 (French CJ).

[102] See text to n 90 et post. There are clear logical links between this approach and one which makes all matters justiciable unless parliament has provided a specific defence of statutory authorisation. I am grateful to Donal Nolan for drawing my attention to this point.

[103] *Stovin* (n 2) 953 (in cases involving failure to exercise a power, it must be the 'policy [ie the intention] of the statute' to require compensation to be paid).

[104] *Heyman* (n 2) 482–83.

[105] *Barclay* (n 2) 597.

[106] *Gorringe* (n 2) [3].

[107] *Pyrenees* (n 2) 346 (Brennan CJ); *Crimmins* (n 2) 19 (Gaudron J), 39–40 (McHugh J), 72, 76–77 (Kirby J); *Sullivan* (n 2); *Barclay* (n 2) 597 (Gummow and Hayne JJ;); *Gorringe* (n 2) [3] (Lord Steyn); *Mitchell* (n 45) [63] (Lord Rodger). The requirement of 'compatability' has now also been made the subject of enactment in some Australian States and Territories: see, eg, Wrongs Act 1958 (Vic), s 84 (3).

this is the key proposition. Indeed, according to her Honour, all the other distinctions to which I have adverted—between policy and operation, or between 'discretionary' and 'non-discretionary' decisions—are, in substance, getting at the same, basic question of whether or not the statute in question intended to 'exclude the common law in whole or in part'.[108]

In considering whether or not Parliament intended to grant a privilege from any duty of care to a body in respect of the exercise of a power, courts consider a number of factors, including the 'background statutory framework',[109] and whether the purpose of the statute was to protect particular individuals or groups, or to benefit the public as a whole.[110] The language of the provision, its scope and its substantive purposes, as revealed by its legislative history, are also clearly important.

The advantages of this approach are that it makes all duty decisions in respect of statutory power particular to the power in question and it uses familiar tools of statutory interpretation to determine outcomes. Both features commend it to courts in the modern age. It roots tort privileges and immunities in a definite democratic source; and it uses reasoning that is equally applicable in claims against public and private parties, thereby formally treating government and its citizenry in much the same way. Rules of statutory interpretation are of course no guarantee of certain results. Statutes will often be genuinely unclear as to whether or not a privilege was intended to attach to the exercise of the power in question and judges may differ in their interpretation of parliamentary intentions. For example, Lord Browne-Wilkinson in *X* clearly assumed that Parliament only generally intends to immunise exercises of power that are not wholly unreasonable,[111] whereas Lord Jauncey thought that it cannot intend to protect those that are careless.[112]

There may be a case for presuming no privilege to be intended by a statute unless the language is especially clear; so as thereby to prevent unintentional derogations from private rights. This presumption would also encourage governments to obtain a specific and express electoral mandate for any exemptions from private law duties that it requires in order to go about its business for the public good. In practice, however, it seems more likely that courts will deploy the full and normal range of statutory interpretation guidelines without recourse to any fixed rule of this kind. It is possible that, in the process, they will read many of

[108] *Crimmins* (n 2) 19 (Gaudron J). See, similarly, *Stuart* (n 2) 239 (French CJ). This cannot be the whole truth, since sometimes public bodies do not derive their powers from statute, but from prerogative. In all and any such cases, immunities and privileges from private duties must have a non-statutory source.

[109] *X* (n 2); *Sullivan* (n 2); *Crimmins* (n 2) 77–78 (Kirby J); *Barclay* (n 2) 596–97 (Gummow and Hayne JJ) (look at the terms scope and purpose of the provision), 630 (Kirby J).

[110] In *Heyman*, this question was thought to be irrelevant by both Gibbs CJ (436) and Mason J (465) (although *cf* Brennan J (347)), but it is now clearly accepted: see, eg, *X* (n 2) [762] (Lord Browne-Wilkinson); *Pyrenees* (n 2) 347 (Brennan CJ); *Crimmins* (n 2) 39 (McHugh J) (power to protect a 'specific class' rather than the 'public at large'), 77 (Kirby J); *Barclay* (n 2) 564 Gleeson CJ, 576 (McHugh J), 658 (Callinan J); *Becker* (n 107) [110].

[111] *X* (n 2) 736.

[112] ibid, 728. See also, taking the same view, *Heyman* (n 2) 484 (Brennan J); Nolan (n 3) [17.16].

their own, conventional assumptions into Parliament's will, such as the assumption that Parliament would not intend any duty to attach to 'policy' decisions, as opposed to matters of 'operation'. If this happens, then, sadly, the approach will not greatly assist in clarifying outcomes and will simply clothe the uncertainties of traditional conventional justiciability doctrine in the new language of democratic intent. Nonetheless, the focus on particular statutory contexts, language and background does seem to promise, on balance, a more precise approach. By simply applying the normal techniques of statutory interpretation and assimilating the way in which decisions about privilege are made in respect of public and private parties, it also accords more closely with the Diceyan conception of the rule of law. The growth of this technique, and the decline of that which is based purely and simply on higher-level, vaguer conventions regarding the separation of powers is therefore to be cautiously welcomed. It can only work fully effectively, however, if greater measures are taken at the legislative stage to specify privileges and immunities in advance at the time that statutory powers are enacted.

IV. Financial Crisis and Legislative Backlash

As we have seen, the approach of courts in both Australia and the UK in recent years has been to regard the 'discretionary' nature of public powers as less and less of a problem from the constitutional point of view. Judges have placed more emphasis on the practical difficulties of judging certain types of public decision and on ensuring that duties of care are not imposed contrary to parliamentary intentions. This has corresponded with a shift in legal reasoning away from the grant of tort immunities, toward the grant of fact-specific privileges and the deployment of realistic attitudes towards breach questions that takes account of the special difficulty and complex nature of many public tasks, as well as of the limits placed on public resources. This more open, flexible approach treats public bodies—perhaps more than at any previous time in the history of Australia and the United Kingdom—in a way that mimics the approach that private law courts take in respect of private parties wielding similar power.

This trend has proven decidedly unpopular with governments, especially in the wake of the global financial crisis. The reaction in Australia has been particularly outspoken and blunt. The existence of crisis in the insurance industry in the early part of the new millennium brought about significant rises in public liability insurance premiums in Australia. These pressures, combined with intensive political lobbying by a powerful insurance industry rapidly (many would say precipitously) persuaded governments to implement a series of measures to limit private law claims in negligence cases, including claims against public authorities.[113]

[113] For critical commentary on the reforms, see R Davis, 'The Tort Reform Crisis' (2002) 25(3) *University of New South Wales Law Journal* 865; H Luntz, 'Reform of the Law of Negligence: Wrong

Whatever the truth of the matter, perceptions apparently abounded amongst governments in the wake of the *Brodie* case that all public 'policy' decisions might give rise to negligence liabilities and that this was likely to send public liabilities spiralling out of control, so as to seriously curtail governments' ability to offer front-line public services.[114] In consequence, when the Ipp Committee was commissioned in 2002 to recommend ways in which civil liability could be cut back, it sought to meet these concerns by recommending the introduction throughout Australia of protection for public decisions of a 'policy' type.[115] The protection recommended may well, in truth, have offered no further succour to authorities than already existed at common law. The recommendation was not for any extra privileges or immunities for policy decisions, but for the introduction of a public law test of Wednesbury unreasonableness as an additional threshold requirement for civil actions in respect of them.[116] Ironically, the prompt for introducing this public law test into private law actions was taken from the United Kingdom,[117] where that approach was raising its head at the time, but where it has since been firmly rejected, as we saw in Part III.

As things turned out, governments were never able to agree on what to do about discretionary public decisions. They hurried down their own political paths amidst the febrile atmosphere of crisis, casting barely a sideways glance. Many clearly did not regard the Ipp recommendation as radical enough, or else they misinterpreted it. The full range of the reforms is too great to expatiate here, but it is interesting to highlight some of the main contrasts between the legislation as a corpus and the approach developing prior to this time at common law.

Many jurisdictions have now introduced statutory immunities for public decisions involving 'general allocations of resources'.[118] At best, these measures probably replicate patterns of protection for 'discretionary' decisions that already existed at common law, using slightly different language and thereby adding an additional layer of complexity and potential confusion. But there is also a possibility that they have actually reversed a strategy of increased scrutiny and public accountability that the High Court had been deliberately setting in place (albeit obiter)

Questions—Wrong Answers' (2002) 25(3) *University of New South Wales Law Journal* 836; P Cane, 'Reforming Tort Law in Australia: A Personal Perspective (2003) 27 *Melbourne University Law Review* 649; K Burns, 'Distorting the Law: Politics, Media and the Litigation Crisis: An Australian Perspective' (2007) 15 *Torts Law Journal* 195; E Carroll, 'Wednesbury and Reasonableness as a Limit on the Civil Liability of Public Authorities' (2007) 15 *Tort Law Review* 77; Aronson (n 3); Bell-James and Barker (n 36).

[114] *Ipp Review* (n 4) [10.3].

[115] ibid, Rec 39. The definition of 'policy' decisions was virtually identical to that proffered at common law by Mason J in *Heyman* (text to n 99) namely, 'decisions based substantially on financial, economic, political or social factors or constraints': ibid, [10.22].

[116] ibid.

[117] In particular, Lord Hoffmann's judgment in *Stovin* (n 2): *Ipp Review* (n 4) [10.26].

[118] Civil Liability Act 2002 (Qld), s 35(b); Civil Liability Act 2002 (Tas), s 38(b); Civil Law (Wrongs) Act 2002 (ACT), s 110(b); Civil Liability Act 2002 (NSW), s 42(b); Civil Liability Act 2002 (WA), s 5W(b).

in *Brodie*.[119] Most jurisdictions have also introduced provisions that provide extra protection for road traffic authorities against liability for failure to exercise their road maintenance powers.[120] Most have introduced measures that allow public authorities to admit evidence of compliance with their own procedures as evidence that their decision in a given case was not negligent.[121] Three have introduced additional limitations on public authorities' liability for omitting to exercise their regulatory powers, which make liability for failing to exercise (or consider exercising) them dependent on a plaintiff proving that, if he or she had applied to an administrative court, he or she would have been able to obtain a public law writ of mandamus compelling the authority to use the power.[122] A wide range of jurisdictions have also introduced something akin to the administrative law Wednesbury unreasonableness test recommended by the Ipp Review as an added restriction on private law liability. Some of these provisions appear to be confined, rather bizarrely one might think given the aims of the legislation,[123] to actions for breach of statutory duty, but those extant in at least two States apply to negligence claims in respect of the exercise of a public body's functions.[124] An extraordinary feature of many of these provisions is that (like those relating to road maintenance) they apply to protect the sorts of actions and decisions that common law courts would probably previously have regarded as falling squarely within the 'operational' sphere and which would be unlikely to raise significant judicial concerns at common law.[125] In such instances, the provisions' effect has been significantly to restrict liability, accountability and victim compensation within domains of public decision-making that were not previously regarded as problematic, or controversial.

Many detailed criticisms can be made of these measures.[126] Here I shall merely comment on their broader, more controversial implications. First, it is clear that

[119] *Brodie* (n 2).

[120] Civil Liability Act 2002 (Qld) s 37; Civil Liability Act 2002 (Tas) s 42; Civil Liability Act 2002 (NSW) s 45; Civil Law (Wrongs) Act 2002 (ACT) s 113; Civil Liability Act 2002 (WA) s 5Z. There is no provision in VIC, SA or NT.

[121] Civil Liability Act 2002 (Qld) s 35(d); Civil Liability Act 2002 (Tas) s 38(d); Civil Liability Act 2002 (NSW) s 42(d); Civil Law (Wrongs) Act 2002 (ACT) s 110(d); Civil Liability Act 2002 (WA) s 5W(d); Wrongs Act 1958 (Vic) s 83(c). There is no provision in SA or NT.

[122] Civil Liability Act 2002 (NSW) s 44; Civil Liability Act 2002 (Tas) s 41; Civil Law (Wrongs) Act 2002 (ACT) s 112.

[123] The legislation was designed to cut back on public authority liabilities, but as Aronson points out (n 3, 76), liabilities for breach of statutory duty are exceptionally rare outside of the health and safety context.

[124] The position is still unclear in QLD, TAS and the ACT, although a first instance decision has suggested (obiter) that the QLD provision applies only to actions for breach of statutory duty: *Hamcor Pty Ltd v Queensland* [2014] QSC 224 (affirmed without deciding the point [2015] QCA 183). The provision in VIC has been held only to apply to such actions. In NSW, a provision covering negligence cases was subsequently introduced in the form of s 43A of the Civil Liability Act 2002 (NSW). In WA, the provision clearly applies to negligence actions. See further Bell-James and Barker (n 36).

[125] See, eg, *Hamcor* (n 123) (obiter); *Lee v Carlton Crest Hotel (Sydney) Pty Ltd* [2014] NSWSC 1280; *Curtis v Harden Shire Council* [2014] NSWCA 314.

[126] See n 113.

the re-introduction into the law, via statute, of public-law thresholds for civil actions in respect of discretionary public decision-making cuts directly against the trend at common law and accords public bodies special treatment. The 'mandamus' requirement in actions for omissions to exercise a regulatory power is especially striking in this regard and flies in the face of the reasoning of Mason J in *Heyman*[127] and Lord Hoffmann in *Stovin*.[128] True it is, that the existence of some pre-existing duty to act can help solve traditional objections to omissions liabilities in cases between private parties, but so too can a defendant's special control over the risk in question, so it is clearly not a necessary requirement in such cases. There is therefore no good reason why the absence of any public law duty to act should preclude a public body having a private law duty to act. Similarly, it is clear that courts themselves entertain serious doubts as to whether it is appropriate to introduce Wednesbury unreasonableness standards into the law in the way that governments have done. They have accordingly done their best to interpret the provisions in a way that severs them from these, public law roots.[129] If additional deference to a public decision is needed on account of its particular, practical difficulty and sensitivity, then the more appropriate approach would surely be to accord public bodies the same protection as is provided to expert private decision-makers under *Bolam* and its statutory equivalents,[130] not to reference public law standards.

All of this ignores the lessons of the common law about the importance of distinguishing the functions and purposes of public and private law and diverges from the Diceyan ideal that the obligations of the state and its citizens ought to be approached in basically the same way in analogous cases. It may not be going too far to say that it signals a privileged and self-preferential attitude on the part of government towards its own civil obligations. To my mind, this is telling and regrettable in equal measure. When viewed in the stark light of their effects on the civil rights of citizens, the Australian reforms take on a rather sinister hue—the aspect of an opportunistic grab by government of privileged status at a time of financial crisis. Even if it is regarded, less cynically, as a democratic readjustment of resources from the compensation of individual tort victims to the provision of front-line public services, one must wonder whether the former goal is really a lesser public good than the latter—is corrective justice really a lesser priority than social welfare, or an important part of it? Whatever one thinks about this, the recent adjustments are unlikely to be easily reversible, despite the fact that the insurance 'crisis' has now receded, because government interests are now far too firmly captured.

127 *Heyman* (n 2) 465.

128 *Stovin* (n 2) 950 (Lords Goff and Jauncey agreeing).

129 See, eg, *Allianz Australia Insurance Ltd v RTA of New South Wales* [2010] NSWCA 328 [89] (Giles JA, McColl JA and Sackville AJA agreeing); *Grant v Roads and Traffic Authority of New South Wales* [2014] NSWSC 379 [144]-[159] (Rothman J); *Curtis* (n 124) [5]–[6], [261]–[262] (Bathurst CJ).

130 See nn 34–35.

The second observation is that the reforms are so extensive and far reaching in their scope that they cannot generally claim to concern themselves centrally with the problems of 'discretionary' 'policy' decision-making, even though it was the threat to such decision-making that supposedly caused governments to ask the Ipp Committee to review public authority liability in the first place. Rather, they are a blunt instrument aimed at reducing public authority debts across the board and protecting the public purse. They are also so varied in content and form as to leave the private law rights of Australian citizens more uncertain than ever, and sometimes completely different, as between different states and territories. Democratic as it apparently is, this is also, in its own way, a denial of equality to citizens in terms of the respect accorded to some of their most basic interests, such as person and property. The strength of the common law system, for all its ragged uncertainties, was not simply that it tried to treat public bodies in as nearly-as-possible-the-same way as private parties, but also that, as a unitary system with the High Court of Australia at its head, it was able to treat all citizens in the same way too. To my mind, the fact that very basic private interests such as person and property can receive such different levels of protection before the law, depending on where in Australia one chooses to reside, signals that something has gone awry in the operation of the Australian, democratic system. This is not something that any private citizen would sensibly choose.

V. Conclusions

Discretionary public power is an essential building block of the modern administrative state, but the relationship between public discretion and private law rights continues to cause confusion and starkly divide interests. That confusion can be partly reduced in the common law, I have suggested, by more careful and more disciplined thinking about what courts mean when they describe public powers as discretionary. The language of discretion itself is of little assistance in articulating the circumstances in which governments and other public bodies owe duties of care in respect their special powers and should be dropped from courts' legal reasoning, as should references to the question whether a decision fell 'within' or 'outside' a body's power. Instead, we must look directly to the substance of courts' concerns about their constitutional relationship to the state.

Whilst courts have shown themselves less shy about this relationship in recent years and more prepared to treat public bodies in as-nearly-as-possible-the-same way as they treat ordinary, private parties who are tasked with making especially difficult judgements, their gradual progression towards the basic, Diceyan vision has proven simply too threatening to some governments in the wake of the recent global financial crisis. At the first sign of serious economic strife and the first distress call from their insurers, governments appear to have run for the hills, not only reverting to regrettable, ancient patterns of immunity and privilege, but also, in some cases, redefining the relationship between public power and private liability with a trenchant, utilitarian conservatism that undermines the more liberal movements of the common law in recent years. Had this blunt, utilitarian shift toward the curtailment of private rights to compensation and corrective justice been based on sound, empirical data about the effect that private law duties and liabilities were having on the capacity of governments to make political judgements for the public good, or on the capacity of insurers to insure their public activities, this might still have been justified. But the evidence is missing[131] and it is private rights and interests that have been left to shorten their breath in the meantime, or quietly suffocate in the vacuum.

[131] In the UK, the extent of public compensation payouts is apparently not properly recorded, much to the recent frustration of the Law Commission (Law Comm Rep no 322 (n 4) [1.45]). In Australia, the link between private tort litigation and the 'insurance crisis' has never been empirically validated: see Cane, Burns (n 113).

10

The Legitimacy of the Company as a Source of (Private) Power

ROSS GRANTHAM

Companies have always been sources of great wealth and power. From the earliest chartered corporations that ran entire countries,[1] through the great railway companies of the nineteenth century, to the modern social media mega-corporations, companies have been in a position to influence the day-to-day lives of people in ways at least as profound as any government.[2] This power has presented society and the law with a challenge in terms of the political and moral legitimacy of corporate power: why should such enormous power be in private hands, and to what ends ought that power be used? This chapter will begin by exploring the extent and nature of corporate power in the twenty-first century, highlighting the growing power companies now have over society as a whole—power to affect the environment, political decision-making and, increasingly, the norms and behaviours of society.

Turning to the justifications of corporate power, most accounts have tended to see the company as either a private economic institution or as a quasi-public political institution.[3] The economic power of the company is legitimated either by being grounded in the private rights of the individuals involved or as being constrained by an overriding need for that power to be used in the public interest. None of these justifications, however, are complete or entirely satisfactory and they each tend to reflect a prior and unarticulated conviction as to how the company should be viewed.[4] Moreover, attempts to justify corporate power have largely failed to consider the purposes for which the corporate form does and should exist, or the distinction between the economic and social power of the company. The result is that the various accounts of the legitimacy of corporate power have tended to talk past one another, or have shared a dubious willingness

[1] The British East India Company effectively governed India from 1757 to 1858, during which time it maintained a civil service and an army. See C Philips, *The East India Company: 1784–1834* 2nd edn, (Manchester, Manchester University Press, 1961).

[2] A Jay, *Management and Machiavelli* (London, Hutchinson, 1987) 27–28.

[3] M Eisenberg, 'Corporate Legitimacy, Conduct, and Governance—Two Models of the Corporation' (1983) 17 *Creighton Law Review* 1.

[4] ibid, 17.

to accept that the economic benefits of the company can be properly offset against its social costs.

As an economic institution, the company represents the most effective and successful mechanism yet devised for the creation of wealth and its superiority in this respect seems ample justification for the *economic* power it holds. However, it is the legitimacy of the company as a social actor and the holder of increasing power to affect society that presents the real challenge. While it may already be too late to renege, as a society we need to recognise and understand the implications of the bargain we are being presented with: that, in return for access to the power of the information age, to Google's search engine, and Facebook friends, we are trading off more and more of our autonomy as individuals and the choices that we have as to the nature of the society in which we live.

I. Nature and Extent of Corporate Power

The concept of power is a difficult and contested idea and has been the subject of extensive consideration and theorisation. It is not proposed here to engage with these debates, but rather to adopt what is arguably the most widely accepted notion of power as a working premise. John Kenneth Galbraith, following Weber, defined power as existing where 'someone or some group is imposing its will and purpose or purposes on others, including on those who are reluctant or adverse. The greater the capacity to impose such will and achieve the related purpose, the greater the power.'[5] Understood in these terms, a company may be said to have power if it has the ability or capacity to make decisions, take action, or have an impact upon the will or autonomy of others regardless of the agreement, approval or willingness of those affected.[6] Moreover, that power may exist not only in relation to those with whom the company directly transacts, but may also exist in relation to the wider community.

In considering the nature and extent of corporate power, we can broadly distinguish between, on the one hand, economic power and, on the other, non-economic or societal power. Although this distinction is perhaps more accurately represented as points on a spectrum or range of effects, rather than exclusive categories, the distinction, it will be suggested later, is important in considering whether and how we can legitimate the power held by companies. It should also be noted that

[5] JK Galbraith, *The Anatomy of Power* (Boston, Houghton Mifflin, 1983) 2. See also R Dahl, 'The Concept of Power' (1957) 2 *Behavioral Science* 201. In the context of companies, see J Parkinson, *Corporate Power and Responsibility* (Oxford, Oxford University Press, 1993) 8–9; M Moore, *Corporate Governance in the Shadow of the State* (Oxford, Hart Publishing, 2013) 17–18; S Bowman, *The Modern Corporation and American Political Thought: Law, Power and Ideology* (University Park, Pennsylvania State University Press, 1996) ch 1.

[6] This follows the conception of corporate power adopted by both Parkinson, ibid, 8, and Moore, ibid, 17.

our concern in this chapter is with large and very large companies. This is because power is primarily a function of the enormous wealth and resources accumulated in their hands. In this sense, the issue is not so much one with the corporate form *per se*, but with the aggregation of wealth. However, the company is the dominant form for the conduct of business and is ideally suited to the aggregation of wealth. Thus, for all practical purposes the issues of corporate power and the corporate form are the same.

A. Economic Power

Economic power is defined here as the power that flows from the ownership and control of wealth to affect the economic interests of others. This includes those with whom the holder of the power deals directly. The resources available to the company and the control that its ownership affords over the use of those resources means a large company is able to dictate the terms and price to those with whom it directly transacts: smaller traders, retail customers, and its employees. It also includes those who do not deal directly with the company. Thus, for example, a decision by a company to relocate its factory will impact upon the livelihood of others in the local community (or country as a whole) whose economic interests depend on the custom of the employees of the factory for its revenue or the availability of goods and services for its own business. Thus, when a car manufacturer in Australia recently decided to cease operations, it was estimated that this would result in the failure of 100 other businesses in that city and the loss of 90,000 jobs.[7]

The modern registered company was conceived as a vehicle to facilitate the aggregation of capital and it is thus not surprising that companies have always been repositories of significant wealth. However, since the end of the Second World War in particular, increasing amounts of wealth, and thus power, have been aggregated in the hands of the largest multinational companies. Such is the scale of the largest multinationals that their wealth now surpasses that of the majority of countries. It is now the case that of the 100 largest economies in the world, 51 are companies.[8] The largest company in the world in 2013, Walmart, was the 28th largest economy in the world. It was closely followed by Shell Oil (29th), Exxon (30th), and China Petroleum & Chemical Corporation (Sinopec) (31st). Walmart's global revenue is roughly that of Sweden's GDP, while Shell's is larger than Austria's, and Toyota's revenues exceed the GDP of Ireland. By the mid-1990s, the annual sales of global

[7] General Motors Holden announced in 2014 that it would cease car manufacturing in Adelaide. See P Brain, 'The Impact on the Australian Economy of the Closure of GMH Production Facilities in Australia' (Victoria, NIEIR, 2013) 2; R Ranasinghe, A Hardacre, and J Spoehr, 'Impact of the Auto Industry Closure' *Workplace Futures Survey—Playford and Salisbury Wave* (Australian Workplace Innovation and Social Research Centre, The University of Adelaide, 2014).

[8] M Steger, *Globalisation: A Very Short Introduction*, 2nd edn, (Oxford, Oxford University Press, 2008) 51; L Chen, 'The World's Largest Companies 2015' *Forbes*, 6 May 2015; *Forbes Global 2000* available at www.forbes.com/global2000/list.

multinationals accounted for more almost two-thirds of the total world GDP[9] and it has been estimated that the top 500 companies in the US account for 82 per cent of all sales in that country.[10]

The power that their massive wealth affords individual companies is greatly multiplied by the fact that in a wide range of industry sectors there is a very high degree of concentration of ownership in the hands of a remarkably small number of multinationals. A recent study has found that a mere 147 multinationals control 40 per cent of the total value of all multinationals globally.[11] Moreover, the ownership and control of whole industry sectors worldwide is dominated by only a handful of companies. Thus, for example, the largest eight car and truck makers account for 60 per cent of global production.[12] In the food sector, the degree of concentration has spawned the term 'agropoly'. In 2013, it was reported that the 10 largest multinationals accounted for 75 per cent of seed production, with one company, Monsanto, alone accounting for 26 per cent of world seed production. Global pesticide production is almost completely concentrated in the hands of 10 companies, while global coffee production, although involving 25 million small farmers, is effectively controlled by the three major roasting companies and the five companies that control 55 per cent of all trade in coffee beans.[13] The technology sector is equally closely held. In the field of computers, Microsoft products account for over 90 per cent of computer operating systems in use,[14] while Google so completely dominates the field of internet search engines that we now speak of searching the internet as 'googling'. In the mobile telephone market, Google (Android) accounts for 83 per cent of operating systems used worldwide, while handset sales are dominated by Samsung, Microsoft, and Apple.[15]

It may be argued that companies, no matter how large, do not have economic power as defined above because their decisions and behaviour are constrained by market forces.[16] In competitive markets, the forces of demand and supply, and the

[9] United Nations Conference on Trade and Development, *World Investment Report 1995: Transnational corporations and competitiveness* (Geneva, United Nations, 1995) 39. See also R Schaeffer, *Understanding Globalization: The Social Consequences of Political, Economic, and Environmental Change* 2nd edn (Lanham, Rowman & Littlefield, 2003) 238.

[10] Bowman (n 5) 17.

[11] S Vitali, J Glattfelder and S Battiston, 'The Network of Global Corporate Control' (2011) *PLoS One* 6(10) 4.

[12] Statista, 'Global market share of the world's largest automobile OEMs as of August 30, 2014' available at www.statista.com/statistics/316786/global-market-share-of-the-leading-automakers.

[13] H Paul and R Steinbrecher, *Hungry Corporations—How Biotechnology Companies Colonise the Foodchain* (London, Zed Books, 2003); United Nations Conference on Trade and Development, 'Tracking the Trend Towards Market Concentration: The Case of the Agricultural Input Industry', UNCTAD, 2006; EcoNexus, 'Agropoly—A Handful of Corporations Control World Food Production' (Berne Declaration, September 2013).

[14] Statista, 'Microsoft: statistics and facts' available at www.statista.com/topics/823/microsoft.

[15] Statista, 'Vendors' market share of mobile phone unit sales to end users worldwide from 1997 to 2014' available at www.statista.com/statistics/271574/global-market-share-held-by-mobile-phone-manufacturers-since-2009.

[16] See, generally, Parkinson (n 5) 10–15; M Stokes, 'Company Law and Legal Theory' in W Twining (ed), *Legal Theory and Common Law* (Oxford, Blackwell, 1986) 157.

availability of alternative providers means that companies are unable to charge more for their goods and services than the prevailing market price and firms that do try to do so will fail as consumers go elsewhere for cheaper options. Likewise, companies cannot skimp on quality as consumers will abandon the firm's products. It follows, so the argument goes, that companies in fact have little or no power to impose their will on those with whom they deal. Rather, they are at the mercy of popular will as expressed through the mechanism of the market. As regards those with whom they deal directly, they must produce goods and services at a cost and of a quality that meets the market, and in respect of the wider community, the demands of efficiency mean they cannot afford[17] to act other than in ways that are socially acceptable.[18]

The argument that market forces deny the existence of corporate economic power rests on the assumptions of full competition and perfect information.[19] In some markets at some times, these assumptions may be justifiable. However, in many other markets these assumptions are likely to be rather heroic. First, many markets are simply not fully competitive. Even putting aside those relatively rare cases of a technical monopoly, many markets are dominated by a small number of large companies. As we saw above, in the automotive, food products, technology, and social media sectors, global markets are controlled by a handful of mega-companies. Secondly, few, if any, markets ever reach a state of perfect information. A more reasonable assumption, therefore, is that of bounded rationality,[20] where market participants have either, or both, limited information and a limited ability to understand or process the available information. It is for this reason that much of modern consumer law is concerned with imposing obligations of information disclosure: it is accepted that market forces alone will not produce an optimal amount of comprehensible information. Thirdly, consumers are likely to have only a very limited ability to influence resource allocation or production decisions. While consumers may have a power of veto over products that are brought to market, in the sense that they may not buy the product or buy it at the price

[17] 'Afford' is used here in two senses. First, companies cannot afford financially to divert significant resources from their most efficient use as this would jeopardise their profitability. Secondly, companies cannot afford the reputational losses that would flow from acting in a socially irresponsible way: being socially responsible is part and parcel of good business.

[18] See, for example, the various consumer boycotts that have brought large companies to heel, such as the long- running campaign against the use of animal fur in clothing and the 2010 boycott of Nestlé in response to deforestation and its palm oil supply chain.

[19] Neoclassical economics seeks to model problems rather and the real world. Accordingly, it makes a number of key assumptions in building its model. These include that actors act rationally and with full information and that markets are competitive in the sense that there are numerous firms and there are no barriers to entry and exit from the market. See, generally, E Weintraub, *General Equilibrium Analysis* (Cambridge, Cambridge University Press, 1985); S Dow, 'Mainstream Economic Methodology' (1997) 21 *Cambridge Journal of Economics* 73, 83; R Cooter and T Ulen, *Law and Economics*, 6th edn, (Boston, Prentice Hall, 2012) 28, 41.

[20] A term coined by H Simon, 'A Behavioral Model of Rational Choice' (1955) 69 *Quarterly Journal of Economics* 99 and *Models of Man, Social and Rational: Mathematical Essays on Rational Human Behavior in a Social Setting* (New York, Wiley, 1957).

being asked, consumers' choices are often subject to extensive manipulation.[21] The purpose of the $1.5 trillion spent worldwide each year on advertising[22] is precisely to create and shape consumer demand so that it matches what firms have to sell. Consumers also lack any positive say as to what products and services they want firms to develop and bring to market. In this sense, companies have significant power to shape the range of opportunities available to consumers and when and how they might meet consumer demand. Thus, for many years US car manufacturers simply refused to build small cars,[23] and there have long been suspicions that the oil industry has sought to frustrate development of alternative sources of energy.[24] Accordingly, while market forces clearly offer some restraint on corporate economic power, it seems equally clear that defects in markets mean that companies have considerable discretion in resource allocation and production decisions, and thus extensive economic power.

B. Non-Economic or Societal Power

Non-economic or societal power has three aspects.[25] First, a company may have power in the sense that its activities may impact upon the physical environment. That a company's activities may affect local and global eco-systems is all too apparent from disasters such as the Exxon Valdez oil spill in Alaska in 1989 and the Deepwater Horizon oil spill in the Gulf of Mexico in 2010. These disasters not only affect the natural environment, but also the heath of local communities. Equally profound for both local eco-systems and local communities are the changes brought about through activities such as the clearance of rainforests to make way for commercial plantations[26] and the taking of farming land for mining and coal seam gas. These commercial developments not only impact on the natural environment, but also the way of life of those who live on the land.[27]

[21] Parkinson (n 5) 13.

[22] Chief Marketing Officer Council, 'Marketing Spend' available at www.cmocouncil.org/facts-stats-categories.php?view=all&category=marketing-spend.

[23] C Lindblom, *Politics and Markets* (New York, Basic Books, 1977) 153.

[24] E Black, *Internal Combustion: How Corporations and Governments Addicted the World to Oil and Derailed the Alternatives* (New York, St Martin's Press, 2006); P Roberts, *The End of Oil: the Decline of the Petroleum Economy and the Rise of a New Energy Order* (London, Bloomsbury, 2004).

[25] Bowman (n 5) 16: 'Corporate power affects virtually aspect of social existence—work, education, the arts, leisure, communication, transportation, entertainment'. The Corporations and Markets Advisory Committee, 'The Social Responsibility of Corporations' (December 2006) 14, distinguishes economic and societal impacts, and includes within societal impacts environmental and social impacts, but curiously omits political impacts.

[26] See, eg, P Nelson et al, 'Oil Palm and Deforestation in Papua New Guinea' (2014) 7 *Conversation Letters* 188; N Gilbert, 'Palm-oil Boom Raises Conservation Concerns: Industry Urged Towards Sustainable Farming Practices as Rising Demand Drives Deforestation' (2012) *Nature* vol 487, no 7405, 14.

[27] They may be physically displaced, their health may be affected, and their livelihoods may be affected. A major concern with coal seam gas in Australia is the pollution of ground water and the

Although by no means limited to developing nations, the impact of the power of multinationals is arguably felt most in developing nations, where local communities and governments are less able or willing to resist the power of large companies. A notorious example of this was the plight of the Ogoni people of Nigeria. Shell discovered oil on their land in the 1950s and, over a 40 year period, the land became severely contaminated by a series of large oil spills. In the 1990s, a protest movement arose, but rather than requiring Shell to clean up the contamination, the Nigerian government forcibly suppressed the protests, with more than 2,000 people killed and 80,000 displaced.[28]

Secondly, there is the power of companies to shape and influence the policy decisions and law-making by government. As Marsh and Locksley note, companies may exercise this power in two ways: 'directly through interest groups and structurally because of the crucial role boards and managers exercise over production, investment and employment decisions which shape the economic and political environment within which Governments make policy'.[29] Direct influence involves the lobbying of government and donations to political parties. It has been estimated that there are more than 30,000 corporate lobbyists in Washington and Brussels and between 1997 and 2000 US corporations spent $9.7 billion lobbying the US Congress.[30] Structural influence relies on the need for governments to maintain business confidence and a strong economy if the government is to be re-elected. In the large economies of the West, which might hitherto have been thought to be immune to corporate power, the global financial crisis of 2008 brought home the dependence of the world economy and national governments on companies that were now too big and too central to the economy to be allowed to fail. In the developing world and smaller economies, pressure from large multinational companies, whose revenues may be much greater than the country's entire GDP, may be both direct and irresistible.[31] It has thus been said that there

loss of quality farming land. See W Rifkin, V Uhlmann, J Everingham, K May, 'Tracking the Boom in Queensland's Gasfields' (2014) *International Journal of Rural Law and Policy* 3; T Nunan, 'Legal Issues Emerging from the Growth of the Coal Seam Gas Industry in Queensland' (2006) 25 *Australian Resources and Energy Law Journal* 189.

[28] C Obi, 'Globalisation and Local Resistance: The Case of the Ogoni Versus Shell' (1997) 2 *New Political Economy* 137; C Parker, *The Open Corporation* (Cambridge, Cambridge University Press, 2002) 2 and 161.

[29] D Marsh and G Locksley, 'Capital in Britain: Its Structural Power and Influence Over Policy' (1983) 6 *West European Politics* 36, 59.

[30] L Drutman, 'How Corporate Lobbyists Conquered American Democracy' *The Atlantic*, 20 April 2015; Statista, 'Total Lobbying Spending in the United States from 1998 to 2015' available at www.statista.com/statistics/257337/total-lobbying-spending-in-the-us.

[31] The influence of multinationals is not always negative. Despite the popular belief that multinationals only ever invest in dictatorships, empirical evidence suggests that the prospect of investment by multinationals may encourage regimes to behave better: N Jensen, 'Democratic Governance and Multinational Corporations: Political Regimes and Inflows of Foreign Direct Investment' (2003) 57 *International Organization* 587.

'has been no greater challenge to nation states sovereignty since the middle of the 20th century than the threat of MNCs [multinational corporations]'.[32]

Finally, companies are increasingly acquiring influence over the nature of our society and culture. A feature of the last 20 years has been the rise of social media and social networking. In 2015, there were 1.5 billon Facebook users (almost a quarter of the world's population), 555 million users of Tumblr, 320 million users of Twitter, 400 million users of Instagram, and Netflix, the TV and film streaming service, had 26 million users worldwide. The Apple music download app, iTunes, accounts for almost 70 per cent of all legally downloaded music in the US.[33] Likewise, the e-book market now accounts for almost a third of all book sales in the UK.[34]

As our social interactions, leisure activities and knowledge of the world around us becomes more virtual and technology-dependent, so too does the power of the social media mega-companies such as Google, Microsoft, Amazon, and Netflix to influence society and cultural norms. While we are accustomed to, and sceptical of, the manipulation of news by newspapers and television, we seem less aware of the extent to which our virtual, online selves are being watched[35] and influenced by social media companies.[36] Our reliance on the internet and internet-enabled technology for so much of what we do and know, and our apparent preference for virtual social interaction, means that what we know of the world is now mediated through the Google search box and the Facebook message wall. The power of Google and Facebook, among others, to shape our world is, therefore, enormous and there is already evidence that Google manipulates its search engine results. In 2015, the Federal Trade Commission found that Google had been manipulating search results to promote its services and demote those of its competitors.[37] However, much more insidious are the in-built biases that prefer

[32] K Irogbe, 'Global Political Economy and the Power of Multinational Corporations' (2013) 30 *Journal of Third World Studies* 223. See also S Cohen, *Multinational Corporations and Foreign Direct Investment: Avoiding Simplicity, Embracing Complexity* (Oxford, Oxford University Press, 2007) ch 10; R Bryant and S Bailey, *Third World Political Ecology* (London, Routledge, 1997).

[33] Statista, 'Facts on the Digital Music Industry' available at www.statista.com/topics/1386/digital-music.

[34] L Campbell, 'E-book Market Share Down Slightly in 2015' *The Bookseller*, 8 June 2015; M Ingram, 'No, e-book Sales are not Falling, Despite What Publishers Say' *Fortune*, 24 September 2015.

[35] See, eg, the description of B Schneier, *Data and Goliath: The Hidden Battles to Collect Your Data and Control Your World* (New York, W W Norton, 2015) of the extent to which we are all, quite voluntarily, under the closest surveillance by private organisations.

[36] R Epstein and R Robertson, 'The Search Engine Manipulation Effect (SEME) and its Possible Impact on the Outcomes of Elections' *Proceedings of the National Academy of Sciences of the United States of America* 4: 'Resent research has demonstrated that the rankings of search results provided by search engine companies have a dramatic impact on consumer attitudes, preferences and behaviour … this is presumably why North American companies now spend more than 20 billion US dollars annually on efforts to place results as the top of rankings'.

[37] R Winkler and B Mullins, 'How Google Skewed Search Results' *Wall Street Journal*, 19 March 2015; Federal Trade Commission, 'Google Agrees to Change Its Business Practices to Resolve FTC Competition Concerns In the Markets for Devices Like Smart Phones, Games and Tablets, and in Online Search' Press Release, 3 January 2013.

popularity over accuracy, and established websites over new ones, and the direct human intervention in the operation of the search engines.[38] As Vaidhyanathan notes, Google's 'process of collecting, ranking, linking, and displaying knowledge determines what we consider to be good, true, valuable, and relevant. The stakes could not be higher.'[39] And while Google may thus far have chosen not to exercise this capacity, the very fact the capacity to influence our view of the world exists is of great significance.[40]

Google, along with many companies, collects vast amounts of information about us from our online presence and the sensors embedded in our homes, cars, mobile phones, and workplaces[41] which it analyses so as to be able to identify and categorise us and predict and shape our behaviour and preferences.[42] This so-called 'Big Data Analytics' is being used to select the advertisements that pop up when we access our Gmail, decide who we want to employ,[43] and what we want to watch on television.[44] Richards and King suggest that the issue of Big Data goes to the very essence of who we are, to our sense of individual identity, and to who controls our identity:

> With even the most basic access to a combination of big data pools like phone records, surfing history, buying history, social networking posts, and others, 'I am' and 'I like' risk becoming 'you are' and 'you will like.' Every Google user is already influenced by big-data-fed feedback loops from Google's tailored search results, which risk producing individual and collective echo chambers of thought.[45]

The Information Age in which we now live has vested in private companies (arguably even more so than the state) a capacity to influence and shape information about us and what we know of the world around us that hitherto existed only within the pages of dystopian works of fiction such as *1984* and *A Brave New World*.

[38] S Vaidhyanathan, *The Googlization of Everything: (And Why We Should Worry)* (Berkeley, University of California Press, 2011) 7 and 66–67.

[39] ibid, 7.

[40] For example, research by Epstein and Robertson (n 36) has demonstrated the capacity of search engines like that of Google's to significantly affect the outcomes of national elections.

[41] M Andrejevic and M Burdon, 'Defining the Sensor Society' (2015) 16 *Television and New Media* 19, describe the process by which sensors that are connected to the internet are being embedded in our homes and how the data generated by these sensors is being used to monitor, predict and modify our behaviour.

[42] See, generally, M Burdon and P Harpur, 'Re-conceptualising Privacy and Discrimination in an Age of Talent Analytics' (2014) 37 *University of New South Wales Law Journal* 679; F Pasquale, *The Black Box Society: The Secret Algorithms That Control Money and Information* (Cambridge, Harvard University Press, 2015); V Mayer-Schönberger and K Cukier, *Big Data a Revolution that Will Transform How we Live, Work, and Think* (Boston, Houghton Mifflin Harcourt, 2013).

[43] One of the examples given by Burdon and Harpur, ibid, 685, is the use of analytics to make predictions about the suitability of job applicants on the basis of the web browser they used to upload their job applications. Those using Firefox or Chrome were identified as more effective than those using Internet Explorer or Safari.

[44] A Leonard, 'How Netflix Is Turning Viewers into Puppets' *SALON* (1 February 2013) available at www.salon.com/2013/02/01/how_netflix_is_turning_viewers_into_puppets.

[45] N Richards and J King, 'Three Paradoxes Of Big Data' (2013) 66 *Stanford Law Review Online* 41, 43–44.

II. The Legitimacy of Corporate Power

It is a fundamental premise of modern Western liberal society that power must be legitimated.[46] That is, it must be justified and those who exercise it must be constrained in how they use it. For liberalism, unbridled and arbitrary power is a threat to the foundational values of society of liberty and equality of the individual. Historically, most of the focus has been on the power vested in the hands of state. In large measure this reflected an assumption that all important power in society was held by the state.[47] And quite clearly the extensive legislative and coercive powers of the state mean there are still good reasons to be concerned about state power. However, the state is no longer the sole (and perhaps now not the most important) repository of power in society. As the previous section demonstrated, the capacity of large companies to influence the daily lives of ordinary individuals is now, arguably, at least as great as that of the state. The multinational company now has significant power in respect of not only those with whom it directly transacts, but virtually everyone in society. The economic power of the company, and the increasing impact over the last 20 years that companies have on society as a whole, therefore, gives rise to the question of whether, and how, that power can be justified or legitimated: how do we explain the aggregation of economic, political, social and cultural power in the hands of ostensibly private entities that are legally accountable to only a small group of shareholders (who in many cases are other companies) and in practice are accountable to no-one?[48]

Over the course of the history of the modern registered company there have been various attempts to legitimate its power. These accounts reflect three broad conceptions or models of the company. The first is that the company is a fundamentally private institution that serves the economic interests only of those directly involved. On this view, the legitimacy of the wealth and power of the company is grounded in the private rights and autonomy of the individuals who come together to form the corporation. If we accept the legitimacy of wealth and power held by the individual, then, the argument goes, we must also accept the legitimacy of the wealth and power that arises when individuals band together and act collectively. The arguments that seek to legitimate the company in private rights do so either in terms of the property or the contractual rights of the shareholders. The second model is that the company is a public or political institution in which all of the society has a stake. This argument takes two forms: the 'concession theory' of the corporation and the idea of the company as a social enterprise. The third

[46] Stokes (n 16) 156; JW Hurst, *The Legitimacy of the Business Corporation* (Charlottesville, University Press of Virginia, 1970) 58.

[47] Stokes (n 16) 156.

[48] As a result of the separation of ownership and control identified by A Berle and G Means, *The Modern Corporation and Private Property* (New York, Harcourt Brace, 1968) shareholders lack the capacity or incentive to actually hold corporate management accountable.

model is that however one characterises the company, its power is justified by the benefits it produces for society as whole. This argument is both empirical and consequentialist and legitimates corporate power in terms of its superior capacity to increase the total wealth of society, even allowing for the costs associated with creating that wealth.

A. Ownership as the Basis of Legitimacy

One of the earliest attempts to legitimate the power of the company focused on the property rights of the shareholders as the owners of the company.[49] As conceived by Blackstone, property confers on its holder near absolute rights to use that property, including joining with other individuals to aggregate their property. As long as it was owned by individuals (legally or at least economically) the economic and political power of the company was, therefore, morally justified as an emanation of the autonomy of the individual and the bargain upon which society itself was founded. Corporate power was also rendered benign by focusing on the property rights of individuals. As nothing more than the aggregate of the rights of individuals, corporate wealth did not threaten individual liberty or the democratic basis of the state any more than private wealth did. Indeed, the corporation understood as private property rights was part and parcel of the guarantee of individual autonomy against state interference that the institution of property provided.[50]

If we accept, for the purposes of argument, the absolute nature of Blackstone's conception of property rights,[51] the major difficulty facing the property rights basis of legitimation is that it seems now hopelessly implausible to contend that shareholders own the company or its assets in any meaningful sense. While it is true that in the old deed of settlement company, the members, like ordinary partners, held an equitable interest in the assets of the company,[52] from the early nineteenth century, the courts began to reject the idea, first, of shareholders as owners of the company's assets and then later the idea of the shareholders as the owners of the company. Instead, the emphasis shifted away from idea that the rights of shareholders were an 'interest in the company' whereby the 'company itself is treated not merely as a person, the subject of rights and duties, but also as a *res*, the object of rights and duties',[53] to the ownership only of the particular rights encompassed in the share. This analysis reached its high point in *Short v*

[49] See, generally, R Grantham, 'The Doctrinal Basis of the Rights of Company Shareholders' (1998) *CLJ* 554.

[50] Stokes (n 16) 156–57; Parkinson (n 5) 33–40; C Reich, 'The New Property' (1974) 73 *Yale Law Journal* 733.

[51] This is of course a highly contested vision of property rights. For a very different perspective, see M Davies, *Property: Meanings, Histories, Theories* (Abingdon, Routledge-Cavendish, 2007).

[52] *Buckeridge v Ingram* (1795) 2 Ves Jun 652; *Howse v Chapman* (1799) 4 Ves Jun 542.

[53] P Davies and S Worthington, *Gower & Davies' Principles of Modern Company Law* 9th edn (London, Sweet & Maxwell, 2012) 861.

Treasury Commissioners[54] where, in assessing the compensation payable for the compulsory acquisition of the company's shares, the Court of Appeal held that shareholders were not entitled to compensation for the value of the company as a whole, but only for what was being expropriated—their shares.[55] Shareholders were thus transformed from owners of the assets and undertaking to owners merely of certain rights against the company.

It may be argued that, even if shareholders are no longer the owners of the company in a strict legal sense, their position is nevertheless like that of an owner in that they have control of the company and its assets and that, therefore, their quasi-proprietary control over the company legitimates its power. While such an argument had considerable force in the mid-nineteenth century, by the early twenty-first century it is no longer legally or practically tenable. In a series of decisions starting with *Automatic Self-Cleansing Filter Syndicate Co Ltd v Cuninghame*[56] and *Salmon v Quin & Axtens Ltd,*[57] the courts began to reconceive the relationship between the shareholders, the directors, and the company. This new model took as its starting point the separateness of the corporate entity from those persons who constituted the organs through which the company must necessarily act (the shareholders and directors). Thus, rather than the right to bind the company arising, as it does with a partnership, from a delegation by the members, the rights (of both the board and shareholders) were conceived of as flowing from the company itself. The legal personality of the company was thus the ultimate source of rights and the company's internal governance rules were transformed from mere agreement to something akin to the constitution of the state.[58] The important implication of the new analysis was that those to whom the constitution had granted control rights—primarily the directors—held those rights free from encroachment by other agencies.[59] In the standard arrangement under which the management of the company was vested in the directors, the shareholders therefore had no control.

The change in the legal analysis of where control lay was accompanied and necessitated by profound changes in the nature and size of companies. During the twentieth century companies grew much larger, often having many thousands

[54] [1948] 1 KB 122. In *Mellon v Alliance Textiles Ltd* (1987) 3 NZCLC 100,086, 100,092, Hardie Boys J said 'when the subject matter is a holding in a large public company, the share can only be regarded as an investment …'.

[55] This conclusion also seems to be reflected in the principles which govern the valuation of shares. The shares will only be valued on an asset-backing basis where the company is unlikely to continue as a going concern.

[56] [1906] 2 Ch 42 (CA). In this line of authorities see also: *Thomas Logan Ltd v Davis* (1911) 104 LT 14; *Scott v Scott* [1943] 1 All ER 582; *Breckland Group Holdings Ltd v London & Suffolk Properties Ltd* (1988) 4 BCC 542; *Black White and Grey Cabs Ltd v Fox* [1969] NZLR 824; *Clifton v. Mount Morgan Ltd* (1940) 40 SR(NSW) 31; *Winthrop Investments Ltd v Winns Ltd* [1975] 2 NSWLR 666; *Massey v Wales* [2003] NSWCA 212.

[57] [1909] 1 Ch 311 (CA), affirmed [1909] AC 442 (HL).

[58] Davies and Worthington (n 53) 65.

[59] *Clifton v Mount Morgan Ltd* (1940) 40 SR (NSW) 31.

of shareholders. Building on this observation, Adolf Berle and Gardner Means concluded that in large public companies there had occurred a separation of the ownership of the investment by shareholders from the control of that investment by management.[60] This separation existed because of the large size of the company's capital and from the small stakes held in that capital by individual shareholders. No individual shareholder had either the power, or the incentive, to exercise any control. Control of the company and its wealth and power thus rested solely with management. The important implication of this observation was that the rational passivity of shareholders effectively freed corporate management from direct oversight and accountability to shareholders and meant that the legitimacy of the power of these new large companies could not be grounded in the property rights of shareholders.

B. Contract as the Basis of Legitimacy

The registered company that emerged in 1844 has always had a strong contractual flavour. In large measure this is due to the origins of the company in the deed of settlement company and the law of partnership. The earliest attempts to conceptualise the company as a mere association of contracting individuals, however, floundered on the apparently crucial role of the state in conferring legal personality on the association and, perhaps even more importantly, on the realisation that the limited liability of the shareholders could not in any practical sense be achieved purely by contract.

A new and more sophisticated contractual conceptualisation of the company was, however, developed by the law and economics movement in the 1970s. The 'nexus of contracts theory'[61] treats the company as little more than a collective noun for the web of contracts that link the various participants, which include

[60] This was an empirical observation based on Berle and Mean's study (above n 46) of the structure of the corporate economy in the United States in the 1920s. Whether the focus on public companies was a representative sample of the corporate economy is a matter of debate. See, generally, D Millon, 'Theories of the Corporation' (1990) *Duke Law Journal* 201, 220 and W Werner, 'Corporation Law in Search of its Future' (1981) 81 *Columbia Law Review* 1161. For an account of the enduring influence of Berle's and Means' work, see W Bratton, 'Berle and Means Reconsidered at the Century's Turn' (2001) 26 *Journal of Corporation Law* 737.

[61] The leading advocates of this approach are F Easterbrook and D Fischel, *The Economic Structure of Corporate Law* (Cambridge, Harvard University Press, 1991) and 'The Corporate Contract' (1989) 89 *Columbia Law Review* 1416. See also J Macey and G Miller, 'Corporate Stakeholders: A Contractual Perspective' (1993) 43 *University of Toronto Law Journal* 401; M Jensen and W Meckling, 'The Theory of the Firm: Managerial Behaviour, Agency Costs and Ownership Structure' (1976) *Journal of Financial Economics* 305 and B Cheffins, *Company Law: Theory Structure and Operation* (Oxford, Clarendon Press, 1997). For outlines of the history and structure of the contractual analysis by non-believers, see W Bratton, 'The New Economic Theory of the Firm: Critical Perspectives from History' (1989) 42 *Stanford Law Review* 1471 and J Parkinson, 'The Contractual Theory of the Company and the Protection of Non-Shareholder Interests' in D Feldman and F Meisel (eds), *Corporate and Commercial Law: Modern Developments* (London, Lloyds of London Press, 1996) 121.

shareholders, management, employees, and creditors. The function of company law is thus conceived of as the facilitation of the parties' bargains. Unlike previous legal theories, the nexus of contracts analysis had no place for a reified notion of the company and, as such, there was nothing to own.[62] The privileged position which the nexus of contracts analysis affords shareholders to have the company run to maximise the return to them is explained as a contractual entitlement to which all the parties would agree *ex ante*.[63] The important (and intended) normative implication of the nexus of contacts analysis was that the company was an entirely private arrangement and thus the power of the company was fully and completely justified in terms of the private rights of those involved in it. As a web of private relationships, any form of direct state intervention and oversight of the internal affairs of the company beyond that which could be justified in respect of individuals was, therefore, wholly impermissible.

Although dominating company law debate for most of the last 30 years, and likely influencing a range of company law reform initiatives, the nexus of contracts theory and the legitimation of corporate power in the contractual rights of those involved in the company has not, however, proved compelling. At the normative level,[64] the vision of the company as a purely private association remains hotly contested. There is a growing tide of opinion that stresses the social importance and institutional nature of the company and conceives of the company in 'communitarian' terms where the interests of all groups must be respected.[65] Indeed, one communitarian scholar has already (though somewhat prematurely) pronounced contractarianism in company law dead.[66]

From a descriptive perspective the nexus of contracts analysis is also problematic. As Brian Cheffins notes, the contractual 'characterization is at odds with the legal conceptualization of the company'.[67] This manifests itself principally in three areas. First, the nexus approach relies on a conception of contracting that modern contract scholars would find quaintly old-fashioned. In its reliance on consent

[62] F Easterbrook and D Fischel, 'Voting in Corporate Law' (1983) 26 *Journal of Law and Economics* 395, 396; E Fama, 'Agency Problems and the Theory of the Firm' (1980) 88 *Journal of Political Economy* 288, 290; Parkinson, ibid, 123.

[63] Rationally, all of the parties to the nexus of contracts would grant shareholders the right to have the firm conducted so as to maximise their profits. This is because shareholders are the residual risk bearer (the return to shareholders arises only after all other claims have been satisfied). Thus, by maximising the return to shareholders, the parties would ensure that all of their claims were also maximised.

[64] At least in the hands of Easterbrook and Fischel (n 61) the contractual analysis is intended as both a normative principle as well as an explanatory one: D DeMott, 'Trust and Tension Within Corporations' (1996) 81 *Cornell Law Review* 1308, 1312.

[65] See the essays in L Mitchell (ed), *Progressive Corporate Law* (Colorado, WestView, 1995) and the scholarship collected in the bibliography in D Millon, 'New Directions in Corporate Law: Communitarians, Contractarians, and the Crisis in Corporate Law' (1993) 50 *Washington and Lee Law Review* 1373.

[66] D Branson, 'The Death of Contractarianism and the Vindication of Structure and Authority in Corporate Governance and Corporate Law' in Mitchell, ibid, 93.

[67] Cheffins (n 61) 32.

as both the descriptive and normative basis of contracting, the nexus approach is clearly out of step with modern contract law that increasingly accommodates mandatory or overriding rules without seemingly sacrificing its 'contractual core'.[68] Furthermore, in order to accommodate awkward features of the extant law, the contractual analysis has been forced to adopt an extremely expansive notion of contract. In particular, it is clear that, even if technically a contract, the company's constitution is heavily overlaid by statute and that for most companies the constitution does not result from the sort of actual bargaining between the participants[69] that the nexus approach needs to support its normative conclusions.[70] In expanding the notion of contract, the contractual analysis has thus lost much of its explanatory and moral force.

Secondly, and most importantly, the contractual analysis simply does not accurately describe the content of company law. In particular, the presence in the law of non-excludable mandatory rules, such as the fiduciary duties of directors,[71] mandatory rules relating to takeovers,[72] derivative actions and rules around financial assistance[73] is at odds with the central prediction of the contractual analysis. If the purpose or function of company law was simply to facilitate the parties' bargain there would be little room for rules which the parties cannot modify or exclude. While corporate contract scholars have advocated the removal of such rules,[74] these exhortations have largely fallen on deaf ears.

[68] J Coffee, 'No Exit?: Opting Out, the Contractual Theory of the Corporation, and the Special Case of Remedies' (1988) 53 *Brooklyn Law Review* 919, 937. See, generally, P Atiyah, *The Rise and Fall of Freedom of Contract* (Oxford, Clarendon Press, 1979) and 'Contracts, Promises and the Law of Obligations (1978) 84 *LQR* 193.

[69] M Eisenberg, 'The Structure of Corporation Law' (1989) 89 *Columbia Law Review* 1641; V Brudney, 'Corporate Governance, Agency Costs, and the Rhetoric of Contract' (1985) 85 *Columbia Law Review* 1403. While in Australia and to a lesser extent the UK, the constitution is still couched in largely contractual language, in counties such as New Zealand and Canada, the core internal governance rules are given their force directly by statute: Companies Act 1993 (NZ), s 128.

[70] If the corporate governance structure does not result from actual consent, it is difficult to infer that the resulting structure is efficient. Contract theorists have responded, however, that so long as the governance structure is 'priced', through the value of the shares on the stock market, then it is possible to infer efficiency. The validity of this assumption depends on two further assumptions. First, that the stock market is efficient and, secondly, that shareholders trade on the basis of this information rather than 'noise'. Both assumptions are controversial. See Cheffins (n 61) 55–58.

[71] That a fiduciary's obligations are not entirely excludable was confirmed by the Court of Appeal in *Armitage v Nurse* [1998] Ch 241 where Millett LJ said: 'there is an irreducible core of obligations owed by trustees …'. In those jurisdictions, such as Australia, where the directors duties exist both as common law rules and legislation (Corporations Act 2001 (Cth), ss 180–187) there can be no question of these duties being excluded or modified by the parties. For an overview of the arguments, see J Coffee, 'The Mandatory/Enabling Balance in Corporate Law: An Essay on the Judicial Role' (1989) 89 *Columbia Law Review* 1618 and I Ramsay, 'Models of Corporate Regulation: The Mandatory / Enabling Debate' in R Grantham and C Rickett (eds), *Corporate Personality in the 20th Century* (Oxford, Hart Publishing, 1998) 226.

[72] For example, the requirement in *The Takeover Code* (10th edn, 2011) of equal treatment of shareholders (General Principle 1) and mandatory bids (Rule 9).

[73] Cheffins (n 61) 228.

[74] Easterbrook and Fischel (n 61).

Finally, the contractual analysis does not accurately describe the processes underlying the development of company law. It is simply not plausible, even in the United States where the nexus approach originated, to suggest that the legislature and the courts have sought to develop the law exclusively on the basis of what, *ex ante*, the parties would have agreed to, had transaction costs not been prohibitive. On the contrary, it is clear that both Parliament and the courts have been motivated by other considerations. As Cheffins explains,[75] legislatures in most jurisdictions have been concerned with issues of fairness,[76] social justice[77] and the effects on society of corporate transactions.[78] Thus, for example, concerns with morality underpin the Company Directors Disqualification Act 1986,[79] and the oppression remedy in section 994 of the Companies Act 2006 (UK) has been said to be concerned with 'a visible departure from the standards of fair dealing and a violation of the conditions of fair play …'[80] The approach of Commonwealth courts is also informed, explicitly on occasion, by notions of fairness, propriety, and morality. In *Northside Developments Pty Ltd v Registrar-General*, Mason CJ invoked principles of 'commercial morality' to justify the balance struck between corporate insiders and creditors by the rule in *Turquand's case*.[81]

A purely contractual analysis of the company and corporate power has a strong provenance in the original building blocks of the modern company.[82] However, the twentieth century saw a fundamental change in the underlying conception of the company from that of an association to that of a corporation: the company was no longer a 'they,' but an 'it'.[83] Entailed in this change were an abandonment of contract as the primary legal basis in favour of a more institutional basis and the subordination of the position of shareholders. Although the full implications of this change are still being worked through, it has rendered a purely contractual analysis, even one as sophisticated as the nexus of contract analysis, incapable of legitimating the power of the modern company.[84]

[75] Cheffins (n 61) 228.

[76] ibid, 142ff.

[77] At one time UK company legislation made special provision for consideration of the interests of employees: Companies Act 1985, s 719. The current Act also mentions employees' interests but only as a factor to be taken into account by directors in determining how best to promote the success of the company for the benefit of shareholders: Companies Act 2006, s 172.

[78] This seems to underlie the anti-takeover or 'constituency' statutes in America. These statutes were introduced by a number of US states following the rash of hostile takeovers in the 1980s. These statutes allowed, and in some cases required, directors to take account of constituencies other than shareholders when assessing how to respond to the bid: D Millon, 'Redefining Corporate Law' (1991) 24 *Indiana Law Review* 223; J Gordon, 'Corporations, Markets, and Courts' (1991) 91 *Columbia Law Review* 1931.

[79] F Wheeler, 'Directors' Disqualification: Insolvency Practitioners and the Decision-Making Process' (1995) 15 *Legal Studies* 283, 289.

[80] *Elder v Elder & Watson Ltd* [1952] SC 49, 55 (Lord Cooper), speaking of an earlier formulation.

[81] (1990) 170 CLR 146, 164–65.

[82] R Grantham, 'The Proceduralisation of Australian Corporate Law' (2015) 43 *Federal Law Review* 233.

[83] L Sealy, 'Perception and Policy in Company Law Reform' in D Feldman and F Meisel, *Corporate and Commercial Law: Modern Developments* (London, Lloyds of London Press, 1996) 26.

[84] See, generally, Moore (n 5).

C. The Corporation as a Concession from the State

One of the oldest arguments seeking to legitimate the company and corporate power is the 'concession theory'.[85] The grant of separate legal personality and limited liability to those involved in the company was regarded as a privilege from the state and in return for that privilege the otherwise private association would carry out public functions and would be subject to on-going oversight by the state. In the late eighteenth and early nineteenth centuries, when corporations were created by specific statutes or charters for purposes such as building canals, bridges, roads, and railways, or of exploiting foreign trading opportunities, this made a lot of sense. These corporations were routinely granted quasi-public powers, such as levying tolls and taxes and compulsorily acquiring land. Many corporations in this period, especially the overseas trading corporations such as the East India Company, were granted monopoly rights and were effectively the agent of British national foreign policy. The public nature of these corporations was also evident in bodies that functioned as national regulators of professional standards such as the various trade guilds. The strongly public flavour of the purposes for which corporations were established in this period gave weight to the view that corporations were essentially public institutions that should, therefore, act in the interests of society as a whole. Corporate power was thus legitimated on fundamentally the same basis as the power of the state.

The concession theory of the legitimacy of corporate power was, however, doomed by the advent of a general right to incorporate, introduced first in 1844. The Joint Stock Companies Act 1844 (UK) and the Limited Liability Act 1855 (UK)[86] made it possible for anyone wishing to pay the modest fee and complete the relevant paperwork to bring a limited liability company into existence. Although the Act of 1844 may, on a close reading, have been less revolutionary than is often thought,[87] by the time the House of Lords decided *Salomon v A Salomon & Co Ltd*[88] in 1897 the right of a single individual to bring forth a registered company was such that to claim that it was the conferral of a special privilege was simply no longer plausible. Trading in corporate form was now a right and the vast majority of companies now being established existed for purely private purposes and gain. While the state might retain power to ensure the corporate form was used for the purposes for which it was provided, the mere fact of the state's provision of the corporate form could not sustain an argument that the state retained a general right to intervene to impose public constraints on individual companies.[89]

[85] See, generally, Millon (n 60) 207; R Dias, *Jurisprudence* 5th edn (London, Butterworths, 1985) 265–69; Stokes (n 16) 162.

[86] The first general grant of limited liability. This Act remained in force for only a few months before being replaced by the Joint Stock Companies Act 1856.

[87] R Grantham, 'The Limited Liability of Company Directors' (2007) *LMCLQ* 362.

[88] [1897] AC 22.

[89] Parkinson (n 5) 30.

D. The Corporation as Social Enterprise

The influential political scientist Robert Dahl claimed that 'every large corporation should be thought of as a *social enterprise* that is, as an entity whose existence and decision can be justified only insofar as they serve the public or social purpose'.[90] This claim rests on two main premises. The first is that in modern society companies have enormous power to affect the societies in which they exist, a power that goes well beyond the direct provision of goods and services to those with whom they contract. Companies may thus be said to have social decision-making power.[91] Implicit here also is the claim that the activities of companies are not otherwise constrained by factors such as market forces. The second premise is the more philosophical one that all power, both state power and power in private hands, is legitimate only in so far as it is used for the benefit of society. In his seminal work, *The Legitimacy of the Business Corporation*, Hurst articulates this premise as follows:

> What law permits or accepts, what it enforces or compels should be socially useful and socially responsible. These have been prime elements in the demand for legitimacy which has been an insistent theme in our legal order. Legitimacy means that no arrangement of relations or of power recognized in law should be treated as an end in itself or as autonomous. An institution must be legitimated by its utility to some chosen end other than its own perpetuation. An institution which wields practical power—which compels men's wills or behaviour—must be accountable for its purposes and its performance by criteria not wholly in the control of the institution itself. That legitimacy should derive from utility expresses the pragmatism bred of our experience in opening up a raw continent, through generations in which we were under pressure to improvise and make do with resources frustratingly short of the opportunities. That legitimacy means responsibility—that an institution with power must be accountable to some judgment other than of the power holders—expresses the prime emphasis this culture puts on the individual as the ultimate measure of institutions.[92]

From these basic premises, theorists have drawn a number of sometimes conflicting conclusions. First, that as a social enterprise, the company cannot be regarded simply as a set of private contractual and property relations, but rather as a public or at least quasi-public institution. Accordingly, the state is justified in intervening in the affairs of the company to ensure that it in fact serves the public interest and that its power is subject to the same constraints and oversight as that of any public body. Secondly, that at least in those societies premised on democratic principles, where power is ultimately legitimated by the approval of the members of the society, corporate power must also be permeable to democratic oversight and control: 'In order to match the power and consequences of corporate action on social and

[90] R Dahl, 'A Prelude to Corporate Reform' (1972) *Business and Society Review* 17. See also Parkinson (n 5) 23.

[91] Parkinson (n 5) 23.

[92] Hurst (n 46) 58.

political relations, management decision-making should be open to democratic influences.'[93] This in turn entails implications about the governance structures of the company and the objectives of corporate regulation.[94] Thirdly, some theorists have argued that the power and influence of the company means that the purposes of the company should be freed from the sole pursuit of the maximisation of profit for the benefit of shareholders, in favour of the interests of society as a whole. For Berle and Means, this meant that corporate management should be seen as a 'purely neutral technocracy balancing a variety of claims by various groups in the community and assigning to each a portion of the income stream on the basis of public policy rather than private cupidity'.[95] For other scholars, it means that the company must be seen as a socially responsible citizen that is either free, or required, to take into account the social and environmental impacts of its actions on society and, where necessary, to forgo the pursuit of profits in favour of the non-economic interests of society.

Although the analysis of the company as a social enterprise or socially responsible citizen has many advocates[96] and in some jurisdictions these ideals have been incorporated into company law,[97] as a basis for legitimating the power of the company the social enterprise analysis faces a number of criticisms and obstacles. First, few, if any, doubt the efficiency of the company as a means of creating wealth, or that the creation of wealth is valuable to society. The critique most often levelled at the social enterprise analysis is that once one qualifies the goal of the company, so that it is not solely the pursuit of wealth for the benefit of shareholders, then one fundamentally compromises the efficiency of the corporate form, which in turn is contrary to the interests of society. Secondly, even if one accepts that corporate behaviour should take account of the public interest, it is inappropriate for corporate managers to decide what the public interest requires. Corporate managers are unelected, unrepresentative of society, are not accountable to the public, and the formulation and implementation of public policy ought to be left to those institutions, such as government, that are representative and accountable. While this criticism perhaps has less force in relation to that conception of social responsibility that merely requires the company to take account of the long-run benefits

[93] Parker (n 28) 2.

[94] One possible implication of this is that the regulation of companies should focus more on procedures that insure stakeholder involvement in corporate decision-making: Grantham (n 82).

[95] Berle and Means (n 48) 312–13.

[96] See, for examples, B Horrigan, *Corporate Social Responsibility in the 21st Century* (Cheltenham, Edward Elgar, 2010) and Corporations and Markets Advisory Committee (n 25). The European Union has been a strong advocate of corporate social responsibility: European Union, *Green paper—Promoting a European Framework for Corporate Social Responsibility* COM/2001/0366; and *Communication From The Commission To The European Parliament, The Council, The European Economic And Social Committee And The Committee Of The Regions—A Renewed EU Strategy 2011–14 for Corporate Social Responsibility* COM/2011/0681.

[97] For example, India has introduced a mandatory corporate social responsibility obligation in its legislation: Companies Act 2013, s 135.

to wealth generation from being seen to act in a responsible manner,[98] it clearly carries much more weight in respect of the stronger form of social responsibility that requires the company to actively engage with social issues. The prospect of corporate power being actively deployed by a handful of senior managers to shape society and social issues is almost as concerning as the unconstrained pursuit of profit.

A third and related criticism is that which ultimately persuaded Berle and Means that freeing corporate managers to pursue goals other than profit created more problems than it solved. As the custodians of other people's money (the shareholders' money), there is a risk that managers will pursue their own, particular goals and interests.[99] This may range from inefficient empire building, to lavishing upon themselves expensive offices and corporate jets, to managers using company funds and power to pursue their own, particular social or political agenda. The costs associated with this sort of managerial behaviour are termed 'agency costs' and represents a cost to society in that resources are being used in a less than efficient way. It is also morally objectionable in that it represents a non-consensual transfer of wealth from shareholders to managers. Where the sole goal of the company is the maximisation of profits this represents a simple yardstick against which shareholders can monitor and assess the behaviour of management. Shareholders are thus enabled to call management to account, thereby reducing agency costs. The concern of Berle and Means was that, if the company had multiple, potentially conflicting goals, any meaningful control over management would be lost. It would be possible for management to play off the various goals against one another and justify almost any action as being in one or more of the interests that are meant to inform corporate behaviour.

Finally, for better or worse, the idea that a company should act in a socially responsible way and, in pursuit of that, forgo profit maximisation, has simply not caught on in the common law world. The history of the company is one of a succession of scandals, from the South Sea Bubble through Enron and the GFC, and from Bhopal[100] to Love Canal,[101] to Exxon Valdez, to the James Hardie saga in Australia.[102] Yet, despite all of this, we seem content with the idea that the company

[98] This so-called 'enhanced shareholder value' model is reflected in section 172 of the Companies Act 2006 (UK).

[99] A Berle, 'Corporate Powers as Powers in Trust' (1931) 44 *Harvard Law Review* 1049 and 'For Whom Corporate Managers Are Trustees: A Note' (1932) 45 *Harvard Law Review* 1365.

[100] In December 1984, 500,000 people were exposed to toxic gases to a leak from the Union Carbide India Ltd pesticide plant in Bhopal, India.

[101] See, generally, A Levine, *Love Canal: Science, Politics and People* (Lexington, DC Heath and Company, 1982); C Colten and P Skinner, *The Road to Love Canal: Managing Industrial Waste Before EPA* (Austin, University of Texas Press, 1996); E Blum, *Love Canal Revisited: Race, Class, and Gender in Environmental Activism* (Kansas, University Press of Kansas, 2008).

[102] D Jackson, *Report Of The Special Commission Of Inquiry Into The Medical Research And Compensation Foundation* (21 September 2004, NSW Government); H Glasbeek, 'Contortions of Corporate Law: James Hardie Reveals Cracks in Liberal Law's Armour' (2012) 27 *Australian Journal of Corporate Law* 132.

is a valuable tool for the generation of wealth, whose utility is not sufficiently diminished by the occasional excesses to warrant a fundamental change in the goal of the company. Although there has been some tinkering around the edges in some common law jurisdictions, such as the 'constituency statutes' in the US[103] and the adoption of an enlightened shareholder value metric in section 172 of the Companies Act 2006 (UK), we have not yet been prepared to fundamentally depart from a conception of the company as an essentially economic institution that exists as a vehicle for the pursuit of profit for shareholders. Unless and until that happens, the legitimacy of the company as a social enterprise remains theoretical and aspirational at best.

E. The Maximisation of Wealth as the Basis of Legitimacy

In keeping with the prevalence of neo-liberal politics over the last three decades and the pragmatism which has always surrounded debates about the company, the most widely accepted basis of the legitimacy of corporate power rests not on the rights of individuals, or of society, but on the desirable consequences that flow for society as a whole from the activities of the corporate form.[104] The argument runs as follows. The efficient utilisation of scarce resources and the maximisation of the wealth of society is a good and important thing, both as a means to other substantive goals (such as happiness) and as an end in itself.[105] The pursuit of the maximisation of social wealth is, therefore, in the public interest and, being in the public interest, serves to legitimate those institutions that bring about that goal. The modern registered company, trading with the benefit of limited liability, has proven itself to be the most efficient means of producing wealth. Although it is not perfect, and the power that is inevitably vested in the company may generate costs, those costs are more than justified by the gains. Thus, the power that arises from the placing of the means of production in the hands of the private company is legitimated by its superiority in maximising social wealth.

As a consequentialist argument about the benefits to society of the corporate form, the legitimacy of the company necessarily turns on whether—and to what extent—the company is efficient. While the efficiency of the corporate form, and of market forces generally, to produce an efficient utilisation of resources is a basic article of faith of neo-liberal philosophy and law and economic analyses of the company, some commentators have raised doubts about this premise. John Parkinson, for example, identifies three reasons why we ought to doubt the efficiency of the company as a creator of wealth.[106] First, as discussed above, in reality in

[103] See n 78 above.
[104] Eisenberg (n 3); Parkinson (n 5) 48–49.
[105] Despite its claims to normative neutrality, neo-classical economics has tended to treat efficiency as an independent goal and virtue. See A Ogus, *Costs and Cautionary Tales* (Oxford, Hart Publishing, 2006) 26.
[106] Parkinson (n 5) 305.

many if not most markets there are significant barriers to entry[107] with the result that most markets display some element of oligopoly and firms in those markets have some element of discretion over production and pricing. Secondly, the inferences we draw as to the efficiency of the resource allocation decisions of those involved in markets assume they are truly consensual and are based on perfect information. However, this is likely to be true only in the rarest of cases. Thirdly, firms are often able to externalise some of the costs of their production onto third parties. Thus, where a firm is able to discharge fumes from its factory into the atmosphere, the firm passes the costs of refining that discharge onto the local community or indeed the world as whole. The result is that the firm produces goods at a cost that does not truly reflect the actual costs of production and thus the production is not allocatively efficient.

There is much force in Parkinson's analysis, but to the extent that Parkinson's critique relies on the corporate form and the market conditions within which they operate being perfectly efficient, Parkinson may be attacking a straw man. For the purpose of the argument that the company is legitimated by being an efficient creator of social wealth, it is surely enough that the company is the *most efficient* institution for the creation of wealth that presently exists. To judge the company against a standard of perfection seems an unrealistically high bar to set. Parkinson's critique also seems to focus on the losses attributable to corporate power in isolation from any gains. In doing so, Parkinson may overlook the truism that there are no omelettes without broken eggs and that in assessing the company as a generator of wealth, we must look at net wealth—gains less losses. It follows that, if the company generates more gains than losses, then it must be regarded as efficient and that, if it generates more net wealth than any other alternative institution, then we must accept its superiority and that the premise of the argument in favour of the legitimation of the corporate power is made out.

The much more significant concern with the wealth maximisation justification lies in a consideration of the nature, or type, of the costs imposed by the operation of the corporate form. As suggested above, the power of the company may exist in respect of the economic interests of those impacted, or it may exist in respect of the non-economic or societal impacts of corporate activity. In the case of corporate economic power, whether that is a power in relation to those with whom the company directly transacts or others in the economic system, economic power and the costs imposed by the company seem relatively easy to justify on a cost-benefit basis. Although the global ubiquity of the corporate form[108] means that there is no counter-factual to compare it against, overall the corporate form does seem to have proven itself as an efficient creator of profits: it is more likely than not that it generates more wealth than the costs it imposes in producing that wealth.

[107] These may be legal (eg licensing requirements or the existence of monopoly rights); financial (eg expensive plant and equipment) or reputational (eg there is a dominant existing market participant).

[108] The corporate form is recognised just about everywhere in the world, including such far off sounding places as Burkina Fasso, Kyrgyzstan, and North Korea.

The costs that it does generate are either the result of consensual transactions, or are economic or financial costs imposed on other participants in the economic system. At the level of the system at least, there seems no real objection to the neo-classical calculus that sets economic benefits off against economic costs.[109]

The real difficulty lies in the emergence of the non-economic or societal power of the company. In respect of the costs arising from the company's societal power—the impact on the environment, on our health, and on our opportunities to flourish as fully rounded, intellectual and social beings—the argument for the legitimacy of the company as a generator of wealth requires us to accept that economic benefits are properly set off against impacts on these other non-economic interests. The difficulty in doing this, however, is that the interests or costs being set off against one another may be incommensurable. The benefits to society of the survival of a small town, or the rural way of life, or the reduction in greenhouse gas emissions, or the right of the individual to be forgotten,[110] and the increases in profitability of the decision to move a major source of employment off-shore, or the invasion of our privacy so as to more precisely target marketing seem to be expressed in fundamentally different currencies. The increase in one cannot bear upon, or make up for, losses in the other. Therefore, while as a purely economic institution the corporate form's preeminent capacity to generate material wealth seems to more than adequately justify the economic power it has come to hold, these economic benefits cannot, without more, justify or legitimate the social power and impact of the company.

III. Conclusion

The identification of, on the one hand, the economic power of the company and, on the other hand, the emergence of the company as a major environmental, political and social force reveals the central challenge posed by the corporate form today: can we justify the social power now in the hands of the company? Presently, we have no satisfactory answer to that question. The company as a source of social power has crept up on us unawares. Over the decades, the flexibility of the corporate form and our tendency to see the company as an all-or-nothing concept—it exists for all purposes or for none—have allowed it to be used for, and to be

[109] Parkinson (n 5) 49, also critiques this analysis on the basis that even if total aggregate social wealth is increased it ignores the distributional issues that this wealth is held for the benefit only of a small group of shareholders. However, increasingly this is less of a concern as increased shareholding by institutional shareholders (especially pension funds) means that whether we know it or not, we are probably all shareholders now.

[110] The proposed European Union General Data Protection Regulation would allow an individual to request their erasure from metadata held by companies such as Google. See European Commission, 'Agreement on Commission's EU data protection reform will boost Digital Single Market' Press Release, 15 December 2015 (IP/15/6321).

influenced by, all manner of non-economic purposes and considerations. That a corporation might enjoy the right to the freedom of religion[111] would surely have dumbfounded Robert Lowe,[112] the father of the modern company.[113]

If we are to address the question of the company's social power, the first step must be to think deeply and broadly about what the company is really for—for what purposes ought we to recognise the corporation as an institution and what are we prepared to trade for ever increasing material and technological well-being. Do we really want to trade off individual autonomy, choices about the structure of society and how we live our lives for the convenience and power of the Google search engine, Wi-Fi enabled refrigerators, on-line shopping, and virtual friends? That we may wish to do so is certainly not inconceivable, but the risk we face today is that we may not even understand that there is a bargain to be made.

[111] In *Burwell v Hobby Lobby Inc* 573 US (2014) the US Supreme Court upheld the claim by a closely held corporation to protection under the Religious Freedom Restoration Act 1993 (42 USC ch 21B).

[112] As Vice President of the Board of the Trade, Robert Lowe, later First Viscount Sherbrooke, was the leading figure in the introduction of the statutes granting the general right to incorporation and limited liability.

[113] J Micklethwait and M Wooldridge, *The Company: a Short History of a Revolutionary Idea* (London, Phoenix, 2005) 51.

11

Reshaping Responsibility: The Emerging Private Law of Institutional Wrongs

MAYO MORAN

I. Introduction

Private law, especially negligence, has witnessed a dramatic expansion in the past few decades. Among other tasks it is being asked to take on increasingly complicated questions of responsibility many of which implicate key social and political institutions. Once, not so very long ago, it was relatively unusual for an institution to be held liable. This was true for all kinds of institutions, including those that pursued both public and private purposes. In the traditional picture, power within institutions was controlled by a number of forces most prominently governance mechanisms, administrative law and political mechanisms. However, the private law of responsibility was generally not an important means by which power was disciplined within institutions. That, however, has changed. A whole range of important social and political institutions have found themselves subject to significant new private law liability for a range of activities. A few examples will serve to illustrate this shift.

Whereas once both churches and governments were shielded from private law liability, that is no longer the case. In 1996, twenty-seven former students of an Indian Residential School (IRS) sued the Government of Canada and the United Church along with the dormitory supervisor who had recently been criminally convicted of their sexual abuse.[1] Complex questions about the responsibility of the Church and the federal government were at the heart of the case. *Blackwater v Plint* reached the Supreme Court of Canada nearly ten years after the filing of the statement of claim. It involved hundreds of days of court hearings, thousands

[1] *Blackwater v Plint* 2005 SCC 58, [2005] 3 SCR 3. For a more detailed discussion of the *Blackwater* litigation, see M Moran, 'The Role of Reparative Justice in Responding to the Legacy of Indian Residential Schools' (2014) 64 *University of Toronto Law Journal* 529, 550–53.

of paragraphs of judicial reasoning, and of course very significant monetary and non-monetary costs. Many of the most difficult questions were matters of institutional liability. These included issues about which of the institutional defendants was vicariously liable for the criminal acts of the supervisor, how liability ought to be apportioned between the various defendants, and the role of institutional immunities if any. Ultimately, both the Church and the federal government were held vicariously liable for the assaults because of their long history of joint involvement in the education of Aboriginal children. The question of exactly what duties were owed was the subject of extensive argument and judicial reasoning. On that issue, Brenner J held that Canada owed 'a duty of special diligence to the plaintiffs' because of its complete control over their lives and education and that it 'fell short of discharging its duty'.[2] Awards of between $10 000 and $150 000 were made to the six plaintiffs who were ultimately found entitled to damages. Fault was apportioned 75 per cent to Canada and 25 per cent to the Church. The Supreme Court of Canada also rejected the doctrine of charitable immunity.[3] But the matter did not end there. *Blackwater* and similar cases set off a flood of litigation that resulted in the Indian Residential Schools Settlement Agreement, which has an estimated value of five billion dollars. The Agreement set up a Truth and Reconciliation Commission, a compensation tribunal and a range of other remedies. It thus forms an important chapter in the story of institutional liability.[4]

Complex questions of institutional liability and political action were also at the heart of the decisions in *Mutua and Others v The Foreign and Commonwealth Office*.[5] In that case, a group of survivors of the suppression of the Mau Mau uprising in the 1950s Kenya sued the British Government in UK courts for brutalities they suffered at the hands of the authorities. The case involved extensive consideration of the relationship between the Colonial Administration and the UK government at the time. The role of the perpetrators themselves and of the Kenyan Human Rights Commission were also the subject of much discussion. The case inevitably drew the courts into the complexities of the politics and processes of colonial institutions and indeed into the question of institutional responses to insurrection. In these and many other ways, the case of the *Mutua* claimants must have seemed insuperably difficult. Yet after two important decisions that were decided largely in their favour, in 2013 the British government settled the action. It agreed to pay £13.9 million to 5,228 veterans, thus amounting to £2,658 per victim. As part of the settlement, the government also paid £6 million to the Leigh Day law firm, a matter which was later the subject of dispute and more

[2] *WRB v Plint* 2001 BSSC 997, 93 BCLR (3d) 228 [259].

[3] *Blackwater* (n 1) [39]–[44].

[4] *Indian Residential Schools Settlement Agreement* (May 2006), available at www.residentialschoolsettlement.ca/settlement.html. For more information regarding the IRSSA, see the special issue of the University of Toronto Law Journal devoted to the residential school litigation and settlement: (2014) 64 *University of Toronto Law Journal*. See also: Moran (n 1).

[5] *Mutua and Others v The Foreign and Commonwealth Office* [2011] EWHC 1913 (QB); *Mutua and Others v The Foreign and Commonwealth Office* [2012] EWHC 2678 (QB).

litigation. In announcing the settlement to Parliament, Foreign Secretary William Hague acknowledged 'the pain and grievance felt by those who were involved in the events of the Emergency in Kenya'.[6] He also said that the British Government regretted that Kenyans were subject to torture and other forms of ill-treatment at the hands of the colonial administration, although he continued to deny British Government liability for the actions of the colonial administration. The British High Commissioner in Nairobi also made a public statement to members of the Mau Mau War Veterans' Association in Kenya, explaining the settlement and 'expressing [Britain's] regret for the events of the Emergency Period'.[7] Thus in *Mutua* we see the reach of private law into the most protected domain of political institutions, even at their most difficult moments.

The institutional abuse of children has prompted a great deal of legal activity and has given rise to considerable innovation in the developing case law on institutional wrongs. This is true across common law jurisdictions including the United States, which has seen an enormous amount of activity involving the Catholic Church in particular, in Canada as the residential schools and other cases demonstrate and also in the United Kingdom. Australia, however, is particularly interesting on the question of institutional responsibility because of the Royal Commission that specifically addresses institutional questions. In Australia, as in other places, recent decades have witnessed a growing awareness of the scope and the seriousness of institutional abuse, particularly sexual abuse of children. A number of these cases came before the courts, but the results were unclear and the processes difficult.[8] The implications for victims of childhood sexual abuse, particularly in the wake of revelations about the prevalence of sexual abuse of children in institutions and the unsatisfactory institutional responses, prompted the Australian Government to appoint the Royal Commission into Institutional Responses to Child Sexual Abuse, in 2013. The programme of the Commission is an ambitious one and beyond the scope of this chapter. However, its detailed consideration of institutional liability and proposals for reform released in its

[6] Foreign & Commonwealth Office and The Rt Hon William Hague, 'Statement to Parliament on Settlement of Mau Mau claims', (6 June 2013), available at www.gov.uk/government/news/statement-to-parliament-on-settlement-of-mau-mau-claims.

[7] Foreign & Commonwealth Office and Dr. Christian Turner, 'Launch of the Mau Mau Memorial in Kenya', (22 May 2014), available at www.gov.uk/government/speeches/launch-of-the-mau-mau-memorial-in-kenya.

[8] For example, in *New South Wales v Lepore* [2003] HCA 4, 212 CLR 511, the High Court considered a claim for compensation against a school authority in the case of a student who was abused by a teacher. Although the case resulted in six separate judgments and disagreement concerning an appropriate standard, four of the seven justices held that it was possible, under certain circumstances, to hold an institution liable for the sexual abuse of a child in its care. Similarly, in *The Salvation Army (South Australian Property Trust) v Graham Rundle* [2008] NSWCA 347, the New South Wales Court of Appeal upheld the lower court's discretionary extension of the relevant limitations period, permitting the plaintiff's untimely claim to proceed. Ultimately, the Salvation Army agreed to an undisclosed 'substantial financial settlement' out of court.

2015 report entitled *Redress and Civil Litigation*, mark perhaps the most sustained and thoughtful consideration of the changing nature of institutional liability to date.[9] In addition to the novel discussion of the principles of redress schemes and related recommendations, the recommendations regarding law reform in areas touching on institutional liability could dramatically alter the legal landscape for institutions. Although it is too early to tell what exactly will emerge from the many recommendations, it is fair to say that the Report itself is certainly an important development in the emerging law of institutional liability.

Dramatic situations like these involving complex claims of institutional liability, are in many ways the new normal for private law. Indeed, they now count among the most difficult sets of issues across common law jurisdictions. This chapter examines how these cases came to be with particular focus on the evolution of the duty of care and related doctrines. The gradual erosion of the immunities that specifically protected key institutions is an important part of the story of how the private law of institutional wrongs began to emerge.[10] But in addition to private law's increasing willingness to reject procedural barriers and delve into the substance of the issue, something deeper was also at work. The conceptual underpinnings of the duty of care in negligence were shifting. Over the course of the last century, that duty has emerged as an especially powerful branch of private law: it now counts among the most potent forces in shaping how institutions exercise their power. But this growth was only possible because of the way that the duty of care, along with other related doctrines, gradually altered its understanding of fault and responsibility. The doctrinal shifts in the duty of care, vicarious liability and other related rules gradually opened up the law of negligence to whole new categories of claims, including complex claims of institutional responsibility. These cases consistently number among the most difficult that courts have to confront and it is fair to say that task of developing tools to respond to them is very much a work in progress. The aim of this chapter is to assist that work in progress by outlining an important dimension of how those cases came to be.

II. The Emergence of the General Duty

This expansion of private law liability came about as a result of a number of factors, but perhaps none of them is as important as the emergence of negligence

[9] Commonwealth Royal Commission into Institutional Responses to Child Sexual Abuse, *Redress and Civil Litigation Report* (Sydney, Commonwealth of Australia, 2015).

[10] I explore these developments and some of their ramifications in the context of the Indian Residential Schools Settlement Agreement as well as in the broader context of the emergence of the past as a legal problem: Moran (n 1); M Moran, 'The Problem of the Past and How to Fix It' (draft manuscript on file with the author); Leora Bilsky, 'Transnational Holocaust Litigation' (2012) 23 *European Journal of International Law* 349.

as a cause of action. At its core, the new 'general' duty of care in negligence began to give serious legal expression to the idea that an actor had a private law duty to repair the harm caused by her wrongs.[11] As this fundamental reparative justice idea began to take hold of the legal imagination, it exerted a very different kind of pressure on the structures and doctrines of private law. And this reparative impulse has, of course, particular significance for the expansion of the law of negligence. The idea that there is a broad reparative principle, traceable from international human rights law through to domestic private law is especially apparent in many aspects of the growing jurisprudence on institutional liability. Significantly, the Australian Royal Commission into Institutional Responses to Child Sexual Abuse in *Redress and Civil Litigation* seems to accept the view that basic principles concerning 'the right to a remedy and reparation for victims of gross violations of international human rights law' have salience for shaping the principles of redress, compensation and even institutional liability rules in domestic private law.[12] But if the general duty, in that sense, has come a long way toward expressing its underlying reparative ideal in its origins it looked very different. Perhaps due to anxiety about the implications of a broadly-articulated duty of care in negligence, the common law was initially wary about expansiveness. The early law of negligence was respectful of contract law, avoided complicated relations with criminal law and administrative law, and stayed away from the niceties of institutional decision-making.

The emergence of a generalised duty of care for negligence is, in private law terms, a relatively recent phenomenon. When Lord Atkin stated, in his famous 1932 opinion in *Donoghue v Stevenson,* that there 'must be, and is, some general conception of a duty of care of which these are particular instances...'[13] he set in motion a virtual revolution in private law. From the very beginning institutions were implicated and were asked new, perhaps unforeseen, questions. Lord Buckmaster's anxious dissent foresaw some of these implications, asking whether, for instance, in the case of accidents, railway companies would now suddenly be subject to whole new lines of inquiry and much expanded liability. As he acutely foretold, the general duty to take care would indeed open the door to vast new forms of liability.

Courts struggled to come to terms with the implications of this new generalised duty of care in the form of the 'neighbour' principle. For institutions in

[11] In 'The Role of Reparative Justice', I discuss how over time the Canadian civil redress model has gradually moved into closer alignment with the reparative ideal: Moran (n 1) 556.

[12] Royal Commission (n 9) 59–63. The van Boven principles include the victims' rights to equal and effective access to justice; adequate, effective and prompt reparation for harm suffered, and access to relevant information concerning violations and reparation mechanisms: Theo van Boven, 'The United Nations Basic Principles and Guidelines on the Right and Reparation for Victims of Gross Violations of International Human Rights Law and Serious Violations of International Humanitarian Law' (adopted by the General Assembly of the United Nations in 2005). The van Boven principles highlight the fact that remedies are not limited to monetary payments but also include a number of other forms of reparation: Royal Commission (n 9) 62–63.

[13] *Donoghue v Stevenson* [1932] AC 562 (HL), 580.

particular, with their complex decision-making structures and attendant agency issues, the potential implications were monumental. How, for example, was a railway company to act like a 'reasonable man' in identifying, weighing and responding to systemic risk? The ordinary standard developed in the context of individual agents was strained in the application to institutions, particularly large ones. The problems were especially acute for wrongs of omission—those instances where the institution may have failed to recognize or prevent a risk posed by an individual, system or process within their purview. While such duties were certainly not unproblematic in cases involving individuals, the challenges they posed for institutions were of a different magnitude entirely. Perhaps for these reasons, and no doubt for others, as the generalised duty of care came into being it was initially accompanied by a fair amount of protection, much of which benefited institutions.

Sometimes this protection was quite explicit, such as when it took the form of immunities. Indeed, for most of our legal history, immunities were the primary technique used to protect key institutions from the scrutiny of the law and private law in particular. Thus charitable immunity long prevented the application of the law of negligence, for instance, to a charitable entity. While the contours of charitable immunity were always complex, it typically provided significant protection to charitable institutions. Across common law jurisdictions, important changes occurred in the 1980s and 1990s in the wake of a number of sexual abuse scandals involving churches and other institutions. These cases were instrumental in opening up a whole category of institutions to private law liability. This is especially true in the United States, where the Catholic Church sex abuse scandal has had a profound effect on charitable immunity as well as other doctrines.[14] The situation there is much litigated and remains complex. However, the general trend there as elsewhere is a distinct movement away from immunities in general and charitable immunity in particular. For example, in Canada, courts refused to allow the Catholic Church to invoke charitable immunity in order to avoid paying damage awards arising out of sexual and physical abuse cases.[15] The inapplicability of

[14] For examples of charitable immunity in the United States see: M Cobb, 'A Strange Distinction: Charitable Immunity and Clergy Sexual Abuse in Picher v Roman Catholic Bishop of Portland' (2010) 62 *Maine Law Review* 703, 704–05, 708. See Law Council of Australia, *Redress and Civil Litigation Consultation Paper* (Submission to the Royal Commission into Institutional Responses to Child Sex Abuse) (Canberra, March 19, 2015) 14 for a discussion regarding the immunity afforded to unincorporated institutions in Australia. For a more detailed account of the erosion of the charitable immunity doctrine see: Moran (n 1) 539–40.

[15] For instance, *Re Christian Brothers of Ireland* involved a court-ordered winding up of a charitable corporation for the purpose of compensating the victims who had been abused at the Mount Cashel Orphanage. The Christian Brothers argued that two, valuable British Columbia schools were not assets that were available to pay the Mount Cashel victims. The chambers judge held that while there was no doctrine of charitable immunity, the assets that were held upon a special purpose trust that could only be used to compensate persons for wrongs done in the context of that specific trust. But the Ontario Court of Appeal reversed, rejecting the existence of charitable immunity as well as the "special purpose trust" exemption. Justices Abella and Feldman noted that the exception threatened to undermine the principle that there is no doctrine of charitable immunity. The Supreme Court of Canada denied leave to appeal: *Christian Brothers of Ireland in Canada* 37 OR (3d) 367; *Re Christian Brothers of Ireland in Canada* 47 OR (3d) 674. See further Moran (n 1) 539.

charitable immunity in the Indian Residential Schools context was also specifically affirmed in the Supreme Court of Canada decision in *Blackwater v Plint*. While the BC Court of Appeal had held that charitable immunity protected the United Church from liability, the Supreme Court overturned this and clearly stated that the doctrine of charitable immunity was no longer viable. It observed that exempting non-profit organizations when government was present would undermine the policy of protecting children from abuse.[16] The doctrine of charitable immunity has also virtually been abolished in the UK and in other parts of the common law world as well.[17]

Other, related developments were also important, in particular the abrogation of the immunities that protected the Crown and its emanations. Derived from the English doctrine of sovereign immunity, the government or Crown was historically understood to be immune from liability in tort. Well into the 20th century, there was no remedy against the sovereign unless the law expressly provided for it. However in the mid-twentieth century, this idea also began to erode and legislation started to eliminate the broad presumption against government liability. In 1947, England adopted the Crown Proceedings Act 1947; legislation that was emulated throughout the Commonwealth.[18] Typically, such legislation provides that the state is liable for damages committed by a servant of the Crown for which, if it were a person, it would be liable in tort.[19] The general effect of such legislation was thus to remove the special cloak of protection that immunities traditionally conferred on not only the state itself, but also on public authorities writ large. Despite the formal abrogation of Crown immunity, however, courts continued to offer the state special protection when the complained-of action was undertaken in pursuit of a policy objective or under statutory authority.[20] While the evolution in this body of law is complex, the general trend has been to limit the specialised exemptions available to governments and to treat their liability on an increasingly

[16] *Blackwater* (n 1) [41].

[17] In the UK, the House of Lords abolished the doctrine of charitable immunity in 1946: *Mersey Docks and Harbour Board v Coggins and Griffith (Liverpool) Ltd* [1947] AC 1 (HL). Although, in some cases, Australian law provides the right to indemnity from a trust, there is no general conception of charitable immunity: Hon Justice M McMurdo AC, 'Faith Hope and Charity: The Resilience of the Charitable Trust from the Middle Ages to the 21st Century' (2013) 13 *Queensland University of Technology Law Review* 1, 12.

[18] Crown Proceedings Act 1947 (UK).

[19] ibid; RSC, 1985, c C-50 s 1; 1990, c 8 s 21(3)(b)(i); Crown Proceedings Act 1988 (NSW), ss 3, 5; Crown Proceedings Act 1980 (Qld) ss 7–8; Crown Proceedings Act 1992 (SA) ss 4–5; Crown Suits Act 1947 (WA) s 5; Crown Proceedings Act 1993 (Tas) ss 4–5; Crown Proceedings Act 1993 (NT) ss 4–5; Crown Proceedings Act 1992 (ACT) ss 3, 5.

[20] The legacy of *Anns* discussed below is perhaps the most notable example of the efforts to reshape tort law to make it more apt to application in a wide array of institutional settings, including of course, the state. While, as discussed, the evolution of that law has been very complex, the overall trend has been one of diminishing distinctive institutional protections as the domain of the 'general' duty of care expanded.

similar basis to that of other institutions.[21] So, as with charitable immunity, the decline of sovereign immunity and related doctrines meant that public institutions were newly exposed to private law duties, especially the duty of care in negligence. In this sense, the decline of specific, institutional protections traditionally extended through immunities was a key step in the emergence of the private law of institutional wrongs.

But just as important as the decline of these explicit doctrines that protected institutions were the conceptual shifts in the unstated assumptions that shaped the duty of care itself. Particularly significant in this regard was the fact that the duty of care began with a relatively simplified idea of wrong. This is hardly surprising, given that the new kind of wrong most centrally implicated in the emerging duty of care—inadvertent wrongdoing—was somewhat untilled terrain for private law. Thus, while private law had long responded to intentional wrongs, negligence was more complicated, in part because of its central yet attenuated fault requirement—it was a 'species of *culpa*', as Lord Atkin noted in *Donoghue v Stevenson*.[22] Unlike the more traditional nominate torts, which focused on the invaded interest of the plaintiff, the duty in negligence shifted its gaze to the defendant.[23] As the general duty in negligence gradually came to replace the nominate torts, this new emphasis on fault had serious ramifications. However, these ramifications were not so apparent in the early days because of other features of the emergent duty of care that contained its impact. Among these, the animating idea of a single wrongdoer was especially important. This deep, unstated commitment meant that there was hesitation, if not outright rejection of the idea that there could be multiple, overlapping and different duties of care engaged in a single accident. Though never articulated explicitly, the force of the animating idea of the single wrongdoer could be felt in various doctrines, and perhaps came closest to the surface in the doctrines of contributory or comparative negligence and in the related doctrine of the last clear chance.

Although the idea of comparative fault is now well-entrenched as a principle of attribution of liability, this was not the case in the early law of negligence. As Fleming James Jr explained in an influential 1953 article on the subject, the prevailing view at the time was that negligence on the part of the plaintiff was

[21] For a history of the decline of sovereign immunity in the US, see: L Jaffe, 'Suits Against Governments and Officers' (1963) 77 *Harvard Law Review* 1; W Gellhorn and C Schenck, 'Tort Actions Against the Federal Government' (1947) 47 *Columbia Law Review* 722. For Australia, see: C Mantziaris, 'The Executive: A Common Law Understanding of Legal Form and Responsibility' in R French, G Lindell and C Saunders (eds), *Reflections on the Australian Constitution* (Sydney, Federation Press, 2003), 154–57. For the UK, see: P Leyland, *The Constitution of the United Kingdom: A Contextual Analysis* (Portland, Hart Publishing, 2012) 100. For Canada, see: R Decary, 'Compensation Against the Federal Crown' (1976) 22 *McGill Law Journal* 321; G Heckman, 'Canada (Attorney General) v Telezone: Jurisdiction in Actions against the Federal Crown' (2011) 38 *Advocates' Quarterly* 111, 114–16.

[22] *Donoghue* (n 13) 580.

[23] For example, torts that protected security of the person such as assault and battery, false imprisonment, etc. See for instance: D Nolan and J Davies, 'Torts and Equitable Wrongs' in A Burrows (ed), *Oxford Principles of Law: English Private Law* 3rd edn (Oxford, Oxford University Press, 2013).

a complete bar to recovery.[24] After pointing to some of the difficulties with this rule, he noted that it was perfectly consistent with tort law to have a rule whereby the plaintiff's own negligence diminishes, without entirely defeating, the claim to damages against a wrongdoer (effectively what is now the modern trend). His exploration of the reasoning underlying the traditional rule serves to illuminate the operating preconceptions of the early accounts of negligence. Speaking of Lord Wright's efforts to explain the 'complete bar' rule in terms of its procedural origins, he makes the following point:

> ...that plaintiff's allegation that his injury was 'due to the defendant's negligence' could only have meant that it was due solely to that cause....What the point really shows then is that the habit of thinking in terms of a single legal cause too often underlay procedural as well as substantive law.[25]

Interestingly, Fleming James Jr also detects the (unstated) effect of the single legal cause paradigm in the contours of the "last clear chance" doctrine. In particular, he notes how the inquiry into what conduct was culpable tended, instead, to focus on the question of 'whose act was last'.[26] Rather than assessing fault or culpability, he suggests, much of the analysis instead focused on directness, sometimes phrased as proximate cause. Again, what this reveals, among other things, is the commitment to the single wrongdoer model. And it is perhaps not coincidence that this restrictive approach arose in the context of the shifting demands being made of tort law. Whereas it had originally been preoccupied with accidents between neighbour and neighbour, matters changed as industrialisation took hold.[27] In this context, the commitment to a 'single legal cause' and its confining effect on the law of negligence served to protect both public and private institutions from the impact of potentially debilitating new duties.

The gradual shift from that commitment to the single legal cause to the current situation where the dominant rule is comparative negligence had significant implications for institutional liability. At an obvious level, it increased the number of parties who could plausibly be responsible and gave rise to more liability because of its elimination of a particularly powerful defence. But, beyond increasing liability in negligence, the demise of those, old rules also held deeper significance—it signalled a move away from the single wrongdoer paradigm. That paradigm had tended to focus legal scrutiny on the search for a culpable individual wrongdoer. But as this understanding started to weaken, a larger array of actors,

[24] Fleming James Jr, 'Contributory Negligence' (1953) 62 *Yale Law Journal* 691, 691 citing *The Restatement of Torts*, §467 (1934):

> Except as stated in §§ 479 and 480, the plaintiff's contributory negligence bars recovery against a defendant whose negligent conduct would otherwise make him liable to the plaintiff for the harm sustained by him. (§§ 479 and 480 concern 'last clear chance' situations.)

[25] ibid 694, citing Lord Wright, 'Contributory Negligence' (1950) 13 *MLR* 2, 5.

[26] Fleming James Jr, 'Last Clear Chance: A Transitional Doctrine' (1938) 47 *Yale Law Journal* 704, 705.

[27] L Green, 'The Duty Problem in Negligence Cases' (1929) 29 *Columbia Law Review* 255, 260.

along with institutions themselves, started to fall within the purview of the private law regime of responsibility.

Even as this larger vista of institutional accountability opened up however, other mechanisms kept duty confined. Just as the search for a single wrongdoer tended to rule out liability where a plaintiff herself had also made a mistake, it also had serious ramifications for how the negligence of the defendant was understood. Inspired by the idea of *culpa*, the simplest cases of breach for this emerging duty of care were those involving serious individual wrongs. It is hence not surprising that in paradigmatic early cases like *Vaughan v Menlove*,[28] the reasonable man was adopted as the common law vehicle for expressing the standard appropriate to the duty of care. In the context of individual accidents, such as the property damage that Menlove's carelessness caused to his neighbour in *Vaughan*, the reach for the reasonable man was understandable. But it is also worth noting how that fiction fixes the search for culpability on the acts or omissions of a single individual. Efforts to reshape the reasonable person into an appropriate standard for the inquiry at hand have involved the courts in some leaps of imagination.[29] However, it is one thing to endow the fictional person with the attributes of other persons and quite another to adapt it to situations that involve a large number of agents whose choices taken together resulted in the acts or omissions in question. The emergence of the Learned Hand test in *Carroll Towing*[30] was thus important for a range of reasons, among them the fact that it signalled a move away from the relatively simple single wrongdoer model, towards a more multi-faceted understanding of wrongdoing. Whatever the worries about some of the economic interpretations later given Justice Cardozo's famous formulation of what constitutes reasonable care, its focus on a depersonalised language associated with assessing the risk of an accident and balancing that against the difficulty of its prevention certainly also represented a broader movement towards a duty of care that made more sense within an institutional setting.

III. The Evolution of the Duty of Care: The Legacy of Dorset Yacht

As the law of negligence began to countenance multiple, distinct and possibly overlapping duties of care along with a proliferation of possible defendants, private law liability for institutional wrongs became a serious prospect. In the

[28] *Vaughan v Menlove* (1837) 132 ER 490, 3 Bing NC 468.

[29] M Moran, *Rethinking the Reasonable Person: An Egalitarian Reconstruction of the Standard of Care* (Oxford, Oxford University Press, 2003). See also: J Gardner, 'The Many Faces of the Reasonable Person' (2015) 131 *LQR* 563.

[30] *United States v Carroll Towing Co* 159 F2d 169 (2d Cir 1947).

common law world, a key moment in this evolution came with the articulation of the duty of care in *Home Office v the Dorset Yacht Co Ltd.* Even a law professor would be hard pressed to devise a case that posed more complexity for the private law of negligence than *Dorset Yacht.* The plaintiffs claimed private law damages against a prison authority for the negligent supervision of a group of borstal boys who were on an island facility. When the guards went to bed, the unsupervised boys stole a yacht and damaged the yacht of the respondents while escaping. In traditional duty of care terms, the problems were legion: multiple different wrongs and wrongdoers; claims of civil liability for the criminal acts of a third party; and wrongs of omission, not commission. To complicate matters further, the private law claim was against a public authority engaged in distinctively public activities. In the Court of Appeal, Lord Denning denied the claim on public policy grounds, noting that there was no precedent for the idea that a prison authority could be liable for the damage caused by an escapee.[31] However, the House of Lords reversed this holding and found that a duty did indeed exist. Lord Reid's comments are illuminating:

> ... there has been a steady trend toward regarding the law of negligence as depending on principle so that when a new point emerges one should ask not whether it is covered by authority but whether recognised principles apply to it. *Donoghue v Stevenson* may be regarded as a milestone, and the well-known passage in Lord Atkin's piece should I think be regarded as a statement of principle ... it ought to apply unless there is some justification or valid explanation for its exclusion.[32]

When the majority went on to hold that these circumstances could give rise to a private law duty of care, the decision heralded a new era in institutional accountability. In part this arose because of the effect of the decision on the private law liability of public authorities and in part because of the way that it contemplated liability for the acts of third parties. Let us briefly examine each of these developments.

A. Private Law Liability for Public Authorities

First and most obviously perhaps, the decision allowed that a private law duty could exist against a public authority even in a case where it was engaged in what one could think of as distinctively public activities. So one important result of *Dorset Yacht* was that it complicated the traditional distinction between public law and private law accountability. Despite the decline of the formal doctrine of sovereign immunity, public authorities had continued to be protected by rules that distinguished sharply between private law duties and public law duties, as Lord Denning's reasoning in the Court of Appeal decision in *Dorset Yacht* illustrates.

[31] *Home Office v the Dorset Yacht Co Ltd* (1969) 2 QB 426, 1015.

[32] *Home Office v The Dorset Yacht Co Ltd* [1970] AC 1004 (HL), 1005.

But in *Dorset Yacht* the House of Lords rejected that sharp distinction. It held that, under certain circumstances, a public authority exercising public powers could be subjected to a private law duty of care, thus giving rise to damages in negligence. This aspect of the *Dorset Yacht* decision brought a whole new class of institutional actors within the scope of private law duties, and for a whole new range of institutional undertakings. Thus, a very important branch of the emerging law of institutional wrongs was born—that large and significant part of tort law that deals with the liability of public authorities.

Although the House of Lords attempted to circumscribe the duty by limiting it in a number of ways,[33] the case set in motion a fundamental reconfiguring of the relationship between private law and institutions, particularly, but not only, public ones. Efforts to delineate the zone of private law liability from the zone of public law accountability have continued to pose serious challenges for courts and institutions across the Commonwealth (and beyond). The complicated legacy of the famous decision in *Anns* v *Merton London Borough Council*, which found that a county council was liable for shoddy house inspections, serves as an example. In that case, Lord Wilberforce suggested that the law of negligence had evolved from the neighbour principle in a distinctive way that favoured the 'general' duty of care discussed above, but that also suggested some limits:

> In order to establish that a duty of care arises in a particular situation, it is not necessary to bring the facts of that situation within those of previous situations in which a duty of care has been held to exist. Rather the question has to be approached in two stages. First one has to ask whether, as between the alleged wrongdoer and the person who has suffered damage, there is a sufficient relationship of proximity or neighbourhood such that, in the reasonable contemplation of the former, carelessness on his part may be likely to cause damage to the latter—in which case a prima facie duty of care arises. Secondly, if the first question is answered affirmatively, it is necessary to consider whether there are any considerations which ought to negative, or to reduce or limit the scope of the duty or the class of person to whom it is owed or the damages to which a breach of it may give rise.[34]

Lord Wilberforce's innovation was borne of an impulse to re-work the duty in terms that made sense of the increasing array of institutions and issues to which it was being asked to apply. The neighbour principle simply did not seem capable of doing all of the work that duty was increasingly being asked to do. However, problems quickly began to emerge. Some of these related to the fact that on some readings of Lord Wilberforce's test foreseeability of harm alone seemed to be enough to ground a prima facie duty of care. The danger of excessive reliance on foreseeability of harm was not so apparent when the duty in negligence was cabined by immunities and by the limitations of the early common law imagination, focused as it was on a single wrongdoer. However, without these restrictions, it soon became evident that foreseeability alone gave rise to a *prima facie* duty

[33] ibid 36.

[34] *Anns v Merton London Borough Council* [1978] AC 728 (HL), 751–52.

of care that was far too broad. This was problematic for public authorities since negligence in the discharge of their duties almost inevitably gave rise to foreseeable harm. But the Stage One duty as articulated in *Anns* did not seem to have the conceptual tools to assist a court in determining what relationship a public authority needed to have with an injured plaintiff in order to generate a private law duty. Under Lord Wilberforce's formulation, the corrective to this overbreadth was of course found in Stage Two of the test, where policy considerations were invoked to reduce or limit the prima facie duty of care. But the broad category of 'policy' has also proved of uncertain assistance to courts trying to determine when to limit that broad *prima facie* duty. It has thus turned out to be extremely challenging to draw a convincing line between the distinctive nature and role of public institutions and the role of private law liability. Public authorities as wide-ranging as those involving prisons and child welfare, health, financial and market regulation, and housing have increasingly been brought under the scrutiny of private law. The results have been, to say the least, uneven.

Indeed, in the United Kingdom, *Anns* was the subject of controversy almost from the time it was handed down until it was overruled by the House of Lords in 1990 in *Murphy v Brentwood District Council*.[35] Yet despite the fact that *Anns* was overruled in the United Kingdom, it has continued to be a major precedent elsewhere in the Commonwealth. The Supreme Court of Canada has repeatedly affirmed the vitality of the *Anns* test, including in cases involving the liability of public authorities such as *City of Kamloops v Neilson*.[36] It has also continued to use the modified *Anns* test for establishing new duties of care, most often in an institutional setting and frequently involving public authorities. For example, in *Canada v Imperial Tobacco*,[37] the company was sued both by consumers and by a provincial health authority to recover health-related costs of tobacco use. In turn, it claimed contribution from the Government of Canada as regulator. The Supreme Court of Canada rejected the private law duty claim based on Stage Two of the *Anns* test. It held that a public authority had protection from civil liability for decisions 'based on public policy considerations, such as economic, social and political factors, provided they are neither irrational, nor taken in bad faith'.[38] In a similar vein, the *Anns* test has continued to be relied upon in other Commonwealth jurisdictions including Australia.[39] As this suggests, whatever its strengths

[35] *Murphy v Brentwood District Council* [1991] 1 AC 398 (HL).

[36] [1984] 2 SCR 2 (SCC). The approach was later modified in *Cooper v. Hobart* 2001 SCC 79, [2001] 3 SCR 537.

[37] *R v Imperial Tobacco Canada Ltd* 2011 SCC 42, [2011] 3 SCR 45.

[38] ibid [88].

[39] The High Court reaffirmed an *Anns*-style two stage approach to duty of care in *Bryan v Maloney* (1995) 182 CLR 609 (HCA), shortly after the House of Lords itself had overruled *Anns*. Since then, the test has remained a source of judicial authority, although the High Court has been divided on its application in relation other issues, such as the role of proximity. See, eg: *Woolcock Street Investments Pty Ltd v CDG Pty Ltd* (2004) 216 CLR 515 (HCA); *Brookfield Multiplex Ltd v Owners Corporation Strata Plan 61288* [2014] HCA 36. In New Zealand, the High Court has affirmed a comparable approach. In *South Pacific Manufacturing Co Ltd v New Zealand Security Consultants & Investigations Ltd*, Cooke P endorsed the *Anns* approach and reformulated the questions asked during each stage of the inquiry.

and weaknesses, the *Anns* test was an effort to rationalise the work begun in *Dorset Yacht* by bringing together the broad language of a general duty of care with a principled limitation on that duty that could be invoked for policy reasons, particularly in complex institutional settings characterized by complicated and variable duties. Its complicated legacy illustrates the deep challenges faced by the private law of responsibility as it attempts to re-shape itself to the complicated terrain of institutional wrongs.

B. Liability for Acts of Third Parties

Thus, one important role that *Dorset Yacht* played in the emergence of the private law of institutional wrongs is found in fact that it brought public authorities squarely within the private law duty of care. Since that case was decided, as noted above, courts have struggled with the appropriate limits of liability for public institutions, which have become perhaps the most 'sued' of all institutions and which are commonly joined with other defendants in a wide array of cases. Important as this element of the case has turned out to be, however, there is a second equally powerful reason why *Dorset Yacht* can be seen as a key moment in the emerging private law of institutional liability. This reason is subtler and has implications for a much wider array of institutions. Recall that the traditional picture of the duty of care rested on a rather unitary and simplified idea of '*culpa*', hence the judicial search for a single most culpable wrongdoer. This simplified picture of wrong entailed a unitary concept of duty that was inhospitable to complex and overlapping claims of negligence or other wrongs. On this ground too, *Dorset Yacht* was a moment of dramatic change.

One need only recall that for a long time even the plaintiff's own negligence was enough to relieve a defendant of liability, to see the significance of *Dorset Yacht* to the understanding of wrong in negligence. *Dorset's* facts involved both the intentional criminal acts of the (un-sued) borstal boys who did the physical harm to the plaintiff's property, as well as the supervisory failures of the defendant's employees, which gave the borstal boys the opportunity to escape and cause harm. Before *Dorset Yacht*, the dominance of the idea of *culpa* engaged courts in a search for the most culpable actor—a search that would have ruled out liability on the complex facts of the case. But *Dorset* directed attention to the other part of Lord Atkin's description of the duty in negligence. Negligence, he said, is 'a species of *culpa*' (emphasis added). Until *Dorset Yacht*, the judicial imagination had fixed on one part of that phrase—the more familiar terrain of *culpa*. However, *Dorset* signalled a willingness to consider the meaning of the other part of that famous phrase, thus entertaining the notion of a more complex theory of fault. The possibility thus began to present itself that the general duty in negligence could countenance the co-existence of various different kinds and degrees of culpability, some of omission, some of commission, some even criminal, that together coalesce in the injury to the plaintiff. Parsing out the degrees and forms of responsibility in this new multifaceted understanding thus came to be an important role for duty in negligence. So when *Dorset Yacht* opened up the prospect of liability in negligence for the acts of third parties, it also gave rise to another powerful feature that shaped the emerging private law of institutional liability. Because institutions necessarily act through employees or other agents, they will often be in positions where their supervision (or their failure to supervise) could result in foreseeable harm. The holding that such failures could give rise to a duty of care in negligence even for the criminal acts of third parties opened up new branch of the duty of care that had special ramifications for institutions of all kinds.

Following *Dorset Yacht*, there was dramatic growth in the field of institutional liability for the acts of third parties. As long as negligence was focused on the search for the most culpable wrongdoer, institutions both public and private enjoyed significant liability protection. But with the rise of a more multifaceted concept of fault all of that changed. Institutions were regularly joined with other defendants (or sued on their own, in the case of impecunious defendants) and were suddenly subject to private law duties of an entirely new kind. For example victims of violence sued police authorities for failures to warn them, for negligent supervision that permitted escape, and for shoddy investigations, among other things.[40] Health authorities and service agencies, whether public or private, began to be pursued for the acts, criminal or otherwise, of those in their employ. In contexts that ranged from the intricacies of financial regulation to the details of building code enforcement, regulatory bodies were sued when unscrupulous or hapless third parties caused harm. Of course, often these new categories of cases had an uncertain trajectory. Some succeeded, some did not. One thing is certain—however—the rise of the prospect of institutional liability occasioned by these shifts in the duty of care has prompted some of the most complex and controversial jurisprudence facing courts in all common law jurisdictions. And parsing responsibility among multiple wrongdoers, only some of whom may be before

[40] For example, in the UK, the House of Lords rejected the idea that the police owed a member of the public a private law duty of care during the course of an investigation into a serial killer (*Hill v Chief Constable of West Yorkshire* [1989] AC 53 (HL)). However, the European Court of Human Rights in *Osman v The United Kingdom* ECHR 1998-VIII 3124 later critically examined this decision on the basis that it operated as an immunity that was inconsistent with the European Convention. *Osman* itself was later reconsidered to some degree in the case of *Z and Others v The United Kingdom* App no 29392/95 (ECtHR, 10 May 2001).The situation in the UK remains complicated: *Smith v Chief Constable of West Sussex* [2008] UKHL 50. Other jurisdictions also continue to wrestle with these questions. Canadian courts have declined to apply blanket protections from private law to the exercise of police power, although they have been circumspect in how they have applied private law. Thus, for instance, in *Jane Doe v Metropolitan Police* (1998) 39 OR (3d) 487, 160 DLR (4th) 697 police were found to owe the likely targets of a serial rapist a private law duty to warn. The situation in Australia is considered by the Royal Commission, which noted in *Redress* and *Civil Litigation* (n 9) that, despite the general reluctance of Australia to make the institutions liable for the deliberate criminal act of one of its members or employees, the situation is different, with at least some forms of institutional negligence, particularly in the setting of a school or ward situation (at 461–64 citing cases including *S* v *The Corporation of the Synod of the Diocese of Brisbane* [2001] QSC 473).

the court, in contexts that involve overlapping, but distinct duties for omissions, commissions and other wrongs is now a major task of the law of negligence.

Lord Atkin's important articulation of the broad legal duty of care that we owe each other just in virtue of our proximity and interaction was originally limited by factors both outside and also within the developing law of negligence. Among the most important was the simplified picture of wrongdoing that played a central role in confining the duty of care to relatively uncomplicated responsibility problems, hence narrowly reading the scope of institutional liability. But as this picture slowly began to change, the concept of the general duty and the question of just what it was that we owed each other came to the fore. Courts, especially following the landmark House of Lords decision in *Dorset Yacht*, had to confront a set of overlapping multi-faceted questions about responsibility that were radically different than those that had fallen within their traditional purview. And unlike the early days of the law of negligence, almost all of these questions implicated institutions to some degree.

IV. Institutional Liability: Vicarious Liability and Non-Delegable Duties

In addition to the reshaping of duty itself, there was another closely-related shift that was extremely important in the emerging private law of institutional liability. It concerns the liability rules that are specific to institutions, namely vicarious liability and the closely connected non-delegable duty. As we have seen, the law of negligence gradually adopted a more complex model of fault, better suited to assessing institutional decision-making. At the same time, courts began to articulate a generalised duty of care that aspired to apply broadly, including to a wide array of institutions. Alongside these developments in the all-important law of negligence, there were also background changes taking place in the rules that concerned attribution of liability. The most important of these dealt with vicarious liability.

The common law had long recognised vicarious liability. In fact, that doctrine was an extremely important source of liability for institutions both public and private long before the duty of care itself began to move beyond the single wrongdoer model. Traditionally, the doctrine of vicarious liability attributed responsibility to the master/employer in situations where the servant/employee committed a tort in the course of employment. However, for most of the period of its operation, the terms on which it did so were extremely narrow. In part, this was because of the fact that the doctrine of vicarious liability also shared an attachment to the single wrongdoer model. This was especially apparent in its approach to cases where the employee engaged in criminal wrongs. Thus, the more egregious and intentional the underlying employee wrong, the less willing courts were to pass liability on to the master or institution. One important reason for this was found in the fact that the underlying rationale for passing on liability was based on the idea of an implicit command from the employer. But the notion of implied command quite naturally disinclined courts to pass liability on to employers where the employee wrong was egregious or intentional. So even where the wrong was committed during the course of and was enabled by the employment relationship, there was notable reluctance to pass liability on to the institution. However this eventually began to change as well, with dramatic consequences for institutions both public and private.

The overall nature of these this change is well captured by the United Kingdom Supreme Court in *JGE v Trustees of Portsmouth Roman Catholic Diocesan Trust:*

> By the end of the eighteenth century there was a shift away from the notion of implied command arising from the relationship of master and servant. In its place grew an acceptance by the middle of the next century, aided by the great Victorian judges and the recognition of a changing and developing industrial society, that the existence of the master/servant relationship was itself enough to impose liability on the master if the servant was acting within the scope of his employment. Lord Brougham explained, 'The reason I am liable is this, that by employing him I set the whole thing in motion; and what he does, being done for my benefit and under my direction, I am responsible for the consequences of doing it.' So it should be: the master has the 'deeper pockets' per Willes J in *Limpus v LGO Co* (1862) 1 H & C 526, 539.[41]

Many of the cases that reshaped the law on vicarious liability and opened up institutions to private law involved underlying substantive wrongs and injuries of the most serious kind. Horrific violations of children and of relationships of profound trust and dependency were at the core of many of the cases that began to open up the doctrine of vicarious liability.[42] Once this door began to open, however, it soon became apparent that it would be a means, if not the major means, by which institutional liability would be established. The Australian Royal Commission notes that, in both the UK and Canada, the law has reached the position where, generally speaking an institution will be vicariously liable for the criminal acts of its members or employees that cause harm to children either where there is a close connection between the act that caused the harm and the tortfeasor's employment, or where 'in the operation of its enterprise the employer has created or significantly increased the risk of their employee causing harm'.[43]

With regard to vicarious liability, *Mutua* is a rather dramatic illustration both of the complexities of this new category of private law claims and of the growing centrality of the doctrine of vicarious liability to institutional liability. As noted above, *Mutua* was an action for damages against the United Kingdom

[41] *JGE v Trustees of Portsmouth Roman Catholic Diocesan Trust* [2012] EWCA Civ 938 [20].

[42] As I discuss in detail elsewhere, across a number of jurisdictions the institutional sexual abuse of children and the ensuing litigation was an extremely important catalyst in changing the law not only of vicarious liability but also limitations periods and other dimension of the private law of institutional wrongs: Moran (n 1) 587; Moran (n 10).

[43] Royal Commission (n 9) 489–90.

Government for brutality suffered by the claimants during the suppression of the Mau Mau rebellion in Kenya in the 1950s. Among other complexities, the case involved questions of institutional and indeed state liability for the criminal wrongdoing of others. On this latter issue, dramatic shifts in the law of vicarious liability were absolutely central to *Mutua's* rather surprising success. When the statement of claim was filed in June 2009, vicarious liability was seen as unpromising. But the dynamic state of that law was such that, as the case moved forward, vicarious liability emerged as the most important institutional claim against the UK government. McCombe J describes the changes in the following terms:

> … the law in this area is in a continuous state of development. Four days before the hearing of this matter, the Court of Appeal handed down its judgment in *JGE v The Trustees of the Portsmouth Roman Catholic Diocesan Trust* [2012] EWCA Civ 938, in which Ward LJ delivered a very full and (if I may very respectfully say so) masterly review of the law in this area. In addition, on 23 July 2012, as I was informed, the Supreme Court was scheduled to hear an appeal from the Court of Appeal's earlier decision in *Various Claimants v The Catholic Child Welfare Society and the Institute of Brothers of the Christian Schools & ors.* [2010] EWCA Civ 1106. Each of these cases sought to apply the law of vicarious liability as developed in relation to the criminal acts of an employee perpetrated on an innocent victim in his care: *see Lister v Hesley Hall Ltd* [2001] UKHL 22.[44]

Indeed, the shift in vicarious liability doctrines in response to institutional child abuse cases prompts McCombe J to comment as follows:

> The combination of these two developments of the law show that the idea that we learnt as students, that (subject to very limited exceptions) vicarious liability for a tort only arises where the primary tort is committed by an employee within the scope of his employment, is now far too narrow. The law has progressed well beyond liability solely for employees doing precisely what they were employed to do and beyond the acts and defaults of employees under a contract of service.[45]

It is this, dramatic expansion that prompts McCombe J to find that, during the course of litigation itself, vicarious liability transformed in such a way that it became central to concluding that the *Mutua* claims should not be dismissed at this stage. As he observes, the changes in vicarious liability reveal a shift in its underpinnings that bring it closer to other forms of liability in tort and further away from the more contractual notion of implied command.[46]

This suggestion that the distance between the institutional duty of care itself and the basis for attributing vicarious liability may indeed be narrowing, echoes a theme in the emerging law of institutional liability. As duty rules broaden to countenance the possibility of overlapping liability for different actors within an institution, vicarious liability rules have undergone a similar, but more dramatic expansion. The old, more personalised idea that vicarious liability would generally

[44] *Mutua* [2012] (n 5) [78].
[45] ibid [80].
[46] ibid [84].

only apply where the employee was given specific orders has been replaced by broader and more specifically institutional notions like enterprise risk. In the process, the exposure of institutions to liability for wrongs committed by those in their employ has greatly expanded. The conceptual apparatus of vicarious liability, which once depended on the logic of implied contract, has thus gradually been transformed into something with closer relations to the concept of duty itself with its emphasis on risk analysis and principles related to undertakings and other fiduciary-like obligations. All of these issues are, of course, part of the growing vocabulary of duty and of negligence, not of contract.

That the doctrine of vicarious liability is moving into a duty-like rather than a contract-like analysis is perhaps especially evident in the complex law on the issue in Australia. There, as a result in large measure of the complicated legacy of the High Court decision in *Lepore*, the question of institutional liability, especially for the criminal acts of employees, has been discussed both in terms of vicarious liability and in terms of what has come to be called the 'non-delegable duty'. This is 'a personal duty borne by the institution' which cannot be delegated. As the Royal Commission notes 'Where this duty is recognised, the institution must ensure that reasonable care is taken by those to whom it entrusts the performance of its duty of care.'[47] That Report illustrates how important a principle institutional liability has become. While acknowledging that the non-delegable duty imposes strict liability, the Report points to the growing importance of institutional liability and its role in realising the reparative ambitions of the law of negligence. Liability for the wrongful acts of third parties, the Report observes, is now so deeply entrenched in the common law that the refusal to extend it to cases of institutional sexual abuse of children actually offends the principles underlying the law of negligence:

> We have been influenced by the decisions of the courts in which strict liability has been recognised. If the law makes a solicitor liable for the criminal act of his clerk and the dry cleaner liable for the criminal act of his employee, could it be argued that it is not appropriate for institutions to be liable for the criminal abuse of a child when in their care? If the protection of an individual's property is an important priority of the common law, the protection of children should at least have the same priority. In our opinion the community would today expect that the care of children should attract the highest obligation of the law.[48]

It is for this reason that, rather than wait for the common law of Australia to catch up with the United Kingdom and Canada on this important question of institutional duty, the Royal Commission instead recommends legislation that would impose a non-delegable duty on certain institutions for institutional child sexual abuse despite it being the deliberate criminal act of a person associated with the institution.[49] It also recommends that in such cases, a 'reverse onus' should be

[47] *Redress and Civil Litigation* (n 9) 490.
[48] ibid, 490–91.
[49] ibid.

imposed on all institutions, including those institutions for which the Commission did not recommend the legislative imposition of a non-delegable duty.[50]

The move from the language of vicarious liability to the language of duty captures much of the underlying conceptual shift in the principles underlying institutional liability. When problems of individual liability were at the centre of the understanding of duty, attribution of that liability to institutions was exceptional and was understood in the individually-oriented paradigm of contract (however fictional this vocabulary might have been, even then). But as institutional liability claims, under pressure from the reparative ambitions of the negligence principle, began to assume more dominance, this paradigm has worn increasingly thin. Alongside the willingness to attribute liability to institutions, courts have sought more satisfying language than the fiction of implied command. The analysis of attribution problems has thus come to more closely resemble the duty analysis itself. This is apparent, of course, in the obvious case in Australia and elsewhere, where the idea of a non-delegable duty is coming to the fore as the basis for attributing liability to an institution. However, a similar shift is equally underway, though perhaps more subtly, in the changing nature of vicarious liability itself. In that case as well, the dominant tools of analysis are increasingly duty-like—concerned with analysis of the proximity of relationship and the creation of risk, the very features central to the general negligence duty itself.

V. Conclusion

Traditionally, private law was kept away from important institutions through a whole range of mechanisms. In addition to explicit barriers like immunities, there were also subtler protections including, most fundamentally, how the duty of care itself was understood. As the concept of duty began to be re-worked and developed in a manner that was more apt to the institutional setting, the law of negligence became a more and more important force in institutional life. Private law today, and especially the law of negligence, exerts an undeniable power over institutions and affects many of their basic operations and features in the process. It should come as no surprise that many of the most challenging issues of contemporary tort law—and indeed of private law more generally—are directly related to the rise of the generalised duty and its gradual entry into the terrain of institutional responsibility. As institutional liability in negligence began to take hold, it raised difficult questions about the relationship between public and private law (administrative law and the liability of public authorities, for example), between the law of negligence and human rights guarantees, and between tort law and other areas, including not only contract, but also criminal law. It is no accident then that

[50] ibid, 495.

issues of institutional liability currently number among the most complex faced by the law of negligence. These new and difficult questions strain the relatively under-developed conceptual model of negligence. Duty analysis, as we have noted, has come under particular stress as it is being asked to do more and more complex analytical work. Developing a model of duty equal to the array of questions being demanded of it is of course very much a work-in-progress. It is my hope that tracing how these challenges arose and outlining some of their prominent features will assist with that work-in-progress and aid in understanding this critical new mode of private law.

12

Class Actions: Uses and Abuses of the Process of Courts

JUSTICE PHILIP MCMURDO

The body of laws which creates obligations for individuals or corporations, effectively defines a balance of power between them, for every circumstance in which such a law is engaged. Those relations of power are continuously affected by changes to private law, and those changes are now effected mainly by parliaments, rather than by courts. For example, the so-called 'tort law reforms', which resulted from legislative responses to perceived crises in the availability of liability insurance, have had a wider and deeper impact on tort law than any development in the common law by the High Court of Australia. And the impact on commercial law, particularly that governing the enforcement of contracts, by legislation proscribing certain conduct, most importantly misleading or deceptive conduct, has been greater than that from the development of the common law affecting the formation and enforcement of contracts.

Relations of power between private persons and corporations are regulated also by the body of laws which affects the *enforcement* of private law rights and obligations. Of the many modern developments in that body of laws, both by parliaments and courts, at least potentially the most significant are those involving group or class actions and the external funding of litigation. The development of the law for class actions has been largely by legislation. But the practical viability of those cases is commonly dependent upon the provision of external funding for the prosecution of a suit and a substantial market has developed in which financiers, who are strangers to the cause, fund the litigation in return for a share of the proceeds of a successful claim. The development of the law about litigation funding has been by the courts and largely by judgments of the High Court in *Campbells Cash and Carry Pty Ltd v Fostif Pty Ltd* (which I will call '*Fostif*').[1]

The first of the legislative schemes to facilitate class actions was the introduction of Part IVA of the Federal Court of Australia Act 1976 (Cth) in 1992. This

[1] *Campbells Cash and Carry Pty Ltd v Fostif Pty Ltd* [2006] HCA 41, (2006) 229 CLR 386 ('*Fostif*').

legislation was recommended by the Australian Law Reform Commission.[2] At the core of its reasoning, the Commission said that a new procedure was required to provide 'access to a court-based remedy' in the many types of cases where that access was effectively denied because of the high cost of proceedings relative to the amount which could be claimed by an individual claimant.[3] Another reason which the Commission identified was that 'increased access to legal remedies in court proceedings could render the substantive law more enforceable and must encourage a greater degree of compliance with laws the purpose of which is to prevent or discourage activities which cause loss or injury to others'.[4] Whilst there were further reasons given by the Commission, these two considerations were concerned with a perceived power imbalance between those with actionable rights but with no practical remedy and those against whom the rights should be enforced.

As I will discuss, *Fostif* involved the application of a procedural rule, common to most Australian superior courts, governing so called representative claims. But these comments by Kirby J in *Fostif* describe the policy arguments for the facilitation of both representative and class actions:

> [I]t is necessary to keep in mind the particular demands inherent in representative proceedings: the need to marshal effectively substantial resources; to gather voluminous evidence; to retain and pay competent counsel over a significant period; often to provide in advance substantial security for costs; to attend both to the general issues and to those particular to identified subcategories and individual cases; and to prove consequential losses usually with the evidence of several experts. In proceedings such as the present, faced with such daunting requirements, the ordinary tobacco retailer would commonly give up. If the only way to vindicate legal rights was to bring individual proceedings or to find others with exactly the same interest, most ordinary retailers would abandon hope. They would not enforce legal rights of action belonging to them … They would withdraw rather than venture upon such expensive, stressful, perilous litigation … Individually, for most or all of them, enforcement of legal rights would not be worth the cost, risk and effort.
>
> It is against the inherent inequalities, presented by these litigious facts of life, that a representative action may, under proper conditions, afford a litigant with an individual claim a justifiable prospect to secure practical access to that litigant's legal rights in association with many others.[5]

The Law Reform Commission's report discussed the possible means of financing grouped actions. But it did not anticipate that this might include the provision by a non-party of funding for a share of the proceeds of the claim. Indeed, the Commission's anticipation was the opposite because it adhered to its previously stated view that the tort of maintenance should be abolished as a crime and as

[2] Australian Law Reform Commission, *Grouped Proceedings in the Federal Court* (Report No 46, 1998).
[3] ibid, 27 [63].
[4] ibid, 33 [67].
[5] *Fostif* (n 1) 386, 448–49 [137]–[138] (citations omitted).

a tort but not where it amounted to champerty.[6] The Commission wrote in its 1988 report:

> *Effect of implementing these recommendations.* Private financing of proceedings is now accepted as a legitimate means of enabling less wealthy individuals or groups to gain access to the courts. The abolition of maintenance to the extent recommended would allow private financing of grouped proceedings by, for example, consumer organisations or environmental groups in every case, as long as the agreement to maintain the action was not made in consideration of a share in the proceeds or subject matter of the action. While this may be appropriate for agreements between solicitors and clients it should not be extended to third parties.[7]

Consequently, there was no legislative anticipation of the rise of third party litigation funding. It was, and remains, relevantly unregulated. Although the prevalence of class actions can be at least partly attributed to the provision by third parties of litigation funding, it had not been thought that such funding was an appropriate, let alone necessary, element in such litigation.

I. *Fostif*

The origin of the claim in *Fostif* was a judgment of the High Court in 1997, *Ha v New South Wales*[8] in which it was held that State tobacco licensing schemes were invalid as involving unconstitutional excises. Then in 2001, in *Roxborough v Rothmans of Pall Mall Australia Ltd*,[9] the High Court held that a retailer who had bought tobacco products from a wholesaler on terms where there was a distinct component of the price which represented the (invalid) licence fee, could recover from the wholesaler, as money had and received, the amount of that component if it had not been remitted by the wholesaler to the taxing authority. The action for money had and received was not precluded by the fact that the retailer had passed on the same burden of the invalid tax to its customers and therefore had suffered no loss. Gummow J there wrote that, 'the action for money had and received is not concerned with recovery as compensation for loss or damage suffered by the plaintiff'.[10]

The outcome in *Roxborough* presented a great opportunity for an entrepreneurial litigation funder. In the year following *Roxborough*, one such funder, a company called Firmstones, set about encouraging tobacco retailers to make claims against

[6] Australian Law Reform Commission (n 2) 129 [317], quoting from Australian Law Reform Commission, *Standing in Public Interest Litigation* (Report No 27, 1985) 176–80 [335]–[341].

[7] Australian Law Reform Commission (n 2) 129 [318].

[8] (1997) 189 CLR 465.

[9] (2001) 208 CLR 516.

[10] ibid, 542 [68].

their wholesalers for the refund of licence fees. Firmstones retained a solicitor who commenced several relevantly identical proceedings in the Supreme Court of New South Wales, each in the name of a retailer. One was Fostif Pty Ltd and it claimed to be suing as a representative.

At that time, there was no legislation or procedural rule by which class actions could be brought in the Supreme Court of New South Wales.[11] *Fostif* was commenced as a purported representative action under Part 8, r 13(1) of the Supreme Court Rules (NSW) which then provided:

> Where numerous persons have the same interest in any proceedings the proceedings may be commenced, and unless the Court otherwise orders, continued, by or against any one or more of them as representing all except one or more of them.

That procedural rule was not unique to New South Wales. It came from a substantially similar rule in England and had equivalents in other jurisdictions.[12] In the summons by which the proceeding was commenced, no person was named or otherwise identified as a retailer for whom Fostif Pty Ltd sued as a representative. Rather, the summons provided for an 'opt in' process by which retailers could agree to be represented and the plaintiff sued as the representative of any retailer who opted in.

Therefore, when the proceeding was commenced, Fostif Pty Ltd was not representing anyone. Instead it was claiming that it would prosecute the case as a representative if and when another person or persons chose to be so represented. The High Court held that this was fatal to the proceeding being a representative proceeding under that procedural rule. For that reason, the High Court allowed the appeal from the Court of Appeal and restored the order which had been made by the primary judge (Einstein J), which was that the claim not continue as a representative proceeding. Consequently, the relevant analysis within the judgments in the High Court in *Fostif* was *obiter dicta*.

At first instance, there were other reasons given for the proceeding not to continue as a representative claim. Einstein J held that there was an insufficient common interest between the plaintiff and any other retailer. He also held that the litigation funding arrangements for the plaintiff were 'against public policy as well as comprising an abuse of the court process'.[13]

The Court of Appeal unanimously disagreed with that characterisation of the case.[14] In the High Court, Gummow, Hayne and Crennan JJ and, in separate judgments, Gleeson CJ and Kirby J also rejected it. But in their judgment, Callinan and Heydon JJ held that the proceeding was an abuse of process because of the funding arrangements.

[11] The enactment of legislation for class actions in the Supreme Court of New South Wales did not occur until 2010, when Pt 10 was inserted into the Civil Procedure Act 2005 (NSW) by the Courts and Crimes Legislation Further Amendment Act 2010 (NSW). By this amendment, 'representative proceedings' became available in New South Wales courts from 4 March 2011.

[12] The present Queensland rule being r 75 of the Uniform Civil Procedure Rules 1999 (Qld).

[13] *Keelhall Pty Ltd v IGA Distribution Pty Ltd* [2003] NSWSC 816; (2003) 54 ATR 75, 103–04 [72].

[14] *Fostif Pty Ltd v Campbells Cash & Carry Pty Ltd* (2005) 63 NSWLR 203 (CA NSW).

The defendants' argument for this characterisation of the proceeding focused upon elements of Firmstones' participation in the litigation. The various proceedings, of which the *Fostif* claim was one, had been commenced by solicitors who had been retained by Firmstones as a principal and not as the nominal plaintiff's agent. The case was to be prosecuted entirely according to Firmstones' instructions. The 'opt in' procedure contained terms under which Firmstones would pay all of the costs of the prosecution of the case and meet all costs orders made against the plaintiff. In return, Firmstones would receive one third of any amount recovered from the defendants by way of a judgment or settlement.

Einstein J described this arrangement as 'trafficking in the retailers' litigation'.[15] The Court of Appeal asked whether the participation of Firmstones 'had corrupted or [was] likely to corrupt the processes of the court to a degree that attracts the extraordinary jurisdiction to dismiss or stay permanently for abuse of process' and concluded that there was no abuse of process.[16] Gummow, Hayne and Crennan JJ summarised the facts which were identified by the Court of Appeal in reaching that conclusion as being:

> First, the proceedings were under judicial supervision; secondly, Firmstones' control of the litigation was not 'excessive'; thirdly, Firmstones' fees were not excessive; fourthly, there was a solicitor on the record; and fifthly, the individual claims were small (making separate recovery processes unlikely)[17]

Einstein J had also described Firmstones' conduct as constituting 'champertous intermeddling'. In that description, Einstein J was well aware that the torts of maintenance and champerty had recently been abolished in New South Wales.[18] But he reasoned that public policy considerations which were thought to have founded the common law's development of those torts were relevant in the consideration of whether the proceedings offended public policy and were an abuse of process.

In the judgment of Gummow, Hayne and Crennan JJ, those policy considerations for the torts of maintenance and champerty, at least by the time of their statutory abolition in New South Wales, were not apparent. After discussing some of the cases on maintenance and champerty, their Honours said:

> What this brief and incomplete survey of the state of the English law, as it stood by the early years of the twentieth century, may be understood as revealing is that the law of maintenance and champerty depended more upon assertion of consequences said to follow from the existence of the common law criminal offences of maintenance and champerty, than it did upon any close analysis or clear exposition of the policy to which the rules were intended to give effect.[19]

[15] *Keelhall* (n 13) 100 [60].
[16] *Fostif v Campbells* (n 14) 234 [132].
[17] *Fostif* (n 1) 424 [63] (citations omitted).
[18] Maintenance, Champerty and Barratry Abolition Act 1993 (NSW), s 4.
[19] *Fostif* (n 1) 429 [77].

Gummow, Hayne and Crennan JJ summarised the appellants' argument as follows:

> Shorn of the terms of disapprobation, the appellants' submissions can be seen to fasten upon Firmstones' seeking out those who may have claims, and offering terms which not only gave Firmstones control of the litigation but also would yield, so Firmstones hoped and expected, a significant profit to Firmstones ...[20]

before holding that:

> ... none of these elements, alone or in combination, warrant condemnation as being contrary to public policy or leading to any abuse of process.[21]

Their Honours continued:

> Two kinds of consideration are proffered as founding a rule of public policy—fears about adverse effects on the processes of litigation and fears about the 'fairness' of the bargain struck between funder and intended litigant. ...
>
> Neither of these considerations, whatever may be their specific application in a particular case, warrants formulation of an overarching rule of public policy that either would, in effect, bar the prosecution of an action where an agreement has been made to provide money to a party to institute or prosecute the litigation in return for a share of the proceeds of the litigation, or would bar the prosecution of some actions according to whether the funding agreement met some standards fixing the nature or degree of control or reward the funder may have under the agreement. To meet these fears by adopting a rule in either form would take too broad an axe to the problems that may be seen to lie behind the fears.[22]

Their Honours considered a number of arguments which suggested that the conduct of the proceedings in these circumstances could be corrupted by the funder's intervention, including an excessive temptation to dishonestly or improperly conduct the case, a risk of 'blackmail settlements' and the causation of lengthy and expensive litigation.[23] Each of these concerns was to be met, in their view, by the court's controlling its own process rather than by the application of 'some general rule of public policy that a defendant may invoke to prevent determination of the claims that are made against that defendant'.[24]

II. *Fostif*—The Minority View

Callinan and Heydon JJ observed that there had been 'an excessive concentration in the arguments of the appellants, and hence in the minds of those concerned to

[20] ibid, 433 [88].
[21] ibid.
[22] ibid, 434 [90]–[91].
[23] ibid, 435 [93]–[95].
[24] ibid, 436 [95].

refute those arguments, with questions about how far the public policy relating to maintenance and champerty survives', and that it was 'preferable to consider the matter from the point of view of abuse of process generally'.[25] But they said that it was:

> ... clear that in particular cases the facts which make an agreement champertous, whether taken by themselves or taken with other facts, may also cause the prosecution of proceedings under the agreement to be an abuse of process.[26]

They observed that the expression 'abuse of process' was 'a wide one, capable of application in very diverse circumstances'.[27]

Their Honours then identified the way in which these proceedings constituted an abuse of process:

> [T]he aspect of 'abuse of process' which is relevant for present purposes is that the process of the court is abused when it is employed for some purpose other than that which it is intended by the law to effect.[28]

In essence, Callinan and Heydon JJ reasoned that this was litigation which was not being conducted for the resolution of a dispute or disputes between the parties, namely the nominal plaintiff and any persons to be represented as plaintiffs and the defendants; rather it was litigation which was commenced and to be prosecuted for the distinct and improper purpose of profit-making by the litigation funder. They said:

> [T]he function of court proceedings is to provide a means of quelling real and active controversies that have arisen between persons who are unfortunate enough to have fallen into disputes with each other and that exist independently of and anterior to the commencement of the proceedings. The purpose of court proceedings is not to provide a means for third parties to make money by creating, multiplying and stirring up disputes in which those third parties are not involved and which would not otherwise have flared into active controversy but for the efforts of the third parties, by instituting proceedings purportedly to resolve those disputes, by assuming near total control of their conduct, and by manipulating the procedures and orders of the court with the motive, not of resolving disputes justly, but of making very large profits. Courts are designed to resolve a controversy between two parties who are before the court, dealing directly with each other and with the court: the resolution of a controversy between a party and a non-party is alien to this role.[29]

The reasoning of Callinan and Heydon JJ was not so much concerned with potential for the misconduct of otherwise valid proceedings by the facts and circumstances of Firmstones' participation, or the 'fairness of the bargain', but rather with the use of the court and its process, including its coercive powers, for an improper purpose. Whether the proceeding was effectively brought for a collateral

[25] ibid, 486 [263].
[26] ibid, 486 [265].
[27] ibid, 486 [266].
[28] ibid.
[29] ibid, 487–88 [266].

and improper purpose was not a question which was specifically discussed in the other judgments or in the judgments in that case, of the Court of Appeal.

Speaking extra-curially in 2009, Keane J expressed apparent support for the view of Callinan and Heydon JJ:

> In the traditional conception the courts are an arm of government charged with the quelling of controversies. In this paradigm, the courts, in exercising the judicial power of the state, … are not 'providing legal services'. The parties to litigation … are being governed—whether they like it or not. The torts of maintenance and champerty, whatever their historical origins, served the important purpose of protecting the administration of justice from having to deal with suits which would not be brought were it not for the funding provided by the intermeddler …
>
> It is unattractive that the exercise of judicial power should be viewed as a tradable commodity and that officers of the courts should act, or be thought to act, as factors for those engaged in the trade. It is, moreover, odd that when the judicial arm of the state is straining to meet its constitutional obligation to quell the controversies which come before it in the ordinary way, the courts must also devote meagre resources to dealing with suits that are brought only because a trader can make a profit from the exercise.[30]

III. A Further Decision of the High Court

In 2009, in *Jeffery & Katauskas Pty Ltd v SST Consulting Pty Ltd*,[31] the High Court again considered whether the circumstances under which a third party funded a plaintiff's claim made for an abuse of process. After a lengthy trial in that case, the plaintiff's claim was dismissed, as was its appeal against that judgment. The plaintiff's case had been funded by a non-party, SST Consulting, which had been granted a charge over all of the plaintiff's assets. The defendant had obtained orders for security of costs of the trial and of the appeal, but there was a substantial shortfall between its costs and the security which had been provided. The defendant therefore applied for orders for costs against SST and its directors.

Under its relevant procedural rules, the Supreme Court of New South Wales was precluded from making an order for costs against a person who was not a party, except in certain exceptional circumstances of which the relevant one was said to be that provided by r 42.3(2) of the Uniform Civil Procedure Rules 2005 (NSW). The rule provided that the prohibition of an award of costs against a non-party did not limit the power of the court:

> (c) to make an order for payment, by a person who has committed contempt of court or an abuse of process of the court, of the whole or any part of the costs of a party to proceedings occasioned by the contempt or abuse of process …

[30] P Keane 'Access to Justice and Other Shibboleths' (a paper presented at the Colloquium of the Judicial Conference of Australia, Melbourne, 10 October 2009).

[31] [2009] HCA 43, (2009) 239 CLR 75.

The question was whether the Supreme Court had power to order costs against SST because it was a non-party which, for a contingency fee, had funded an impecunious corporate plaintiff without providing it with an indemnity for adverse costs orders. That turned upon whether SST had 'committed … an abuse of process of the court'. The High Court (French CJ, Gummow, Hayne and Crennan JJ, Heydon J dissenting) held that there had not been an abuse of process. The majority judgment confirmed the effect of *Fostif* as follows:

> [T]he abolition of the offences and torts did not preclude the possibility that non-party funding of legal actions for reward or otherwise might give rise to an abuse of process. But to acknowledge that possibility is not to hold non-party funding of a litigant for reward to be an abuse of the process of the court. That proposition could not stand with the decision of this Court in *Campbells Cash and Carry Pty Ltd v Fostif Pty Ltd*. …
>
> … Gummow, Hayne and Crennan JJ (with whom Gleeson CJ agreed in this respect) declined to formulate an overarching rule of public policy that would, in effect, bar the prosecution of an action involving an agreement to provide money to a party to institute or prosecute the litigation in return for a share of the proceeds of the litigation. Nor would they accept that there should be a rule which would bar the prosecution of some actions according to whether the agreement met some standards relating to the degree of control or the amount of the reward the funder might receive under the agreement. It was not shown that apprehensions that the funder might improperly interfere with the conduct of the proceedings could not sufficiently be addressed by 'existing doctrines of abuse of process and other procedural and substantive elements of the court's processes'.[32]

The majority discussed the wide variety of circumstances which might result in an abuse of process, noting that the categories of abuse of process are not closed.[33] In particular, they noted that an abuse of process can extend to proceedings which are 'seriously and unfairly burdensome, prejudicial or damaging' or 'productive of serious and unjustified trouble and harassment'.[34] They held that 'an agreement by a non-party, for reward, to pay or contribute to the costs of a party in instituting and conducting proceedings is not, of itself, an abuse of the court's processes'.[35]

IV. The Irrelevance of Champerty

There is no reason to suppose that a different view about abuse of process would have been reached by the majority in *Fostif*, had the case come to the High Court from a jurisdiction, such as Queensland, where maintenance and champerty

[32] ibid, 92–94 [26]–[29] (citations omitted).

[33] ibid, 93 [28].

[34] *Jeffery* (n 31) 93–94 [28], citing *Batistatos v Roads and Traffic Authority (NSW)* [2006] HCA 217, (2006) 226 CLR 256, 267 [14].

[35] *Jeffery* (n 31) 94 [30].

remain actionable torts. Gummow, Hayne and Crennan JJ saw no clear basis in policy for the torts, at least nowadays. They suggested that maintenance and champerty were rules which had remained 'unchallenged long after the reason for them has disappeared'.[36] They also noted that, prior to the legislative abolition of the torts and offences of maintenance and champerty in New South Wales and the United Kingdom, maintenance or champerty had not been held to constitute a defence to an action on the claim that was maintained, or to be a ground for staying such an action.[37]

Indeed, in several Australian jurisdictions which had not abolished the torts, there had been recent cases in intermediate courts of appeal where the court had refused to stay an action which was funded on a champertous basis. In one such case in 1997,[38] *Magic Menu Systems Pty Ltd v AFA Facilitation Pty Ltd*,[39] the Full Court of the Federal Court (Lockhart, Cooper and Kiefel JJ) recognised a more liberal approach of courts to proceedings which were funded in that way. The Court said:

> It may be said that public policy considerations shaped the attitude of the Courts towards agreements to maintain litigation. The concern early expressed was that the remedial processes of the law might be used as a tool of oppression. … What maintained actions were thought likely to produce, and which was inimical to the public interest, altered over the course of time and with changing social conditions, as did the recognition of interests which were sufficient to justify interference in another's litigation by supporting it. … It may now be observed, for example, that concerns expressed earlier this century, as to the potential for the maintenance of actions to give rise to an increase in litigation, might now be considered of lesser importance than the problems which face the ordinary litigant in funding litigation and gaining access to the Courts. … [S]upport of legal proceedings based upon a bona fide common interest, financial or philosophical, must be permitted if the law itself [is] not to operate as oppressive. The Courts today, in our view, are likely to take an even wider view of what might be acceptable, particularly if procedural safeguards are present or able to be applied.[40]

Another of those cases was the decision in 2003 of the Queensland Court of Appeal in *Elfic Ltd v Macks*.[41] The appellants were defendants in what became very extensive and expensive litigation in the Supreme Court of Queensland, brought by some companies in liquidation. The claims failed entirely, including claims of fraud which, in the view of the trial judge, were so devoid of any foundation that he ordered indemnity costs against the plaintiffs.[42] The proceedings were funded

36 *Fostif* (n 1) 431 [78].

37 ibid, 432 [82].

38 Involving the funding of proceedings in the Queensland Registry of the Federal Court.

39 (1997) 72 FCR 261.

40 ibid, 267.

41 [2003] 2 Qd R 125.

42 *Emanuel Management Pty Ltd (in liquidation) v Foster's Brewing Group Ltd* (2003) 178 FLR 1. In relation to costs, see *Emanuel Management Pty Ltd (in liquidation) v Foster's Brewing Group Ltd and Coopers & Lybrand* [2003] QSC 299.

on the plaintiffs' side upon terms which were clearly champertous, except that the Federal Court had directed the liquidators of the plaintiff companies that such terms could be agreed. The defendants sought an injunction to restrain the performance of the litigation funding arrangements. They failed at first instance and on appeal. Special leave to appeal to the High Court was refused upon the basis that an appeal would not enjoy sufficient prospects of success to warrant a grant of special leave.[43] In the Court of Appeal, McMurdo P said:

> The mere fact that proceedings are financed by third parties with no interest in the outcome other than repayment and profit from the litigation is not itself sufficient to invoke the jurisdiction of the court. Courts should be careful not to use that power to deny access to justice to a party who has sought to fund bona fide proceedings in a way which may be contrary to public policy unless that which has been done amounts to an abuse of the court's own process ...[44]

In that case, it was considered that the liquidator retained sufficient control of the litigation, notwithstanding the terms of the provision of the funding. In that respect, Davies JA said:

> In this case the conduct of all proceedings and settlement negotiations is in the hands of experienced lawyers who can be expected not to act improperly or abusively. ... Regardless of the funding arrangement, [the liquidator] can apply to the Court for directions at any time. Under the [Corporations] Law any substantial compromise requires approval of the court, committee of inspection or resolution of the creditors. Under the funding arrangement, any dispute between [the liquidator] and [the funder] is to be resolved by an independent senior counsel. Mansfield J was satisfied that ultimate control of the litigation under the funding arrangement remained with the liquidator.[45]

The next case was the subject of a series of three judgments in the Court of Appeal of Western Australia: *Clairs Keeley (A Firm) v Treacy*.[46] In the first of these cases, the Court by a majority ordered a stay of an action by Ms Treacy and others against their former solicitors, upon the ground that it was champertously maintained and an abuse of the process of the Court. In the second case, a differently constituted court dismissed the plaintiffs' application to lift the stay. In the third decision, a further application by the plaintiffs to lift the stay succeeded, upon the basis that the arrangements between the litigation funder and the lawyers to conduct the plaintiffs' case had been sufficiently amended in respect of the control of the litigation to prevent the case being an abuse of the process of the Court. In the second of these cases, the Court (Steytler, Templeman and McKechnie JJ) said:

> It is acceptable for the litigation to be pursued by plaintiffs who, although funded by a third party, are acting in their own interests in the pursuit of justice in their respective

[43] (2002) 23(6) Leg Rep SL4.

[44] *Elfic* (n 41) 137–38 [67]. This passage was quoted with approval by Mason P in *Fostif v Campbells* (n 14) 225 [99].

[45] *Elfic* (n 41) 145 [107] (citations omitted).

[46] [2003] WASCA 299, [2004] WASCA 277 and [2005] WASCA 86.

> causes, and are so acting on the advice of independent solicitors. It is not acceptable for the litigation to be pursued in such a way that the interests of the plaintiffs are subservient to those of the funder. That would be an abuse of process. The Court cannot know how, or on what basis, the plaintiffs are being advised. It can have regard only to the potential for abuse.[47]

In the New South Wales Court of Appeal in *Fostif*, Mason P disagreed with the second and third sentences within that passage, saying:

> I observe that this was a decision in a State where the tort has not been abolished. In my opinion, a conclusion about abuse of process must stem from a finding directed at the actual or likely conduct of the party in whose name the litigation is brought (or its agents). The court is not concerned with balancing the interests of the funder and its clients. Indeed, it is not concerned with the arrangements, fiduciary or otherwise, between the plaintiff and the funder except so far as they have corrupted or have a tendency to corrupt the processes of the court of the particular litigation. It is only when they have that quality that the defendant has standing to complain about them.[48]

Although that passage from *Clairs Keeley* was not discussed in the majority judgments in the High Court in *Fostif*, it is inconsistent with them.

A case which might have provided a good occasion for the court's intervention was *Hall v Poolman*.[49] This was not a class action. It involved claims by liquidators in respect of insolvent trading and unfair preferences, which were brought ostensibly for the benefit of a group constituted by unsecured creditors. As Palmer J discussed, in reality the case was brought for the benefit not of the creditors, but the liquidators, their lawyers and the litigation funders. Full recovery of the liquidators' claims, including costs and interest, after payment of funder's costs and its success fee and the costs of the liquidators and their solicitors would have yielded no more than a fraction of a cent in the dollar for unsecured creditors.[50] The defendants argued that it was relevant to the exercise of the court's discretionary powers under sections 1317(2) and 1318 of the Corporations Act 2001 (Cth) to relieve them from liability, that the true beneficiaries of the claims would not be the creditors.[51] Palmer J observed that it was 'fair to say that courts in Australia have not yet fully explored the ramifications of litigation funding'.[52] After discussing the majority judgments in *Fostif*, Palmer J said that those views did not 'yet command universal acceptance' and that the minority judges 'were eloquent in their condemnation of the concept of litigation fund as merely another form of business investment'.[53] Palmer J said also that 'if access to justice for the creditors were the justification for these proceedings, that justification fails when creditors

[47] [2004] WASCA 277 [71].
[48] *Fostif v Campbells* (n 14) 229 [114].
[49] [2007] NSWSC 1330 (2007) 65 ACSR 123.
[50] As Palmer J found, ibid, [70].
[51] ibid, [368].
[52] ibid, [370].
[53] ibid, [373].

will be lucky to get anything at all, and the amounts which they will receive are, in most cases, derisory…' Nevertheless he held that the majority judgment in *Fostif* required a conclusion that the defendants could not have a defence on this basis.[54] With respect, the conclusion of Palmer J that the circumstances could not be used as part of a substantial defence under the Corporations Act 2001 (Cth) to the liquidators' claims may have been correct. However the circumstances of those claims may have justified the court's intervention at an early stage of that litigation in order to protect against an abuse of its own process.

V. Is The Law Settled?

The minority judgment in *Fostif* explained a basis, in an appropriate case, for a court to intervene to prevent an abuse of its own process, which was not a basis which was discussed and rejected in the majority judgments. There is therefore a prospect for the minority reasoning to be employed, as it was, in the strong dissenting judgment of Rares J in *Deloitte Touche Tohmatsu v J P Morgan Portfolio Services Ltd.*[55] Rares J expressed this reasoning within his judgment under the heading 'The "Real" Litigant Issue'. His Honour set out a passage from the judgment of Gleeson CJ, Gummow, Hayne and Heydon JJ in *D'Orta-Ekenaike v Victoria Legal Aid*[56] as follows:

> [T]he central concern of the exercise of judicial power is the quelling of controversies. Judicial power is exercised as an element of the government of society and its aims are wider than, and more important than, the concerns of the particular parties to the controversy in question …[57]

Rares J then discussed the relative positions of the nominal litigant and its funder:

> Here the nominal litigant, Portfolio Services, has no interest in litigating the proceedings against the vendors on its own account. Nor did it have any interest, on its own account, to commence the proceedings. There is no controversy between Portfolio Services and the vendors which existed at the time the proceedings were instituted or now and which those parties wished to have resolved or quelled.
>
> Rather, Westpac has sought to exploit the potential causes of action which Portfolio Services could have litigated, but has no interest to litigate, on its own account. …

[54] ibid, [379]. Still, Palmer J held that the court should enquire into the liquidators' conduct in the prosecution of these claims under its power under section 536(1) (a) of the Corporations Act 2001 (Cth). On an appeal against that order for an enquiry, the order was set aside because it was relevant only to what order for costs should be made and the parties had by then reached a settlement compromising the liquidators' rights.

[55] (2007) 158 FCR 417; 240 ALR 540.

[56] (2005) 223 CLR 1, 16 [32].

[57] *Deloitte* (n 55) 432 [104].

> I am of opinion that there is no controversy which is before the Court. Rather, the proceedings have been brought for the dominant purpose of enabling Westpac, and not Portfolio Services, to take advantage of a potential controversy in order that Westpac will enrich itself to the entire exclusion of any benefit to Portfolio Services. …
>
> The abuse of the process of the court in this proceeding consists in the manufacturing of the litigation by Westpac. It has used Portfolio Services' name and possible causes of action in circumstances where Portfolio Services has no purpose in its own right or, independent of the litigation agreement, on behalf of Westpac to have the judicial power used to resolve anything.[58]

Rares J compared that case with the conduct of litigation by an insurer exercising its right of subrogation to commence proceedings and litigate in the insured's name. In such (insurance) cases, he noted, there is 'a real controversy between the nominal parties (including the insured)'.[59]

In *Deloitte Touche*, Tamberlin and Jacobson JJ held that, on the facts, the nominal litigant was the 'real litigant' because, although it was bringing the proceedings to benefit another party, it was doing so pursuant to an agreement by its parent company to bring such proceedings, if required by the financier, pursuant to a certain contract which was not simply for the funding of litigation. Tamberlin and Jacobson JJ did not seem to reject the relevance of an inquiry as to whether the nominal litigant was a 'real' litigant in the sense described by Rares J.

In the New South Wales Court of Appeal in *Jeffery and Katauskas*, it was said that the High Court's decision in *Fostif* 'makes success on an argument that litigation funding with or without control constitutes an abuse of process extremely difficult if not impossible'.[60] That may well overstate the position. The reasoning of Callinan and Heydon JJ is yet to be specifically considered and rejected in the High Court. As I have discussed, the joint judgment of Gummow, Hayne and Crennan JJ in *Fostif* did not do so, but instead addressed arguments which were perceived to relate to a risk of some abuse in the particular conduct of a case. The categories of abuse of process are not closed and the majority view in *Fostif* did allow for the possibility of an abuse of process in the individual case. In particular, there is some prospect for a finding of an abuse of process according to the terms of the retainer of lawyers on the record for a funded plaintiff or group.

As the majority judgments in the High Court in *Fostif*, and that of Mason P in the Court of Appeal in that case, explained, the arguments of defendants in these cases have often focussed on a purported concern for the position of the nominal litigants in their relationship with the litigation funder, instead of focussing upon the genuine interests of defendants in the proper conduct of the proceedings against them. But there is a third interest, which is the public interest in the

[58] *Deloitte* (n 55) 432–33.

[59] ibid, 433 [111].

[60] *Sub nom Rickard Constructions Pty Ltd v Rickard Hails Moretti Pty Ltd* [2008] NSWCA 283 [79]. The comment drew strong criticism in that case from Heydon J in *Jeffery* (n 31) 101 [49].

proper exercise of judicial power and, in particular, by that being confined within its proper limits. The boundaries of judicial power are defined by reference to the quelling of disputes according to law. And the dispute must be between the parties to the litigation, albeit that in some cases a nominal party will hold the cause of action for another. But that is not the case where the litigation funder's entitlement is not as the equitable owner of a cause of action, but instead to the whole or a part of the proceeds of a judgment or settlement.

There is also a pragmatic reason for courts to be concerned with the misuse of their process in the ways suggested by Callinan and Heydon JJ and Rares J. It is that the resources of courts are finite and the employment of those resources for cases involving no real controversy between the nominal litigants is likely to be at the expense of other litigants with genuine controversies to be resolved.

The present tolerance of litigation funding owes much to the faith placed by courts in the proper performance by the lawyers conducting the case of their duties to the nominal litigant and to the court. It cannot be thought that a court would permit a proceeding to be prosecuted by a lawyer who disavows the established duties which are owed in the conduct of litigation by a lawyer on behalf of a party. Courts rightly depend upon the performance by lawyers of their duties, not only to the court, but to the parties whom they represent, because it is upon that assumption that the lawyer's conduct of the case at every step can be attributed to the litigant. The majority view in *Fostif* was that the lawyers might discharge their duties to the nominal litigant (as well as to the court) whilst being retained by the litigation funder as a principal. But there may arise particular cases where that acceptance is tested by evidence which suggests a particular likelihood of a neglect of the duty to the nominal litigant. Such a case may well be that described by the Western Australia Court of Appeal in the passage from *Clairs Keeley (No 2)* which I have set out above.[61] In such cases, the basis for the court's intervention might be found in an abuse of process. But it might also be found in the court's control of its own officers.

Third party litigation funding has facilitated extensive litigation through group and representative proceedings on a scale and in legal contexts which could not have been anticipated when class actions were first facilitated in the 1990s. This has occurred without legislative action and with the imprimatur of the courts. It is relevantly regulated only by the courts' powers to control their own processes, according to what they perceive to be the proper use of those processes and the due limits of judicial power. Third party funding thereby profoundly shifts the balance of power between, on one hand, impecunious claimants, or claimants with small claims measured individually and, on the other hand, defendants. It empowers outsiders to litigate the claims of others.

As I have tried to explain, there are unresolved legal questions. But beyond them clearly there are issues of policy which may well warrant legislative intervention.

[61] *Clairs* (n 47).

Thus far the legislative response has been to facilitate the growth of the litigation funding industry by a response to a judgment of the Federal Court which held that the funding agreement for a class action constituted a 'managed investment scheme' that required registration under the Corporations Act 2001 (Cth).[62] The government's response was first to introduce the Corporations Amendment Regulation 2012 (No 6) (Cth), excluding funded class actions from the definition of a managed investment scheme. The explanatory statement to the regulation said:

> The Government considers that these requirements are not appropriate for litigation funding schemes. The Government supports class actions and litigation funders as they can provide access to justice for a large number of consumers who may otherwise have difficulties in resolving disputes.[63]

Shortly after his appointment, the current Attorney-General for the Commonwealth announced an interest in considering the regulation of the industry of third party litigation funding. More recently, at the end of 2014, the Productivity Commission recommended that litigation funders be licensed.[64] Changes which may come from legislation may or may not address the potential for abuse of the process of courts.

[62] *Brookfield Multiplex Ltd v International Litigation Funding Partners Pte Ltd* (2009) 180 FCR 11; 260 ALR 643.

[63] Explanatory Statement, Corporations Amendment Regulation 2012 (No 6) (Cth) 'Select Legislative Instrument 2012 (No 172)' 1.

[64] Productivity Commission, *Productivity Commission Inquiry Report—Access to Justice Arrangements* (No 72, 5 September 2014) Vol 2.

INDEX

abuse of power, 15–16, 25–26
  see also misfeasance in public office
abuse of process, 22
  Fostif case, 288–91
abuse of rights doctrine, 198
advertising controls, 78, 81
  inequalities of informational power, 76–77
Anns test, 223–24, 226, 274–76
Australia:
  Anns test, 275–76
  class actions, 285–86
  institutional child abuse, 265–66, 279
  justiciability, 222–25
  misfeasance in public office, 177
    vicarious liability, 203
  public discretion and private law duties of care, 209–10, 232–33, 235–36
  public liability law, 91, 93–94, 213, 215–17, 220
    responsibility model, 97–100
  vicarious liability, 281–82
availability of personal information, 247

bad faith, 226, 275
  misfeasance in public office, 179–80, 185, 193
bargaining power, *see* inequalities of bargaining power
big data, 247

Catholic Church, 22
  institutional child abuse, 4, 265, 268
  private law liability:
    charitable liability, 268–69
champerty
  class actions and, 286–87, 289, 293–97
Chancery Amendment Act 1858, *see* Lord Cairns' Act 1858
charitable liability, 268–69
civil regulation:
  control of public power, 83–84
class actions, 285–87
  champerty and, 293–97
  Fostif case:
    background, 287–90
  litigation funding, 299–300
  subsequent cases, 292–93
  see also abuse of process
commercial jurisprudence, 41–42
conceptions of power in private law, 26–28
  ability to influence, 7–8
  capacity and ability, 7
  Hohfeld's analysis, 8–9
concession theory and corporate power, 248–49, 255
consideration doctrine, *see* doctrine of consideration
constitutional justiciability, 221–23
  criteria:
    decisions falling within or outside powers, 226–28
    decisions not justiciable, 228–29
    policy/operation distinction, 223–25
    separation of powers, 227–28
  immunity and, 221–22
  parliamentary intentions and, 229–32
  privilege and, 222–23
consumer credit, 10–11, 53–54, 79–82
  financial literacy, 78–79
  history, 56–59
    fragmentation of legislative rules, 59–60
    regulatory philosophy, 60
  regulation, 60, 76
    informational inequalities, 72–73
consumerism, 53–54
  inequalities:
    bargaining power, 54, 61–72
    informational power, 54–56, 72–79
contract law:
  development, 32–37
  equity and, 32–33
  fairness, 32–37
  fraud, 34–35
  legal procedure and fairness, 46–47
    juries, 47–49
  legitimacy of corporate power and, 251–54
  merchants and, 37–40
    commercial jurisprudence, 41–42
    doctrine of consideration, 40–41
    insurance, 41–43
    negotiable instruments, 41–42
    promissory notes, 40–41
  modern conceptions, 50–51
  'moral economy', 33–34
  public policy, 43–46
  'sound price' doctrine, 35–37
cooling-off periods:
  inequalities of informational power, 77–78

corporate power, 240–48
economic power, 240–43
legitimacy, 248
benefit for society, 249
concession theory and, 255
contract and, 251–54
fundamentally private institutions, 248
maximisation of wealth and, 259–61
ownership and, 249–51
public or political institutions, 248
social enterprise and, 256–59
non-economic/societal power, 240–41, 244–47
corporations and companies, 23–24, 239–40, 261–62
corporate power, 240–48
economic power, 240–43
legitimacy, 248–61
non-economic/societal power, 240–41, 244–47
economic power, 240
competition and markets, 242–43
consumer influence, 243–44
control of wealth, 241–44
ownership, 241–42
legitimacy of corporate power, 248
concession theory and, 255
contract and, 251–54
maximisation of wealth and, 259–61
models of company:
benefit for society, 249
fundamentally private institutions, 248
public or political institutions, 248
ownership and, 249–51
social enterprise and, 256–59
non-economic/societal power, 240–41
environmental impact, 244–45
nature of society and culture, influence over, 246–47
policy decisions and law-making, impact on, 245–46
corrective justice:
unjust enrichment and, 160, 167, 170–72, 175
corrective model of public liability law, 100–02
Critical Legal Studies movement, 31–32
Crown immunity, *see* sovereign immunity
Crowther Committee, 10, 53–55, 56, 57–58, 60, 62

damages in lieu of injunctions, 111–12
discretion, 207–10, 236–37
conceptual analysis, 210–11
immunity, discretion as, 211–13
judgement, discretion as, 214–18
power, discretion as, 211
privilege, discretion as, 213–14
financial crisis and, 232–36
granting damages in lieu of injunctions, 111–12
early case law, 112–13
Shelfer case, 113–14
governmental discretion, 16–18
immunity, as, 211–13
judgement, as, 214–18
power, as, 211
privilege, 213–14
Shelfer case, 113–14
judicial scepticism, 114–18
rejection of judgment, 130–31
statutory powers and, 207–08
discretionary powers:
immunity and, 211–13
judgement and, 214–18
power and, 211
privilege and, 213–14
doctrine of consideration, 40–41, 50
Dorset Yacht case:
evolution of duty of care, 272–73
private law liability, 273–74
third party liability, 276–78
doorstep credit, 58–59
inequalities of informational power, 77–78
duty of care, 218–19
constitutional justiciability, 221–23
criteria, 223–29
immunity and, 221–22
parliamentary intentions and, 229–32
privilege and, 222–23
discretion and, 219–20
financial crisis and, 232–36
institutional duty of care
negligence and, 272–73
private law liability, 273–76
third party liability, 276–78
limitations, 220–21
see also Anns test; discretion

ecclesiastical institutions, 24–26
private law liability, 263–64
see also Catholic Church
economic power, 240
competition and markets, 242–43
consumer influence, 243–44
control of wealth, 241–44
ownership, 241–42
equality principle, 95–97, 103, 213
equitable relief from unconscionable bargains, 72–73
European Convention for Human Rights:
state liability and, 103
EU law:
state liability and, 103

exemplary damages:
misfeasance in public office and, 183–84, 187, 191–92, 200

fairness:
contract law, 32–37, 46–47
financial crisis:
impact on discretion and duty of care, 232–36
negligence cases and, 232–33
public liability insurance, 232
public/private law dichotomy, 235
reforms, impact of, 236
statutory immunities and, 233–34
thresholds for civil actions, 235
financial literacy and capability:
inequalities of informational power, 78–79
Fostif case, 285–87
background, 287–90
impact, 292–93, 297–300
minority view, 290–92
France:
public liability law, 13–14, 17, 88–89
instrumental/functional model, 103, 104
responsibility model, 94–95
separation of powers and, 95–96
UK compared, 89
fraud, 34–35, 45–46
'fraud on the power', 145–46
usury laws, 61
functional model of public liability law, 102–04

gain-based relief, 120
Shelfer case and, 131–34
'good working rule', 115–17
judicial scepticism, 114–15
onus of proof and, 127–28
release-fee relief in lieu of injunctions, 124–25
governmental discretion, 16–18
see also discretion
governmental power, 12–13
abuse of power, 15–16
governmental discretion, 16–18
liability rules, 13–15, 83
government tort liability:
legal history:
Crown immunity, 87
development of legal categories, 86
development of tort, 86–87
feudal societies, 84–85
independence of executive, 85–86
Petition of Right, 85–86
sovereign immunity, 87

hire-purchase, 4, 58–59, 75–76, 77–78
Hohfeldian analysis, 8–9, 15, 23–24, 110, 210
right-duty relation, 188, 196–97

illegality, 44, 94–95
knowledge of, 185
misfeasance in public office, 179–80, 185, 192, 197–98
immunity, 211–19
Crown immunity, 85–87
discretion as, 211–13
Federal immunity (USA), 14, 103
justiciability, 221–29
mirror principle, 212–13
privilege and, 213–14, 221–29
sovereign immunity, 85–87, 91–93, 99–100
individual power:
social power compared, 9–12
inequalities of bargaining power, 54
redressing inequalities, 79–82
statutory relief from unconscionable bargains, 67–72
usury laws, 61–67
statutory relief from unconscionable bargains and:
interest and statutory controls, 67–72
usury laws and:
canon law, 63–65
circumvention of usury laws, 65–67
effect of voidness, 64–65
equitable fraud, 61–62
offence of usury, 63–64
unconscionable bargain doctrine, 62
inequalities of informational power, 54–56
redressing inequalities, 79–82
controls on advertising, 76–77
cooling-off period, 77–78
doorstep credit, 77–78
equitable relief from unconscionable bargains, 72–73
formality requirements, 73–76
improving financial literacy and capability, 78–79
information disclosure, 73–76
statutory relief from unconscionable bargains, 73
information disclosure:
availability of personal information, 247
inequalities of informational power, 73–76
informational power, *see* inequalities of informational power
institutional child abuse, 265–66, 279
non-delegable duty and, 280–82
vicarious liability and, 280–82
institutional liability, *see* non-delegable duties; vicarious liability
institutional power, 22–23, 263–66, 282–83
accountability, 272
comparative fault, 270–72
immunities, 268
charitable immunity, 268–69
sovereign immunity, 269–70

negligence, 266–67, 272–73
'general' duty of care, 267
'neighbour' principle, 267–68
private law liability, 273–76
third party liability, 276–78
see also Church; corporations and companies; trusts law
instrumental model of public liability law, 102–04
insurance markets, 17, 41–43

judgement/discernment:
discretion as, 214–18
judicial power:
access to justice, 21–22
common law and, 107–08
court processes, 21–22
legislative power and, 18–19, 107–08
property rights and, 19–20, 109–11
juries:
declining use, 107–08
fairness, 47–49
legal procedures, 47–49

Lawrence v Fen Tigers, 19
Shelfer case and, 126–27
legal procedure and fairness, 46–49
litigation funding, 299–300
Lord Cairns' Act 1858, 111–12
release-fee awards, 119–20
trespass and, 120–23

malice:
misfeasance in public office, 179–80, 197
malicious prosecution:
misfeasance in public office and, 189–90
mercantile interests and contract law, 37–40
commercial jurisprudence, 41–42
doctrine of consideration, 40–41
insurance, 41–43
negotiable instruments, 41–42
promissory notes, 40–41
mirror principle, 212–13
misfeasance in public office, 204–05
conceptual analysis, 178–79
bad faith, 179–80
illegality, 180
malice, 179–80
legal history, 177–78
limitations, 180–81
public law conception, 181–86
private law conception compared, 196–98
tort law conception compared, 193–96
'standing' and bringing a claim, 199–200
tort, as a, 186–87
justifications for tort remedy, 187–89
types of misconduct, 201–03
vicarious liability, 203–04
who is liable, 200–01
Molony Committee, 75, 77–78, 79

negligence:
discretion and duty of care, 232–33
'general' duty of care, 267
institutional duty of care and, 266–67, 272–73
private law liability, 273–76
third party liability, 276–78
'neighbour' principle, 267–68
private law liability, 273–76
third party liability, 276–78
negotiable instruments, 38, 41–42, 50
New Deal, 110
non-delegable duties:
institutional liability, 278–82

ownership:
corporate power, 241–42, 249–51
Hohfeld, 110–11

parliamentary intentions, 229–30
relevance to duty of care issue, 230–32
power:
abuse of power, 15–16, 25–26
conceptions of power in private law, 7–9, 26–28
concession theory and corporate power, 248–49, 255
discretionary powers:
immunity and, 211–13
judgement and, 214–18
power and, 211
privilege and, 213–14
inequalities of bargaining power, 54
redressing inequalities, 61–72, 79–82
statutory relief from unconscionable bargains, 67–72
usury laws, 61–67
inequalities of informational power, 54–56
controls on advertising, 76–77
cooling-off period, 77–78
doorstep credit, 77–78
equitable relief from unconscionable bargains, 72–73
formality requirements, 73–76
improving financial literacy and capability, 78–79
information disclosure, 73–76
redressing inequalities, 72–82
statutory relief from unconscionable bargains, 73
undue influence, 169–70
unconscionable bargain doctrine, 62
inequality of bargaining power, 67–72
inequality of informational power, 72–73

see also corporate power; economic power; governmental power; individual power; judicial power; social power
privilege:
  discretion as, 213–14
promissory notes, 40–41
public interest, 19, 88
  Shelfer case and, 123, 128–30
public nuisance:
  misfeasance in public office and, 190–91
public policy:
  contract law and, 43–46
public tort law:
  Australia, 93–94
  corrective model, 100–02
  France, 88–89
    UK compared, 89
  instrumental/functional model, 102–04
  responsibility model, 94–100
  UK, 89–91
  USA, 91–93

Rawlsian theory of social justice:
  challenges, 152
    Cohen, 152–54, 158
    other criticisms, 156–58
    Pogge, 154–56
  theory of social justice, 147–48
    division of labour argument, 148–49, 152
    family, 149
    implications for trusts law, 149–52
  Two Concepts of Rules, 156–57
release-fee awards, 119–20
  Shelfer case, 124–25
responsibility model of public liability law:
  arguments against Dicey, 96–97
  Australia, 97–99
  Dicey, 94–96
  elements, 94–95
  equality principle, 95
  fault and illegality, 95
  France, 94–95
  UK, 95–97
  USA, 99–100
rule of law theory, 90–91, 93, 101, 232

Shelfer case:
  discretion to grant damages in lieu of injunctions, 113–14
  'good working' rule, 114–15
  judicial scepticism, 114–15
  nuisance and, 123, 134
  rejection of judgment, 126–34
    celebration of discretion, 130–31
    gain-based relief, 131–34
    Lawrence v Fen Tigers, 126–27
    relevance of public interest, 128–30
    use of 'good working rule' and onus of proof, 127–28
  release-fee awards, 124–25
social enterprise and legitimacy of corporate power, 256–59
social justice, 147–48
  challenges, 152
    Cohen, 152–54, 158
    other criticisms, 156–58
    Pogge, 154–56
  division of labour argument, 148–49, 152
  family, 149
  implications for trusts law, 149–52
social power:
  individual power compared, 9–12
'sound price' doctrine, 35
sovereign immunity, 85–87, 91–93, 99–100, 269–70
  see also public liability law
sovereign liability, *see* sovereign immunity
state entities:
  corporatist approach, 83–84
  individualist approach, 83–84
  models of allocation of public power
    concentration, 84
    diffusion, 84
  see also government tort liability
state power to regulate property, 134–35
  judiciary, 19–20, 109–11
  legal realism, 110
  redistribution of property rights, 110–11
  USA, 109–10
statutory relief from unconscionable bargains, 73

third party liability:
  duty of care, 276–78
'ticket cases', 54
tort liability, *see* government tort liability
trespass and Lord Cairns' Act 1858, 120–23
  nuisances distinguished, 19, 120, 134
trustees, 137–38
  administrative powers, 138–39
    case law, 139–43
  dispositive powers, 143–47
  Rawls' approach to social justice and, 147–52
    challenges, 152–58
trusts law, 24
  discretionary trusts, 143–47
  pursuit of ethical and social considerations, 138–43
  Rawls' approach, 147–52
    challenges, 152–58
  social justice and, 137–38
  trustees' powers:
    administrative powers, 138–43
Two Concepts of Rules (Rawls), 156–57

unconscionable bargain doctrine, 62
inequality of bargaining power:
interest and statutory controls, 67–72
statutory relief from 67–72
inequality of informational power:
equitable relief from unconscionable bargains, 72–73
statutory relief from unconscionable bargains, 73
statutory relief, 67–72, 73
undue influence, 159–60
definition, 162
foundations of, 165–67
unjust enrichment analysis, 170–74
wrongs analysis of, 167–70
large group awareness training courses (LGAT) and, 162, 164–65, 174
category 2A undue influence, 162–63
Rebekah Lawrence case, 160–62
rebutting influence, 162
unjust enrichment and, 170
corrective justice, 171
equity, 172–74
wrongs, 170–72
wrongs analysis of:
deferential trust in relationships, 167–68
equitable wrongs, 168–69
interpersonal dynamics, 167
power relationships and relationships of authority, 169–70
Universal Principle of Right, 172–74
unjust enrichment:
corrective justice, 160, 167, 170–72, 175
USA:
Federal immunity, 14, 103
public liability law, 91–93
instrumental/functional model, 103–04
responsibility model, 99–100
state power to regulate property, 109–10
usury laws and bargaining power:
canon law, 63–65
circumvention of usury laws, 65–67
effect of voidness, 64–65
equitable fraud, 61–62
offence of usury, 63–64
unconscionable bargain doctrine, 62

vicarious liability, 95, 203–04. 266
institutional liability, 278–82
UK and USA law compared, 87